MOON

W9-CIC-188

GIFT OF
DOROTHY CLEMENS
FUND
THE PUBLIC LIBRARY OF BROOKLINE

Where stories begin

ACADIA
NATIONAL PARK

HILARY NANGLE

Contents

Although every effort was made to make sure the information in this book was accurate when going to press, research was impacted by the COVID-19 pandemic and things may have changed since the time of writing. Be sure to confirm specific details, like opening hours, closures, and travel guidelines and restrictions, when making your travel plans. For more detailed information, see p. 295.

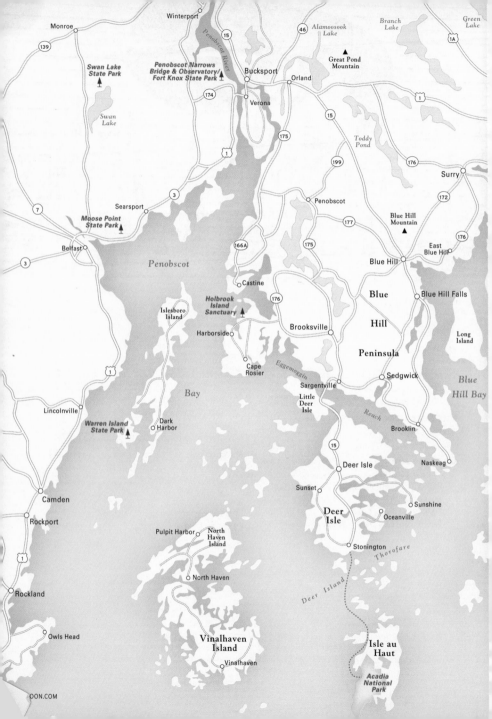

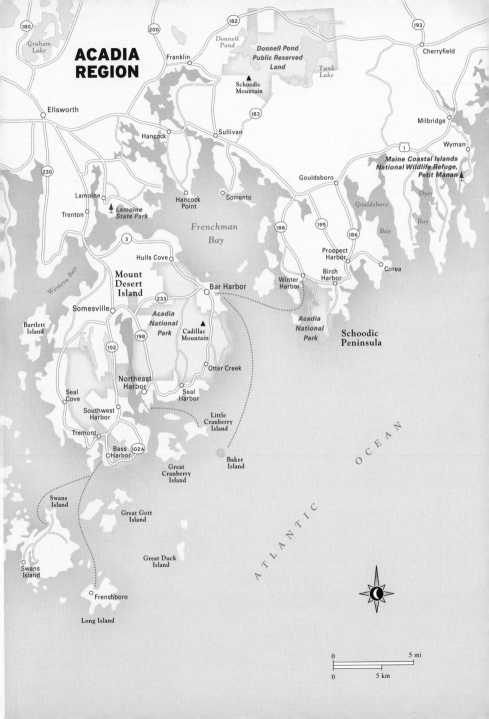

MOUNT DESERT ISLAND

Bartlett
Island

Pretty
Marsh

PRETTY MARSH RD

102

Bartlett Narrows

Western Bay

Black
Island

Alley
Island

Green
Island

Blagden
Preserve

Squid
Cove

Round
Pond

INDIAN POINT

OAK HILL CROSS RD

Somes
Pond

OAK HILL RD

Somesville

198

102

Indian
Point

Mount Desert Narrows

THOMPSON ISLAND
INFORMATION CENTER ■

102

198

Town
Hill

CROOKED RD

198

Somes

National

Sargent
Mountain

The
Bubbles

Aunt
Betty
Pond

233

Acadia

NORWAY DR

Lake
Wood

Witch Hole
Pond

Eagle
Lake

PARK LOOP RD

Bubble
Pond

SIEUR DE MONTS
SPRING ■

Dorr
Mountain

★

▲ Cadillac
Mountain

Champlain
Mountain ▲

SCHOONER HEAD

3

Bar Harbor

BAR HARBOR CHAMBER
INFORMATION CENTER ■

College of the
Atlantic

Bar
Island

Porcupine
Islands

The
Thrumcap

Schooner
Head

HULLS COVE
VISITOR CENTER ■

Salisbury
Cove

Hulls Cove

Hulls Cove

RD

3

Eastern Bay

Trenton

BAR HARBOR
AIRPORT ✈

230

Union River Bay

To Ellsworth →

3

Lamoine

Lamoine
State Park

Maribro

Hancock
Point

Frenchman Bay

Sorrento

DISCOVER

Acadia
National Park

Mount Desert Island has been luring visitors since French explorers first answered the island's siren song in 1604. Seductively remote, it dangles like a pendant into the Atlantic, flashing its profile to passing navigators and mainland drivers. Although only 15 miles from north to south and 12 miles from west to east, the island is home to more than 30,000 of Acadia National Park's roughly 37,000 acres. It's a miniature masterpiece that's laced with hiking trails and carriage roads, etched by a craggy coastline, sprinkled with ponds, and lorded over by bald peaks.

Acadia's appeal is contradictory: It's accessible, and yet it's not. More than three million visitors annually arrive on Mount Desert by car, bus, plane, or cruise ship, all eager to view the park's icons. The Park Loop Road makes that easy. But even on the most crowded days, it's possible to slip away and find peace and quiet on a hike, paddle, or bike ride. Step off the major thoroughfares, and birdsong replaces idle chatter, pine perfumes the air, and signs of civilization disappear from view. Off-the-beaten-path gems might lack the drama of the icons, but they feed the soul, ease the mind, and restore much-needed balance to a hectic life.

Clockwise from top left: Claremont Hotel; a dock in Claremont; cormorants; Abby Aldrich Rockefeller Garden; Pigeon Hill; Corea Harbor.

Beyond Mount Desert Island, other sections of the park beckon. Islesford and Baker Island are connected by passenger ferries and excursion boats; oh-so-remote Isle au Haut lets the curious view from the safe confines of a boat while inviting the hardy to hike and camp in near solitude; and the mainland Schoodic section's pink granite shores receive far fewer visitors than Mount Desert Island.

While the park is the region's flawless gem, it's set amid other precious ones. If stretched taut, Hancock County—with Acadia as its centerpiece—would have more than 1,000 miles of coastline. No saltwater locale on the Eastern Seaboard can compete with the region's variety of scenery or its natural resources, which also include the Maine Coastal Islands National Wildlife Refuge, the Donnell Pond Public Reserved Land, three scenic byways, and countless preserves. This inspiring scenery feeds dozens of artists and artisans, whose galleries and studios pepper the region.

"Maine is so lovely," a British visitor to Acadia sighed nostalgically, "I do wish England had fought harder to keep it."

Clockwise from top left: Thunder Hole; a collection of buoys; Waterfall Bridge; a Park Ranger Program.

10 TOP EXPERIENCES

1 **Drive the Park Loop Road:** Many of Acadia's iconic sights can be seen along this 27-mile road (page 46).

2 **Take in the Views from Cadillac Mountain:** While sunrise and sunset get all the raves, the views from Cadillac's open summit are spectacular anytime (page 52).

3 **Visit Schoodic Point:** Drive to the park's only mainland section or hop a ferry from Bar Harbor to spend the day along this rugged pink granite shoreline (page 143).

4 Pedal Acadia's Carriage Roads: The best way to travel the park's 45-mile car-free road network and see its 17 arched bridges is by bicycle (page 75).

>>>

5 Paddle a Sea Kayak: The serpentine coastline, with its countless coves, harbors, bays, and islands, is ideal for experienced sea kayakers (page 95, page 189, and page 223).

<<<

6 Take a Hike: Whether you're a first-time hiker or a pro, there's a trail for you (page 31).

>>>

7 **Explore Isle au Haut:** Spend a day hiking the remote island and spend a night under the stars at a rustic campsite (page 230).

8 **View Whales and Puffins:** Take guided excursions to view whales, seals, and sea birds (page 96 and page 158).

9 **Feast on Lobster:** Enjoy Maine's signature crustacean the way locals do—fresh from the sea (page 246).

10 **Admire Stunning Fall Foliage:** Stop by Acadia in the fall for some of the most beautiful foliage around (page 33).

Planning Your Trip

Where to Go

Acadia on Mount Desert Island

Mountains tumbling to the sea, ocean waves crashing on granite ledges, serene ponds, and wildflower-filled meadowlands—the Mount Desert Island section of the park has it all, in spades. Watch the sun rise out of the Atlantic from **Cadillac Mountain's summit,** drive along the icon-rich **Park Loop Road,** hike trails through forestlands and up coastal peaks, scale granite cliffs, or paddle the coastline's nooks and crannies. Intimate yet expansive, wild yet civilized, Acadia is as accessible or as remote as you desire.

Mount Desert Island Communities

Excursions into the park depart from the surrounding communities, which have attractions of their own: museums, gardens, shops, and theaters. **Bar Harbor** is the island's hub; tony **Northeast Harbor** is located at the mouth of Somes Sound, a rare fjard; **Southwest Harbor** is the heart of the island's quiet side. These communities, along with the smaller fishing villages, are where you'll find **lobster dinners** with all the fixings.

Schoodic Peninsula

Everything changes when you continue north on Route 1: the pace slows, fast-food joints and even stoplights disappear, and independence reigns. **Schoodic Point's pink granite shores** are undoubtedly the highlight of the park's only

the view from Cadillac's summit in summer

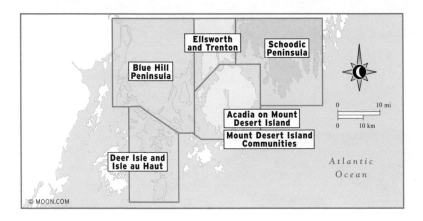

© MOON.COM

mainland section, but there are other reasons to mosey **off the beaten track.** Back roads and scenic byways loop through fishing villages, bisect a mountain- and lake-speckled wilderness preserve, access a national wildlife refuge, and edge those pink shores. It's a bonanza for **hikers, bikers, anglers, boaters,** and **bird-watchers.**

Blue Hill Peninsula

Water, water everywhere. Around nearly every bend of the Blue Hill Peninsula is a **river** or **stream,** a **cove,** a **boat-filled harbor,** or a **serene pond.** It's an inspired and inspiring landscape dotted with **historic homes and forts.** The locals, a blend of summer rusticators, genteel retirees, artists, boatbuilders, and back-to-the-landers, have worked diligently to preserve not only the landscape but also the heritage. It's a fine place to kick back, relax, day-trip to Acadia National Park, and savor the good life.

Deer Isle and Isle au Haut

If Deer Isle isn't the end of the world, there's a sense that you can see it from here. Tethered to the mainland by a bridge soaring over Eggemoggin Reach, Deer Isle and Little Deer Isle are fishing centers accented by a **vibrant arts community.** Depart the island's tip by ferry for Isle au Haut, where the most **remote and rugged** piece of Acadia National Park awaits **hikers** and those for whom even Deer Isle is a bit too crowded.

Ellsworth and Trenton

To visit Mount Desert Island, you must pass through the madness of Ellsworth and Trenton, a traffic-clogged, curse-inducing strip of mini malls and big-box stores. There are a few gems hidden amid the sprawl, including **historic buildings,** trails for **hiking,** and lakes for **boating.** Perhaps most delightful is **Birdsacre,** the former home of ornithologist Cornelia Stanwood, now a preserve with nature and bird rehab centers.

a nature-viewing cruise

- **Bicycling:** Pedaling Acadia's famed **carriage roads** takes you into the heart of the park. Forty-five of the 57 miles of gravel roads are open to bicyclists, and many are accented with rough stone bridges. All are mapped and sign-posted, so you won't get lost. While there are some ups and downs, none of the roads are very steep.

- **Birding:** Twenty warbler species are among the 338 bird species that have been sighted on Mount Desert Island. Plan a day with **Down East Nature Tours** to sight eagles, ospreys, peregrine falcons, shorebirds, and warblers as well as rare birds such as the Nelson's sharp-tailed sparrow.

- **Camping:** Make advance reservations for Acadia's **Blackwoods** or **Seawall Campgrounds** on Mount Desert Island, which has the greatest concentration of trails, with options for all abilities. Consider adding a night or two at the **Schoodic Woods Campground** on the Schoodic Peninsula, and three nights on **Isle au Haut** for a primitive escape.

- **History:** Don't miss **Castine,** a seemingly bucolic town fought over by the French, British, and Dutch thanks to its strategic location.

- **Rock Climbing:** No experience is required to climb Acadia's cliffs, but you will need a guide or a lesson. **Acadia Mountain Guides Climbing School** and **Atlantic Climbing School,** both in Bar Harbor, will tailor instruction to your needs and help you find the perfect route.

- **Scenic Driving Tour:** Drive the **Park Loop Road** on Mount Desert Island and then loop together the **Schoodic National Scenic Byway,** wrapping around the Schoodic Peninsula, with the inland **Blackwoods Scenic Byway.**

- **Sea Kayaking:** One of the best ways to see Acadia is from the water, and paddling a sea kayak along the shoreline allows you to explore all the nooks and crannies. Outfitters in Bar Harbor, Southwest Harbor, Hancock, Deer Isle, and Castine offer **guided trips.** Experienced kayakers seeking island-hopping experiences should join the Maine Island Trail Association.

- **Solitude:** Plan well in advance to book a campsite on **Isle au Haut,** home to a remote section of Acadia National Park that sees fewer than 130 visitors daily.

- **Whale-Watching:** Whale-watching excursions venture up to 20 miles out to sea, which means not only will you likely spot whales, seals, and seabirds, but you'll also get grand views of the island-salted seascape.

When to Go

If you yearn to be car-free on Mount Desert, plan to be here in summer, particularly between **late June and mid-October,** when Acadia's **Island Explorer shuttle service** operates.

If you plan to visit the Isle au Haut section of the park, time a visit for **early June-mid-September** to coincide with the **Isle au Haut passenger ferry service** to the park dock; otherwise you'll have a nearly 10-mile round-trip hike to Duck Harbor.

High Season (July-mid-Oct.)

July and August means plentiful **festivals and fairs, nightlife** in Bar Harbor, **nature tours, concerts** (jazz, classical, and pop), **carriage rides, hiking,** and **whale-watching trips.** The downside is the crowds, although the surrounding towns on Mount Desert Island as well as those on the Schoodic and Blue Hill Peninsulas and on Deer Isle are far quieter.

Fall is my favorite season here. September and October are fantastic in the park and on the island. **Nights are cool** (mid-40s to mid-50s), days are often brilliant, and the **fall foliage** vistas are dramatic (see www.mainefoliage.com). The word has spread, though, and fall is **popular with bus tours and cruise lines,** so you won't be alone—but the visitor head count is still lower than in July and August.

Mid-Season (late Apr.-June)

Spring tends to be something of a blip in Maine; the park starts reawakening around **mid-late April,** when the entire **Park Loop Road reopens** (including the Cadillac Mountain Road), although the Island Explorer bus service doesn't start until mid-June. In early spring, some of the carriage roads tend to be fragile and open only for foot traffic, not for bicycles; **trails can be muddy** and ice still coats some of the rocks, but you'll be rewarded by hardy **wildflowers** poking up here and there. Until about mid-May, you'll also be spared the annoying blackflies. In May the **weather can be unpredictable,** and many **businesses still haven't opened** for the season. The reward is far fewer people, making it easier to get around and enjoy the park's splendors in solitude.

Low Season (Nov.-mid-Apr.)

Although Acadia is open in winter for **cross-country skiing, snowshoeing, snowmobiling** (with some restrictions), and **hiking,** there are few services and no programs; even the surrounding towns all but roll up the sidewalks. Plan ahead, come prepared for all weather, and you can enjoy Acadia as few people see it.

Before You Go

Park Fees and Passes

The entrance fee is **$30 per vehicle** ($25 for motorcycles) late June-mid-October, and it is valid for seven days. Acadia's other fee options include:

- **Individual Pass** ($15): Valid for seven days.

- **Acadia Annual Pass** ($55): Valid for one year from the day of purchase.

- **Interagency Annual Pass** ($80): Allows unlimited entrance for one year to all national parks.

- **Access Pass** (free): Lifetime access to all national parks for any blind or permanently disabled U.S. citizen or permanent resident.

- **Senior Pass** ($80/lifetime): Entrance to more than 300 national parks for U.S. citizens and permanent residents age 62 or older.

- **Interagency Volunteer Pass:** Accumulate 250 service hours to earn this one-year pass valid for all federal recreation sites.

- **Interagency Annual Military Pass:** free pass for active-duty military personnel and dependents; valid documentation required (CAC Card or DD Form 1173).

- **Every Kid in a Park 4th Grade Pass:** free for any U.S. fourth-grade student; allows entry with family: www.everykidinapark.gov

Camping Reservations

There is **no lodging** within Acadia National Park. **Campground reservations** for Seawall and Blackwoods Campgrounds on Mount Desert Island, Schoodic Woods Campground on the Schoodic Peninsula, and Duck Harbor Campground on Isle au Haut are available online at www.recreation.gov or by calling 877/444-6777.

Deer Isle in the spring

Vehicle Reservations

Timed-entry vehicle reservations are required for driving the **Cadillac Summit Station,** which covers the Park Loop Road spur ascending Cadillac Mountain. In the future, the park also plans to implement reservations for the Sand Beach Entrance Station, which covers the one-way Park Loop Road section edging the coastline to Otter Creek Road. Make reservations online at www.recreation.gov. The proposed fee is $6 per reservation, but that is subject to change.

In the Park

Visitors Center

Hulls Cove Visitors Center (Rte. 3, Hulls Cove, 207/288-3338, open daily Apr. 15-Oct. 31) is eight miles southeast of the head of Mount Desert Island. Day-trippers can leave their cars in the lot and hop on the Island Explorer bus, which stops at the base of the stairway from the parking lot to the center.

Schoodic Woods Campground (54 Far View Dr., Winter Harbor, 207/288-3338) doubles as the visitors center on the Schoodic Peninsula. It's signed off the Park Loop Road.

Where to Stay

MOUNT DESERT ISLAND

Advance reservations are needed for **Blackwoods Campground** and **Seawall Campground.**

The island has **hotels, motels, inns, B&Bs, cottages,** and more than a dozen **private campgrounds** and **glampgrounds.** Lodging can be scarce at the height of summer, particularly during the first two weeks in August, when room rates also spike. Off-season rates are always lower. Only a handful of accommodations remain open year-round.

ISLE AU HAUT

Advance reservations and permits are required at **Duck Harbor Campground** (open May 15-Oct. 15).

SCHOODIC PENINSULA

Advance reservations are needed for **Schoodic Woods Campground** (open late May-mid. Oct.). A handful of inns and B&Bs pepper the Schoodic Peninsula and surrounding region; it's best to make advance reservations for them as well, especially in August.

Getting Around

The free **Island Explorer** (www.exploreacadia. com) shuttle bus runs **June-mid-October.** The hub is the Bar Harbor Village Green, where all of the routes (except Schoodic) begin or end. The service covers most of Mount Desert Island, as well as the Gateway Center and Bar Harbor Airport in Trenton. From **mid-June to late September,** the **Bar Harbor Ferry** connects with the Island Explorer's Schoodic Peninsula route.

From **early June to mid-September,** the **Isle au Haut Boat Company** operates a passenger ferry to the park's Duck Harbor dock in addition to its year-round service to the Town Dock.

The Best of Acadia National Park

You can pack a lot into five days, even getting a taste of the more remote sections of the park. If you have limited time, stick to Mount Desert Island. For easiest park access, base yourself in Bar Harbor; even better, stay at one of the park's campgrounds. If you plan on visiting Isle au Haut, plan a night closer to Stonington to catch the early boat. Be sure to plan ahead and make reservations for the Sand Beach Entrance Station, Acadia Summit Road, and Jordan Pond North parking lot.

Acadia on Mount Desert Island
DAY 1
Pack a picnic, head to the park's Hulls Cove Visitors Center, purchase a pass, pick up a schedule of ranger-led activities, and then drive or pedal the **Park Loop.** You can complete the loop itself in about two hours, but it'll take the better part of the day if you stop at all the sights, including the Acadia

Nature Center, Wild Gardens of Acadia, and Abbe Museum at **Sieur de Monts Spring,** as well as **Sand Beach, Thunder Hole, Jordan Pond House,** and **Cadillac Mountain** (best at sunset, or save it for sunrise tomorrow). Make it a whole day by adding a hike. Perhaps stretch your legs with a **walk along the Ocean Path** or an ascent of Great Head or Gorham Mountain. If time permits, visit the Seawall area and **Bass Harbor Head Light.** In the evening, if you're not completely exhausted, perhaps attend a ranger-led program at either Blackwoods or Seawall Campground.

DAY 2
Rise early and catch sunrise from the summit of **Cadillac Mountain.** Enjoy the morning and early afternoon exploring one of the park's outlying holdings aboard a ranger-narrated cruise to **Baker Island** or **Islesford.** On returning, head

Jordan Pond House

Best in One Day

If you only have one day to explore Acadia National Park, spend it on Mount Desert Island.

- Rise early and welcome the day from the summit of **Cadillac Mountain.** Descend to Bar Harbor for breakfast, and pick up a picnic lunch to enjoy during your park explorations.

- Begin at the **Hulls Cove Visitors Center,** where you can check out exhibits.

- Spend the morning driving the coast-hugging section of the **Park Loop Road,** stopping to take in the sights at **Sieur de Monts Spring,** including the **Abbe Museum** and **Wild Gardens of Acadia.**

- Wriggle your toes in the sands of **Sand Beach.**

- Hike the **Ocean Path, Great Head,** or **Gorham Mountain,** and view **Thunder Hole.**

sunset from Cadillac Mountain

- Continue to Jordan Pond House for a walk or pedal on the **carriage roads,** followed by popovers on the lawn.

- Loop over to the quiet side of the island, perhaps stopping to visit **Asticou** or **Thuya Gardens** in Northeast Harbor, then edging around the shoreline of **Somes Sound** on Sargent Drive.

- Loop out through Southwest Harbor to the **Seawall** section of the park to view **Bass Harbor Head Light,** perhaps hiking **Wonderland** or **Ship Harbor Nature Trail** en route.

- End the day with a sunset paddle, a dinner cruise to **Islesford,** or a **ranger-led program** at one of the park's campgrounds. If you didn't rise early to catch sunrise from Cadillac's summit—or even if you did—consider returning for sunset.

to the **Jordan Pond House** for tea and popovers on the lawn. Work it off with a sunset walk or pedal on the carriage roads.

DAY 3

Pursue your interests, mixing and matching any of the following: Take a guided **sea kayaking** tour; enjoy **bird-watching** with Michael Good of Down East Nature Tours; **hike** Acadia, St. Sauveur, Mansell, or Flying Mountain, followed by a refreshing **swim** in Echo Lake; reserve a **horse-drawn carriage ride** to the Day Mountain summit; scale Acadia's cliffs on a **climbing** lesson; take a sunset cruise aboard the *Margaret Todd*; or join one or more **ranger-led programs.**

Acadia on the Schoodic Peninsula
DAY 4

Pack a picnic and catch a ferry to Winter Harbor and spend the day exploring the **Schoodic** section of the park, either by **bicycle** or via the **Island Explorer.**

Acadia on Isle au Haut
DAY 5

Rise early, pack a picnic and plenty of water, and catch the morning park boat out of Stonington to **Isle au Haut** for a **day hike.** Consult with the ranger upon arrival to determine which trails are best for your abilities and schedule.

Hidden Acadia

Though the park's new transportation plan will help reduce crowding at Acadia's most popular sights, sometimes you simply want to slip away from the madding crowd. Here are a few ways to do just that. For each, the days and activities are interchangeable, so you can mix and match at whim.

Schoodic Peninsula

Even though the mainland Schoodic section of Acadia National Park is easily accessible, it sees far fewer visitors than Mount Desert Island. If even this area feels a bit crowded, both the **Maine Coastal Islands National Wildlife Refuge,** a birder's bonanza, and the **Donnell Pond Public Reserved Land,** a wilderness reserve laced with hiking trails and splashed with lakes and ponds, are within easy reach. While the region offers plentiful elbow room, it doesn't have a lot of overnight accommodations, so be sure to book a camping site or accommodations before arriving.

DAY 1

Pack a picnic lunch and snacks, and spend your first day in the **Schoodic section of Acadia National Park.** Drive, bike, or use the Island Explorer bus to explore the park's nooks and crannies. Hike the **Schoodic Head Loop** or the **Buck Cove Mountain Trail,** visit the **Rockefeller Welcome Center,** pedal the biking paths, stroll along or hang out on the pink granite shoreline, and maybe catch sunset, either from **Schoodic Point** or by hiking to the shoreline from the **Sundew Trail** on the **Schoodic Institute** campus.

DAY 2

Drive Route 1 north to Pigeon Hill Road in Steuben to **Maine Coastal Islands National Wildlife Refuge,** on Petit Manan, for bird-watching and easy hiking. En route, you'll pass the trailhead for **Pigeon Hill,** a moderate hike with great views from the summit. You can

Schoodic Point

Acadia National Park is a great place to introduce children to the great outdoors. Between park visits, you'll find plenty of other activities with real kid appeal. Here are a few sure bets.

IN THE PARK

Before arriving, register either by phone or online for **Acadia Quest,** an experiential scavenger hunt in the park. At park headquarters, sign kids up as **Junior Rangers.** Then pick and choose from the **ranger-led activities** that appeal to your family's interests and abilities. Good choices for **easy family hikes** include the Ocean Path, Jordan Pond Nature Trail, Ship Harbor Nature Trail, and Wonderland. If you're into **geocaching,** ask about the park's EarthCache Program (www.nps.gov/acad/planyourvisit/earthcache.htm).

Kids can handle something slimy on Diver Ed's Dive-In Theater Boat Cruise.

SLIMY SEA CREATURES

You can't beat the wow appeal of **Diver Ed's Dive-in Theater Boat Cruise** (207-288-3483 or 800/979-3370, www.divered.com). Ed dives to the depths with an underwater camera while you wait on board and watch the action. When he resurfaces, he brings along with him a variety of creatures from the depths for passengers to see, feel, and learn about.

LOBSTER LORE

Even if the kids won't eat lobster, they'll be fascinated by the information presented during the two-hour cruises aboard the **Lulu** (56 West St., Bar Harbor, 207/963-2341 or 866/235-2341, www.lululobsterboat.com).

HANDS-ON NATURE

"Please touch" is the philosophy at the **George B. Dorr Museum of Natural History** (105 Eden St./Rte. 3, Bar Harbor, 207/288-5015, www.coa.edu), a small museum on the College of the Atlantic campus in Bar Harbor. Kids have the opportunity to touch fur, skulls, and even whale baleen.

FERRY HOPPING

Spend the better part of a day on the **Cranberry Isles,** visiting both Big and Little Cranberry and walking or biking around, or take a passenger ferry to **Winter Harbor** and hop on the Island Explorer bus to visit the Schoodic section of Acadia National Park. En route, watch for seals, seabirds, and lobster boats hauling traps.

NATIVE AMERICAN CULTURE

Check with the **Abbe Museum** (26 Mt. Desert St., Bar Harbor, 207/288-3519, www.abbemuseum.org) about scheduled special programs for kids, and time your visit to take advantage of them. There's a resource room for children downstairs and a few other kid-friendly exhibits at this Native American history museum, but the events bring it all to life.

LAUGH FEST

Improv Acadia (15 Cottage St., Bar Harbor, 207/288-2503, www.improvacadia.com) stages a family-friendly show every evening.

I SCREAM, YOU SCREAM

The ultimate kid-in-a-candy-store experience is at **Ben & Bill's** (66 Main St., Bar Harbor, 207/288-3281 or 800/806-3281), where you can buy not only chocolates made on-site but also to-die-for ice cream in both adult- and kid-pleasing flavors.

OLYMPICS OF THE FOREST

Expert lumberjack Tina Scheer and her crew demonstrate their amazing skills at **The Great Maine Lumberjack Show** (Rte. 3, Trenton, 207/667-0067, www.mainelumberjack.com). During the 75-minute performance, two teams compete in 12 events, including ax throwing and log rolling. You can participate in some and even arrange for your youngster to learn how to log roll. Talk about a great story for that "what I did on my summer vacation" assignment.

continue north to Cherryfield and Route 182, the **Blackwoods Scenic Byway,** to the **Donnell Pond Public Reserved Land** for a day hike followed by a swim. If you've brought a kayak or canoe, you'll find plenty of inviting lakes and ponds along the way. Don't forget a picnic lunch.

DAY 3

Plan a morning hike on the **Northern Corea Heath** trail to explore the diverse ecosystems and the rare plateau bog. Have lunch at **Corea Wharf Gallery,** and then spend a leisurely afternoon browsing the numerous **artisans' galleries** tucked throughout the Schoodic region.

Quiet Side of Mount Desert Island

The western side of Mount Desert Island draws fewer visitors, not because it lacks hikes, paddles, and scenery, but rather because the park's hub is on the eastern side. Southwest Harbor anchors the region, but the village is much smaller than Bar Harbor. Few commercial bus tours motor through and no cruise ships dock here, which keeps crowds at bay. Many of the park's trails draw hikers, but there are places to slip way.

DAY 1

Rise early if you want to hike any of the more popular trails on this side of the island, including **Acadia, St. Sauveur,** and **Flying Mountains.** After refreshing yourself with a dip in **Echo Lake,** loop out to the park's picnic area at **Seawall** to enjoy your pre-packed lunch. Afternoon options include **bird-watching** from Seawall's shore, at the adjacent brackish pond, and along the **Hio Road;** viewing **Bass Harbor Head Light;** and visiting the **Wendell Gilley Museum** or the **Maine Granite Industry Historical Society Museum.**

DAY 2

Explore one or more of Acadia's islands. Hop aboard a passenger ferry to the **Cranberry Isles** from Southwest Harbor and visit both **Great Cranberry** and **Islesford,** where the park maintains a small museum. Or, take the luncheon nature cruise from Bass Harbor to **Frenchboro**

bird-watching on Mount Desert Island

10 Best Hikes

MOUNT DESERT ISLAND

Ocean Path
This popular trail is both easy and easy to reach. Plan an early-morning arrival for this **4.4-mile round-trip** that mirrors the shore, taking in Sand Beach, Thunder Hole, Otter Cliffs, and Monument Cove (page 58).

Jordan Pond Shore Path
A mostly level **3.2-mile loop,** the shore path navigates a counterclockwise circuit of **Jordan Pond.** Plan your hike for fall, for a supremely colorful palette, and reward your efforts with popovers at **Jordon Pond House** (page 62).

Gorham Mountain Loop
This **3.5-mile loop** hike summits 525-foot **Gorham Mountain,** for views of Sand Beach, Egg Rock Light, the Beehive, and Champlain Mountain, continues to the **Bowl,** a lovely pond, and then descends to the Park Loop Road (page 63).

Beachcroft Path
Fifteen hundred beautifully engineered pink granite steps and slabs ease the moderate **2.4-mile round-trip** climb to **Huguenot Head** on the west side of Mount Desert's **Champlain Mountain.** Savor the views over Frenchman Bay before making the more difficult ascent to the summit, where the vistas are even more spectacular (page 65).

Penobscot and Sargent Mountains
This **6-mile round-trip** hike takes in two summits on the west side of Mount Desert Island. The terrain is difficult to strenuous, but you can take a swim break between peaks in **Sargent Pond,** and the views are worth the effort (page 65).

Flying Mountain Trail
Despite being the lowest of Acadia's 26 peaks, this west-side mountain delivers gorgeous views over the mouth of Somes Sound via this **1.5-mile loop.** The descent brings you to **Valley Cove,** a place to cool tootsies, before the easy walk back to the parking lot (page 70).

Perpendicular and Razorback Trails
Ready for a workout on one of the park's most engineered trails? Start on the Perpendicular Trail, which has more than 1,000 steps and snakes up

Jordan Pond Shore Path

Mansell Mountain from the shores of Long Pond. Return via the steep Razorback Trail to make it a **2.7-mile loop** (page 73).

SCHOODIC PENINSULA

Schoodic Head Loop
The Schoodic Head Loop connects three trails for a **2.7-mile round-trip** hike that travels from woods to the summit for expansive views (page 147).

Schoodic Mountain
Not to be confused with the Schoodic Head Loop, this moderately difficult **2.8-mile loop** in the Donnell Pond Public Reserved Land rewards hikers with panoramic views of Acadia's peaks on Mount Desert Island across Frenchman Bay (page 154).

ISLE AU HAUT

Western Head and Cliff Trails
For terrific shoreline scenery, take a day trip to Isle au Haut and hike these two trails for a nice loop around **Western Head.** The route follows the coastline, ascending ridges and cliffs and descending to rocky beaches, with some forested sections (page 231).

with **Island Cruises** (be sure to make advance reservations). If you're an experienced cyclist, you could take a bike aboard the state ferry to **Swans Island** for the day.

DAY 3

Choices, choices: If you're yearning to hike, consider off-the-beaten-path **Mansell Mountain** or **Great Notch.** If you prefer to paddle, join **Maine State Kayak** on a **guided sea-kayaking trip,** or combine paddling with **bird-watching** at **Bass Harbor Marsh,** a tidal marsh within the park that's a breeding area for American black ducks and Nelson's sharp-tailed sparrows. **Pretty Marsh Picnic Area** is a fine place for a picnic, and a stairway accesses the pebbly shoreline.

Isle au Haut Getaway

When you really want to slip away, Isle au Haut is the answer. The section of Acadia on this remote, wooded island is considered the park's backcountry. Because access is limited, it's an especially quiet part of Acadia. The spectacular scenery includes cliffs and crashing surf, mountains, woodlands, and inviting Long Pond, which is as close as you'll get to a shower. If you spend a few days here camping and hiking, you must bring everything you might need with you (and back) and make camping and boat reservations in advance.

HIKING

Although most of the island's 18 miles of trails are rated moderate, they're not as well maintained as those on Mount Desert Island, so they may seem more strenuous. If you're staying overnight, you don't have to worry about missing the ferry, so you can link trails together for long hikes. If you're only here for the day, confer with the ranger who meets the boat about the best options for your abilities and desires. If you want to cool off, follow the unpaved road eastward for roughly 2.5 miles to **Long Pond,** the local swimming hole.

CAMPING

The only way to stay overnight in the park on Isle au Haut is at one of the five lean-tos in the primitive **Duck Harbor Campground.** Reservations are required, and you should make campground reservations before making boat reservations. The campground's season runs May 15-October 15. Unless you want to schlep your gear 4-5 miles from town, depending upon the route, confirm when the **Isle au Haut Boat Company** runs its park boat to Duck Harbor—usually early June to mid-September—and plan your trip within those dates.

GETTING THERE

Unless you have your own boat, the only way to get to Isle au Haut is with the **Isle au Haut Boat Company** in Stonington, located at the tip of Deer Isle. From early June to mid-September, there's twice-daily boat service to the park's dock in Duck Harbor. (Don't mix it up with the company's other route, which goes to the town dock, 4-5 miles from the campground.)

Fall Foliage

The timing and quality of Maine's fall foliage owes much to the summer weather that precedes it, but the annual spectacle never disappoints. In early September, as deciduous trees ready themselves for winter, they stop producing chlorophyll, and the green begins to disappear from their leaves. Taking its place are brilliant reds, yellows, oranges, and purples that paint the leaves and warm the hearts of every "leaf-peeper."

PLANNING TIPS

- The colorful display begins slowly, reaches a peak, and then fades—starting in Maine's north in early-mid-September and working down to the southwest corner by mid-October. Peak foliage in Acadia typically occurs in early-mid-October, with the color hanging on almost until the end of the month.

- Trees put on their most magnificent show after a summer of moderate heat and rainfall. Excessive heat and scant rainfall means colors will be less brilliant and disappear more quickly. Throw a September or October northeaster or hurricane into the mix, and estimates are up for grabs.

- All this means that predictions are imprecise, so allow some schedule flexibility to take advantage of optimum color. Early September-mid-October, check the foliage section on the state Department of Conservation's website (www.mainefoliage.com) for frequently updated maps, recommended driving tours, and weekly reports on the foliage status (this is gauged by the percentage of "leaf drop"). Sign up via the website for weekly email reports (Acadia straddles zones 1 and 2 in the report maps). The state's toll-free fall foliage hotline is 888/624-6345.

- Fall foliage trips are extremely popular, so lodging can be scarce. Plan ahead and make reservations; sleeping in your car can be mighty chilly at that time of year.

TOP LEAF-PEEPING SPOTS

- On Mount Desert Island: Hike any of the trails that don't drop to the oceanfront; the

autumn on a carriage trail on Mount Desert Island

more inland, the better. You'll still get ocean views from most summits, but you'll see more vibrant color in the mountains. Good bets are Mansell, Beech, and South Bubble Mountains. The carriage trails are also good bets for color. I especially like Witch Hill Pond, where you see not only the foliage, but also the pond and a few bridges.

- In the Schoodic region: By far, the best color is along the Blackwoods Scenic Byway, which noodles between mountains and ponds. Up the ante by hiking Schoodic or Black Mountains—you'll take in views over Mount Desert Island and Frenchman Bay.

- In the Blue Hill/Deer Isle region: Begin with the Penobscot Narrows Bridge Observatory; on a clear day, the sweeping views range from Katahdin, Maine's highest peak, to Cadillac, the highest on the Eastern Seaboard. Mosey down the peninsula for more up-close views, especially where there are fresh-water ponds.

Acadia by Sea

Yes, the waters lapping Acadia's shores are chilly, but don't let that keep you away from them. One of the best ways to see this national park is from the water—either from the comfort of an excursion boat or up close and personal on a sea kayaking tour.

Mount Desert Island

BAR HARBOR WHALE WATCH COMPANY

(1 West St., Bar Harbor, 207/288-2386 or 800/942-5374, www.barharborwhales.com)

Have a whale of a time looking for humpback, finback, and minke whales while aboard a high-speed catamaran staffed by knowledgeable guides, some affiliated with Allied Whale. In season, opt for the whale and puffin trip, which includes viewing of the puffin colony on Petit Manan Island.

LULU LOBSTER BOAT

(55 West St., Bar Harbor, 207/288-3136, www.lululobsterboat.com)

You'll learn about every aspect of Maine's tasty crustacean as you cruise the waters around the Porcupine Islands.

DIVER ED'S DIVE-IN THEATER BOAT CRUISE

(207/288-3483 or 800/979-3370, www.divered.com)

Go down to the bottom of the sea with Diver Ed. Although geared to kids, adults will also enjoy this fun and educational cruise aboard the *Starfish Enterprise*.

SEA VENTURE CUSTOM BOAT TOURS

(207/412-0222, www.svboattours.com)

Charter a custom, nature-focused trip with Registered Maine Guide and committed environmentalist Captain Win Shaw and learn about sea life, coastal birds, and marine habitats.

SEA PRINCESS

(207/276-5352, https://barharborcruises.com)

A park ranger narrates a 2.5-hour afternoon

kayaking around Bar Harbor

Acadia In-Park Lodging

	Location	Price	Season	Amenities
Blackwoods	Mount Desert Island, east side	$30	early May- mid Oct.	tent and small RV sites (35-feet max)
Seawall	Mount Desert Island, west side	$22-30	late May- mid Oct.	tent and small RV sites (35-feet max)
Schoodic Woods	Schoodic Peninsula	$22-40	late May- mid Oct.	tent and RV sites
Duck Harbor	Isle au Haut	$20	mid May-mid Oct.	lean-tos

cruise around the mouth of Somes Sound and out to Islesford. The tour includes a stop on the island, allowing enough time for a quick look-about and a visit to the museum.

ISLAND CRUISES
(Little Island Marine, Shore Rd., Bass Harbor, 207/244-5785, www.bassharborcruises.com)
Join Captain Eli Strauss on a lunch tour to Frenchboro. En route, learn about island communities, sea critters, and coastal birds. On the return trip following lunch on the island, Strauss will haul a lobster trap or two and explain the process.

NATIONAL PARK KAYAK TOURS
(39 Cottage St., Bar Harbor, 800/347-0940, www.acadiakayak.com)
Explore the waters on the western side of Mount Desert Island with a guided kayaking trip, ranging from four hours to multiple days.

COASTAL KAYAKING TOURS
(48 Cottage St., Bar Harbor, 207/288-9605 or 800/526-8615, www.acadiafun.com, $49-61)
Dip a paddle into Bar Harbor's waters with an introductory, family, or sunset guided tour.

Blue Hill/Deer Isle
THE PERFECT TOUR
(207/479-3000, https://theperfecttour.com)

Join captain Linda Greenlaw, of *Perfect Storm* fame, for a custom tour aboard the *Earnest*, during which you might catch your dinner, enjoy a floating picnic, or savor a sunset while fishing, bird-watching, and wildlife-watching.

CASTINE KAYAK ADVENTURES
(17 Sea St., 207/866-3506, www.castinekayak.com)
All of Kayak Karen's tours are great, but for a different experience, consider the Bioluminescent Night Paddle tours, which happen under the stars (weather permitting).

ISLE AU HAUT BOAT COMPANY
(27 Seabreeze Ave., Stonington, 207/367-5193 or 207/367-6516, www.isleauhaut.com)
During Isle au Haut Boat Company's narrated 1.25-hour Scenic Harbor Cruise, the crew hauls a string of lobster traps as the boat weaves a course through the islands salting Stonington's harbor.

Schoodic Region
HANCOCK POINT KAYAK TOURS
(58 Point Rd., Hancock, 207/266-4449, http://schoodicmaineguide.com)
Join Registered Maine Master Guide Antonio Blasi on a guided sea kayaking excursion of Frenchman Bay. Trips operate on a flexible schedule and usually include a stop on an island. Multiday expeditions are available.

Acadia on Mount Desert Island

Rather like an octopus, or perhaps an amoeba, Acadia National Park extends its reach here and there and everywhere on Mount Desert Island. The park was created from donated parcels—a big chunk here, a tiny chunk there—and slowly but surely fused into its present-day size of more than 50,000 acres, of which 36,968 acres are owned by the National Park Service (the balance is privately owned land under conservation easements managed by the park). Permanent boundaries do exist—Congress certified them in 1986—but they can be confusing to visitors. One minute you're in the park, the next you've stepped into one of the island's towns. This symbiotic relationship is a reminder that Acadia National Park, covering a third of the island, is the major presence on Mount Desert. It affects traffic, indoor

Highlights

Look for ★ to find recommended sights, activities, dining, and lodging.

★ **Park Ranger Programs:** Join one of the numerous programs, from guided hikes and photography tours to natural history programs and children's activities, offered daily by park rangers (page 44).

★ **Park Loop Road:** If you do nothing else on Mount Desert Island, drive this magnificent road that takes in many of Acadia National Park's highlights (page 46).

★ **Sieur de Monts Spring:** This lovely oasis is home to the Wild Gardens of Acadia, the Acadia Nature Center, and the original Abbe Museum, and is the base for hiking Dorr Mountain (page 48).

★ **Sand Beach:** Spread a blanket on one of the few beaches in this part of Maine (page 49).

★ **Thunder Hole:** Time your visit to see the tide surge and explode through this geological formation (page 50).

★ **Cadillac Mountain:** Acadia's prime feature is the highest point on the Eastern Seaboard, allegedly where the sun's first rays land in the United States. Drive, bike, or hike to the 1,530-foot summit for stunning views (page 52).

★ **Eagle Lake:** A mountain backdrop and undeveloped shores contribute to Eagle Lake's popularity. A boat launch and a carriage road make it easy to explore (page 54).

★ **Gorham Mountain Trail:** This trail requires minimal effort to reap maximum rewards. It's an excellent family hike—kids love the Cadillac Cliffs (page 63).

★ **Biking Carriage Roads:** Fifty-seven miles of meandering crushed-stone paths crossing 17 handsome stone bridges welcome cyclists (page 75).

Acadia on Mount Desert Island

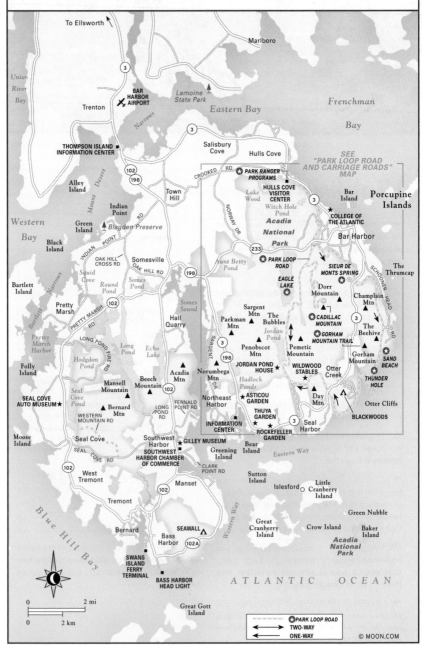

To Ellsworth

Marlboro

3

Union
River
Bay

Lamoine
State Park

BAR
HARBOR
AIRPORT

Trenton

Eastern Bay

Frenchman

Narrows

3

Bay

THOMPSON ISLAND
INFORMATION CENTER

Salisbury
Cove

Hulls Cove

102
198

Town
Hill

SEE
"PARK LOOP ROAD
AND CARRIAGE ROADS"
MAP

Alley
Island

CROOKED   RD

PARK RANGER
PROGRAMS

Lake
Wood

HULLS COVE
VISITOR
CENTER

Bar
Island

Porcupine
Islands

Indian
Point

Witch Hole
Pond

3

Western
Bay

Green
Island

Blagden Preserve

NORWAY DR

Acadia

COLLEGE OF
THE ATLANTIC

Black
Island

Somesville

OAK HILL
CROSS RD

OAK HILL RD

National

Bar Harbor

Squid
Cove

Round
Pond

Somes
Pond

198

Park

Aunt Betty
Pond

233

PARK LOOP
ROAD

SIEUR DE
MONTS SPRING

The
Thrumcap

Bartlett
Island

Pretty
Marsh

PRETTY MARSH   RD

Somes
Sound

EAGLE
LAKE

Dorr
Mountain

Champlain
Mtn

SCHOONER HEAD RD

Pretty
Marsh
Harbor

LONG POND FIRE RD

Long
Pond

Echo
Lake

Hall
Quarry

Sargent
Mtn

The
Bubbles

Jordan
Pond

CADILLAC
MOUNTAIN

3

The
Beehive

Parkman
Mtn

GORHAM
MOUNTAIN TRAIL

Folly
Island

Hodgdon
Pond

SARGENT DR

Penobscot
Mtn

Pemetic
Mountain

Gorham
Mountain

SAND
BEACH

Acadia
Mtn

JORDAN POND
HOUSE

WILDWOOD
STABLES

SEAL COVE
AUTO MUSEUM

Mansell
Mountain

Beech
Mountain

102

Norumbega
Mtn

198

3

Otter
Creek

THUNDER
HOLE

Moose
Island

Seal
Cove
Pond

Bernard
Mtn

WESTERN
MOUNTAIN RD

FERNALD
POINT RD

Northeast
Harbor

Hadlock
Ponds

ASTICOU
GARDEN

Day
Mtn

Otter Cliffs

BLACKWOODS

Seal Cove

SEAL COVE RD

LONG POND
RD

Southwest
Harbor

GILLEY MUSEUM

Greening
Island

THUYA
GARDEN

3

Seal
Harbor

West
Tremont

102

SOUTHWEST
HARBOR CHAMBER
OF COMMERCE

CLARK
POINT RD

Bear
Island

Eastern Way

INFORMATION
CENTER

ROCKEFELLER
GARDEN

Tremont

102

Manset

Sutton
Island

Islesford

Little
Cranberry
Island

Western Way

Green Nubble

Bernard

Bass
Harbor

SEAWALL

102A

Great
Cranberry
Island

Crow Island

Baker
Island

Acadia
National
Park

SWANS
ISLAND
FERRY
TERMINAL

BASS HARBOR
HEAD LIGHT

ATLANTIC   OCEAN

Blue Hill Bay

0   2 mi

0   2 km

Great Gott
Island

Great
Gott
Island

PARK LOOP ROAD

TWO-WAY

ONE-WAY

© MOON.COM

and outdoor pursuits, and in a way, even the climate.

Acadia's history is unique among national parks and is indeed fascinating. Several books have been written about the high-minded (in the positive sense) and high-profile personalities who provided the impetus and wherewithal for the park's inception and never flagged in their interest and support. To spotlight a few, we can thank George B. Dorr, Charles W. Eliot, and John D. Rockefeller Jr. for the park we have today.

The National Park Service began keeping track of Acadia's visitors in 1919, when 64,000 people were counted. Given Acadia's complicated boundary, an exact count is impossible now, but in the past few years the number of annual visitors has exceeded 3.5 million. You'll understand why when you visit for yourself.

Exploring the Park

INFORMATION CENTERS

There are two major centers on Mount Desert Island for Acadia National Park information. Some Acadia information is also available from the Bar Harbor Chamber of Commerce Visitor Center, the Southwest Harbor Chamber of Commerce, and the Mount Desert Island Chamber in Northeast Harbor. The park also maintains a small info center facing the Village Green in Bar Harbor.

Thompson Island Information Center

As you cross the bridge from Trenton toward Mount Desert Island, you might not even notice that you arrive first on tiny Thompson Island, site of **Thompson Island Information Center** (8am-6pm daily mid-May-mid-Oct.), established jointly by the Mount Desert Island Regional Chamber of Commerce and Acadia National Park.

The rustic building, on your right as you head south on Route 3, has walls lined with brochures for accommodations, restaurants, and activities. There are also restrooms. Across Route 3 is a picnic area overlooking Mount Desert Narrows.

If you've arrived without a place to stay (particularly in July-Aug.), the welcoming staffers here are incredibly helpful. They keep track of lodging vacancies throughout Mount Desert Island and will go to great lengths to funnel you somewhere. In high season, don't expect to be overly choosy, though—room rates are high, vacancies are few, and you will be forced to take your chances.

In season, a park ranger is sometimes posted on Thompson Island to answer questions and provide basic advice on hiking trails and other park activities, but consider this a stopgap—also be sure to continue on to the park's main visitors center. You can purchase your Acadia pass here as well.

NOTE: Implementation of the park's new transportation plan includes replacing this info center with a planned Acadia Gateway Center, on Route 3 in Trenton in 2023.

Hulls Cove Visitors Center

The **Hulls Cove Visitors Center** (25 Visitor Center Rd., Bar Harbor, 207/288-3338, daily Apr. 15-Oct. 31), eight miles southeast of the head of Mount Desert Island, is well signposted. Hours vary by season and staffing availability. Here you can buy your park pass; rendezvous with pals; buy books, park souvenirs, and audio guides; and use the restrooms. Pick up a schedule for the excellent **Island Explorer** shuttle bus system, which operates late June-Columbus Day.

Previous: view from Baker Island to Mount Desert Island; Acadia's rugged coastline; bicycling along the carriage roads.

If you have children, enroll them in the park's free **Junior Ranger program.** To earn a Junior Ranger patch, they must complete the activities in an age-appropriate workbook, attend ranger-led programs, and promise to take care of Acadia. Once they've completed the book, stop by the **Junior Ranger Table** (8:30am-10:30am and 2pm-4pm daily) to be sworn in by a ranger.

As part of Acadia's new transportation plan, parking at the visitors center is expanding, which will make it easier for those stopping in for info as well as for day-trippers to leave their vehicle and hop on the Island Explorer bus. The bus stops at the base of the winding stairway from the parking lot to the center.

Bar Harbor Village Green

The park staffs a small **information center** (8am-5pm, late June-mid Oct.) in downtown Bar Harbor on the Village Green, adjacent to the Island Explorer bus stop on Firefly Lane. Park and bus information, as well as visitor passes, are available here.

PARK ENTRANCE AND ROAD FEES

Avoid lines by buying your pass online and printing it out at home. Passes are required when in the park, and rangers check cars left at trailheads. Buying a pass not only gives you access to all the wonders of Acadia, but also supports much needed projects and repairs.

- **Entrance fee:** $30 per car or RV, $25 per motorcycle late June-mid-October (when the Island Explorer is running). It covers everyone in the vehicle and is valid for seven days. If want to buy an individual pass that will not cover a car (best if you're traveling on foot or by bicycle or using the Island Explorer for transportation), the fee is $15 for seven days (free for ages 15 and younger).

- **Acadia Annual Pass:** $55, valid for one year from the day of purchase. If you're in Acadia more than one week in any given year, this is the cheapest option. It covers

the pass holder and passengers in a non-commercial vehicle.

- **Interagency Annual Pass:** $80, allowing unlimited entrance for one year from date of purchase to all national parks and other federal recreation sites.

- **Senior Pass:** At $80, this is an incredible bargain for U.S. citizens and permanent residents who are age 62 or older, allowing lifetime entrance to more than 300 national parks, historic sites, and monuments. It also entitles you to half-price camping. Purchase must be made in person with proof of age (a driver's license, passport, etc.). The pass covers everyone in the pass holder's vehicle. You will need to show an ID at the park's gate.

- **Access Pass:** free for any U.S. citizen or permanent resident who is blind or permanently disabled (a temporary disability, such as a broken arm or leg, does not qualify). It allows lifetime entrance to all national parks as well as Fish and Wildlife, Forest Service, and Bureau of Land Management sites. It also allows half-price camping. The pass covers everyone in the pass holder's vehicle.

- **Interagency Annual Military Pass:** free pass for active-duty military personnel and dependents; valid documentation required (CAC Card or DD Form 1173).

- **Interagency Volunteer Pass:** Accumulate 250 service hours and you'll be rewarded with a one-year pass valid for federal recreation sites.

- **Every Kid Outdoors Fourth Grade Pass:** free for any U.S. fourth-grade student; allows entry with family: www.everykidinapark.gov

Where to Buy Passes

- **Avoid lines and purchase** your weekly or annual pass **online** at www.yourpassnow.com.

- **Hulls Cove Visitors Center,** the park's

Park Rules

Most rules at Acadia are just common sense; some are specific to Acadia's situation and needs.

- It's forbidden to disturb or remove any **public property**—plants, minerals, artifacts, animals, and so forth. This extends to the rocks on the beaches.

- **Pets** are allowed in Acadia, with some exceptions, but they must be on a leash (6 feet or shorter). They must not be left unattended. Pets are not allowed on Sand Beach or at Echo Lake May 15-September 15, in the Wild Gardens of Acadia; on ranger-led programs; or in the Duck Harbor Campground on Isle au Haut. They are also banned from the park's ladder trails and from the visitors centers and other public buildings. Service dogs, of course, are always exempt from the rules.

- **In-line skating, roller skiing,** and **skateboarding** are allowed only on roads closed to automobiles.

Be sure to purchase a park pass before entering Acadia.

- **Bicycles** are not allowed on any hiking trails. They're allowed on 45 miles of park carriage trails, but not on 12 miles of signposted carriage roads in the Land and Garden Preserve.

- **Motorized vehicles** are not allowed on park trails and carriage roads; **ATVs** are not allowed anywhere in the park. **Class 1 e-bikes** are allowed on the carriage roads; heed 20mph speed limit.

- **Camping** within park boundaries is allowed only at the park's two campgrounds on Mount Desert Island, one on Isle au Haut, and one on the Schoodic Peninsula. There is no backcountry camping in the park or anywhere else on Mount Desert Island, but outside the park there are commercial campgrounds. Visitors with horses can camp at Wildwoods.

- **Camp stoves** and **grills** are allowed only in designated campgrounds and picnic areas; fires are allowed only in fire rings and fireplaces at these sites.

- **Alcohol** use is not allowed in the public buildings or facilities, at parking lots and pullouts, at Sand Beach and Echo Lake Beach, along the Lake Wood shoreline, or within 0.25 mile of the swimming areas at the southeastern end of Long Pond.

- **Hunting** is not allowed in the park.

- **Fireworks** are not allowed in the park.

- **Feeding of wildlife,** including gulls, is prohibited.

- Federal law requires the use of **seatbelts** by drivers and passengers in all national parks.

visitor information center. Be prepared to wait for a parking slot in high season.

- The Acadia National Park information office on Firefly Lane, opposite the **Village Green** in downtown Bar Harbor; the office faces the hub for the Island Explorer bus system.

- **Sand Beach Park Entrance Station,** on Park Loop Road between the Schooner Head Overlook and Sand Beach.

- **Blackwoods and Seawall Campgrounds,** the only park camping areas on Mount Desert Island.

- **Thompson Island Information Center** (Rte. 3, Trenton).

- The **Jordan Pond Gift Shop** and the **Cadillac Mountain Gift Shop.**

- Local **chambers of commerce** also sell passes.

Vehicle and Parking Reservations

In 2019, Acadia implemented a new transportation plan to reduce congestion in the park. The timed-entry plan requires **vehicle reservations** for two sections of the Park Loop Road. Once you've entered either, you may remain as long as you like, but if you leave, you'll need another reservation to reenter. Reservations must be made online (www.recreation.gov); they are not available at the park. The proposed reservation fee ($6, subject to change) is nonrefundable. The vehicle reservation is not a substitute for a park pass; you'll need both.

While no vehicles greater than 38 feet in length and 11 feet, 8 inches in height have been permitted on the Park Loop Road, the park plans to begin phasing this requirement out and allowing such vehicles in—check with the park for current status. The park also will begin requiring reservations for the Jordan Pond North parking lot.

Vehicle and parking reservations will be available on a rolling basis as much as six

months in advance, although a portion will be held back and released 48 hours in advance. Reservations are not needed for pedestrians or bicyclists on Park Loop Road, or for other sections of the park.

SAND BEACH ENTRACE STATION

Reservations are not required for 2021, but likely will be for 2022. When implemented, they will be required (7am-5pm daily) for the one-way section of the Park Loop Road edging the ocean from the Sand Beach Entrance Station to Otter Cliff Road. This section accesses Sand Beach and Thunder Hole as well as the trailheads for Great Head, The Beehive, Ocean Path, and Gorham Mountain. All of these also can be reached on the Island Explorer bus.

CADILLAC SUMMIT ROAD

Reservations are required (4:30am-6:30pm daily) for the 6.4-mile round-trip Cadillac Summit Road, so if you're planning to catch the sunrise from the summit, plan accordingly. There are about a half dozen viewpoints along the road, as well as the Blue Hill Overlook (best for sunsets) and the summit. The Island Explorer does not service this road. Note: RVs and trailers are prohibited on this road.

Supporting the Park

A single glance at the map of Acadia National Park immediately raises the question: How do you sell passes and count heads in a park that has patches of land here and there and everywhere—even on a section of the mainland and on offshore islands? The answer: not easily.

So, let's look at the picture another way. It's important to know that 100 percent of the entrance fees stays in the National Park Service. Of that, 80 percent stays in Acadia National Park. The private Friends of Acadia organization and other donors often match these funds to make the money even more effective. Consider just a few of the projects your pass helps fund:

Island Explorer Routes

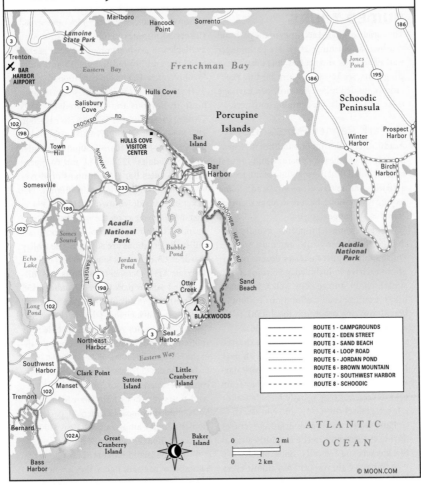

ROUTE 1 - CAMPGROUNDS
ROUTE 2 - EDEN STREET
ROUTE 3 - SAND BEACH
ROUTE 4 - LOOP ROAD
ROUTE 5 - JORDAN POND
ROUTE 6 - BROWN MOUNTAIN
ROUTE 7 - SOUTHWEST HARBOR
ROUTE 8 - SCHOODIC

© MOON.COM

- Trail and carriage road reconstruction and rehabilitation
- The Island Explorer bus system
- New and improved restroom facilities
- Repairs to historic stone bridges
- New and improved informational exhibits
- Improvements in accessibility
- Lifeguards at Sand Beach and Echo Lake Beach
- Interpretive programs
- Campground, building, and picnic area improvements and rehabilitation
- Paved roads and parking areas

At many of the project sites, you'll see brown National Park Service signs that read "This Project Funded by Your Park User Fee." Think of them as Acadia's thank-you note for your support.

Do note that the park is enforcing passes. If

you don't display some type of pass in vehicle, you're subject to citation.

GUIDED TOURS

The variety of guided activities in the park and nearby is astonishing: There are park ranger walks and talks and cruises, bus tours, bicycling tours, sea kayaking tours, birding expeditions, guided hikes, horse-drawn carriage rides, and even deluxe camping outfitters.

★ Park Ranger Programs

Acadia offers plentiful possibilities for learning more about the park's natural and cultural history. You'll find the schedule of ranger-led activities online (www.nps.gov/acad). Some require reservations; be sure to make them for activities that appeal to you.

The park ranger programs, usually lasting 1.5-3 hours, are great—and most are free. During July-August there are dozens of programs each week. Included are birding, dusk, sunset, photo, and geology walks; mountain hikes; carriage road explorations by foot or bike; stargazing programs; touch tank talks; and activities geared to young families.

Reservations are required and fees charged for several different boat cruises with park rangers, who provide natural history narration. The specific cruises can vary from year to year, but they usually include **Baker Island, Frenchman Bay,** and **Islesford.**

Park rangers also give evening lectures during the summer in the amphitheaters at Blackwoods and Seawall Campgrounds.

And best of all, you can join almost every ranger program via an Island Explorer bus (late June-mid-Oct.).

Bus, Trolley, and Van Tours

The veteran of the Bar Harbor-based bus tours is **Acadia National Park Tours** (ticket office Testa's Restaurant, Bayside Landing, 53 Main St., Bar Harbor, 207/288-0300, www.acadiatours.com, May-Oct., $35 adults, $20 under age 13). A 2.5-3-hour naturalist-led tour of Bar Harbor and Acadia departs at 10am and 2pm daily from Testa's Restaurant, across from

Agamont Park near the Bar Harbor Inn, in downtown Bar Harbor. Reservations are advised in midsummer and during fall foliage season (late Sept.-early Oct.); pick up reserved tickets 30 minutes before departure. Also available is a 3.5-hour premium tour geared to adults and limited to ages 13 and older ($60pp), offered on an air-conditioned coach.

If you have a time crunch, take the one-hour trolley-bus tour operated by **Oli's Trolley** (ticket office 1 West St., Bar Harbor, 207/288-5443 or 866/987-6553, https://olis-trolley.com, 4 trips 10am-3:30pm daily July-Aug., $33 adults, $23 ages 11 and younger), which includes Bar Harbor mansion drive-bys and the Cadillac Mountain summit. The ticket office is downtown at Harbor Place, next to the town pier on the waterfront. Dress warmly if the air is at all cool; it's an open-air trolley. Reservations are advised. The trolley also does 2.5-hour park tours two to five times daily late April-October ($48 adults, $33 children) and 4-hour park tours ($73 adults, $58 children). Call in advance for specific departure times, which change from week to week. The bus and trolley routes both include restroom stops. Tours depart from the boardwalk at the Harborside Hotel, 55 West Street.

MDI Tours (207/808-0413, www.mditours.com) offers private 3- to 5-hour park and island tours in Chevy Suburban SUVs. The tours, guided by local islanders, depart from Hadley's Point Campground. Rate is $100 per vehicle per hour.

While the Island Explorer buses do reach a number of key park sights, they are not tour buses. There is no narration, the bus cuts off the Park Loop at Otter Cliffs, and it excludes the summit of Cadillac Mountain.

Bird-Watching and Nature Tours

For private tours of the park and other parts of the island, contact Michael Good at **Down East Nature Tours** (150 Knox Rd., Bar Harbor, 207/288-8128, www.downeastnaturetours.com). A biologist and Maine Guide, Good is simply batty about birds. He has

Getting Around the Car-Free Park

Since 1999, when the fare-free, propane-fueled buses began running throughout Mount Desert Island, more than eight million riders have used the Island Explorer bus system, reducing car and RV usage and its resultant pollutants and greenhouse gases. The Island Explorer transports passengers to ferry landings, saves hikers and bikers from backtracking, gets commuters to work, and has revolutionized the summertime traffic patterns on Mount Desert Island.

The service has been dramatically expanded since it began on an experimental basis. Service on Mount Desert Island now begins in late June and lasts until Columbus Day. The Schoodic Peninsula route, which coordinates with the Bar Harbor-Winter Harbor ferry, continues through August; the Ellsworth Express operates once a day in each direction through early September.

Why spend valuable vacation time looking for a place to park your car? Why be disappointed when you reach a trailhead and find the parking lot full? Take the bus. Feeling unsteady and unable to hike or bike? Tour the park and the island on the bus. Each bus can handle up to six bikes and a wheelchair, and there are even dedicated bike shuttles operating between Bar Harbor and Eagle Lake.

The nonprofit Downeast Transportation (207/667-5796, www.exploreacadia.com) operates the fleet, with support from your park entrance fees, Friends of Acadia, L.L.Bean, and area towns and businesses.

Two caveats: First, these aren't tour buses, and there is no narration, nor do they climb Cadillac Mountain, so don't use them as a substitute for a guided tour or as a way to see all park highlights. Second, although the buses are free, riders traveling into the park must have a park pass.

The Island Explorer hub is the Bar Harbor Village Green, where all of the routes (except Schoodic) begin or end. Late June-Labor Day, service begins at 6:45am daily, although not every route starts that early. The last bus leaves downtown Bar Harbor about 10pm for the campgrounds at the northern end of the island. A geolocation system provides tracking information at the Village Green, at the Hulls Cove Visitors Center, and online.

Specific stops are listed on the schedule, but drivers will pull over and pick you up or drop you off anywhere they feel it's safe. Don't hesitate to request a stop or flag down a bus.

So pick up a schedule—copies are everywhere on Mount Desert—and use the Island Explorer to explore the island.

spent more than 25 years studying the birds of North America and has even turned his home property on Mount Desert Island into a bird sanctuary. Good specializes in avian ecology in the Gulf of Maine. Whether you're a first-timer wanting to spot eagles, peregrine falcons, shorebirds, and warblers or a serious bird-watcher seeking to add to your life list, perhaps with a Nelson's sharp-tailed sparrow, Good is your man. Prices begin at $135 per person for four hours and include transportation from your lodging; kids are half price. Bring your own binoculars; Good supplies a spotting scope.

Carriage Tours

To recapture the early carriage roads era, take one of the horse-drawn open-carriage tours offered from Wildwood Stables (Wildwood Stables, 21 Dane Farm Rd., Seal Harbor), one mile south of the Jordan Pond House. Best choices are the two-hour Day Mountain Summit and Mr. Rockefeller Bridges tours. The concessionaire is expected to change in 2021 or 2022, so check the park's website for updated info. Two carriages are wheelchair accessible, carrying up to two wheelchairs and four additional passengers; call in advance to reserve space on these.

DRIVING TOURS

The ideal way to fully appreciate Acadia is to hike the miles of trails, bike the carriage roads, canoe the ponds, swim in Echo Lake, and camp overnight. It seems rather a shame to treat Acadia as a drive-through park, but circumstances—time, health, and other factors—sometimes dictate that.

★ Park Loop Road

Logically, a driving tour of Acadia would follow the 20-mile **Park Loop Road** (Apr. 15-Nov. 30, weather permitting). It begins at the Hulls Cove Visitors Center, winds past several of the park's scenic highlights (with parking areas), ascends via a 3.2-mile spur to the summit of Cadillac Mountain, and provides magnificent vistas. Allow a couple of hours so you can stop along the way.

Start at the parking lot below the Hulls Cove Visitors Center and follow the signs; part of the loop is one-way, so you'll be traveling clockwise. Time your drive to your Sand Beach Entrance reservation, allow about 20-30 minutes from the Hulls Cover Visitor Center via Paradise Hill to Park Loop roads. The maximum speed is 35 mph, but be alert for gawkers and photographers stopping without warning and pedestrians dashing across the road from stopped cars or tour buses. If you're out at midday in summer, don't be surprised to see cars and RVs parked in the right lane in the one-way sections; it's allowed unless posted otherwise (although right-lane parking will be eliminated in the future).

Along the route are trailheads and overlooks, as well as **Sieur de Monts Spring,** home to the Acadia Nature Center, Wild Gardens of Acadia, Abbe Museum summer site, and the convergence of several spectacular hiking trails (Sieur de Monts is before the Sand Beach Entrance Station, so consider visiting here at a different time); **Sand Beach; Thunder Hole; Otter Cliffs;** the **Fabbri Picnic Area,** with one wheelchair-accessible picnic table; **Jordan Pond House; Bubble Pond; Eagle Lake;** and the summit of **Cadillac Mountain.** Just before you get to Sand Beach, you'll see the park entrance station, where you'll need to purchase a pass if you haven't already done so. If you're here during nesting and fledging season—April-mid-August—be sure to stop in the Precipice Trail Parking Area to view the peregrine falcons with spotting scopes provided by park staff.

Island Tour

If you still have time for and interest in more driving after you've done the loop, take a spin around the rest of the island. Exit the Park Loop Road near Bar Harbor onto Route 233, heading west. Continue to Route 198 and turn left (south). After just over one mile, watch for a smallish sign for **Sargent Drive.** Only cars are allowed on this road—no RVs. Take Sargent Drive, skirting gorgeous **Somes Sound,** into Northeast Harbor.

Leave Northeast Harbor via Route 198 northbound, and drive until you reach the head of Somes Sound. Go left around the head of the sound to **Somesville,** a gem of a historic hamlet, and then continue south on Route 102 to Southwest Harbor. If you have time, take the Route 102A loop, which offers a chance to see **Bass Harbor Head Light.** You'll want to walk from the parking lot to get the best view; one trail has you scampering down steps to the ledges and rocks below it, while the other is a paved drive to near the light's base. Otherwise, continue on Route 102 to Tremont, with a possible detour into Bernard for great lobster on the wharf, and then go clockwise around to West Tremont, Seal Cove, and Pretty Marsh, and back to Somesville. From here, you can go directly north to leave the island via Route 102/198, or go to Bar Harbor by heading east.

ACADIA QUEST

Acadia Quest (207/288-3340, www.friendsofacadia.org) is a terrific way for families to explore the park. The free scavenger hunt encourages participants to collect experiences in Acadia. Teams must include at least one adult older than 18 and one child younger than 18. To complete the quest, teams undertake and document activities; the theme and specifics change each year. Doing so immerses you in the park, engaging everyone in fun and in

Park Loop Road and Carriage Roads

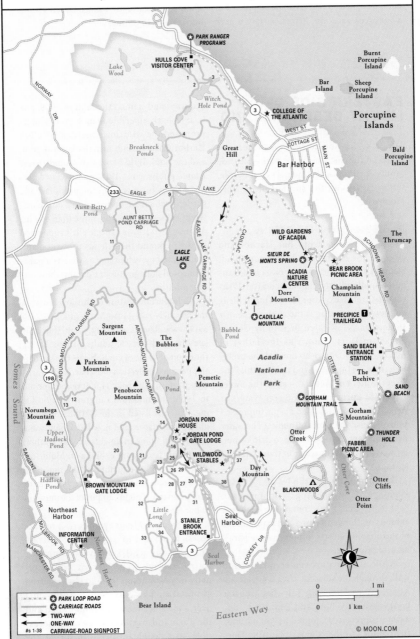

PARK RANGER PROGRAMS

HULLS COVE VISITOR CENTER

Lake Wood

Witch Hole Pond

Breakneck Ponds

COLLEGE OF THE ATLANTIC

Great Hill

WEST ST

COTTAGE ST

Bar Harbor

LAKE RD

NORWAY DR

EAGLE LAKE

AUNT BETTY POND CARRIAGE RD

Aunt Betty Pond

EAGLE LAKE

EAGLE LAKE CARRIAGE RD

CADILLAC MTN RD

WILD GARDENS OF ACADIA

SIEUR DE MONTS SPRING

ACADIA NATURE CENTER

Dorr Mountain

BEAR BROOK PICNIC AREA

Champlain Mountain

CADILLAC MOUNTAIN

PRECIPICE TRAILHEAD

AROUND-MOUNTAIN CARRIAGE RD

Sargent Mountain

The Bubbles

Bubble Pond

Acadia National Park

SCHOONER HEAD RD

The Thrumcap

SAND BEACH ENTRANCE STATION

The Beehive

SAND BEACH

Parkman Mountain

Jordan Pond

Pemetic Mountain

Penobscot Mountain

GORHAM MOUNTAIN TRAIL

Gorham Mountain

OTTER CLIFF

Norumbega Mountain

Somes Sound

Upper Hadlock Pond

Lower Hadlock Pond

JORDAN POND HOUSE

JORDAN POND GATE LODGE

WILDWOOD STABLES

Day Mountain

Otter Creek

THUNDER HOLE

FABBRI PICNIC AREA

Otter Cliffs

BROWN MOUNTAIN GATE LODGE

BLACKWOODS

Otter Point

Northeast Harbor

Little Long Pond

STANLEY BROOK ENTRANCE

Seal Harbor

Otter Cove

SARGENT DR

MANCHESTER RD

MILLBROOK RD

INFORMATION CENTER

Northeast Harbor

Seal Harbor

COOKSEY DR

Porcupine Islands

Burnt Porcupine Island

Bar Island

Sheep Porcupine Island

Bald Porcupine Island

Legend

- PARK LOOP ROAD
- CARRIAGE ROADS
- TWO-WAY
- ONE-WAY
- #s 1-38   CARRIAGE-ROAD SIGNPOST

Bear Island

Eastern Way

0   1 mi

0   1 km

© MOON.COM

some cases educational activities. The quest runs from late spring until early November, but is designed so that it can be completed in a one-week vacation. Prizes, such as a park pass, Acadia Quest patch, or raffle items, are awarded. Register in person at the Hulls Cove, Thompson Island, or Village Green visitor/info centers, or online.

Sights

EASTERN SIDE OF MOUNT DESERT ISLAND
The Park Loop Road

The Park Loop Road loops through the major sights on the east side of the park—Sieur de Monts Spring, Sand Beach, Thunder Hole, Otter Cliffs, and the summit of Cadillac Mountain.

★ SIEUR DE MONTS SPRING

About two miles from Bar Harbor and close to the often-busy Park Loop Road, Sieur de Monts Spring is an oasis in a tranquil woodland setting. Named after 17th-century French explorer Pierre Dugas, Sieur de Monts, the spring is the centerpiece of a 10-acre parcel donated in 1916 by George Bucknam Dorr, known as the father of Acadia. It was Dorr who erected the pretty Italianate springhouse and dubbed this "the Sweet Waters of Acadia"—after the Sweet Waters of Europe and the Sweet Waters of Asia, two springs that had deeply impressed him on a visit to Constantinople. (The water here, incidentally, is not safe to drink—nor, for that matter, is the water in those Istanbul springs.)

Also here is the **Acadia Nature Center** (9am-5pm daily June-Aug., 9am-4pm daily Sept.-early Oct., free), containing hands-on exhibits on flora and fauna and explanations of the ongoing efforts to preserve the park's natural resources.

While at the nature center, take time to walk through the adjacent **Wild Gardens of Acadia** (9am-5pm daily July-Aug., shorter hours mid-May-June and Sept.-Oct., donation appreciated), touted as "an outdoor field guide" to the island's plantlife. Dorr

acquired and named the land in 1909, and in 1961 park superintendent Harold Hubler proposed the wildflower garden. The Bar Harbor Garden Club initially sponsored it, and the book *Wild Flowers of Mount Desert Island,* published in 1918, was used to determine the plantings. Walking paths lace the gardens, which are divided into a dozen different habitats containing more than 400 indigenous wildflower species. It's supported by the park and the Friends of Acadia and maintained by volunteers as well as a park-sponsored college student during the summer months.

An important feature of this lovely area is the privately run **Abbe Museum** (207/288-3519, www.abbemuseum.org, 10am-5pm daily late May-mid-Oct., $3 adults, $1 ages 11-17), the original home of Dr. Robert Abbe's extensive personal collection of archaeological artifacts, some dating back 11,000 years. Opened in 1928, the museum outgrew this building, which is listed in the National Register of Historic Places, and now has a handsome year-round home in downtown Bar Harbor. Inside this facility are exhibits on Maine archaeology and the history of the museum. Tickets purchased here can be applied toward admission to the main campus of the museum in Bar Harbor.

The Sieur de Monts Spring area provides access to several hiking trails. Moderate to strenuous trails, many with granite stairs, ascend **Dorr Mountain** (originally Dry Mountain, then Flying Squadron Mountain). The easy **Jesup Path**—just over a mile between Park Loop Road and the Tarn and partially wheelchair accessible—is a delightful stroll. In spring, the

- Acadia National Park was **established by Congress in 1929,** after previous incarnations as Lafayette National Park (1919) and Sieur de Monts National Monument (1916).

- Acadia covers nearly **50,000 acres** on the mainland and islands, including about 13,000 acres protected by conservation easements. Acadia's permanent boundaries were established by Congress in 1986, but it is allowed to acquire offshore easements from the Penobscot Bay shipping channel and throughout Hancock County, and mainland easements on the Schoodic Peninsula. No other U.S. national park has as large an easement program in terms of percentage of total acreage.

- Acadia has **26 mountains** ranging in height from 284 feet (Flying Mountain) to 1,530 feet (Cadillac Mountain). Cadillac is the highest point on the Eastern Seaboard of the United States.

- Nine **"great ponds"** (covering more than 10 acres) lie within the park boundaries. Five others abut parkland. The depths of these lakes and ponds range from 7 feet (Aunt Betty Pond) to 150 feet (Jordan Pond). Mount Desert Island's lakes and ponds have restrictions on swimming and personal and motorized watercraft.

- Acadia has more than 130 miles of **hiking trails** on Mount Desert Island. At the height (so to speak) of trail construction, in the early 20th century, there were some 230 miles. Some of the discontinued trails are being rehabilitated via the Acadia Trails Forever program, a joint project of the park and Friends of Acadia.

- Acadia officials estimate an average of more than **3.5 million park visits** each year, most in the months of July, August, and September.

- The **"creature counts"** in Acadia, on Mount Desert Island, and in the surrounding waters include 338 species of birds, 17 species of amphibians, 5 reptile species, 28 species of fish, 47 species of terrestrial mammals, and 12 species of marine mammals.

- The **Park Loop Road** is 20 miles, with an additional 3.5-mile spur to the visitors center, 1-mile spur to Jordan Pond House, and 7 miles for a round-trip to the summit of Cadillac Mountain.

- The park has 45 miles of car-free, broken-stone **carriage roads** for walking, biking, and horseback riding as well as cross-country skiing and snowshoeing in winter; 12 miles of carriage roads south of Jordan Pond are owned by the Land and Garden Preserve and are open to walkers and horses but not bicycles.

- Acadia has four **campgrounds**—two on Mount Desert Island, one on Isle au Haut, and one on the Schoodic Peninsula. All are seasonal. Backcountry camping is not allowed in Acadia. Commercial campgrounds are located on Mount Desert Island outside park boundaries.

- The Schoodic Peninsula is the only park acreage that's on the mainland; all other park properties are on **islands.** A bridge connects Mount Desert Island to the mainland town of Trenton, but other parcels can only be reached by boat.

boardwalk area of the path is a birder's feast. The path in its entirety is particularly spectacular during the fall foliage season. You can also access the Tarn and Hemlock Trails at Sieur de Monts.

Sieur de Monts Spring is on the Island Explorer bus Route 3/Sand Beach and Route 4/Blackwoods.

★ SAND BEACH

Below the Park Loop Road and the park entrance station, Sand Beach is the park's only large sandy beach on salt water—*cold* salt water (about 55°F). Well, it's not really sand, as a sign posted here will tell you—it primarily comprises zillions of crushed shells, pulverized so they look like sand. Despite the frigid waters, Sand Beach can get very crowded on hot days. If you're hankering for a beach day, get there early and bring all the necessities: food, water, sunscreen, and beach gear.

If you haven't purchased your park entrance pass by this point, you'll need to do it here. Sand Beach is about 25 minutes from Bar Harbor via the Island Explorer bus (Route 3/Sand Beach). It's a bit quicker by car before and after the bus season. You can access the **Great Head Trail** and **Ocean Path** from here.

★ THUNDER HOLE

Thunder Hole gets pumped up as a spectacular attraction, and it is—but only if your timing is right. If not, as one ranger snickered, it's more of a gurgling gulch. When the wind is coming from the south or southeast, when a storm has churned up the sea, or when the tide is rushing inward, you'll hear and feel how Thunder Hole got its name. As the water rushes into a narrow slot in the rocks, it creates a powerful roar, shoots into the air, and often showers the closest bystanders.

If your schedule is flexible, check the tide tables in the local paper and try to be here for the incoming tide, preferably about two to three hours before high tide or during a storm.

Because of the sea spray, the steps leading down toward Thunder Hole are often very slippery. Take particular care with small children and anyone who tends to be unsteady. Stay well back from the shoreline when the surf is rough. People have been swept away by rogue waves, and rescue is extremely difficult.

The park operates an information station (9am-5pm daily May-late Oct.) at Thunder Hole.

OTTER CLIFF AND OTTER POINT

Otter Cliff, an impressive, rugged, pink granite headland edged with spruce, rises 110 feet above the shore, making it one of the highest cliffs along the Eastern Seaboard. From here, you can admire the views back to Sand Beach and over to Schoodic and watch climbers scale the crags. Just offshore, a bell buoy marks the Spindle, a ledge where explorer Samuel de Champlain's ship sustained damage in 1604, forcing him to seek refuge in Otter Cove. Park here or continue to Otter Point, and follow the Ocean Path back to the cliff; it's an easy half-mile walk. It can get crowded here, so if possible go in early morning or late afternoon for a more serene experience. Be careful when scampering around, especially if the rocks are wet. And the name? No, there are no sea otters here. It takes its name from Otter Stream, home to river otters, which empties into Otter Cove.

LITTLE HUNTERS BEACH

Shh, don't tell too many people about this small treasure, just before Hunters Head on the Park Loop Road. It is unsigned but is designated on the park map. Watch for a stream crossing with a trail and stairway on the ocean side. Descend the stairs to a cobble beach, where the incoming tide rumbles as it rolls over the smooth, rounded stones. The stairway parallels a cascading stream that disappears into the beach only to resurface a few feet below. Cliffs fringed with spruce trees frame the beach. A trail near the top of the stairway leads out to a point, where views of the surf are especially fine when the tide is surging. Be careful on the path, as erosion has taken its toll, and resist the urge to remove any rocks from the beach area. Not only is it against park rules, but it also threatens the beach's continued existence.

JORDAN POND HOUSE

Jordan Pond House (Park Loop Rd., 207/276-3316, https://jordanpondhouse.com, 11am-9pm daily, late Apr.-late Oct., 11am-7pm daily late Oct., $11-27) began life as a rustic 19th-century teahouse; wonderful old photos line the walls of its current incarnation, built after a disastrous fire in 1979. It's a hub in the hiking and carriage trail network, and the only restaurant within the park, so

---

1: The Abbe Museum 2: Sand Beach 3: Little Hunters Beach

it's usually very busy. Afternoon tea has been a tradition since Nellie McIntire began serving tea, popovers, and strawberry jam on the lawn; service is available until 5pm daily in summer, weather permitting (about $11). Jordan Pond is far from a secret, so expect to wait for seats at the height of summer. Better yet, plan ahead and make reservations. The setting can't be beat; the food is so-so. Jordan Pond House is on Routes 4 and 5 of the Island Explorer bus.

A health note: Perhaps because of all the sweet drinks and jam served outdoors, patrons at the lawn tables sometimes find themselves pestered by bees. They don't usually sting unless you pester them back, but be alert if anyone in your party is allergic to beestings.

TOP EXPERIENCE

★ CADILLAC MOUNTAIN

As the highest point in Acadia, at 1,530 feet, the summit of Cadillac Mountain receives the day's first rays of sunlight. A couple of trails will get you to the summit, including one from Blackwoods Campground, and you can get a good road- or mountain-bike workout on the road (bikes aren't allowed on trails), but in the end, most summiteers tend to get there by car—a seven-mile round-trip on a paved road. The Island Explorer bus does not go to the Cadillac Mountain summit.

Formerly named Green Mountain, Cadillac was once topped by the wooden Summit Hotel, built by an ambitious developer who eventually fell on hard times and went bankrupt. Some might say he deserved it for blighting the landscape. Before its decline in the late 19th century, however, the 6,000-foot Green Mountain Cog Railway transported guests to the summit, where the view was just as spectacular as it is today. (Photos of the cog railway era are part of the collection at the Bar Harbor Historical Society on Ledgelawn Street.) The summit road was built in 1931.

At the height of summer, the busiest times on the summit are sunrise, midday, and sunset; if you don't have your heart set on seeing the sunrise or sunset, the crowds are thinner an hour or two after sunrise or an hour or two before sunset. The best sunset views aren't from the summit, but from the Blue Hill pullout (with parking) and from some of the small pullouts as you descend the road. Go early to snag a parking space.

At the top are head-swiveling vistas along with a gift shop and restrooms. Be sure to walk the paved 0.3-mile Summit Trail loop for the full effect, but stay on the trail to preserve the summit's fragile plants and soil.

The park runs the **Hawkwatch** program (late Aug.-mid-Oct., weather permitting) near the Cadillac summit. The observation site is on the Cadillac North Ridge Trail, about 600 feet from the summit parking lot. Park interpreters are on hand to help you identify the various species of hawks, falcons, and eagles that migrate through Acadia each fall. Since the Hawkwatch project began in 1995, the annual raptor count during the migration season has averaged about 2,500, with a high of 5,422 in 2011. Call or check online for current hours.

Carriage Roads

Acadia's **carriage road system** is one of the park's most valued cultural resources—listed since 1979 in the National Register of Historic Places. Between 1913 and 1940, petroleum heir John D. Rockefeller Jr. was involved in the purchase of acreage and the design and construction of more than 57 miles of carriage roads on Mount Desert Island. Today, thanks to him, we can all walk and bike these roadways, and even go for horse-drawn carriage rides. Not only did Rockefeller conceptualize the project, finance it, and consult on every aspect of the road and bridge designs, he was on hand during the construction and landscaping phases. No detail escaped his scrutiny.

Distinctive features of the roads are 17 handsome rough-stone bridges (with single, double, and triple arches; no two are alike), 16-foot-wide broken-stone roadbeds that

1: Park Loop Road 2: the view from Cadillac's summit in autumn

required countless hours of labor, and tasteful carved trail markers. A holdover from Rockefeller's previous carriage road experience was the use of roadside borders of squared-off granite coping stones—known at Acadia as "Mr. Rockefeller's teeth." The roads were designed to deliver dazzling vistas: bald summits, woodlands, and gem-like ponds.

And then there are the two stone gate lodges, or gatehouses—**Brown Mountain Gate Lodge** (near Northeast Harbor) and **Jordan Pond Gate Lodge** (near Jordan Pond)—heralding entrances to the original carriage road system (many more access points exist today). Designed by Grosvenor Atterbury in a whimsical French Romanesque style (Rockefeller Hall on the Schoodic Peninsula is in the same style), the handsome structures are startling, to say the least. It's hard not to smile when you encounter them. During the construction of the carriage roads, engineer Paul Simpson and his family occupied the Jordan Pond Gate Lodge.

Forty-five miles of the broken-stone roads—all on the east side of the island, between the Hulls Cove Visitors Center in the north and Seal Harbor in the south—are in the park and open for walking, bicycling, and horseback riding, and in winter for cross-country skiing and snowshoeing. Twelve additional miles of roads on private land owned by the Land and Garden Preserve are open for walking and horseback riding but not cycling—be alert for the No Bikes signs when you're cycling. All of the private roads are south of the Jordan Pond House.

If you simply want a peek at a bridge, and don't have the time, inclination, or ability to mosey the carriage roads, head to the Witch Hole Pond loop, where the impressive triple-arched **Duck Brook bridge** is just yards off Duck Brook Road.

★ Eagle Lake

The largest lake on the eastern half of the island, Eagle Lake is entirely within the park, so its shoreline is undeveloped. Cadillac,

Pemetic, and Sargent Mountains and the Bubbles surround it. You can pedal or walk around Eagle Lake on a carriage road, launch a canoe or kayak and paddle its waters, or just find a rock to sit on and enjoy the scenery. You might spot ospreys, eagles, great blue herons, loons, and other wildlife. Two parking lots off Route 233 make access easy—one is by the boat launch, and a larger one is on the other side of the road—but these are often filled during peak season. Consider taking the Island Explorer bus, which offers a Bicycle Express route between Bar Harbor and Eagle Lake.

WESTERN SIDE OF MOUNT DESERT ISLAND

The western half of the island, also known as the quiet side, gets far less traffic and few tour buses. The park sections here may lack the big-name sights or jaw-dropping vistas of the Park Loop Road, but looping around on Route 102 provides ample rewards for those who prefer more intimate park experiences.

Carroll Homestead

Kids especially enjoy stepping back in time at this farmhouse, occupied by four generations of the Carroll family between 1825 and 1917. The park manages the homestead as an educational resource. During open house hours, volunteers tell family stories and teach pioneer games.

Seawall

The remote Seawall section of the park, on the island's west side, feels raw and untrammeled. Here, sea-tossed granite rocks form a natural seawall dotted with rocky pockets and ledges. Most visitors congregate on the ocean side, but on the inland side of the road is Seawall Pond. This freshwater body makes it possible to view freshwater and saltwater birds simultaneously, a rare occurrence. Seawall's picnic area is a fine place to watch waves crash on the rugged pink shoreline. The best time to visit, however, is at night: Seawall is one of the best places in the country for **stargazing.** Also here is one of the park's two campgrounds.

Bass Harbor Head Light

At the southern end of Mount Desert's western "claw," follow Route 102A to the turnoff toward Bass Harbor Head. Drive or bike to the end of Lighthouse Road, walk down a steep wooden stairway, and look up and to the right. Voilà! Bass Harbor Head Light, its red glow automated since 1974, stands sentinel at the eastern entrance to Blue Hill Bay. A paved path with interpretive signage starts from the other end of the parking lot and leads to near the tower's base; for the best views, scramble carefully to the lower rocks. Built in 1858, the 26-foot tower and lightkeeper's house occupy a dramatic setting, making for a photographer's dream. Winter access to the parking lot may be limited, but otherwise the area is open year-round. The park acquired the lighthouse complex, comprising five historic buildings on two acres, from the Coast Guard in 2020. Plans are underway to stabilize the lighthouse, protect it from deterioration, and potentially provide visitor access in the future. Not far from the light (east along Rte. 102A) are the trailheads for the easy Ship Harbor and Wonderland Nature Trails, part of Acadia National Park. The lighthouse is a short walk from Route 102A, on the Island Explorer bus Route 7/Southwest Harbor.

Bass Harbor Marsh

If you're a birder, Bass Harbor Marsh is a must. Both American black ducks and Nelson's sharp-tailed sparrows breed here, as does the elusive least bittern. The best access for bird-watching is via the Marshal Brook fire road, off Seal Cove Road in Southwest Harbor.

Pretty Marsh Picnic Area

Picnic spots are everywhere on Mount Desert, but an Acadia National Park site that many people miss is way-off-the-beaten path Pretty Marsh Picnic Area. When I visited on a hot August day at the height of peak season, only a handful of others were enjoying this wooded waterfront spot. A few picnic sites are roadside, but the best ones require ambling down the fire road to the shore of Pretty Marsh Harbor, where you'll find a pavilion sheltering two tables and a trail to others tucked under trees along the shoreline. Behind the pavilion, a stairway descends to a rocky beach—great for beachcombing and perhaps even braving a swim (no lifeguards). Kids love this place, but come prepared with insect repellent. Don't be misled by the name; the waterfront is not marshy. The picnic area is just west of Route 102 (Pretty Marsh Rd.) on the westernmost shore. Pretty Marsh is not on an Island Explorer bus route; you'll need a car or bike to get here.

OFFSHORE ISLANDS

Islesford Historical Museum

The **Islesford Historical Museum** (207/288-3338, www.nps.gov/acad, free), on Little Cranberry Island and operated by the National Park Service since 1948, displays collections pertinent to the island's history and heritage. Call or check the website for hours, as these vary every year. William Otis Sawtelle (1874-1939), a summer resident of the island, purchased the old island market in 1917. Inside he found artifacts belonging to the Hadlock family, which built the shorefront building in 1850. Among his finds were decoys, which he painted blue and placed around the property, including one over the door. That building, known as the Blue Duck, was where he first displayed his expanding collection of local historical materials. In 1926 he began construction of the current brick-and-slate museum. Inside, pieces from Sawtelle's collection are displayed along with other artifacts related to the Cranberry Isles' heritage.

Accessing the island requires taking one of the passenger ferries, excursion boats, or private boats that depart from Southwest Harbor or Northeast Harbor. The best choice is the ranger-narrated Islesford Historic and Scenic

Cruise aboard the *Sea Princess,* departing from Northeast Harbor (207/276-5352, www. cruiseacadia.com, $32 adults, $29 seniors, $19 ages 5-11, $9 age 5 and younger). You can also do it yourself via passenger ferry from Northeast and Southwest Harbors.

Baker Island

The best way to get to—and to appreciate—history-rich Baker Island is on the ranger-narrated Baker Island cruise booked through **Bar Harbor Whale Watch Co.** (1 West St., Bar Harbor, 207/288-2386 or 888/942-5374, www.barharborwhales.com, mid-June-mid-Sept., $49 adults, $27 ages 6-14, $9 under age 6). The five-hour tours include access via motorized skiff to the 130-acre island, which has a farmstead, a lighthouse, and intriguing rock formations. The return trip provides a view of Otter Cliffs (bring binoculars and look for climbers), Thunder Hole, Sand Beach, and Great Head. Call or check the website for departure times.

History buffs, lighthouse lovers, and naturalists will love this trip. Hannah and William Gilley, who rowed here from Mount Desert Island accompanied by their three young children, goats, and household goods, settled Baker Island in the early 1800s. They built a home and a farm and reared 12 children, with Hannah schooling them in the three R's and rowing them to church in Southwest Harbor every Sunday. When the lighthouse was built on the island in 1828, William became its first keeper, at an annual salary of $350. He was removed from that post in 1848 for political reasons, and that's where the story gets really interesting.

Note that because the National Park Service contracts with an independent boat company, there have been years when this tour hasn't been available. In that case, the only way to reach Baker Island is via charter or your own boat. In any case, pack a lunch. Check the park's ranger program schedule or ask at a visitors center for tour status.

Bass Harbor Head Light

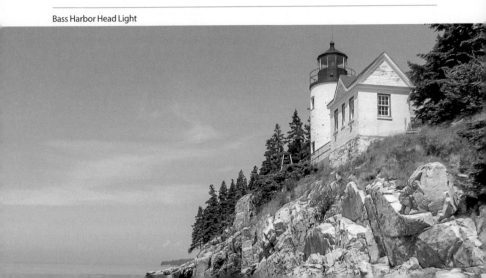

Hiking

It would take weeks of nonstop hiking to cover every trail in the Mount Desert Island acreage of Acadia National Park, and it would consume most of this book to write about them. It's not a bad idea, but few of us have enough free time to manage such a feat. It's best to do as much as you can when you're here, and return as often as possible to do more.

This section contains a selection of choice hikes, ranging from very easy to strenuous. Evaluate your schedule and your skills and limitations (especially the capabilities of your least-sturdy hiking partners), gather your gear, pack a picnic and plenty of water, and head out.

As you take your first step on your first trail, however, keep in mind the Leave No Trace philosophy that governs all recreation in the park. Stick to it for yourself and for the generations to come.

Until the establishment of the Island Explorer bus system, hikers had to do loop trails in order to return to their cars or bikes, or they had to make elaborate arrangements for pickup or shuttling. The bus schedule has created all kinds of other options. It allows you to skip the backtracking—and in some cases lets you pick up transport along the way if you or the kids wear out earlier than expected. This holds true only during the bus season (late June-early Oct., reduced schedule early Sept.-early Oct.). Even if your destination or locale isn't a scheduled bus stop, you can request a stop or flag down a bus anywhere that's safe for the driver to pull over. Pick up the latest schedule at the Hulls Cove Visitors Center or download it before you leave home at www.exploreacadia.com.

The hikes are divided here into two sections—the east side of Mount Desert Island and the west side. Because Somes Sound nearly bisects the island, none of the trails cross from one side of the island to the other,

and almost every one of the peaks' ridgelines runs north-south. The hikes are listed in order of difficulty, from very easy to strenuous; trail lengths vary within each category. Ratings are based on park advisories and personal experience.

Bear in mind that most visitors tend to spend more time on the east side of the island, for a variety of reasons—there are more trails, a range of easy-to-moderate paths, the carriage road network, the auto road to the Cadillac Mountain summit, the Park Loop Road, the park's only restaurant (Jordan Pond House), and so on. Heading for the west-side trails, even at the height of summer, can provide access to quieter spaces and some truly great hikes.

Most trails in Acadia intersect with other trails, making it easy to increase the length and/or difficulty of your hike. A good trail map comes in handy when considering these options (I've included some of these, but there plenty of others).

A number of commercial maps are available. I like the *Acadia National Park Hiking and Biking Trail Map* ($5), published by Map Adventures (www.mapadventures. com), because it's easy to read. The only drawback is that it doesn't include the entire island, making it a bit difficult to figure out locations if you're not familiar with the area. There's also a waterproof version ($10). Another good choice is the waterproof *Appalachian Mountain Club Acadia National Park Discovery Map* ($9.95), a GPS topographic map that includes all of Mount Desert Island and has insets for Isle au Haut and the Schoodic Peninsula.

Note: The park has changed trail names to their historical ones, which can make for some confusion when hiking if you're using old maps or guides. Park rangers will have the latest information.

EAST-SIDE TRAILS

Jordan Pond Nature Trail

Distance: 1-mile loop
Duration: 30-45 minutes
Elevation gain: Minimal
Effort: Very easy
Trailhead: Jordan Pond Parking Area (Island Explorer Route 4 /Loop Road or 5/Jordan Pond)

This oh-so-easy trail is perfect for little ones. You can pick up a brochure ($0.50 donation) at the trailhead detailing 10 numbered sites, so you can pepper the walk with fun info and quiz the kids along the way. Reward them afterward with ice cream at the Jordan Pond House.

The trail loops from the Jordan Pond house through the woods and down to the pond, following the shore for a bit before looping back to the starting point.

Compass Harbor

Distance: 0.8 mile round-trip
Duration: 30 minutes
Elevation gain: Level
Effort: Easy
Trailhead: Compass Harbor section of the park, off Bar Harbor's Main Street approximately one mile south of the intersection with Mount Desert Street

This is an easy stroll through an often-ignored, isolated section of the park. The path loops through old-growth forest to a point on Compass Harbor and by the ruins of George B. Dorr's summer cottage. There are plenty of nice spots for a picnic here, and at low tide you might even brave a swim from the pebbly beach area. The loop at Compass Harbor also connects to the Schooner Head Trail into the main section of the park. You can easily walk to Compass Harbor from downtown, if you want to lengthen the hike without adding any difficulty, and this little park pocket is a great place to escape crowds on busy days.

Ocean Path

Distance: 4.4 miles round-trip
Duration: 1.5-2 hours
Elevation gain: Level
Effort: Easy
Trailhead: Take the Park Loop Road to either the Sand Beach or the Otter Point parking lots. The Island Explorer bus (Route 3/Sand Beach) stops at the Sand Beach and Otter Cliffs parking areas, so you can begin the walk at either end. If you want to do the trail in one direction only rather than backtracking, get off the bus at one end or the other, then pick up another bus when you're ready to continue onward.

Because this trail is so easy and easy to reach, it's extremely popular. In fact, lovely as it is, you'd have to be crazy to be on it 10am-3pm at the height of summer. At the risk of divulging the solution, the last time I walked it, at 7am on a bright June day, I had the path all to myself—a minor miracle, actually—and the tide was at just the right height for Thunder Hole to live up to its name.

The trail runs close to the shore for about half its length and takes in several of the Park Loop Road's highlights—Sand Beach, Thunder Hole, Otter Cliffs, and the giant sea stack in Monument Cove—not to mention gorgeous sea-level views of Frenchman Bay.

Along here, it's especially tempting to "liberate" rocks from the shore, but resist the urge. Remember the slogan, "Leave the rocks for the next glacier." If you forget, a few judiciously placed National Park Service signs will remind you.

Bar Island

Distance: 2 miles round-trip
Duration: 45-60 minutes
Elevation gain: About 170 feet
Effort: Easy
Trailhead: End of Bridge St., Bar Harbor

Check local newspapers or the Bar Harbor Chamber of Commerce visitors booklet for the times of low tide, then walk across the gravel bar to wooded Bar Island (formerly Rodick's Island), which is mostly within the park boundaries. The trail, which begins as an old woods road, zigzags as it rises gently through the woods. Bear right at the first fork, and you'll come to an old homesite with a fine view to Bar Harbor. Return to the main trail, which narrows and steepens, becoming rocky and rooted, as it rises to the island's

East-Side Trails

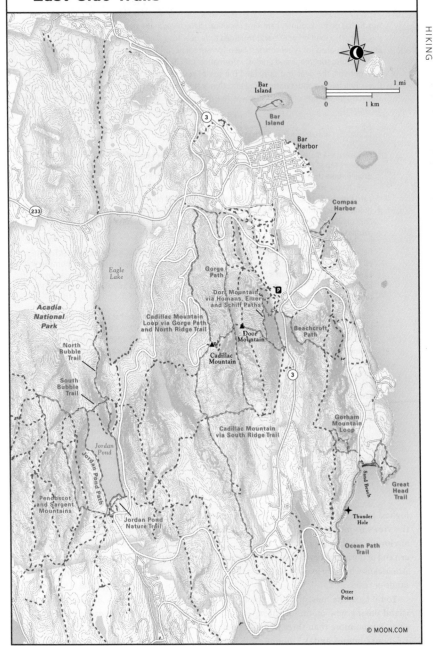

Bar Island

Bar Island

Bar Harbor

Compas Harbor

Acadia National Park

Eagle Lake

Gorge Path

Dorr Mountain via Homans, Emery and Schiff Paths

Cadillac Mountain Loop via Gorge Path and North Ridge Trail

Dorr Mountain

Beachcroft Path

North Bubble Trail

Cadillac Mountain

South Bubble Trail

Jordan Pond

Gorham Mountain Loop

Cadillac Mountain via South Ridge Trail

Penobscot and Sargent Mountains

Jordan Pond Path

Jordan Pond Nature Trail

Sand Beach

Great Head Trail

Thunder Hole

Ocean Path Trail

Otter Point

0   1 mi

0   1 km

© MOON.COM

Day Hiking Tips

Acadia has no backcountry camping, meaning all the hikes in the park are day hikes—guaranteeing, at least, a load off your back. You need little gear for a daylong hike, but use common sense and be prepared for emergencies. Even for experienced hikers and backcountry campers, it's worth noting the "maps and guides" information specific to Acadia.

In general, the gear you carry (and the size of your day pack) depends on your plans for the day—following a short nature trail and then calling it quits; hiking for a few hours and then stopping for a swim; or hiking all day with a noontime picnic. Here's a checklist to help you get organized:

- **Identification,** such as a driver's license, and your **health insurance card.**

- **Maps and guides.** Purchase a trail map at the park's visitors center. The National Park Service map of Acadia that's free at the visitors center is serviceable if you're planning only to drive or bike the Park Loop Road, but do not rely on it for hiking. On the east side of the island, even if you are planning to stick to the hiking trails, be sure also to carry a map of the park's carriage roads to avoid confusion where carriage and hiking trails meet and cross. For trail guides, I recommend *A Walk in the Park* ($12) by Tom St. Germain and *Hiking Acadia National Park* ($17) by Dolores Kong and Dan Ring. Both provide useful detailed maps and elevation profiles for each hike.

- Between late June and Columbus Day, carry a copy of the **Island Explorer bus schedule,** which you can find almost anywhere on the island or download before you leave home (www. exploreacadia.com). Stuff it in your day pack, even if you're getting to your trailhead by car. If someone in your hiking party wants to quit early, you'll want to know the nearest spot (and time) to catch a bus.

- **Water and food.** Even though some ponds in the park are used as drinking-water sources for surrounding towns, the water is treated before they get it. Don't risk intestinal problems; carry your own water. If you're worried about carrying weight and can tolerate the taste, include iodine tablets. To avoid excessive thirst, don't bring salty snacks—carry gorp or energy bars (without chocolate, so you don't have to deal with a melting mush). If you're carrying picnic fare, don't be overambitious or greedy if you're planning a strenuous hike. Be sure to pack any mayo-based food in a flexible insulated bag; peanut butter and jam (jelly for the kids) sandwiches are a safer bet.

- A couple of wastebasket-size **trash bags**—carry in, carry out. A spare bag can also come in handy for protecting maps, a camera, and binoculars in the event of a sudden squall (not unheard of during a Maine summer).

- A **compass or GPS receiver,** particularly if you're directionally challenged or are planning

highest point, marked by a cairn. From here, the views to mountain-backed Bar Harbor are lovely. Shell heaps recorded on the eastern end of the island remind visitors of Native Americans who have lived in Maine for thousands of years.

You'll have the most time to explore the island during new-moon or full-moon low tides, but no more than three hours—about 1.5 hours before and 1.5 hours after low tide. Be sure to wear a watch so you don't get trapped (for up to 10 hours). Every summer, local papers carry stories of people trapped on the island by the tide and pictures of cars parked on the sandbar and forgotten, then flooded by the incoming tide. Don't let it happen to you. Dogs are allowed, but must be tethered on a leash not exceeding six feet.

The bar is also an excellent kayak-launching site.

a lengthy hike. If you own a cell phone, carry it, but turn it off and use it only in an emergency. Wireless service can be iffy in some parts of Acadia; check when you arrive.

- A small first-aid kit (in a waterproof or ziplock bag) containing a few basic items: adhesive bandages, aspirin or acetaminophen, ibuprofen, perhaps an elastic bandage. Even though bees don't tend to be a problem in Acadia (except perhaps on the lawn at Jordan Pond House), be sure you're carrying a prefilled epinephrine syringe to prevent anaphylaxis if you're allergic to beestings (or, for that matter, shellfish). Include a few wooden matches and a whistle in case of emergency.

- Moist towelettes for various cleanup tasks, or for cleansing minor scrapes.

- A Swiss Army knife. Carry the kind with a corkscrew if you're planning on having wine with a picnic. Or you could decant white wine into a plastic water bottle to save weight—but go easy on the alcohol. Not only will it dehydrate you, but it also makes you more prone to tripping and falling.

- A full-brimmed hat and decent hiking shoes (not sandals, which provide no ankle support).

- Sunblock, lip balm (the kind with UV protection), and insect repellent. Lewey's, a natural repellent, is a good choice, especially for children. Repellents by Ben's and Cutter tend to be widely available.

- A camera (with a spare battery and memory card) and binoculars. Most of the island's summits are bare, allowing fabulous views.

- A mini flashlight and spare batteries.

- Clothing. Depending on your plans for the day, carry a change of socks, a rain jacket or windbreaker, maybe a fleece vest, and perhaps a swimsuit for a hike such as Penobscot and Sargent Mountains, where you can pause for a dip in Sargent Pond.

- Most importantly, don't hike alone, or if you do, tell someone—a friend, a relative, your lodging manager, a campground ranger, your shrink, anyone—or leave a note to say where you are headed. If for any reason you don't return, the park rangers at least will know where to start looking.

- Remember, bikes are banned from all hiking trails. Dogs must be leashed (not always convenient on strenuous scrambles), and they are banned from Sand Beach and hiking trails with ladders ("ladder trails"). Best advice: Don't bring a dog. If you do, hike only the shorter, easier trails—and do come equipped to clean up after your pet.

- Lyme disease has been reported here, so when you return, check for ticks.

Great Head Trail

Distance: 1.9-mile loop
Duration: 1 hour
Elevation gain: 145 feet
Effort: Moderate
Trailhead: Take the Park Loop Road to the Sand Beach Parking Area (Island Explorer Route 3/Sand Beach)—the lower parking area is closer to the beach, but it fills up first. Walk down the steps to the beach and across it to the far (eastern) side, where you'll see

the trailhead marker. You'll need to cross a rivulet here to reach the trailhead. If you're not here at low tide and you don't have waterproof shoes, remove your shoes so you won't be hiking with wet feet.

First take the trail to the right, which climbs a few dozen steps (the "moderate" part), then continue right toward the headland ("head"), from which you can see the beach and the prominent mound of the Beehive. Out in Frenchman Bay is Egg Rock Light and beyond it is Schoodic Point. Continue on the trail counterclockwise, following the perimeter of the head, perhaps pausing for a picnic near the ruins of a stone teahouse that was constructed in 1915 by J. P. Morgan's daughter. Continue the loop around the head, then return to Sand Beach.

You can reach Sand Beach (and therefore the Great Head Trail) via the Island Explorer bus, but since the Park Loop Road is one-way at this point, you won't be able to return to Bar Harbor the way you came. You'll need to grab a bus and continue the loop back to Bar Harbor, but the time is the same: 25 minutes from Bar Harbor to Sand Beach, 25 minutes back to the Village Green from Sand Beach.

Another, easier way to hike Great Head is to begin at the trailhead on the north side of the head and go in a clockwise direction. Take Main Street (Rte. 3) south out of Bar Harbor, and about 0.8 mile after the athletic field, bear left onto Schooner Head Road, which roughly parallels the Park Loop Road. Continue past the Schooner Head Overlook. The trail head is on the left, just after a sharp left bend in the road. This is also a great access point for bicycles. There are actually two loops, which could end up taking you 1.8-2 miles. Keep bearing left (clockwise) to skirt the perimeter of Great Head.

Jordan Pond Path

Distance: 3.3-mile loop
Duration: 1 hour minimum
Elevation gain: Level
Effort: Easy-moderate
Trailhead: Jordan Pond. By car from Bar Harbor, take the Park Loop Road (the two-way west side of the loop) to the Jordan Pond parking lot, or take Island Explorer bus Route 4/Loop Road or Route 5/Jordan Pond. In midsummer, another auto option is to take Route 3 south from Bar Harbor to Seal Harbor, then take the Stanley Brook entrance to the park, going north toward Jordan Pond. Park (the Jordan Pond North parking lot requires reservations) and head toward the boat ramp; you'll see the trailhead to the right.

This mostly level, counterclockwise circuit of Jordan Pond is a great way to walk off a Jordan Pond House lunch (including those popovers).

Or do the hike first and reward yourself with afternoon tea. Start on the east side, which is easier; the west side has the only moderate section—rocky and rooted and, depending on recent weather, possibly a bit squishy. Footbridges and boardwalks have been installed in a number of spots.

Jordan Pond is part of the island's drinking-water supply, so no swimming (or even wading) is permitted here.

As if the summer setting here weren't enough, this trail is even more beautiful in the fall, when stands of birches add gold to the palette. Plus, the trail is far less crowded in late September-early October (except perhaps for Columbus Day weekend).

Option: The giant glacial erratic known as **Bubble Rock** is enough of a phenomenon that you may want to detour from the trail to see it via the Bubbles Divide Trail, at the northeast corner of the pond to the South Bubble Trail. Stay on that to return to the Jordan Pond Path by turning right at the intersection with Jordan Pond Carry. At the risk of perpetuating a cliché, I'll add that the classic photo here is a Sisyphus imitation—the mythological fellow relentlessly pushing the boulder up a mountain, only to have it roll back. Fortunately, this one doesn't move, since it's the size of an SUV. There must be thousands of photo albums all over the world containing this image. Needless to say, kids love it. (For an easier hike, use the Bubble Rock trailhead off the Park Loop Road.)

The trail areas around Jordan Pond House and Jordan Pond have been upgraded for wheelchair access, part of a major public-private collaborative effort to increase accessibility in the park. The improved access is on the east side of Jordan Pond.

South Bubble Trail

Distance: 1 mile round-trip
Duration: 1 hour
Elevation gain: 250 feet
Effort: Easy to moderate
Trailhead: Park Loop Road, approximately 2.3 miles south of the Cadillac Mountain turnoff

This relatively easy ascent of South Bubble rewards hikers with views from its scoured granite summit over Jordan Pond and beyond to the Cranberry Isles to the south, Pemetic Mountain to the west, and over Eagle Lake toward Cadillac Mountain to the north. From the parking lot, follow the Bubbles Divide Trail, passing the Jordan Pond Carry Trail and the junction with the North Bubble Trail, and then turning left onto the South Bubble Trail. From the summit, follow a path to the left to find Bubble Rock, a glacial erratic that appears ready to tumble off the cliff and drop onto the cars far below. Return to the main trail and continue to the ledges overlooking Jordan Pond. Be sure to keep an eye on little ones, especially near the cliffs. Return by backtracking via the same trail.

Options: For a longer, more strenuous hike, consider looping in North Bubble and/or descending to Jordan Pond, a steep-ish scramble over and through boulders, with a squeeze through one tight spot.

★ Gorham Mountain Loop

Distance: 3.5 miles round-trip
Duration: 2-3 hours
Elevation gain: 525 feet
Effort: Moderate with strenuous option
Trailhead: On the one-way section of the Park Loop Road, continue past Sand Beach and Thunder Hole to the Gorham Mountain Parking Area. The Island Explorer bus (Route 3/Sand Beach) can drop you off here, or walk a short distance along the Ocean Path after getting off the bus at the Thunder Hole stop. The trailhead is at the back of the parking lot.

This is an especially popular hike, so don't expect to have the trail to yourself. Follow cairns across ledges up from the trailhead to a fork, where you'll see a plaque commemorating Waldron Bates, the ingenious path maker who instigated the strategic use of granite staircases and iron ladders for Acadia's trails. Keep left to stay on the main trail, or detour right for a little adventure. Bates was a lawyer in his day job, but his summer avocation as head of the Roads and Paths Committee for the Bar Harbor Improvement Association

(1900-1909) gave him the greatest pleasure. Think of him if you choose to bear right and navigate the more difficult 0.3-mile Canada Cliff Trail, one of his projects.

The U-shaped Canada Cliff Trail features stairs, a rung and ladders, rocky footing, granite "tunnels," and even an ancient sea cave, now high and dry. The sea cave was once filled with beach cobbles, but it's been cleaned out slowly by hikers—a prime example of the damage done by removing "just one." The Canada Cliff Trail rejoins the Gorham Mountain Trail. For an easier hike, stay on Gorham Mountain Trail.

Whichever route you choose, once you rejoin the Gorham Mountain Trail, continue to the open-ledge summit of Gorham Mountain, at 525 feet the third lowest of Acadia's peaks. A cairn marks the spot. From here, you'll see Sand Beach, Egg Rock Light in Frenchman Bay, the Beehive, Champlain Mountain, and lots more—a fabulous view. Continue along the trail as it descends, hiking straight at the first intersection, where Gorham Mountain Trail splits. The trail will intersect with the Bowl Trail in 0.2 mile; turn right to reach the intersection with the Beehive Trail and the Bowl, a lovely pond for a swim (be forewarned, there are leeches) and a nice spot for lunch. When you're ready, retrace your steps along the Bowl Trail, turning right at the first intersection and then keeping left at the two intersections with the Gorham Mountain Trail, following the Bowl Trail, to the Park Loop Road. Take another right and head for Sand Beach—perhaps dip your toes in the frigid waters—and then follow the Ocean Path back to the Gorham Mountain parking lot.

Option: For a far more strenuous hike, reverse direction using the **Beehive Trail,** one of the park's toughest hikes. Park at Sand Beach and begin on the Bowl Trail until it intersects with the Beehive Trail. One of the park's classics, this trail ascends the Beehive's face via ingenious engineering, including ladders and steps. It can be intimidating and is not one for those scared of heights. Be prepared for slowdowns along the way as more

Volunteering in the Park

As we watch federal funding for national parks lose headway year after year, every park in the United States needs a safety net like Friends of Acadia (FOA, 207/288-3340 or 800/625-0321, www.friendsofacadia.org), a dynamic organization headquartered in Bar Harbor. Propane-powered shuttle-bus service needs expanding? FOA finds a multimillion-dollar donor. Well-used trails need maintenance? FOA organizes volunteer work parties. New connector trails needed? FOA gets them done. No need seems to go unfilled.

FOA—one of Acadia National Park's greatest assets—is both reactive and proactive. It's an amazingly symbiotic relationship. When informed of a need, the Friends stand ready to help; when they themselves perceive a need, they propose solutions to park management and jointly figure out ways to make them happen. It's hard to avoid sounding like a media flack when describing this organization.

Friends of Acadia was founded in 1986 to preserve and protect the park for resource-sensitive tourism and myriad recreational uses. Since then, FOA has contributed more than $35 million to the park and surrounding communities for trail upkeep, carriage road maintenance, seasonal park staff funding, conservation education, and conservation projects. FOA also cofounded the Island Explorer bus system and instigated the Acadia Trails Forever program, a joint park-FOA partnership for trail rehabilitation. More than 40 trails have been rehabilitated or built through the program.

As part of its efforts to reduce traffic congestion on Mount Desert Island, FOA purchased land in Trenton for an off-island transit and welcome center and sold approximately 150 acres to the Maine Department of Transportation for the facility. The organization constructed a community trail on the remaining land. The Acadia Land Legacy Partnership between FOA, Acadia National Park, Maine Coast Heritage Trust, and conservation donors purchases or protects privately held lands in or adjacent to Acadia's borders; recent achievements include the purchase of 62 acres on Seal Cove Pond and the permanent protection of 1,400 acres of intact woods and wetlands bordering Acadia's Schoodic District. FOA also helps fund more than 150 seasonal positions serving the park.

You can join FOA and its roughly 5,000 members and support this worthy cause; memberships start at $40/year. You can also lend a hand while you're here: FOA and the park organize weekly volunteer work parties (8:20am-12:30pm Tues., Thurs., and Sat. June-Columbus Day) for Acadia trail, carriage road, and other outdoor maintenance. Call the recorded information line (207/288-3934) for the work locations, or call the FOA office for answers to questions. The meeting point is park headquarters (Eagle Lake Rd./Rte. 233, Bar Harbor), about three miles west of town. Take your own water, lunch, and bug repellent. Dress in layers and wear closed-toe shoes. More than 12,000 volunteer hours go toward this effort each year.

Each summer, Friends of Acadia also sponsors a cadre of Summit Stewards, who work under park supervision and spend their days on the summit of Cadillac Mountain and out and about on trails repairing cairns, watching for lost hikers, and handing out Leave No Trace information. FOA also hires more than a dozen area teens each summer for the Acadia Youth Conservation Corps, which does trail and carriage road work, and Cadillac Summit Stewards, who work atop Acadia's highest mountain to protect the fragile alpine environment and the visitor experience there. And FOA's seasonal Acadia Digital Media Team captures still photographs and videos to help share the story of the park, the organization, and their programs.

If you happen to be in the region on the first Saturday in November, call the FOA office to register for the annual carriage road cleanup, which usually draws up to 500 volunteers. Bring water and gloves; there's a free hot lunch at midday for everyone who participates. It's dubbed Take Pride in Acadia Day—indeed an apt label.

timid hikers take their time negotiating some of the scarier sections. Stay on the Beehive Trail, passing the Bowl/Connector Trail, until you reach the Bowl. Loop back via the Bowl Trail (1.4 miles round-trip) or Gorham Mountain Trail (3.5 miles round-trip).

Champlain Mountain via the Beachcroft Path

Distance: 2 miles round-trip
Duration: 2-3 hours
Elevation gain: 951 feet
Effort: Moderate
Trailhead: The Tarn Parking Area, on Route 3, just south of the Sieur de Monts Spring park entrance and just north of the Tarn; or take the Island Explorer bus (Route 4/Loop Road or Route 10/Blackwoods).

The Beachcroft Path leads up the west side of Champlain Mountain. Constructed in 1915, the trail is best known for its nearly 1,500 beautifully engineered pink granite steps and slabs.

Start the hike by ascending Huguenot Head via a moderate climb comprising stairs and switchbacks. Take the spur trail over granite ledges to Huguenot Head's 692-foot summit. After enjoying the views over Frenchman Bay, retrace your steps along the spur trail to return to the main trail. From here on, the hiking is more strenuous, so if you're not up for it, return the way you came to conclude your hike. Otherwise, push onward.

After a brief descent, the trail climbs steeply with stairs and scrambles over granite ledges to Champlain's 1,058 summit. The views are stupendous. You can return the way you came or connect with the Champlain North Ridge Trail (0.9 mile to the Park Loop Road), Champlain South Ridge Trail (1.6 miles to The Bowl), or Precipice Trail (This rung-and-ladder trail is not recommended for descending).

Note: Avoid this trail in wet conditions, as the granite becomes quite slippery.

Penobscot and Sargent Mountains

Distance: 4.6 miles round-trip
Duration: 4 hours
Elevation gain: 1,200 feet
Effort: Difficult
Trailhead: Park your car in the overflow lot at Jordan Pond House, go left of the restaurant, and look for the carved trail signpost.

Begin on the Spring Trail. You'll cross Jordan Stream, an intersection with the Jordan Cliffs Trail, and a carriage road before starting on the rough part—heading upward rather steeply along ledges with rocky footing, with some tight squeezes and scrambling required. Handholds and railings have been installed in strategic spots (this part is even less fun on the return route). But the rewards are worth the effort. Turn right on the Penobscot Mountain Trail and continue on to the Penobscot summit (1,194 feet, the fifth highest in the park), which have wide-open views. In August, you'll have wild blueberries (but leave some for others) en route to the top.

The best feature of this hike is that you get to reach one summit and then go for a swim in gorgeous little Sargent Pond before tackling the next one. From Penobscot summit, it's only 10 minutes downhill to the pond. You can even have a second swim on the way back. (This is a long hike, however; if you're hiking with kids, be sure they're up to the challenge. For that matter, be sure you are.)

From Sargent Pond, head upward on the South Ridge Trail to the summit of Sargent Mountain (1,373 feet, the second highest in the park). Don't rush the return—the vistas are superb—but when you're ready, go back the same way.

Options: Instead of returning the way you came, you can create a loop by descending the steep Sargent East Cliffs Trail. At the intersection with Deer Brook Trail and Jordan Cliffs Trail, you can turn right on the Jordan Pond Path to return to the Spring trailhead, or continue straight on the strenuous Jordan Cliffs Trail until it intersects with the Spring Trail, and turn left to retrace the last section of that trail. Past the Deer Brook and Jordan Cliffs junction, the Around the Mountain Carriage Road also intersects with the Deer Brook Trail, offering an easier return.

Cadillac Mountain Loop via Gorge Path and North Ridge Trail

Distance: 4.5-mile loop
Duration: 2.5-4.5 hours
Elevation gain: 1,315 feet
Effort: Difficult
Trailhead: Park Loop Road, on the one-way section before the Sand Beach Entrance Station. From Bar Harbor, take Route 233/Eagle Lake Road and exit right toward the park entrance. Go left on Paradise Hill park road and then take a sharp left on the Park Loop Road and continue 0.3 mile to the North Ridge trailhead.

From the North Ridge trailhead, follow the Kebo Brook Trail 0.4 mile to where they intersect with the Gorge Path. Turn south onto the Gorge Path.

The Gorge Path follows and often crosses the Kebo Stream as it rises through the forested gorge between Cadillac and Dorr Mountains. Expect a lot of stone steps and some boulder scrambles along the way. At the high point, called The Notch, the trail intersects with the Cadillac-Dorr Connector Trail. Turn right to stay on the Gorge Path and continue up the steep face to Cadillac's summit. After looping around the summit, descend via the North Ridge Trail and enjoy the views.

Cadillac Mountain via South Ridge Trail

Distance: 7.1 miles round-trip
Duration: 4 hours
Elevation gain: 1,500 feet
Effort: Moderate, with difficult to strenuous options
Trailhead: Route 3, southwest of Otter Creek and just west of Blackwoods Campground. If you're staying at Blackwood Campground, take the access trail.

The advantage of taking the South Ridge Trail is that it doesn't come close to the Summit Road, with its loud cars and buses, until near the end. The trail departs from across the road from Black Woods Campground, climbs gradually but steadily, and includes a rung section. It begins in the woods and finishes on open granite ledges.

From the trailhead, hike 0.9 miles and you'll reach Eagles Crag (take the loop eastward around it for the views), then continue 1.1 miles to the Featherbed, a pond. Here the South Ridge Trail intersects with the Canon Brook Trail. Continue straight on the South Ridge Trail, passing the intersection with the Cadillac West Face Trail after 0.7 miles. After roughly another half mile, you'll hear the Summit Road traffic. Continue another half mile to the summit parking lot and the Summit Loop. Return via the same trail.

Option: Instead of descending via the South Ridge Trail, you can opt for one of the other trails converging on Cadillac's summit. For a more difficult route that rejoins the South Ridge Trail, take the Gorge Path (also called the Cadillac-Dorr Connector Trail), turning right on the Murray Young Path and bearing right again where it intersects with the Canon Brook Trail. This route requires some scrambling around boulders on the descent to the gorge and then navigating a steep and slippery incline. Watch carefully for trail signs. This option totals 7.5 miles.

Dorr Mountain via Homans, Emery, and Schiff Paths

Distance: 2.8 miles round-trip
Duration: 2.5 hours
Elevation gain: 1,131 feet
Effort: Difficult to strenuous
Trailhead: Take the Hemlock Trail from the beginning of the Sieur de Monts Spring parking lot (look for the split-rail fence) and follow it to the intersection with the Jesup Path. Continue on the Hemlock Trail another few yards to the Homans Path trailhead on your left.

Avid hiker Tom St. Germain, author of *A Walk in the Park,* rediscovered the Homans Path, originally built in 1915, while searching for abandoned trails in the early 1990s and wrote about it in another book, *Trails of History.* He deserves a big thanks, and Friends of Acadia and the Park Service also deserve accolades for restoring this trail.

1: a hiker on the South Ridge Trail **2:** view from South Bubble over Jordan Pond to Cranberry Isles **3:** Dorr Mountain trail

EMERY PATH

DORR MTN.
1.6 MI / 2.4 KM

JESUP PATH

The Homans Path ascends rapidly via steps and switchbacks. Keep right at the intersection with the Emery Path which flows into the Schiff Path (the two were previously known as the East Face of Dorr Trail). From the trailhead, it's 0.3 mile to the intersection with Kurt Diedrich's Climb, which drops to The Tarn. Continue on the Schiff Path 0.5 miles to the intersection with Schiff Ladder Trail. Turn right and continue 0.5 to the Door Mountain Summit. At the intersection with the North Ridge Trail, turn left and continue for 0.1-mile to reach the actual summit. It's a beautiful hike that weaves through narrow passages in the granite ledges and even under slabs of granite. Along the way and especially from the summit of Dorr Mountain, expect nice views over Frenchman Bay. Return the way you came.

Options: Instead of the Homans, you can also ascend via Emery from Sieur de Monts Spring; it's another dandy hike, with steps, balconies, and gorgeous vistas. Another trail connecting Sieur de Monts Spring to the Schiff Path is Kurt Diederichs Climb, the steepest and roughest of the three stair trails. Avoid it when ascending, and be careful on the descent. There are some loose slabs and rocks, and leaf cover in sections can be slippery. There are a few nice glimpses of the Tarn, but for the most part, the better views are on the Emery and Homans Paths.

If you want to ratchet up the difficulty, instead of beginning with the Homans or Emery paths, from Sieur de Monts Springs take the Kane Path along The Tarn 0.5 miles to the Dorr Ladder Trail, which steeply climbs the mountain using rungs and ladders, before intersecting with the Schiff Path and continuing to the summit. If you're not sure about the park's ladder trails, this is a good introduction. The ladders here are easier than those on the Beehive or Precipice trails.

Other Recommended East-Side Trails

The historic Jesup Path, one of the trails added by George Dorr, is partially wheelchair-accessible. Trail crews replaced split logs and muddy sections with a 2,000-foot-long boardwalk that passes through a large grove of white birches. When combined with the Hemlock Trail, it offers nearly 0.75 mile of accessible terrain near Sieur de Monts Spring.

The Seaside Path, or Seaside Trail, runs about two miles through the woods (use insect repellent) between Seal Harbor and the Jordan Pond House. Use the Island Explorer bus to make this a one-way hike, or retrace your route for a longer hike.

In addition to the Beehive, experienced, serious hikers seeking a strenuous challenge should consider the Precipice Trail, which ascends the face of Champlain Mountain via stairs, rungs, ladders, handholds, and bridges, and traverses narrow ledges on cliffs. This trail rises more than 900 feet in less than a mile. Don't even consider this hike if you have a fear of heights. It is usually closed from mid-April into August, to protect nesting peregrine falcons. No pets are allowed. The trailhead is on the Park Loop Road (Island Explorer Route 3/Sand Beach).

If you're looking to escape the sunset-viewing crowds on Cadillac, a short hike (about 20-30 minutes) up either Parkman Mountain or Bald Peak will give you the same views.

WEST-SIDE TRAILS
Wonderland

Distance: 1.4 miles round-trip
Duration: 45 minutes
Elevation gain: Minimal
Effort: Very easy
Trailhead: The Wonderland Trail begins on the south side of Route 102A, one mile west of the Seawall Campground. Walk from Seawall; if you're staying elsewhere, ask the Island Explorer bus driver (Route 7/Southwest Harbor) to drop you off (it's not a regular stop).

The shortest and easiest of the park's trails, Wonderland follows an old fire road and is more a walk than a hike—a great starter hike for a family ensconced at Seawall Campground. Most of the route

West-Side Trails

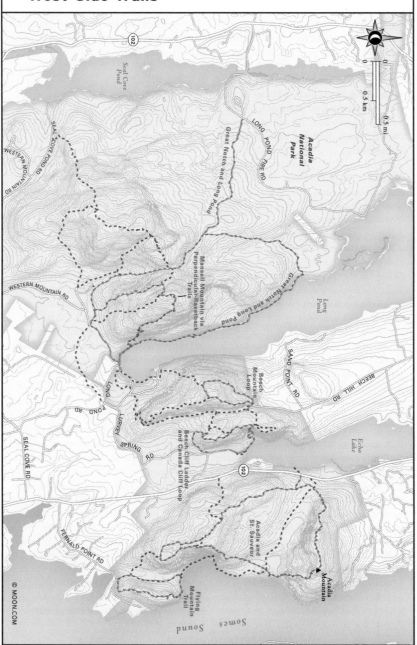

© MOON.COM

is wooded—trees gnarled from the wind, branches laden with moss—with the rugged shoreline and a small cobble beach as your reward at the end.

Across Route 102A from the Wonderland trailhead is the 420-acre Big Heath, considered one of Maine's "critical areas." Avoid it because of its sensitive peatland, wet and squishy and fragile underfoot (not to mention its battalions of mosquitoes). You'll be skirting its edges, though, if you walk the Hio Trail from the back of Seawall Campground.

Ship Harbor Nature Trail

Distance: 1.3-mile loop
Duration: 1 hour
Elevation gain: Level
Effort: Easy, some uneven ground
Trailhead: The parking area (with restroom) for Ship Harbor is less than 0.5 mile west of the Wonderland Parking Area. The trail is on the south side of Route 102A. As with Wonderland, you can be dropped off by an Island Explorer bus (Route 7/Southwest Harbor), or flag one down after your hike.

The Ship Harbor Nature Trail, a figure-eight-shaped loop, isn't quite as easy as Wonderland—roots can snag you along the way, and rocks can be slippery if it has rained or the tide has receded—but it's even more educational as a family hike. At the Thompson Island Information Center, the Hulls Cove Visitors Center, or at Seawall Campground, pick up a copy of the park's 12-page *Ship Harbor Nature Trail* booklet and use it along the way.

Legend has it that the harbor earned its name during the Revolutionary War, when an American privateer, seeking refuge, became stranded here.

If the tide has gone out, follow the trail along the shore first (counterclockwise) so the kids can check out what's been left in the tide pools. If the tide is high, perhaps you'll want to follow the booklet's suggested clockwise route. Or you can do a figure-eight route. In any case, you won't get lost. If you want a

quieter experience, plan a hike for early morning or late afternoon.

Since Wonderland and Ship Harbor are so close together, consider doing both trails in a morning or afternoon. Carry a picnic, and enjoy it on the shore.

Flying Mountain Trail

Distance: 1.5-mile loop
Duration: 1 hour
Elevation gain: 200 feet
Effort: Moderate
Trailhead: The trail begins at the end of Fernald Point Road, 0.8 mile east of Route 102 at the northern edge of Southwest Harbor. If you're driving from the Bar Harbor area, slow down after passing Echo Lake and take the next left. Drive to the end of the road, park in the Valley Cove lot, and begin at the carved signpost. Fernald Point was the site of the early-17th-century St. Sauveur mission settlement established by French Jesuits. The Island Explorer bus headed to or from Southwest Harbor can drop you off or pick you up at the corner of Route 102 and Fernald Point Road; from here, walk down the road to the trailhead.

At 284 feet, Flying Mountain is the lowest of Acadia's 26 summits, so it shouldn't have one of the best views—but it does. With minimal effort (some minor scrambling up and over, but the trail is level at the end), you're surveying the mouth of Somes Sound, including Northeast and Southwest Harbors and Greening Island between them. It is pretty spectacular.

From the trailhead, the rise through the trees is a bit steep, with some stepped ledges, but it's quick and stairs make most of it easy. At the summit, relax and take photos, then descend toward Valley Cove. You'll encounter roots and rocks, and your knees may complain a bit, but again, it's really not strenuous, and it doesn't last long. At the bottom, bear left onto the Valley Cove Road and return to the parking area.

You can hike the Valley Cove Trail as an extension of the Flying Mountain Trail, but it may be closed mid-March-mid-August, as peregrine falcons have been nesting there in recent years.

Beech Mountain Loop

Distance: 1.1 miles round-trip
Duration: 1 hour
Elevation gain: 400 feet
Effort: Moderate
Trailhead: From Route 102 in Somesville, take Pretty Marsh Road west to Beech Hill Road. Turn left and continue to the end, climbing gradually to the parking area for Beech Cliff and Beech Mountain. This trail is not accessible via the Island Explorer.

Several hiking routes merge and converge in the Beech Mountain area. Some begin from a trailhead on the southern side of Beech and can be more strenuous than this one. This hike starts from the northern side.

A short distance from the beginning of the Beech Mountain Trail, you'll reach a fork—the Beech Mountain loop. Bear right to do the loop counterclockwise—the rewarding vistas over Long Pond come sooner, and it's less steep this way.

At the summit (839 feet) stands the park's only fire tower, now disused and rarely open. During unseasonably hot summers, when the fire danger is high, volunteers come up to keep an eye on things, but small charter planes do most of the fire patrols these days. Besides the great views of Long Pond, from here you can see as far as Blue Hill to the northwest and the Cranberry Isles to the south. A knob near the summit is a prime viewing spot for migrating hawks and other raptors in September.

From the summit, continue your counterclockwise route or backtrack the way you came, heading down to the trail junction and back to the parking area.

Option: If you're particularly fascinated by mosses and lichens (and have brought insect repellent), consider a 2.1-mile round-trip to Beech Mountain that begins with a lovely walk in the woods starting at the same trailhead. Instead of taking the Beech Mountain Trail, follow the Valley Trail on fairly level ground for just under one mile. Then bear right onto the Beech Mountain South Ridge Trail and start climbing stone steps (lots of them) toward the summit. Descend from the summit via the Beech Mountain loop route, going clockwise (left) to take advantage of the Long Pond vistas.

Beech Cliff Ladder and Canada Cliff Loop

Distance: 1.8 miles round-trip
Duration: 2 hours
Elevation gain: 485 feet
Effort: Difficult to strenuous
Trailhead: At the southern end of Echo Lake, off Route 102 in Southwest Harbor

This is a ladder trail, so it's not a good choice for acrophobics. From the Echo Lake parking lot, head toward the beach and look for the Beech Cliff trailhead on the left. The trail ascends Beech Mountain via stairs and four ladders. When you reach the intersection with the Beech Cliff Loop Trail, turn right and enjoy the short loop and the views over Echo Lake. When you've completed that loop, and you've returned to the intersection, follow the Canada Cliffs Trail south, which loops back to the Echo Lake Road. At the base of the road, turn left to return to the parking lot.

Options: For a longer hike, when completing the Beech Cliff Loop Trail, continue west on the Beech Cliff trail to get to the intersection at the Beech Hill Road trailhead. From there you can take the Valley Trail to the southern end of Long Pond. At Long Pond, you loop back taking the Beech-West Trail for 0.6 mile. Then turn left on the Beech Mountain Loop Trail for 0.6 mile to the Beech Hill Road trailhead. Alternatively, take the Great Pond Trail to get to the trails up and around Mansell Mountain.

Acadia Mountain and St. Sauveur Loop

Distance: 3.9 miles round-trip
Duration: 4 hours
Elevation gain: 1,167 feet
Effort: Moderate to difficult
Trailhead: From Somesville, west of Bar Harbor, take Route 102 south for just over three miles, alongside Echo Lake, until you see the signposted Acadia

Mountain parking lot. Cross the road to the trailhead. The Island Explorer (Route 7/Southwest Harbor) goes along Route 102; request a stop to start your hike, and flag down the bus when you've finished.

You can hike this loop in either direction. Expect to scramble over rocks in sections. This is a very popular hike, so consider going early in the morning or late in the afternoon to avoid the crowds. It's wise to have a map, as this loop intersects with a number of other trails.

From the trailhead, climb the steps and continue to the junction with the St. Sauveur Mountain Trail. Turn left onto the Acadia Mountain Trail, where it's briefly (deceptively) flat and lovely. After crossing a fire road, begin the rocky ascent along the ledges, following the cairns. Steps ease the way in sections—which is the selling point for hiking this loop in the opposite direction.

It's less than one mile from the trailhead to the open summit of Acadia Mountain, which has fantastic views up and down Somes Sound and out to the Cranberry Isles. There's actually a sort of double summit, with the second one only slightly lower than the 681-foot maximum height. The descent toward the sound is longer and very steep—take it slowly. At the bottom, when you reach the spur to Man O' War Brook, detour briefly to follow the brook east to Somes Sound. Allegedly, Revolutionary War vessels stocked up on water here during their exploits along the Maine coast.

After the detour, return to the trail and continue south on the Valley Peak Trail to the intersection with the St. Sauveur Trail. Turn right on St. Sauveur Trail to return to the trailhead. (For a shorter hike, skip St. Sauveur. After detouring to the overlook, continue on the Acadia Mountain Trail to the Man O' War Brook fire road, and descend that 0.9 miles back to the trailhead.) There's no view from St. Sauveur's summit. When you finish completing the loop, you can cross Route 102 for a swim at Echo Lake Ledges. Note: This trail is not recommended for dogs.

Option: For a longer and more strenuous hike, from the St. Sauveur peak, it's about 0.8 mile via the Valley Peak Trail to the Valley Cove Road. From there, you can loop the 1.5 miles around Flying Mountain, returning via the Valley Peak Trail to St. Sauveur's peak for an additional 3 miles.

Great Notch and Long Pond

Distance: 6.9-mile spur and loop
Duration: 5 hours

the view from the Perpendicular Trail over Long Pond to the Cranberry Isles

Elevation gain: 728 feet

Effort: Moderate

Trailhead: Take Route 102 to the Hodgdon Road end of the Long Pond Fire Road (east side of Route 102, just shy of a mile north of the Seal Cove Auto Museum). Follow Hodgdon Road, take the first right on the unsigned Long Pond Road into the park, and then turn left for the parking area. The trailhead is off the fire road just north of the intersection with the parking area road. This is not on the Island Explorer route.

On a perfect August day, when it may seem as if the entire world has arrived on Mount Desert Island, you can slip away on this hike through the wooded notch dividing Mansell and Bernard Mountains and returning along the shore of Long Pond. Bring plenty of water, a picnic lunch, snacks, and a towel and swimsuit. You may hike this trail with dogs as long as they're on a leash not exceeding six feet.

From the Long Pond Fire Road trailhead, follow the moderate Great Notch Trail (sometimes called the Western Mountain Trail) 2.6 miles to Gilley Field. En route, you'll pass the Long Pond trail intersection at 1.1 miles and the Western Mountain Ridge Trail after 1.5 miles. Continue another 0.4 mile then turn left on the Gilley Trail to Gilley Field, then take the 0.4-mile Cold Brook Trail to the pumping station, turning left to pick up the Long Pond (aka Great Pond) Trail for an easy walk along the lake's shoreline.

Although the waters near the pumping station are closed to swimmers, after hiking the trail another 0.4 mile, you can cool off with a dip and dry off on a nice slab of granite. After about 1.5 miles along the shore, the trail turns away from the lake. At the intersection with the Great Notch Trail, turn right to return to the parking area.

Options: You can increase the distance and/or difficulty of this hike by looping in Knight's Nubble and/or the Sluiceway Trail, among other possibilities.

Mansell Mountain via Perpendicular-Razorback Trails

Distance: 2.7-mile loop

Duration: 2 hours

Elevation gain: 855 feet

Effort: Difficult to strenuous

Trailhead: Take Route 102 to Southwest Harbor, turn onto Seal Cove Road, go right on Long Pond Road, and follow it to the end and park. The Long Pond trailhead is opposite the pumping station.

Frankly, one doesn't hike the Perpendicular Trail for the views, although there are some fine ones to Long Pond, Beech Mountain, and beyond to Somes Sound and the Cranberry Isles. No, one hikes here to admire the trail's magnificent architecture as well as to escape crowds. Constructed by the Civilian Conservation Corps in 1933-1934, the trail, lined with granite coping stones, ascends Mansell Mountain via hundreds of granite steps (a friend counted more than 1,000), along with a few iron rungs and a short ladder.

Follow the Long Pond Trail along the pond's western edge for about 0.2 mile to the Perpendicular trailhead. Continue beyond the forested summit, passing the Mansell Mountain Trail, and turn left at the junction with the Razorback Trail. From here, the descent is steep, but you'll enjoy some nice views before entering the forest. At the intersection with the Gilley Trail, turn left to reach the Cold Brook Trail and follow it back to the Long Pond Trail and the parking lot. No dogs are allowed on the Perpendicular Trail.

Options: For a longer hike, you can loop in Knight's Nubble (929 feet) and Little Notch (889 feet), returning via the Sluiceway Trail, or also add Bernard Mountain (1,070 feet). From the trailhead, you can also loop in Beech Mountain (840 feet) via the Valley Trail to Beech South Ridge Trail and returning via the Beech West Ridge Trail. The figure eight route taking in Mansell, Bernard, and Beech Mountains is about 7.6 miles.

Biking

Bicycling on Mount Desert Island is a joy, but you have to pedal in the right locations. The island is mountainous, and that includes the roads; many have serious ups and downs. Dedicated and experienced road cyclists will have a blast. Mountain bikers, casual bikers, families, and everyone else will be more than pleased with the carriage roads. These gravel roads lace the heart of the park and are punctuated with beautiful stone bridges. They provide a variety of challenges, and you can create a ride of practically any length by linking them together.

You'll find a number of commercial maps available. I prefer the *Acadia National Park Hiking and Biking Trail Map* ($5 paper, $10 waterproof) published by Map Adventures (www.mapadventures.com), because I find it easiest to read, it details in-town roads, and it shows some of the dirt roads described below. One big drawback for cyclists is that this map doesn't include the entire island; the northern third is simply lopped off, so if you're cycling that section, you'll need another map as well.

ROAD BIKING

Road biking on Mount Desert Island is best left to the experienced. Roads are often narrow, shoulders frequently nonexistent or soft, and gawking drivers often aren't paying attention to the road. Families, once-a-year pedalers, and casual bicyclists will do best on the carriage roads. That said, serious road bikers do have a few choices. Stop in at one of Bar Harbor's bike shops for recommendations or to find out about group rides. If you go by yourself, timing is critical. For the best ride with the least traffic, get up at the crack of dawn and start pedaling once it's truly light outside. It's very important to wear reflective clothing on these roads. It's also wise to drive the roads before cycling them to check conditions. If it has been a while since they've been resurfaced, you might be in for a very rough ride.

Park Loop Road

Bikes are not allowed on hiking trails in Acadia, but the Park Loop Road provides a good workout for mountain or road bikers.

bicyclist on carriage roads

Its prime drawback is the volume of car and RV exhaust fumes you'll be inhaling if you take this route in the middle of the day at the height of summer—so don't. Park-wide ozone alerts are not common, but they do occur in Acadia. Nor are the Park Loop's shoulders as wide as they might be to comfortably accommodate many bikes. Besides, on most of the one-way sections of the Park Loop, overflow auto parking is allowed in the right lane, and dodging cars isn't fun. The 27-mile route is indeed spectacular, so if you want to bike it, plan your pedaling for early in the day (around 7am in summer), late in the day (around "happy hour," when everyone else has packed it in and headed for bars or restaurants), or during shoulder months (June, Sept., or even Oct.).

Southeast Quarter of the Island

This route dips in and out of the park. Begin in Bar Harbor and follow Route 3 to Schooner Head Road, then follow signs to Park Loop Road. Ride the Park Loop to the end of the one-way section in Seal Harbor, turn right onto Jordan Pond Road heading to Seal Harbor, and then pick up Route 3 to the intersection with Route 198 in Northeast Harbor. Go left on Route 198 into Northeast Harbor, taking Harborside Road to Joy Road to Manchester Road, and turn right. Manchester Road merges into Sargent Drive. Follow it until it meets Route 198, turn left, and continue to the intersection with Route 233. Turn right and follow Route 233 back to Bar Harbor.

You can increase the mileage by exploring some of the back roads of Seal Harbor (keep an eye out for Martha Stewart) or Northeast Harbor. Another option is to take Duck Brook Road off Route 233, just after the Eagle Lake parking lots. The road meanders into Bar Harbor, merging onto West Street.

Routes 102/102A

Experienced cyclists who are accustomed to traffic might consider this loop around the western half of Mount Desert Island. It passes through Somesville, Southwest Harbor, Bass Harbor, Tremont, and Pretty Marsh. While little mileage on this route is actually in the park, quite a few offshoots do venture into it, in most cases on dirt roads. If you do the full loop, it's about 26 miles. Unless you're intent on getting in mileage, plan time to stop and explore along the way. Expect nonexistent or soft shoulders on much of the route and moderate to heavy traffic.

To add to the distance, venture down some of the side roads along the way, such as Ripples Road to Beech Hill Road (which dead-ends) or Hall Quarry Road (loop), or detour north in Pretty Marsh on Indian Point Road, which ends at Routes 198/102.

TOP EXPERIENCE

★ CARRIAGE ROADS

The better alternative for most aspiring bicyclists is to bring, borrow, or rent a bike and take advantage of the spectacular carriage road system—57 miles of crushed-rock roadways with nary a car in sight. Bikes, including class 1 e-bikes (motorized), are allowed on 45 of the 57 miles; the remaining 12 miles are outside the park on preserve land, so be alert for signs.

At every junction in the carriage road system stands a tall wooden post with a number and directional signs. Use these numbers, together with the park's free carriage road map (download from www.nps.gov/acad or obtain at a visitor center) to navigate the network. Also very helpful are a couple of portable books: *A Pocket Guide to the Carriage Roads of Acadia National Park* by Diana Abrell and *A Pocket Guide to Biking on Mount Desert Island* by Audrey Minutolo.

Periodically, carriage roads and their bridges undergo necessary repairs, and since such work is possible only in decent weather, check online or ask a park ranger about closures.

Some sections of the carriage roads are fine for wheelchairs, particularly near Eagle Lake and Bubble Pond.

Since these are multiuse roadways, bicyclists in particular should remember and adhere to the rules:

- **Bikes yield to everyone** (pedestrians, horses, wheelchairs, strollers); **pedestrians yield to horses.** Horses tend to become skittish around bikes, so be particularly cautious when you're pedaling near them. Better still, pull off to the right, stop, and let them pass.

- **Wear a helmet.**

- **Keep to the right** and signal clearly when passing on the left.

- **Do not speed;** speeders are a danger to pedestrians, horses, children, wheelchair users, and sometimes themselves.

- **Pets** must be on fixed leashes not exceeding 6 feet.

As with the park's hiking trails, it would take a whole book just to focus on all the options on the carriage roads. While the carriage roads make wonderful walking paths, they are the best places in the park for bikes, so most of the route suggestions that follow are geared to cyclists.

It cannot be said often enough: There is no off-road biking in Acadia, and bikes are not allowed on the hiking trails.

Eagle Lake and/or Witch Hole Pond

These two loops are probably the most popular in the park—they're not difficult (good for families) and they're close to Bar Harbor, where so many visitors stay. Thus, if you decide to do either in the middle of summer, get an early start. If you're planning to rent bikes, rent them the night before so you can be on your way right after breakfast.

If you're doing this anytime between late June and Columbus Day, check the schedule for the Island Explorer bus and use it to get to and from your starting and ending points. The Island Explorer Bicycle Express operates between Bar Harbor and Eagle Lake.

Each loop is about six miles. If you'd prefer to double your mileage, do both.

Both loops can be accessed from the Eagle Lake Parking Area on Route 233. Witch Hole also can be accessed from the Hulls Cove Visitor Center, which includes a steep hill. For a shorter loop, begin at the triple-arched Duck Brook Bridge off Duck Brook Road. From here, the main loop is about 1.3 miles.

Jordan Pond and Bubble Pond

To ride this loop, take Island Explorer Route 4/Loop Road or Route 5/Jordan Pond bus to the Jordan Pond Parking Area or drive here via the Park Loop Road (use the Jordan Pond parking lot, not the Jordan Pond House Parking Area). Pedal back along the Park Loop Road (follow bike rules and stay with the traffic; it's two-way here) to the handsome stone Jordan Pond Gate Lodge. From here you have two choices—a clockwise route or a counterclockwise one.

The counterclockwise route allows you a downhill coast along Jordan Pond near the end of your 8.5-mile circuit. Enter the carriage road next to the gatehouse and continue to the junction at signpost 17. Head north, passing Bubble Pond along its west shore—practically in the water—to signpost 7. Bear left around the bottom of Eagle Lake, to signpost 8; continue to signpost 10, and then turn south, skirting Jordan Pond, to signpost 14. Continue south to signposts 15 and 16, exiting onto the Park Loop Road across from where you entered.

After these warm-up rides, you'll have a good sense of this amazing network.

Amphitheatre Loop

This is a fabulous 5.5-mile loop that takes you into the heart of the park, far from the noise of traffic and civilization. You'll pass over two bridges—the gently curving Amphitheatre Bridge, at 236 feet one of the longest in the system, and Little Harbor Brook Bridge, which must be one of the smallest. The route has some steady climbs, but the rewards are panoramic views to the Cranberry Isles. Follow a clockwise route beginning at the Brown Mountain Gatehouse parking lot on Route 198 (one mile north of Northeast Harbor). Enter the carriage road system and bear right at signposts 18 and 19, and keep straight bearing left at signpost 20. Keep right again at signposts 21 and 22. When you return to signpost 20, turn left and keep left until you're back at the parking area. For a longer ride, continue heading clockwise around Upper Hadlock Ponds, adding 4.2 miles. Take the Island Explorer Route 6/Brown Mountain.

Option: Hikers can enjoy the 0.8-mile Amphitheatre Trail connecting the two bridges. It's a lovely walk in the woods paralleling and often crossing Harbor Brook as it babbles and descends over waterfalls into small pools—perfect for cooling hot, tired feet. Don't take this trail during spring runoff periods or after heavy rains, when that sweet brook might be a raging torrent.

Around the Mountain Loop

This 11-mile loop is an outstanding ride for experienced mountain bikers. It circumnavigates several of the park's major peaks, including Sargent, Penobscot, Cedar Swamp, Parkman, and Gilmore, and it passes numerous bridges and waterfalls. The views are glorious. It's not an easy ride, however, as it climbs many hills. Begin at the Parkman Mountain parking lot on Route 198 by heading right. At signpost 13, go left, and then go left at signpost 12. You're now on the Around the Mountain Road. At signpost 10 turn right and keep right, staying on the Around the Mountain Road, at signposts 14, 21, 20, and 19. At signpost 12, turn left, and then turn right at signpost 13 to return to the parking lot. You can also access this route from the Jordan Pond area. Take the Island Explorer Route 6/Brown Mountain.

Hadlock Brook Loop

The rewards for this 3.9-mile loop around Hadlock Pond include views out to the Cranberry Isles, three bridges, and one of the park's highest waterfalls. Begin at the Parkman Mountain parking lot on Route 198, heading right on the carriage road. At the first junction, signpost 13, go left. At the next, signpost 12, go right. The first section is the steepest—you'll reap the benefits of this short climb with a long downhill a bit later. The first bridge you'll come to is Hemlock Bridge over Maple Spring. Take a few minutes and descend the stairs to the spring so you can view this lovely bridge from all angles. Continue on a few hundred yards to aptly named Waterfall Bridge, which crosses Hadlock Brook and provides fine views of a 40-foot waterfall. Again, be sure to hoof it down and under the bridge for the views. Now comes a grin-inducing downhill, a gentle descent to signpost 19; turn right here and again at signpost 18. While nowhere near as impressive as the other two bridges, the small Hadlock Brook Bridge is still lovely. At signpost 13, keep left to return to the Parkman Mountain lot. Take the Island Explorer Route 6/Brown Mountain.

Option: If you're on foot, you can connect to the lower section of the loop and Hadlock Pond by descending the Maple Spring Trail that passes Hemlock Bridge or the Hadlock Brook Trail, under Waterfall Bridge. Each is roughly 0.5 mile long.

FIRE ROADS

Hio Road Trail

Immerse into the Big Heath with an easy walk or bike ride on the park's Hio fire road (also called Hio Truck Road and simply Hio Road). The road, gated at both ends, skirts the Big Heath, a glacial-formed peat bog that's home to insect-eating plants including the pitcher plant. The road passes through lush, mossy woodlands comprising spruce, red and white pine, and balsam fir, along with birch, maple, and cedar. Keep an eye out for animal tracks. Douse yourself liberally with insect repellent. This is a great family ride, with plenty of bird- and wildlife-watching opportunities. The Hio Road runs two miles between the back of the Seawall Campground on Route 102A and Route 102, just north of bridge crossing the Bass Harbor Marsh.

Long Pond Fire Road

The 4.3-mile Long Pond Fire Road loops off Route 102 (take the first, unsigned road south of Pretty Marsh Picnic Area or access it off Hodgdon Road, a little over a mile south of the picnic area). The maintained gravel road loops out to Long Pond and back, including a short section on Route 102. You can break for a swim in the pond. The terrain is moderate, with many long hills; spruce and fir trees line most of the route, and you'll pass boggy areas as well as a few ponds. This is prime moose territory, so be on the lookout for the gangly beasts. If you see one, observe it from a distance; if it starts coming toward you, move away quietly. You can park at Pretty Marsh or at the parking area near the Hodgdon Road end of the park (take the first left).

Water Sports

CALM-WATER PADDLING
Eastern Side of the Island

On the eastern side of the island, both **Eagle Lake** and **Jordan Pond** have boat ramps, making for easy paddles.

EAGLE LAKE

Soak in the views of Cadillac Mountain, Pemetic Mountain, the Bubbles, Sargent Mountain, and Connors Nubble while paddling pristine Eagle Lake. It's wise to stick to the roughly four miles of shoreline, as the wind can rise unexpectedly, creating whitecap conditions. Eagle Lake is a reservoir, so swimming by people or pets is prohibited. Find the Eagle Lake put-in off Route 233 about two miles from Bar Harbor.

JORDAN POND

Jordan Pond's setting, with the Bubbles as backdrop, invites leisurely paddling. Put in at the boat ramp on the southern end of the pond and paddle approximately one mile to the northern end of the lake, where depths can reach 100 feet. You can pull out here for a picnic, but resist the urge to swim (it's not permitted for either people or pets). A hiking path circulates the pond, making it easy to combine a paddle with a walk. Find the Jordan Pond put-in adjacent to the Jordan Pond North parking lot, on the Park Loop Road—you'll need reservations to park here.

Western Side of the Island

The ponds and waterways on the island's western side get far less traffic than those on the eastern side.

SEAL COVE POND

Route 102 skirts the western edge of Tremont's 1.5-mile-long **Seal Cove Pond.** The western shoreline is primarily private property, but the forested eastern shore is in the park. The ledges on this side are a fine place for a picnic or a swim. This long, skinny pond is rather shallow, making it a good home for ducks and wading birds. The primary access point is off Western Mountain Road. To find it, take Seal Cove Road from Seal Cove, go left on the first park road, and follow it to its intersection with Western Mountain Road. Turn left; the road ends at the put-in, where there's limited parking.

BASS HARBOR MARSH

Birders appreciate **Bass Harbor Marsh,** a tidal marsh within the park. It's a breeding area for American black ducks and Nelson's sharp-tailed sparrows, and sightings here may include blue herons, eagles, and ospreys as well as rarities such as the least bittern. You can paddle the shallow open section of the marsh; be wary of tidal currents, and avoid low tide, which can leave you high and dry. Paddle northward, staying on the main channel of Marshall Brook, which narrows and snakes. Access the marsh from the Route 102 bridge in Tremont, just north of the intersection with Route 102A and just south of the Tremont School.

SWIMMING

Acadia has a limited number of swimming areas; their parking lots are mighty crowded on hot days. Go early in the day, or take your chances.

Don't assume you can swim in any freshwater pond or lake you encounter in the park or even elsewhere on the island. Six island locations—Upper and Lower Hadlock Ponds, Bubble and Jordan Ponds, Eagle Lake, and the southern half of Long Pond—are drinking-water reservoirs where swimming and windsurfing are banned (but boating is allowed). Don't let your dog swim in these ponds either. Five of the six are within the park; Long Pond borders the park.

Sand Beach

Located slightly below the Park Loop Road (take Island Explorer Route 3/Sand Beach), **Sand Beach** is the park's and the island's biggest sandy beach. Lifeguards are on duty during the summer, and even then the biggest threat can be hypothermia. The saltwater is terminally glacial—in mid-July it rarely exceeds 55°F. By September it's usually warmer, though the air will be cooler. Even though kids seem not to notice, they can become chilled quickly; keep an eye on their condition. The best solution is to walk to the far end of the beach, where a warmer, shallow stream meets the ocean. Also, if you arrive here at the incoming tide, after the sun has warmed up the sand, the water temperature is marginally higher. On a hot August day, arrive early; the parking lot fills up. Bring a picnic. There are changing rooms and restrooms. Dogs are not allowed on Sand Beach.

After hiking nearby Great Head on a hot day, go for a swim at Sand Beach—you'll be surprisingly grateful for the chilly water.

Echo Lake

The park's most popular freshwater swimming site, staffed with a lifeguard and inevitably crowded on hot days, is **Echo Lake,** south of Somesville on Route 102 and well signposted. Take the Island Explorer bus Route 7/Southwest Harbor. Pets are not allowed on the beach.

Swimming Holes

If you have a canoe, kayak, or rowboat, you can reach swimming holes in **Seal Cove Pond** and **Round Pond,** both on the western side of Mount Desert. Both have shorelines bordering the park. The eastern shore of **Hodgdon Pond,** also on the western side of the island, is accessible by car via Hodgdon Road and Long Pond Fire Road.

Another popular swimming hole is **Lake Wood,** at the northern end of Mount Desert. The 16-acre pond has a small sand beach and a grassy area, a restroom by the parking area, and auto access. To get to Lake Wood from Route 3, head west on Crooked Road for about 0.6 mile to Lake Wood Pond Road. Turn left and continue to the parking area, which will be crowded on a hot day, so arrive early.

Other Recreation

ROCK CLIMBING

Acadia has a number of splendid sites prized by climbers: Otter Cliff, with 60-foot sea cliffs; the Great Head sea cliffs; South Bubble Mountain; South Wall and the Central Slabs on Champlain Mountain; and Canada Cliff on the island's western side. Popular bouldering spots include the shoreline between Sand Beach and Otter Cliff and near Blackwoods Campground. The climbing season usually runs May-October. Occasionally it can start earlier or end later, but you'd have to be on or near the island to be able to catch the decent weather before it deteriorates. This can happen even in summer. Be aware of tides, especially when climbing Otter Cliffs or Great Head.

Some park regulations for Acadia climbing:

- Don't leave your **dog** tied up or on the loose while you're climbing.

- The park's **bridges** are off-limits for climbing or bouldering.

- While **peregrine falcons** are nesting (Apr.-mid-Aug.), the Central Slabs area on the Precipice and the Jordan Cliffs, as well as other areas, are almost always closed.

- Sign in at the registration box at climbing sites—**registration** is required at Otter Cliffs, the South Wall, and Canada Cliff.

- If you're part of an organized commercial or noncommercial group numbering six or more, a **permit** is required for Otter Cliffs. Download it from www.nps.gov/acad.

- At Otter Cliffs, use the **fixed anchors,** not trees, to belay.

If you've forgotten any climbing gear or need replacements, the best source is **Cadillac Mountain Sports** (26 Cottage St., Bar Harbor, 207/288-4532, www.cadillacsports.com), on the ground floor next to Atlantic Climbing School.

Climbing Schools and Guides

If you haven't tried climbing, never do it yourself without instruction. The best advice is to contact one of Bar Harbor's two climbing operations. **Acadia Mountain Guides Climbing School** (228 Main St., Bar Harbor, 207/288-8186 or 888/232-9559, www.acadiamountainguides.com, mid-May-Oct.) offers all levels of instruction and guided climbs for individuals and families. School owner Jon Tierney has been climbing, guiding, and instructing in Acadia since 1983. Rates vary with the number of climbers, but a private full-day guided climb is $270 and a half day is $160. Family rates ($340 half day, $540 full day for up to 4 people) cover up to four family members.

Atlantic Climbing School (ACS, 24 Cottage St., 2nd Fl., Bar Harbor, 207/288-2521, www.climbacadia.com) provides half-day climbing courses for beginners by reservation. You'll learn just enough to introduce you to the sport and do a basic climb—with guides and in line with park rules. ACS also offers a series of courses for intermediate climbers and a half- or full-day guided course for experienced climbers. Half-day courses are $99 per person for three people, $110 per person for two, and $170 for a private course. Full-day guided courses are $150 per person for three, $185 per person for two, or $290 for a private outing.

The best guidebook and app for experienced climbers is *Rock Climbs of Acadia,* by Grant Simmons (Acadia Rock Press, www.rockclimbsofacadia.com, $24.95 book, $15.99 app, $35.99 book and app). The book details routes for nearly 300 climbs, from the well known to the obscure. You can also rent the app for $7.99 for two months.

GEOCACHING

Although traditional geocaching, with hidden prizes, is forbidden in the park, if you have your own GPS unit you can participate in Acadia's EarthCache Program (www.nps.gov/acad/earthcache.htm). Instead of directing you to stashes of trinkets, it leads to some of the park's significant geological sites. Full details, including coordinates for the first stop, are available on the website. It takes an estimated 4-6 hours to complete the program, which will cover much of the park.

Practicalities

FOOD

The only restaurant within the park is the Jordan Pond House (Park Loop Rd., 207/276-3316, www.acadiajordanpondhouse.com, 11am-9pm daily mid-May-late June and late Aug.-late Oct., 11:30am-9pm daily late June-late Aug., $11-33). It's wise to make reservations.

CAMPING

Mount Desert Island has at least a dozen private commercial campgrounds, but there are only two—Blackwoods and Seawall—within park boundaries on the island (a third park campground is on Isle au Haut, and a fourth is in the Schoodic section of the park). You must have a park pass to stay at either.

Blackwoods and Seawall have no hookups. Most sites are for tents, but some do accommodate pop-ups, vehicle campers, and RVs up to 35 feet in length. Both campgrounds have seasonal restrooms (no showers) and dumping stations. Less than 0.5 mile from Blackwoods and 1 mile from Seawall are coin-operated hot showers and small markets for incidental supplies.

Both campgrounds are wooded and have no sea views but are not far from the water. In June, be prepared for blackflies; in July-August, bring insect repellent for mosquitoes. Maximum capacity at each site is six people, one vehicle, and one large tent or two small ones. Quiet time in both campgrounds is 10pm-6am.

Both campgrounds also have amphitheaters, where park rangers present free hour-long evening programs on a variety of natural and cultural history topics.

Noncampers are also welcome at these events, and there's wheelchair access. Some of the programs have included "Forces of Nature," "Avian Mysteries," "Acadia's Treasures," "The French in Acadia," and "All Things Furry." Even sing-alongs are sometimes on the schedule. Blackwoods has programs several nights a week; Seawall programs tend to be on weekend evenings.

Do not bring firewood in from more than 50 miles away. Stop on your way to Acadia and pick up a stash of firewood. All along Route 3 in Trenton and along Route 3 on Mount Desert, near the clusters of commercial campgrounds, you'll see signs for firewood for sale (around $3). Do not bring firewood from home, as it may contain bugs that threaten park resources.

The Island Explorer buses serve both Blackwoods (Route 10/Blackwoods) and Seawall (Route 7/Southwest Harbor) late June-early October. Leave your vehicle at your campsite, and do your park and island exploring by bus.

Blackwoods Campground

Blackwoods Campground has 306 campsites and is located just off Route 3, five miles south of Bar Harbor. Because of its location on the east side of the island, it's also the more popular of the two campgrounds.

If you're staying at Blackwoods, consider adding the strenuous, seven-mile round-trip Cadillac South Ridge Trail to your hiking list. Of course, you can drive to the Cadillac summit and get the same fabulous 360-degree views, but this hike makes it feel like you earned them. Another plus: The park renewed the trail from Blackwoods to Gorham Mountain.

Seawall Campground

Seawall Campground has 214 sites and is located on Route 102A in the Seawall district, four miles south of Southwest Harbor. The fee is $30 per night for drive-in sites and $22 per night for walk-in sites (located 10 to 300 feet from the parking lot; wheelbarrows are available).

Reservations

Reservations for all campgrounds can me made online or by calling the National Recreation Reservation Service (877/444-6777 or 606/515-6777 international or 877/833-6777 TDD, www.recreation.gov, credit or debit card required). Sites are released on a rolling basis and can be made up to six months in advance.

EMERGENCIES

If you have an emergency while in the park, call 911. The park's general information number is 207/288-3338. If you're in a remote location, it helps if you're carrying a cell phone, but keep it turned off while hiking or biking; save it for emergencies. The nearest hospital, in downtown Bar Harbor, is Mount Desert Island Hospital (10 Wayman Ln., 207/288-5081), with a 24-hour emergency room. The nearest major medical center is Eastern Maine Medical Center in Bangor, via a congested route that can take an hour or longer at the height of summer. Bangor, however, is one of the state's bases for a LifeFlight medevac helicopter.

The best advice for averting emergencies is to be cautious and sensible in everything you undertake in the park. Wear a helmet while biking. Don't hike alone or go off the trails and keep back from cliff edges—nearly every year someone is seriously injured or killed falling from the cliffs. Keep a sharp eye on children.

ACCESSIBILITY

The park publishes an *Accessibility Guide* (download from www.nps.gov/acad) that provides accessibility information about general facilities, programs, and services, including accessible trails, carriage roads, scenic sites, and ranger-led activities. Blackwoods Campground has 12 accessible drive-in sites; Seawall Campground has 1 group site and 3 RV, 5 drive-in, and 5 walk-in sites that are accessible. If you have questions, call 207/288-3338, 8am-4:30pm Monday-Friday.

Friends of Acadia has worked with the park, when possible, to make trails restored through the Acadia Trails Forever partnership wheelchair/ADA compliant. These include the Jesup Trail boardwalk, the Jordan Pond Nature Path, and parts of the Ship Harbor Nature Trail. Also accessible and open to motorized wheelchairs is the park's 45-mile carriage road network, although the best choices for wheelchair users are Eagle Lake and Bubble Pond.

There's an accessible path to the water at Echo Lake.

All Island Explorer buses have wheelchair lifts.

GETTING AROUND

The free Island Explorer (207/288-4573, www.exploreacadia.com) operates seven routes on Mount Desert Island that connect villages and campgrounds and access most areas of the park. It operates late June-early October.

Winter in the Park

Winter is off-season in Acadia, but the park remains open. The plus side: You'll have it practically to yourself. The downside: The weather is unpredictable and many services are curtailed.

Acadia's proximity to the ocean and the Gulf Stream current means that you take your chances with snow. Even though the park gets about five feet of snow during an average winter, it's not like a ski resort, where there's a base and more snow keeps piling on top of it. Here, it might snow one day and rain, sleet, or thaw the next. That said, every now and then, a large volume of snow creates a winter wonderland for days or even weeks. January-February can be good for winter sports, but then again, you never know. The park publishes a very handy *Winter Activities Guide,* a foldout map-brochure that explains what you can and cannot do and where you can and cannot go.

In winter, when the Hulls Cove Visitors Center is closed, a park ranger is stationed at the **Bar Harbor Chamber of Commerce Visitor Center** (2 Cottage St., 207/288-5103, 8am-4pm daily).

SIGHTSEEING

Two sections of the Park Loop Road stay open in winter. Access **Ocean Drive**'s two-mile ocean-hugging section from Schooner Head Road, off Route 3, about one mile from downtown Bar Harbor. Note: Keep right, as snowmobilers use the left lane. From Seal Harbor, the **Jordan Park Road** is plowed to the Jordan Pond House Parking Area.

RECREATION
Cross-Country Skiing and Snowshoeing

Acadia's car-free carriage roads are fantastic for cross-country skiing and snowshoeing. Forty-five miles of park carriage trails are open to **cross-country skiing** and **snowshoeing.** The Friends of Acadia partners with the Acadia Winter Trails Association to groom and maintain 32 miles of carriage trails. When time permits and conditions are favorable—the roadbeds must be frozen and snowfall must exceed six inches—volunteers set classic and skating track. Carriage roads designated for grooming are

the carriage roads in winter

serviced from two hubs. In order of grooming priority, trails groomed from the Hulls Cove Visitor Center base are Witch Hole Pond, Eagle Loop Connector, Aunt Betty Pond, and Paradise Hill. Trails groomed from the Brown Mountain Gatehouse base are Hadlock Loop, Amphitheater Loop Parkman Connector, Jordan Pond Connector, and Upper Around Mountain. For current status, check online with the Friends of Acadia (https://friends-ofacadia.org/get-involved/acadia-winter-trails-association). Note: Snowshoers should not step in cross-country ski tracks. Fat-tire bikes are not permitted on groomed carriage roads.

In addition to the carriage roads, skiing and snowshoeing is permitted on unplowed park roads, but note that these are shared with snowmobilers.

Snowmobiling

The 27-mile Park Loop Road, including the summit of Cadillac Mountain, is open to snowmobiling, as are most fire roads. Maximum speed allowed is 35 mph on the Park Loop Road and 25 mph on unpaved roads. Snowmobiles are not permitted off road, on any hiking trails, or on the carriage roads, with the exception of the east side of Eagle Lake to connect the Park Loop Road to Bubble Road. Snowmobilers must yield to hikers, skiers, and snowshoers. Snowmobiler operators must be at least 14 years old, and anyone riding a snowmobile under age 18 must wear a helmet. The best place for snowmobilers to park and access the trail system is from the Hulls Cove Visitor Center. There are no rentals on the island.

Winter Hiking

Winter hiking means navigating often icy and snow-packed trails. Be sure to read the park's *Winter Hiking Tips* before hitting the trail.

Other Activities

Ponds and lakes are open for **ice fishing** usually from January into March, but check with local officials to be sure the ice is thick enough before venturing out on it. **Ice climbing** is permitted. **Dogsledding** and **skijoring** are not allowed.

Outfitters and Instruction

Cross-country skis ($20/day including skis, boots, and poles), snowshoes ($15), and ice skates ($8) are available for rent from **Cadillac Mountain Sports** (26 Cottage St., Bar Harbor, 207/288-4532, www.cadillacsports.com, year-round).

Atlantic Climbing School (ACS, 24 Cottage St., 2nd Fl., Bar Harbor, 207/288-2521, www.climbacadia.com) offers private, customized **ice climbing, mountaineering, snowshoeing, and cross-country skiing** programs for all levels. Prices vary by course and number of participants.

RESTROOMS

Winter toilets are available at the Brown Mountain, Parkman Mountain, and Sand Beach Parking Areas; the Eagle Lake and Jordan Pond boat ramps; Eagle Lake Carriage Road; and Fabbri Picnic Area.

Mount Desert Island Communities

Perhaps no national park has as symbiotic a relationship with its feeder towns as Acadia National Park. Is it a chicken-and-egg situation? Not really. Whereas other national parks have served as magnets for the creation of clusters of new towns, the towns that surround Acadia are longtime communities. These island towns made do and eked out a living from fishing and boatbuilding long before the first 19th-century "rusticators" unloaded their families and steamer trunks and long before the first chunk of pristine island real estate was donated to the nation.

Mount Desert Island's official towns (tax-collecting entities with all the bureaucracy that ensues) are Bar Harbor, Mount Desert, Southwest Harbor, and Tremont. Within each of these towns are villages—some

Highlights

Look for ★ to find recommended sights, activities, dining, and lodging.

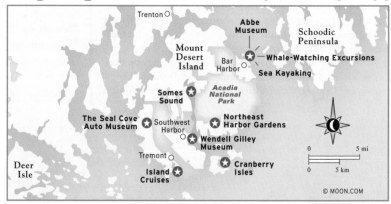

Trenton

Abbe Museum

Schoodic Peninsula

Mount Desert Island

Bar Harbor — Whale-Watching Excursions

Sea Kayaking

Somes Sound

Acadia National Park

The Seal Cove Auto Museum — Southwest Harbor

Northeast Harbor Gardens

Wendell Gilley Museum

Tremont

Island Cruises

Deer Isle

Cranberry Isles

0   5 mi
0   5 km

© MOON.COM

★ **Abbe Museum:** The Abbe Museum and its seasonal facility at Sieur de Monts Spring are fascinating places to learn about Maine's Indigenous people (page 90).

★ **Sea Kayaking:** Head out to sea via kayak on your own or with a guide (page 95).

★ **Dive-in Theater Boat Cruise:** Got kids? Don't miss this tour, where Diver Ed brings the undersea world aboard (page 96).

★ **Whale-Watching Excursions:** Board a high-speed catamaran and cruise well offshore to view whales and the puffin colony at Petit Manan Light (page 96).

★ **Somes Sound:** It's worth the journey to the quiet side of the island to see this spectacular inlet, officially tagged a fjard (page 111).

★ **Northeast Harbor Gardens:** Magical and enchanting best describe **Asticou, Thuya,** and **Rockefeller Gardens.** Zen-like Asticou is best seen in spring; Thuya delivers color through summer; Rockefeller peaks in early August (page 111).

★ **Wendell Gilley Museum:** Gilley's intricately carved birds, from miniature shorebirds to life-size birds of prey, are marvels to behold (page 119).

★ **Island Cruises:** Adults and kids alike enjoy Captain Eli Strauss's extremely informative and fun nature cruises (page 130).

★ **Cranberry Isles:** Make it a point to cruise at least to Islesford for a taste of island life (page 133).

Mount Desert Island Communities

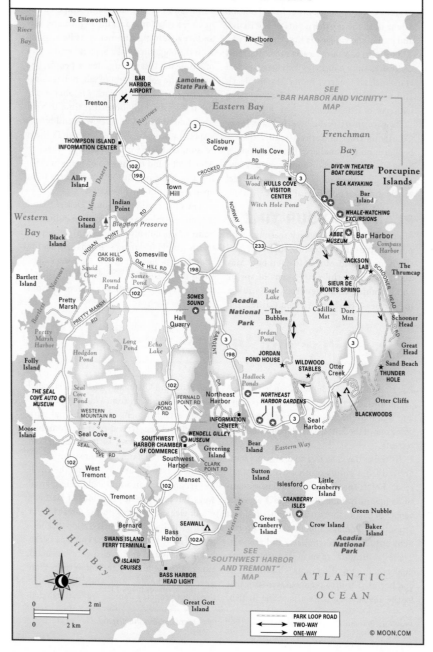

Union River Bay

To Ellsworth

Marlboro

BAR HARBOR AIRPORT

Lamoine State Park

Trenton

Eastern Bay

SEE "BAR HARBOR AND VICINITY" MAP

Frenchman Bay

THOMPSON ISLAND INFORMATION CENTER

Salisbury Cove

Hulls Cove

HULLS COVE RD

Alley Island

Town Hill

Lake Wood

HULLS COVE VISITOR CENTER

Witch Hole Pond

DIVE-IN THEATER BOAT CRUISE

SEA KAYAKING

Porcupine Islands

Bar Island

Indian Point

Green Island

Blagden Preserve

Black Island

WHALE-WATCHING EXCURSIONS

ABBE MUSEUM

Bar Harbor

Compass Harbor

Western Bay

Squid Cove

Somesville

OAK HILL CROSS RD

OAK HILL RD

JACKSON LAB

The Thrumcap

Bartlett Island

Pretty Marsh

Round Pond

Somes Pond

SOMES SOUND

Eagle Lake

SIEUR DE MONTS SPRING

Acadia National Park

The Bubbles

Cadillac Mtn

Dorr Mtn

Schooner Head

Pretty Marsh Harbor

Hall Quarry

Somes Sound

Long Pond

Echo Lake

Jordan Pond

Great Head

Folly Island

Hodgdon Pond

JORDAN POND HOUSE

WILDWOOD STABLES

Otter Creek

Sand Beach

THUNDER HOLE

THE SEAL COVE AUTO MUSEUM

Seal Cove Pond

FERNALD POINT RD

LONG POND RD

Northeast Harbor

Hadlock Ponds

NORTHEAST HARBOR GARDENS

Seal Harbor

Otter Cliffs

BLACKWOODS

Moose Island

WESTERN MOUNTAIN RD

INFORMATION CENTER

Seal Cove

SOUTHWEST HARBOR CHAMBER OF COMMERCE

WENDELL GILLEY MUSEUM

Bear Island

Eastern Way

West Tremont

Southwest Harbor

Greening Island

CLARK POINT RD

Sutton Island

Islesford

Little Cranberry Island

Green Nubble

Tremont

Manset

Western Way

CRANBERRY ISLES

Crow Island

Baker Island

Bernard

SEAWALL

Bass Harbor

Great Cranberry Island

Acadia National Park

SWANS ISLAND FERRY TERMINAL

ISLAND CRUISES

BASS HARBOR HEAD LIGHT

Blue Hill Bay

Great Gott Island

ATLANTIC OCEAN

0   2 mi
0   2 km

PARK LOOP ROAD
TWO-WAY
ONE-WAY

SEE "SOUTHWEST HARBOR AND TREMONT" MAP

© MOON.COM

with post offices and zip codes, some without. Bar Harbor, for instance, includes the villages of Hulls Cove, Salisbury Cove, Town Hill, and Eden, all in the northern part of the island, and part of the village of Otter Creek.

The town of Mount Desert can be the most confusing, since it includes the villages of Seal Harbor, Hall Quarry, Pretty Marsh, Beech Hill, Somesville, and Northeast Harbor, along with part of Otter Creek.

Be sure to drive or bike (or late June-Columbus Day, take the Island Explorer bus) around the smaller villages, especially Somesville, Bass Harbor, and Bernard. Views are fabulous, the pace is slow, and you'll feel you've stumbled on "the real Maine."

PLANNING YOUR TIME

Mount Desert Island is very seasonal, with most restaurants, accommodations, and shops open mid-May-mid-October. May and June bring the new greens of spring and blooming rhododendrons and azaleas in Northeast Harbor's Asticou Garden, but mosquitoes and blackflies are at their worst, and the weather is temperamental—perhaps sunny and hot one day, damp and cold the next, making for a packing nightmare. July and August bring summer at its best, along with the biggest crowds. September is a gem of a time to visit: no bugs, fewer people, less fog, and the golden light of fall. Foliage usually begins turning in early October, making it an especially beautiful time to visit (the Columbus Day holiday weekend brings a spike in visitors). Winter is Acadia's silent season, best left for independent travelers who don't mind making do or perhaps making a meal of peanut butter crackers if an open restaurant can't be found.

The only road onto Mount Desert Island is Route 3. Unless you're traveling in the wee hours of the morning or late at night, expect traffic. Avoid it during shift changes on the island, 8am-9am and 3pm-4pm weekdays, when traffic slows to a crawl. On the island, use the Island Explorer bus system to avoid parking hassles.

Bar Harbor and Vicinity

Bar Harbor (pop. 5,235) was founded in 1796 as the town of Eden. In the late 19th century and well into the 20th, the town grew to become one of the East Coast's fanciest summer retreats.

In those days, ferries and steam yachts arrived from points south, large and small resort hotels sprang up, and exclusive mansions (quaintly dubbed "cottages") were the venues of parties thrown by summer-resident Drexels, DuPonts, Vanderbilts, and prominent academics, journalists, and lawyers. These "rusticators" came for the season with huge entourages of servants, children, pets, and horses. The area's renown was such that by the 1890s, even the staffs of the British, Austrian, and Ottoman embassies retreated here for the summer from Washington DC.

The establishment of the national park in 1919 and the arrival of the automobile changed the character of Bar Harbor and Mount Desert Island. The creation of the income tax, two World Wars, and the Great Depression took an additional toll in myriad ways, but the coup de grâce for Bar Harbor's era of elegance came with the Great Fire of 1947, a wind-whipped conflagration that devastated more than 17,000 acres on the eastern half of the island and leveled gorgeous mansions, humble homes, and more trees than anyone could ever count. Only three people died, but property damage was estimated at

---

Previous: Bernard; Charlotte Rhoades Park and Butterfly Garden; *The Starfish Enterprise.*

Bar Harbor and Vicinity

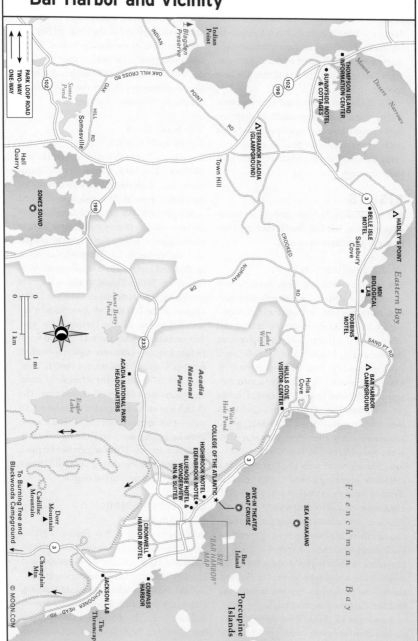

© MOON.COM

more than $23 million. Whole books have been written about the October inferno; fascinating scrapbooks in Bar Harbor's Jesup Memorial Library and exhibits at La Rochelle dramatically relate the gripping details of the story. Even though some of the elegant cottages have survived, the fire altered life here forever.

Bar Harbor often gets a bad rap for crowds. It's the island's largest town and the shopping hub; it's also where tour buses and cruise ships dock. That said, it's not hard to slip away to enjoy the town's sights and charms, of which there are many.

SIGHTS

Acadia National Park comes right up to the edge of town, but the Bar Harbor area has plenty of attractions of its own.

★ Abbe Museum

The fabulous Abbe Museum, Maine's only Smithsonian affiliate, is a superb introduction to prehistoric, historic, and contemporary Native American tools, crafts, and other cultural artifacts, with an emphasis on the Wabanaki, Maine's Micmac, Maliseet, Passamaquoddy, and Penobscot people. Everything about this privately funded museum, established in 1927, is tasteful. It has two campuses: The main campus (26 Mount Desert St., Bar Harbor, 207/288-3519, www. abbemuseum.org, 10am-5pm daily May-Oct., 10am-4pm Thurs.-Sat. Nov.-Dec. and Feb.-Apr., $10 adults, $5 ages 11-17) is home to a collection spanning nearly 12,000 years. In creating the core exhibit, *People of the First Light*, museum staff worked with 23 Wabanaki curatorial consultants and four native artists, among others. Museum-sponsored events include crafts workshops, hands-on children's programs, archaeological field schools, the Abbe Museum Indian Market in May and the Native American Festival (usually the first Sat. after the Fourth of July).

Admission to the in-town Abbe also includes admission to the museum's original site (10am-5pm daily late-May-mid-Oct.), in the park about 2.5 miles south of Bar Harbor at Sieur de Monts Spring, where Route 3 meets the Park Loop Road. Inside a small but handsome building listed in the National Register of Historic Places are displays from a 50,000-item collection. Admission to only the Sieur de Monts Spring Abbe is $3 adults, $1 ages 11-17, and admission paid here can be credited to admission to the main museum.

St. Saviour's Episcopal Church

St. Saviour's (41 Mt. Desert St., Bar Harbor, 207/288-4215, http://stsaviours.me/wordpress, 7am-dusk daily), close to downtown Bar Harbor, is not only the oldest, largest, and tallest public building on the island, it also contains Maine's largest collection of Tiffany stained glass windows. Ten originals are here; an 11th, the Easter Lily Window, was stolen in 1988 and replaced by a locally made window. Of the 32 non-Tiffany windows, the most intriguing is a memorial to Clarence Little, founder of the Jackson Laboratory and a descendant of Paul Revere. Images in the window include the laboratory, DNA, and mice. In July-August, volunteers regularly conduct free tours of the Victorian-era church, completed in 1878; call for the schedule or make an appointment for an off-season tour. The church is open for self-guided tours 8am-8pm daily—pick up a brochure in the back. It's also open for guided tours on Sundays following the 10am service. If old cemeteries intrigue you, spend time wandering the 18th-century town graveyard next to the church.

La Rochelle Mansion & Museum

Immerse yourself in Bar Harbor's gilded age at the Bar Harbor Historical Society, housed in the La Rochelle Mansion and History Museum (127 West St., Bar Harbor, 207/288-0000, www.barharborhistorical.org, hours vary seasonally, $15 adults, $13 seniors and ages 7-12). This 41-room, 13,000-square-foot Georgian Revival waterfront mansion survived the Great Fire of 1947. Exhibits and collections let visitors understand life in the famed summer colony before that devastating event. Exhibitions also highlight renowned landscape designer Beatrix Farrand (who designed and planted the mansion's gardens), architect Frank L. Savage, the grand hotels, and the dairy farms once so prevalent on the island. Do take time to sit a spell on the back porch overlooking Frenchman Bay and Bar Island. Check online or call for the current schedule. Afterward, stroll along upper West Street, which is listed in the National Register of Historic Places, to see other grand cottages that survived the fire.

College of the Atlantic

A museum, a gallery, gardens, and a pleasant campus for walking are reasons to visit the **College of the Atlantic** (COA, 105 Eden St./Rte. 3, Bar Harbor, 207/288-5015, www. coa.edu), which specializes in human ecology, or humans' interrelationship with the environment. Download *A Guide to the COA Campus Landscape: Features, History, and Three-Season Highlights* from the website. It's an excellent companion when exploring the campus and guides visitors to many unexpected treasures, including memorials, terraces, and a shrine. Check the college's calendar of events for lectures, conversations, and other activities.

In a handsome renovated building that originally served as the first Acadia National Park headquarters, the **George B. Dorr Museum of Natural History** (10am-5pm Tues.-Sat., donation) showcases regional birds and mammals in realistic dioramas made by COA students. The biggest attraction for children is the please-touch philosophy, allowing them to reach into a touch tank to feel fur, skulls, and even whale baleen. The museum gift shop has a particularly good collection of books and gifts for budding naturalists. Across the way is the **Ethel H. Blum Gallery** (207/288-5015, ext. 254, 11am-4pm Tues.-Sat. summer, 8am-9pm Mon.-Fri. during the academic year), a small space that hosts some intriguing exhibits.

The campus is home to a number of **gardens** (www.coa.edu/gardens). Find the **Beatrix Farrand Garden,** created by the renowned garden designer in 1928, behind Kaelber Hall. It contains more than 50 varieties of roses and was the prototype for the rose garden at Dumbarton Oaks in Washington DC. Both are known for Farrand's use of garden rooms, such as the walled terraces in this garden.

The **Turrets Seaside Garden,** fronting on the ocean, was restored by a student in 2005. The central fountain, created by alumnus Dan Farrenkopf of Lunaform Pottery, was installed in 2009. Adjacent to the Turrets is a **sunken garden,** created in a foundation. It's been restored a couple of times, and in 2015, the COA Gardening Club started maintaining it, eventually turning it into a sustainable, low-maintenance, edible garden. The 1st floor of the **Turrets,** a magnificent 1895 seaside cottage that's now an administration building, can be explored.

The college also offers excellent and very popular weeklong sessions of **Family Nature Camp** (800/597-9500, www.coa.edu/summer, July-early Aug., $940-1,060 adults, $500 age 15 and younger). It's essential to register well in advance; ask about early-season discounts. Families are housed and fed on the campus and explore Acadia National Park with expert naturalist guides.

Garland Farm

Fans of landscape architect Beatrix Farrand should visit **Garland Farm** (475 Bayview Dr., Bar Harbor, 207/288-0237, www.beatrixfarrandsociety.org), the ancestral home of Lewis Garland, who managed her Reef Point property. When Farrand dismantled that property in 1955, she moved here with the Garlands, engaging an architect to build an addition to the original farmhouse and barn using architectural elements from Reef Point. The property was sold a few times, and greatly reduced in size, until the Beatrix Farrand Society purchased it in 2004. The society aims to restore Garland Farm to its Farrand-era design and

Bar Harbor

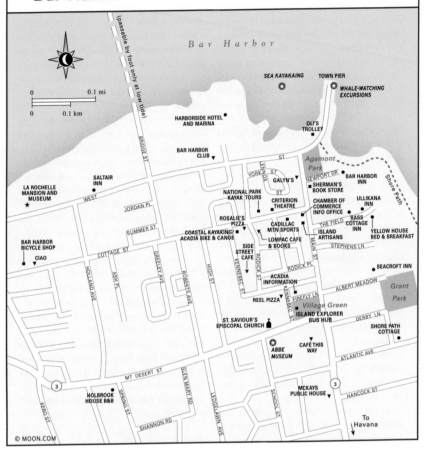

Bar Harbor

SEA KAYAKAING

TOWN PIER

WHALE-WATCHING
EXCURSIONS

HARBORSIDE HOTEL
AND MARINA

OLI'S
TROLLEY

BAR HARBOR
CLUB

*Agamont
Park*

BRIDGE ST

SALTAIR
INN

YORK ST

LENOX ST

GALYN'S

NEWPORT DR

BAR HARBOR
INN

SHERMAN'S
BOOK STORE

Shore Path

LA ROCHELLE
MANSION AND
MUSEUM

WEST ST

NATIONAL PARK
KAYAK TOURS

CRITERION
THEATRE

CHAMBER OF
COMMERCE
INFO OFFICE

ULLIKANA
INN

JORDAN PL

BASS
COTTAGE
INN

SUMMER ST

ROSALIE'S
PIZZA

CADILLAC
MTN SPORTS

THE FIELD

ISLAND
ARTISANS

YELLOW HOUSE
BED & BREAKFAST

BAR HARBOR
BICYCLE SHOP

COASTAL KAYAKING/
ACADIA BIKE & CANOE

LOMPAC CAFE
& BOOKS

STEPHENS LN

CIAO

COTTAGE ST

SIDE
STREET
CAFE

RODICK ST

RODICK PL

MAIN ST

SEACROFT INN

HOLLAND AVE

ASH PL

GREELEY AVE

ROBERTS AVE

HIGH ST

KENNEBEC ST

ACADIA
INFORMATION

KENNEBEC PL

FIREFLY LN

ALBERT MEADOW

Grant
Park

REEL PIZZA

Village Green

ST. SAVIOUR'S
EPISCOPAL CHURCH

ISLAND EXPLORER
BUS HUB

DERBY LN

SHORE PATH
COTTAGE

ABBE
MUSEUM

CAFE THIS
WAY

ATLANTIC AVE

MT DESERT ST

GLEN MARY RD

SPRING ST

3

HOLBROOK
HOUSE B&B

LEDGELAWN AVE

SCHOOL ST

MCKAYS
PUBLIC HOUSE

3

HANCOCK ST

KEBO ST

SHANNON RD

To
Havana

© MOON.COM

0   0.1 mi
0   0.1 km

(passable by foot only at low tide)

condition and to create a center for the study of design and horticulture. The property, now listed in the National Register of Historic Places, hosts special events and programs. Garland Farm is open for visits one or two days per week and tours by appointment ($5 suggestion donation); call or check the website for current schedule. Horticulture-related programs ($20) fill the summer calendar.

Hulls Cove Tool Barn and Sculpture Garden

Part shop, part nature center, part art gallery,

the **Hulls Cove Tool Barn and Sculpture Garden** (17 Breakneck Rd., Hulls Cove, 207-288-5126, www.jonesport-wood.com, free), behind Hulls Cove General Store, is just one of several enterprises of the creative Skip Brack. Inside the barn is an extensive selection of old tools, with an emphasis on woodworking hand tools. The store is open 10am-4pm most days, but call before making a special trip. Paths run through perennial gardens, woods, and fields at the Davistown Museum Sculpture Garden, which surrounds the barn and continues across the street. Throughout the wild gardens are sculptures by noted Maine artists and found-object creations by Brack. Take the Island Explorer bus Route 1/ Campgrounds and request a stop at the Hulls Cove General Store, then walk up the road.

JAX

World renowned in genetic research, scientists at the Jackson Laboratory for Mammalian Research (600 Main St./Rte. 3, Bar Harbor, 207/288-1429, www.jax.org) study cancer, diabetes, muscular dystrophy, heart disease, and Alzheimer's disease, among others—with considerable success. The nonprofit research institution, locally called JAX or just "the lab," is also renowned for its genetics databases and for producing genetically defined laboratory mice, which are shipped to research labs worldwide. The lab offers free one-hour public researcher-led tours (limited to 15 people; min. age 12; preregistration required) one day per week from mid-June to early October. If this is on your must-do list, plan ahead: The tours often sell out well in advance. The visitor program changes every summer, so call for current details.

RECREATION
Parks and Preserves
INDIAN POINT BLAGDEN PRESERVE

In the far northern corner of the island, still within the Bar Harbor town limits, is the lovely Indian Point Blagden Preserve (207/729-5181, dawn-6pm daily year-round), owned by the Nature Conservancy. From the junction of Route 3 and Route 102/198, continue 1.8 miles to Indian Point Road and turn right. Go 1.7 miles to a fork and turn right. Watch for the preserve entrance on the right, marked by a Nature Conservancy sign in the shape of an oak leaf.

Five trails wind through the forested 110-acre preserve, a rectangular parcel with island, hill, and bay vistas and more than 1,000 feet of frontage on Western Bay. Seal-watching and birding are popular—there are harbor seals on offshore rocks, 6 species

of woodpeckers, and 12 species of warblers, plus more than 100 other bird species in blow-down areas. To spot the seals, plan your hike around low tide, when they'll be sprawled on the rocks close to shore. Wear rubberized shoes or boots. Bring binoculars or use the telescope installed here for that purpose. To avoid disturbing the seals, watch quietly and avoid jerky movements. Park near the preserve entrance and follow the Big Woods Trail, which runs the length of the preserve. A second parking area is farther in, but then you'll miss walking through much of the preserve. When you reach the second parking area, just past an old farm field, bear left along the Shore Trail to see the seals. Register at the caretaker's house, which is just beyond the first parking lot, where you can pick up bird and flora checklists. Respect the private property on either side of the preserve.

STONE BARN FARM PRESERVE

The Maine Coast Heritage Trust acquired the 128-acre Stone Barn Farm (Crooked Rd. and Norway Dr., Bar Harbor, 207/729-7366, www.mcht.org) in 2019. The property comprises a stone barn dating from around 1907 and listed on the National Register of Historic Places, an 1840s farmhouse, a carriage house, fields with lupines, woodlands with vernal pools, a mile of marshy frontage on Northeast Creek, and about two miles of walking trails behind the barn connecting it all. It's an especially quiet place to slip away and contemplate nature.

Walks
SHORE PATH

A real treat is a stroll along downtown Bar Harbor's Shore Path (6:30am-dusk daily), a well-trodden granite-edged byway built around 1880. Along the craggy shoreline are granite-and-wood benches, town-owned Grant Park (great for picnics), birch trees, and several handsome mansions that escaped the 1947 fire. Offshore are the four Porcupine Islands. Leashed pets are allowed. Allow about 30 minutes for the one-mile loop, beginning next to the town pier and the Bar Harbor Inn and returning via Wayman Lane (or for maximum views, simply retrace your steps).

GREAT MEADOW LOOP

This easy walk connects downtown Bar Harbor with the park's Jesup Path, which leads to Sieur de Monts Spring. From there, you have access to the Dorr Mountain trails. It's a fine early-morning walk and a gentle introduction to hiking for those nervous about straying too far from civilization.

To find the Great Meadow Loop trailhead, walk up Mount Desert Street from the Village Green to Spring Street. Follow Spring Street to Cromwell Harbor Road and turn left. At the edge of Ledgelawn Cemetery is the signed trail. It meanders through the woods for a bit before emerging on Ledgelawn Avenue (this section doubles as Great Meadow Drive). Turn right and walk along the road until the trail reenters the woods across the road. The trail never strays too far from pavement. It parallels the road for a bit before recrossing it and shadowing the Park Loop Road; the Kebo Valley Golf Club will be on the right. Just before the trail crosses Harden Farm Road, you'll see the Jesup Path trailhead on the left, across the Park Loop Road. Take that if you want to head to Sieur de Monts Spring (0.6 mile). Otherwise, continue along the trail as it follows and crosses Harden Farm Road and wraps around the golf course (there's a portable toilet near one green).

At the intersection with Cromwell Harbor Road, turn right, return to Spring Street, and follow it back to Mount Desert Street and the Village Green. It's just shy of two miles round-trip.

Bicycling

With all the great biking options, including 45 miles of carriage roads and some of the best roadside bike routes in Maine, you'll want to bring a bike or rent one. Two rental firms based in downtown Bar Harbor also handle repairs. Expect to pay around $30 per day for a rental bike, including a helmet, a lock, and a map, and more for a performance or specialty model. It's wise to make advance reservations.

The Minutolo family's **Bar Harbor Bicycle Shop** (141 Cottage St., Bar Harbor, 207/288-3886, www.barharborbike.com), on the corner of Route 3, has been in business since 1977. If you have your own bike, stop here for advice on routes—the Minutolos have cycled everywhere on the island and can suggest the perfect mountain-bike or road-bike loop based on your ability and schedule.

the Shore Path

The shop has rentals varying from standard mountain bikes to full-suspension models and even tandems, as well as all the accessories and gear you might need; electric bikes are $60. Hours in summer are 8am-6pm daily, 9am-5pm daily during spring and fall. Rentals are on a 24-hour basis.

Acadia Bike (48 Cottage St., Bar Harbor, 207/288-9605 or 800/526-8615, www.acadiabike.com) also rents bikes.

If hills are your biking nemesis, consider renting an electric bicycle from **Pedego Electric Bikes Acadia** (55 West St., Bar Harbor, 207/664-9181). These battery-assist bikes let you get as much of a workout as you desire, with six settings ranging from no assist to high assist, as well as a throttle, for an extra push when necessary. Do ask for where these are permitted, as not all are allowed in all parts of the park. Rates begin at $55/four hours or $100/day; reservations are wise.

If you're headed to Southwest Harbor, perhaps for a day trip to Swans Island, see the information on Southwest Cycle in the *Southwest Harbor and Vicinity* section later in this chapter.

TOP EXPERIENCE

★ Sea Kayaking and Canoeing

You can launch your own kayak at **Hadley Point Beach** (Hadley Point Rd., Bar Harbor). This pebbly beach on Mount Desert Narrows has a couple of picnic tables, a portable toilet, and parking. Careful, though—the currents are very strong. To find the put-in, continue south from the Thompson Island Information Center on Route 3 for about four miles. Hadley Point Road is on the left; follow it to the end.

GUIDED TOURS

Sea kayaking is wildly popular along the Maine coast, and Bar Harbor has become a major kayaking destination. No experience is necessary to join tours operated by any of the firms in Bar Harbor.

Since 1993, **National Park Kayak Tours** (39 Cottage St., Bar Harbor, 800/347-0940,

www.acadiakayak.com) has offered Registered Maine Guide-led tours, each limited to a maximum of six tandem kayaks per trip. Four-hour morning, midday, afternoon, or sunset paddles ($55 pp July-Aug., $50 off-season) are offered, including shuttle service, a paddle and safety lesson, and a brief stop. Paddlers are shuttled to the quiet west side of the island (usually Western or Blue Hill Bay, occasionally Somes Sound), with the location determined by wind and weather. Most trips cover about six miles. Multiday camping trips also are offered. It's best if you make reservations at least one day in advance. Trips are offered Memorial Day weekend-early October.

Half-day, full-day, and multiday sea kayak tours are on the schedule organized by **Coastal Kayaking Tours** (48 Cottage St., Bar Harbor, 207/288-9605 or 800/526-8615, www.acadiafun.com, $49-61). The best option for beginners is the 2.5-hour morning harbor tour. A half-day family tour, departing at 1pm, can handle kids age eight and over. A 2.5-hour sunset cruise begins around 5pm, depending on season; a full-day tour covers about 10 miles. All trips are in tandem kayak and are weather dependent; reservations are essential.

Carriage Rides

Tour the countryside via horse-drawn carriage with **Wild Iris Horse Farm** (207/288-5234, www.wildirishorsefarm.com, from $30 adults, $15 kids 12 and younger). The 30- and 45-minute narrated tours depart from 55 West Street, Bar Harbor.

Golf

Duffers first teed off in 1888 at **Kebo Valley Golf Club** (100 Eagle Lake Rd./Rte. 233, Bar Harbor, 207/288-5000, www.kebovalleyclub.com, May-Oct.), Maine's oldest club and the eighth oldest in the nation. The 17th hole became legendary when it took President William Howard Taft 27 strokes to sink the ball in 1911. Kebo is very popular, with a gorgeous setting, an attractive clubhouse, and decent food service, so booking tee times is essential; you can reserve up to six days in advance.

Adopt a Whale

Here's a trump card: When everyone else is flashing photos of kids or grandkids, you can whip out images of your very own adopted whale. And for that, you can thank Allied Whale's **Adopt-a-Whale** program at College of the Atlantic (COA) in Bar Harbor.

In 1972, COA established Allied Whale, a marine-mammal laboratory designed to collect, interpret, and apply research on the world's largest mammal. Although Allied Whale's primary focus is the Gulf of Maine, its projects span the globe, involving international scientific collaboration. Since 1981, part of the research has involved assembling an enormous photo collection (more than 25,000 images) for identification of specific humpback and finback whales (with names such as Quartz and Elvis) and tracking of their migration routes. The photo catalog of finbacks already numbers more than 1,000.

And here's where the adoption program comes in—it's a way to support the important research being done by Allied Whale and its colleagues. If you sign up as an adoptive "parent" for a year, you'll receive a Certificate of Adoption, a North Atlantic whale watch guide, an Understanding Whales: Research Conservation, and Education booklet, and an Adopt a Whale-Allied Whale bumper sticker. It's a superb gift for budding scientists. The adoption fee is $30 for a single humpback or finback or $40 for a mother and calf.

For further information, contact **Allied Whale** (207/288-5644, www.coa.edu/allied-whale).

Mount Desert Island YMCA

Here's a lifesaver on a stormy day: The **Mount Desert Island YMCA** (21 Park St., Bar Harbor, 207/288-3511, www.mdiymca.org, 5:30am-8:30pm Mon.-Fri., 7am-4pm Sat., 7am-2pm Sun. summer) has an indoor pool and a gym, track, fitness room, and recreation room. Weekly rates are $80family, $50/adult, $30-senior or student.

EXCURSION BOATS

Note that prices are given as a guide and will fluctuate with the cost of fuel.

★ Dive-in Theater Boat Cruise

You don't have to go diving in these frigid waters; others will do it for you. When the kids are clamoring to touch slimy sea cucumbers and starfish at various touch tanks in the area, they're likely to be primed for Diver Ed's **Dive-In Theater Boat Cruise** (207/288-3483 or 800/979-3370, www.divered.com), departing from the College of the Atlantic pier (105 Eden St., Bar Harbor). Ed Monat, former Bar Harbor harbormaster and College of the Atlantic grad, heads the crew aboard the 46-passenger *Starfish Enterprise*. The boat goes a mile or two offshore, where Ed, a professional diver, goes overboard with a video camera and a mini-Ed who helps put things in proportion. You and the kids stay on deck, all warm and dry, along with Captain Evil, who explains the action on a TV screen. There's communication back and forth, so the kids can ask questions as the divers pick up urchins, starfish, crabs, lobsters, and other sea life. When Ed resurfaces, he brings a bag of touchable specimens—another chance to pet some slimy creatures (which go back into the water after show-and-tell). It's a great concept. Watch the kids' expressions—this is a big hit. The two-hour trips depart three times daily Monday-Saturday and once on Sunday early July-early September; fewer trips are made in spring and fall. The cost is $42 adults, $37 seniors, $32 ages 5-11, $16 under age 5. Advance reservations are required.

TOP EXPERIENCE

★ Whale-Watching Excursions

Whale-watching boats go as far as 20 miles offshore, so no matter what the weather in Bar Harbor, dress warmly and bring more clothing than you think you'll need—even gloves.

I've been out on days when it's close to 90°F on the island but feels more like 30°F in a moving boat on the open ocean. Motion-sensitive children and adults should plan in advance for appropriate medication, such as seasickness pills or patches. Adults are required to show a photo ID when boarding the boat.

Whale-watching, puffin-watching, and combo excursions are offered by **Bar Harbor Whale Watch Company** (1 West St., Bar Harbor, 207/288-2386 or 800/942-5374, www. barharborwhales.com), sailing from the town pier (1 West St.) in downtown Bar Harbor. The company operates under various names, including Acadian Whale Watcher, and has a number of boats. Most trips are accompanied by a naturalist (often from Allied Whale at the College of the Atlantic), who regales passengers with all sorts of interesting trivia about the whales, porpoises, seabirds, and other marinelife spotted along the way. In season, some trips go out as far as the puffin colony on Petit Manan Light. Trips depart daily late May-late October, but with so many options it's impossible to list the schedule; call for the latest details. Tickets are around $65 adults, $35 ages 6-14, $14 under age 6. A portion of the ticket price benefits Allied Whale, which researches and protects marine animals in the Gulf of Maine. Trips may extend longer than the time advertised, so don't plan anything else too tightly around the trip.

Scenic Nature Cruises (1.5-2 hours) and kid-friendly **Lobster/Seal Watch Cruises** (1.5 hours) are also offered. Rates for these are around $35 adults, $20 ages 6-14, and free-$14 for kids under 6. Also available are 3-hour **Puffin and Lighthouse Cruises** ($54 adults, $27 ages 6-14, and $14 for kids under 6). **Special Lighthouse Photography Tours** are also offered, call or see the website for details.

Sailing

Captain Steve Pagels, under the umbrella of **Downeast Windjammer Cruises** (207/288-4585 or 207/288-2373, www. downeastwindjammer.com), offers 1.5-2-hour day sails on the 151-foot steel-hulled *Margaret Todd,* a gorgeous four-masted schooner with tanbark sails that he designed and launched in 1998, or the *Bailey Louise Todd.* Trips depart at 10am, 2pm, and around sunset daily mid-May-mid-October (weather permitting) from the Bar Harbor Inn pier, just east of the town pier in downtown Bar Harbor. You'll get the best wildlife sightings on the morning trip, but better sailing on the afternoon trip; there's live music on the sunset one. A park ranger narrates some sails, which adds to the experience. Buy tickets at the pier, at the office (27 Main St.), or online with a credit card; arrive at least half an hour before departure. The cost is $42-48 adults, $39-44 seniors, $32-46 ages 6-11, $7-12 ages 2-5. Dogs are welcome on all sails.

Custom Cruises

Captain Winston Shaw's **Sea Venture Custom Boat Tours** (207/412-0222, www. svboattours.com) lets you design the perfect trip aboard *Reflection,* a 20-foot motor launch. Captain Shaw, a Registered Maine Guide and committed environmentalist, specializes in nature-oriented tours. He's the founder and director of the Coastal Maine Bald Eagle Project, and he was involved in the inaugural Earth Day celebration in 1970. He's been studying coastal birds for more than 30 years. You can pick from 10 recommended cruises lasting 1-8 hours, or design your own. In any case, the boat is yours. The boat charter rate is $130/hour for up to two people, $150 for three or four, and $200 for five or six. Captain Shaw can also arrange for picnic lunches. On longer trips, restroom stops are available. The boat departs from the Atlantic Oceanside Hotel pier, off Route 3 in Bar Harbor.

Lobster Cruise

When you're ready to learn *the truth* about lobsters, sign up for a two-hour cruise aboard the *Lulu* (55 West St., Bar Harbor, 207/288-3136, www.lululobsterboat.com), a traditional Maine lobster boat that departs up to four times daily from the Harborside Hotel

and Marina. The captain provides entertaining commentary on anything and everything, but especially about lobsters and lobstering. He hauls a lobster trap and explains intimate details of the hapless critters. This is a real kid-pleaser, but adults are equally entertained. Reservations are required. Cost is $35 adults, $32 seniors and active U.S. military, $20 ages 2-12.

Bay Fishing Trip

Fish for cod, cusk, pollock, mackerel, and other species in Frenchman Bay on a three-hour trip aboard the *Ebb Tide,* operated by **Downeast Windjammer Cruises** (207/288-4585, www.downeastwindjammer.com, $45 adults, $42 seniors, $35 children). Bait and tackle are provided. Morning and afternoon trips depart Tuesday through Saturday from late June through late August.

ENTERTAINMENT

At the height of the summer season, live entertainment includes pub music, films, and classical concerts.

The **Bar Harbor Town Band** performs for free at 8pm Monday and Thursday evenings July-mid-August in the bandstand on the Village Green (Main St. and Mt. Desert St., Bar Harbor).

The **Jesup Memorial Library** (www.jesuplibrary.org) regularly hosts author readings, concerts, and other activities.

Carmen Verandah/Bar Harbor Beerworks (119 Main St., Bar Harbor, 207/288-2886, https://carmenverandahme.com) is the weekend place to see and be seen, with live music, dancing, and more.

You never know quite what's going to happen at **Improv Acadia** (15 Cottage St., Bar Harbor, 207/288-2503, www.improvacadia.com, late May-mid-Oct., $25 adults, $15 age 12 and younger). Every show is different, as actors use audience suggestions to create comedy sketches. Shows are staged once or twice

1: The Abbe Museum 2: La Rochelle Mansion & Museum 3: excursion boats

nightly. Dessert, snacks, and drinks are available. The 8pm show in July and August is family friendly.

Every evening, 7pm-11pm, **pianist Bill Trowell** plays in the Great Room Piano Lounge at the Bluenose Hotel (90 Eden St., Bar Harbor, 207/288-3348, www.barharborhotel.com).

Theaters

Built in 1932 and listed in the National Register of Historic Places, the **Criterion Theatre** (35 Cottage St., Bar Harbor, 207/288-0829, www.criteriontheatre.org) is a beautifully restored, 877-seat art deco classic with an elegant floating balcony. It now hosts performances, movies, and special events.

Combine pizza with your picture show at **Reel Pizza Cinerama** (33 Kennebec Pl., Bar Harbor, 207/288-3811 for films, 207/288-3828 for food, www.reelpizza.net). Two films are screened nightly on each of two screens. Doors open at 4:30pm; get there early for the best seats: tiered rows with counters giving way to comfy couches.

EVENTS

Bar Harbor is home to numerous special events; this is just a sampling. For more information, contact the Bar Harbor Chamber of Commerce (207/288-5103 or 888/540-9990, www.barharbormaine.com).

The mid-May **Taste of Bar Harbor** kicks off the season with cooking classes, brewery tours, tastings, competitions, and other culinary events.

The Abbe Museum's **Native American Indian Market** in mid May attracts many of the country's top Native American artists and artisans.

In early June, the annual **Acadia Birding Festival** (www.acadiabirdingfestival.com) attracts bird-watchers with guided walks, boating excursions, tours, talks, and meals.

The **Fourth of July** is always a big deal in Bar Harbor, celebrated with a 6am blueberry pancake breakfast, a 10am parade, an 11am seafood festival, a band concert, and fireworks. A highlight is the Lobster Race, a crustacean competition drawing contestants such as Lobzilla and Larry the Lobster, who compete in a four-lane saltwater tank on the Village Green. Independence Day celebrations in the island's smaller villages always evoke a bygone era.

The Abbe Museum, the College of the Atlantic, and the Maine Indian Basketmakers Alliance sponsor the annual **Native American Festival** featuring baskets, beadwork, and other handicrafts for sale as well as Indian drumming and dancing, held at College of the Atlantic on a Saturday in early July.

In even-numbered years, the **Mount Desert Garden Club Tour** presents a rare chance to visit some of Maine's most spectacular private gardens on the second or third Saturday in July.

The **Directions Craft Show** fills a weekend in late July or early August with extraordinary displays and sales of crafts by members of the Maine Crafts Guild. You'll find it at Mount Desert Island High School (Rte. 233/ Eagle Lake Rd., Bar Harbor).

The **Acadia Night Sky Festival** (www. acadianightskyfestival.com) in September celebrates Acadia's stellar stargazing with arts and science events, presentations, and activities.

SHOPPING

Bar Harbor's boutiques—running the gamut from attractive to kitschy—are indisputably visitor-oriented; many shut down for the winter, even removing or covering their signs and boarding the windows. Fortunately, the island has enough of a year-round community to support the cluster of loyal shopkeepers determined to stay open all year, but shop-till-you-droppers will be happiest here Memorial Day weekend-Columbus Day, and particularly in July-August. Remember also that Bar Harbor isn't Mount Desert's only shopping area.

Galleries

Downtown Bar Harbor's best crafts gallery is **Island Artisans** (99 Main St., Bar Harbor, 207/288-4214, www.islandartisans.com). More than 100 Maine artists are represented here, and the quality is outstanding—don't miss it. You'll find basketwork, handmade paper, woodcarvings, blown glass, jewelry, weaving, metalwork, ceramics, and more.

It's worth the brief detour off the beaten path to find **Rocky Mann Studio & Gallery** (38 Breakneck Rd., Bar Harbor, 207/288-5478, www.rockymann.com) to see Mann's Saggarware pottery.

Gallery? Nature store? Funky gift store? Museum? It's hard to categorize the **Rock & Art Shop** (23 Cottage St., Bar Harbor, 207/288-4800, http://www.therockand-artshop.com/). Fossils, gems, minerals, bug-filled marbles, and preserved sea horses are part of the intriguing mix, most of which carries educational signs.

Books and Gifts

Toys, cards, and newspapers blend in with the new-book inventory at **Sherman's Book Store** (56 Main St., Bar Harbor, 207/288-3161). It's just the place to pick up maps and trail guides for fine days and puzzles for foggy days.

Find a whodunit at **Bar Harbor Mystery Cove Book Shop** (1 Dewey St., Hulls Cove, 207/288-4665), the overflow of an Internet business specializing in mysteries and detective fiction, from rare books to popular titles. You'll also find plenty of other choices in all genres.

An amazing selection of artisanal olive oils and vinegars, all available for tasting, along with other culinary treasures, fill the shelves of **Fiore** (8 Rodick Pl., Bar Harbor, 207/802-2580, www.fioreoliveoils.com). The store is located behind the police station.

Bark Harbor (150 Main St., Bar Harbor, 207/288-0404) is the place to pick up the perfect souvenir for your cat or dog.

Souvenir shops are everywhere on Mount Desert Island, so why single out one? If you need Maine-made mementos for Uncle Harry and Aunt Mary, or if the kids need trinkets for friends back home, the Acadia Corporation has several shops in downtown Bar Harbor that can cover it all. The price range is broad, quality is fairly high, and clerks are especially friendly at **The Acadia Shop** (85 Main St., Bar Harbor, 207/288-5600, www.acadiashops.com), where the second floor is dedicated to works by Maine artisans. Another branch, **Acadia Outdoors** (45 Main St., Bar Harbor, 207/288-2422), features sportswear and outdoor accessories. The **Acadia Country Store** (128 Main St., Bar Harbor, 207-288-2426) offers Maine-made food, beverages, fudge, and other gifts in a downtown building constructed in the late 1800s.

Outdoor Clothing and Gear

Cadillac Mountain Sports (26 Cottage St., 207/288-4532, www.cadillacsports.com), and its across-the-street specialty Patagonia and North Face stores (39 Cottage St.), can outfit you for hiking, biking, climbing, paddling, swimming, snowshoeing, and other activities and adventures.

FOOD

You won't go hungry in Bar Harbor, and you won't find chain fast-food places. The summer tourism trade and the College of the Atlantic students have created a demand for pizzerias, vegetarian bistros, brewpubs, and a handful of creative restaurants. Of course, almost every restaurant has some kind of lobster dish. Even if you're using Bar Harbor as a base of operations, don't miss opportunities to explore restaurants elsewhere on the island.

For sit-down restaurants, make reservations as far in advance as possible. Expect reduced operations during spring and fall; only a handful of restaurants are open year-round.

Mount Desert Island is a seasonal community, and restaurant days and hours change frequently, so always call ahead. Also note that staffing is always a challenge in the region, and many businesses import workers from overseas. By the time waiters and waitresses have been fully trained, the season is almost over.

Quick Bites

Tastings ($6) are offered daily at **Bar Harbor Cellars** (854 Rte. 3, Bar Harbor, 207/288-3907, www.barharborcellars.com). The winery, located at Sweet Pea Farm, is in the early stages of using organic techniques to grow hybrid grapes. In the meantime, it's making wines from European and California grapes. Also here is a Maine chocolate room and a small selection of complementary foods, such as olives, cheese, and crackers.

Only a masochist could bypass **Ben & Bill's Chocolate Emporium** (66 Main St., Bar Harbor, 207/288-3281 or 800/806-3281, www.benandbills.com, from 10am daily), which makes homemade candies and more than 50 ice cream flavors (including a dubious lobster flavor); the whole place smells like the inside of a chocolate truffle. Closing hours depend on the season and crowds, but it's usually open until late in the evening.

That said, the most creative flavors come from **Mt. Desert Island Ice Cream** (7 Firefly Ln., Bar Harbor, 207/288-0999, and 325 Main St., Bar Harbor, 207/288-5664, www.mdiic.com). It's made in small batches, just five gallons at a time, using the finest ingredients. We're talking creamy, rich, and delicious ice cream in wild flavors.

For longevity and island ties, the winner for house-made ice cream is **Jordan Pond Ice Cream** (34 Main St., Bar Harbor, 207-288-2422).

Inexpensive, but with a healthful menu, is the **Take-A-Break Café** (105 Eden St., Bar Harbor, 207/288-5015, www.coa.edu, 7:30am-9:30am, 11:30am-1pm, and 5:30pm-6:30pm Mon.-Fri. during the academic year) in Blair Dining Hall, at the College of the Atlantic. If you find yourself on the college campus, perhaps for a boat tour or museum visit, consider eating here. The prices are especially inexpensive, there are always vegetarian, vegan, gluten-free, and meat choices, and the selection is organic and local whenever possible.

The **Mount Desert Bakery** (122 Cottage St., Bar Harbor, 207/801-9191, https://mount-dessertbakery.com, 7am-4pm Mon.-Fri.,

8am-3pm Sun.) turns out scrumptious pastries; bagel breakfast sandwiches are available until 11:30am, after that you can order a variety of cold sandwiches and paninis.

Your sweet tooth will delight in the cupcakes, whoopie pies, and other baked goodies available at **The Pink Pastry Shop** (75 Main St., Bar Harbor, 207/288-0110, 8am-9pm daily). Cash only.

After 30 years as a specialty beer pub, the **Lompoc Café & Books** (36 Rodick St., Bar Harbor, 207/901-0004, www.lompoccafe.com, 8am-9pm Tues.-Sun., $9-14) has matured into a casual café and bookshop. Go for soups, salads, sandwiches, and pizzas, along with a small selection of beer and wine. They also serve light breakfast fare.

Another good spot for healthful and vegetarian fare is **Thrive Juice Bar & Kitchen** (51 Rodick St., Bar Harbor, 207/801-9340, http://thrivebarharbor.com, 7am-2pm Wed.-Sun.), which specializes in smoothies, but also has salads, bowls, burritos, and wraps.

When it comes to American pub-grub favorites, such as burgers and fish sandwiches, the **Thirsty Whale Tavern** (40 Cottage St., Bar Harbor, 207/288-9335, www.thirstywhaletavern.com, 11am-9pm daily, $10-24) does it right.

For breakfast or brunch, you can't beat **2 Cats** (130 Cottage St., Bar Harbor, 207/288-2808 or 800/355-2828, http://twocatsbarharbor.com, 7am-1pm daily, $8-15). Fun, funky, and fresh best describe both the restaurant and the food. Dine inside or on the patio.

Choco-Latte (240 Main St., Bar Harbor, 207/801-9179, www.choco-lattecafe.com, 7am-6pm daily) aims to make all of its chocolates in house from organic Criollo cacao sourced from women-owned co-ops in Chiapas and Veracruz, Mexico. Pair them with an organic coffee or a hot chocolate. Also available: breakfast sandwiches, house-made bagels, and grill-press sandwiches ($6-10).

Between Mother's Day and late October, the **Eden Farmers Market** operates out of the YMCA parking lot off Lower Main Street in Bar Harbor, 9am-noon Sundays. You'll find fresh meats and produce, local cheeses and maple syrup, yogurt and ice cream, bread, honey, preserves, and even prepared Asian foods.

Picnic Fare and Prepared Foods

Although a few of these places have some seating, most are for the grab-and-go crowd.

An excellent choice for take-out fare is **Downeast Deli** (65 Main St., Bar Harbor, 207/288-1001, 8am-9pm daily). You can get both hot and cold fresh lobster rolls as well as other sandwiches, soups, and salads.

Peekytoe Provisions (244 Main St., Bar Harbor, 207/801-9161, http://peekytoeprovisions.com, 11am-7pm Wed.-Sat., 11am-5pm Sun., $6-20) is a great spot to pick up prepared as well as made-to-order soups, salads, sandwiches, and specials, most made from local and sustainable ingredients.

Brewpubs and Microbreweries

Bar Harbor Real Ale, Coal Porter, Blueberry Ale and others are brewed by the **Atlantic Brewing Company** (15 Knox Rd., Town Hill, in the upper section of the island, 207/288-2337, www.atlanticbrewing.com). Free brewery tours, including guided tastings, are given daily; call for schedule. Also operating here in summer is **Mainely-Meat Bar-B-Q** (207/288-9200, 11:30am-8pm daily, $8-20), offering pulled pork, chicken, ribs, and similar fare for lunch and dinner.

Atlantic also operates **Atlantic Brewing Midtown** (52 Cottage St., Bar Harbor, 207/288-2326, 11am-9pm daily), where it brews small-batch beers seven barrels at a time. Those as well as other Atlantic beers are offered in the tasting room. There's often live music in the evenings.

Family Favorites

An unscientific but reliable local survey gives the best-pizza ribbon to **Rosalie's Pizza & Italian Restaurant** (46 Cottage St., Bar Harbor, 207/288-5666, www.rosaliespizza.

com, 4pm-9pm Tues.-Sun., $7-20), where the Wurlitzer jukebox churns out tunes from the 1950s. Rosalie's earns high marks for consistency with its homemade pizza (gluten-free crust available), in four sizes or by the slice, along with calzones and subs; there are lots of vegetarian options. The Italian dinners—spaghetti, eggplant parmigiana, and others—are all less than $10, including a garlic roll. Beer and wine are available. Avoid the downstairs lines by heading upstairs and ordering at that counter, or call in your order.

Route 66 Restaurant (21 Cottage St., Bar Harbor, 207/288-3708, www.barharborroute66.com, 11am-9pm daily, $12-25), filled with 1950s memorabilia and metal toys, is a fun restaurant that's a real hit with children (check out the Lionel train running around just below the ceiling). The standard American menu includes kids' choices. No raves here, just okay food in a fun atmosphere.

Efficient, friendly cafeteria-style service makes **EPI's Pizza** (8 Cottage St., Bar Harbor, 207/288-5853, 7am-9pm daily July-Aug., 7am-3pm daily Sept.-June) an excellent choice for budget Italian fare.

On a clear day, you can't beat the panoramic views over Bar Harbor, Frenchman Bay, and the Porcupine Islands from the **Looking Glass Restaurant** (Wonder View Inn, 50 Eden St., Bar Harbor, 207/288-5663, http://www.barharborrestaurant.com, 7am-10:30am, $9-14). The deck is dog friendly.

Most folks come to **Sweet Pea's Café** (854 Rte. 3, Bar Harbor, 207/801-9078, www.sweetpeascafemaine.com, 11am-9pm Wed.-Sun., $15-25) for the wood-oven sourdough pizzas, topped with fresh-from-the-farm greens, veggies, and local seafood, but the mussels and the oyster starters earn raves. The café is located on a working farm, with dining inside or outside looking over pasturelands where horses graze.

Casual Dining

Chef Karl Yarborough draws inspiration for his ever-changing, creative menu at **Ciao** (135 Cottage St., Bar Harbor, 207/801-9110, www.

ciaobarharbor.com, $10-20) from family travels during the winter and pairs it with fresh and local ingredients, resulting in intriguing combos such as lobster and chorizo or pear bruschetta.

When you're craving fresh and delicious fare but not a heavy meal, the ★ **Side Street Café** (49 Rodick St., Bar Harbor, 207/801-2591, www.sidestreetbarharbor.com, 11am-9:30pm daily, $11-26) delivers with an upscale, creative comfort food menu complete with burgers, mac-and-cheese, salads, ribs, Tex-Mex, and even full lobster dinners. The venue tends to be noisy, but you also can sit on the street-side deck. It's open year-round. In 2019, the restaurant opened the **Annex** (51 Rodick St., 4pm-10pm daily), serving craft cocktails and sharable small plates, with live music nightly.

Cocktails, small plates, and crepes are the specialties at **Project Social** (16 Mount Desert St., Bar Harbor, 207/801-9293, www.socialbarharbor.com, 11am-9pm Mon.-Sat., $10-15), a trendy spot facing the Village Green. There's often live music.

Enjoy pub fare, including burgers, scotch eggs, and tacos, as well as vegan, vegetarian, and gluten-free dishes, at **The Black Friar Pub** (10 Summer St., Bar Harbor, 207/288-5091, www.blackfriarinn.com, from 4pm daily, $13-18). Find it tucked just off Cottage Street across from Hannaford.

Set back from the road behind a garden is the very popular **McKays Public House** (231 Main St., Bar Harbor, 207/288-2002, www.mckayspublichouse.com, 5pm-9pm Tues.-Sun., $12-36), a comfortable pub with seating indoors in small dining rooms or at the bar, or outdoors in the garden. The best bet is the classic pub fare, although fancier entrées are also available.

Once a Victorian boardinghouse and later a 1920s speakeasy, **Galyn's Galley** (17 Main St., Bar Harbor, 207/288-9706, www.galynsbarharbor.com, 11am-9:30pm daily Mar.-Nov., $16-31) has been a downtown dining mainstay since 1986. Lots of plants, modern decor, reliable service, and several indoor and outdoor dining areas contribute to the loyalty of the clientele. Reservations are advisable in midsummer. Be seated before 6pm to enjoy the early-bird lobster special.

Casual, friendly, creative, and reliable defines **Cafe This Way** (14 Mt. Desert St., Bar Harbor, 207/288-4483, www.cafethisway.com, 7am-11:30am and 5:30pm-9:30pm Mon.-Sat., 8am-1pm and 5:30pm-9:30pm Sun., $22-30), where it's easy to make a meal out of the small plates ($10-15). Vegetarians will be happy here. The breakfast menu is a genuine wake-up call ($6-12).

Dine inside or on the porch of chef-co-owner Bobby Will's seasonally inspired, New American, farm-to-table restaurant **Salt & Steel** (321 Main St., Bar Harbor, 207/288-0447, www.saltandsteelbh.com, 5pm-9pm Tues.-Sat., $26-37). Can't decide? A four-course tasting menu is available.

International

La Bella Vita Ristorante (55 West St., Bar Harbor, 207/288-5033, www.labellavitaristorante.com, 7am-10pm daily, $15-30), at the Harborside Hotel, does an excellent job with Italian fare, including antipasti, pizzas, pastas, and classics such as veal scaloppini or chicken piccata. Dine inside or out.

For "American fine dining with Latin flair," head to ★ **Havana** (318 Main St., Bar Harbor, 207/288-2822, www.havanamaine.com, 5pm-10pm daily May-Nov. and 9:30am-2pm Sun. late May-late Aug., call for off-season hours, $23-40), where the innovative menu changes frequently to take advantage of what's locally available. Inside, bright orange walls and white tablecloths set a tone that's equally festive and accomplished. There's also garden seating. For a lighter meal, consider **Parrilla** (from 4pm daily and Sunday brunch, $8-39), Havana's street-side outdoor bar with an Argentinian-style wood-fired grill. It serves a selection of small and large plates.

Fine Dining

Five miles south of Bar Harbor, in the village of Otter Creek, which itself is in the town of Mount Desert, is the inauspicious-looking **Burning Tree** (Rte. 3, Otter Creek, 207/288-9331, www.theburningtreerestaurant.com, 5pm-10pm Wed.-Mon. late June-early Oct., closed Mon. after Labor Day, $26-34), which is anything but nondescript inside. Chef-owners Allison Martin and Elmer Beal Jr. have created one of Mount Desert Island's better restaurants, but it can get quite noisy when busy—which it usually is. The specialties are imaginative seafood entrées and vegetarian dishes. At the height of summer, service can be a bit rushed, and the kitchen runs out of popular entrées. Do make reservations

Lobster

Nearly every restaurant in town serves some form of lobster (my top choice for a lobster roll is the Side Street Café).

Dine inside or on the dock at **Stewman's Lobster Pound** (35 West St., 207/288-0346, www.stewmanslobsterpound.com, 11am-10pm daily), where the menu ranges from burgers to lobster.

Although it lacks the oceanfront location, **West Street Café** (76 West St., Bar Harbor, 207/288-5242, www.weststreetcafe.com, 11am-8:30pm daily) is a fine spot for a lobster dinner at a fair price. There are other items on the menu, but the reason to go here is for the lobster (market price). A kids' menu is available. Some upstairs tables have pleasant harbor views. Early-bird specials served 4-6pm.

ACCOMMODATIONS

If you're not planning to camp in one of Acadia National Park's two Mount Desert Island campgrounds (there are no other lodgings, and there's no backcountry camping), you'll need to search elsewhere on the island for a place to sleep. Bar Harbor alone has thousands of beds in hotels, motels, inns, B&Bs, and cottages—and the rest of the island adds to that total, with a dozen private campgrounds thrown into the mix. Nonetheless,

1: Stewman's Lobster Pound 2: Seacroft Inn
3: glamping 4: Terramor Outdoor Resort

lodgings can be scarce at the height of summer, particularly the first two weeks in August, a stretch that coincides with an outrageous spike in room rates. Off-season, there's plenty of choice, even after the seasonal places shut down, and rates are always lower—often dramatically so. Rates noted here reflect peak season, usually July-August. Unless noted otherwise, properties are seasonal.

The **Bar Harbor Chamber of Commerce** (2 Cottage St., Bar Harbor, 207/288-5103, www.barharbormaine.com) and the **Thompson Island Information Center** (Rte. 3, Thompson Island, 207/288-3411) will give you a list of lodgings open year-round, and both offices are helpful for finding beds even at peak times.

Inns and Bed-and-Breakfasts

An in-town find for families, the **Seacroft Inn** (18 Albert Meadow, Bar Harbor, 207/288-4669 or 800/824-9694, www.seacroftinn.com, $130-170) is well situated just off Main Street and near the Shore Path. All rooms in Bunny and Dave Brown's white gabled cottage have refrigerators and microwaves; a continental breakfast is available for $5 per person. Housekeeping is available for $10 per day. Some rooms can be joined as family suites.

A convenient intown location, an inviting front porch, scrumptious afternoon cookies, and gourmet breakfasts contribute to the popularity of the ★ **Holbrook House** (74 Mount Desert St., Bar Harbor, 207-288-4970, www.holbrookhouse.com, from $199), with 12 guestrooms and a two-bedroom cottage. Innkeepers Eric and Michelle Alvin keep updating the 1986 Victorian, maintaining the historical vibe while adding contemporary must-haves. Some rooms have private decks or patios.

Built in 1880, and operated as a B&B by the same family for more than 30 years, the **Shore Path Cottage** (24 Atlantic Ave., Bar Harbor, www.shorepathcottage.com, from $215) offers an enviable location with sighworthy sea views and private access to Bar Harbor's Shore Path. It's secreted away and

yet just a few minutes' walk to all downtown attractions. Comfy and spacious rooms, full breakfasts, afternoon snacks, and on-site bicycle rental are just a few of the plusses of this special spot.

Situated on one oceanfront acre in the West Street Historical District, the ★ **Saltair Inn** (121 West St., Bar Harbor, 207/288-2882, www.saltairinn.com, from $251) was originally built in 1887 as a guesthouse. Innkeepers Kristi and Matt Losquadro and their family now welcome visitors in eight updated guest rooms, most of which are quite spacious, and five of which face Frenchman Bay. Frills vary by room but might include whirlpool tubs, fireplaces, and balconies. A full breakfast is served either in the dining room or on the water-view deck. It's steps from downtown, but really, with a location like this, why leave?

Alpheus Hardy, Bar Harbor's first cottager, built the Tudor-style **Ullikana** (16 The Field, Bar Harbor, 207/288-9552, https://ullikana. com, from $319) in 1885. It's tucked in a quiet downtown location close to the Shore Path and neighboring **Bass Cottage** (14 The Field, Bar Harbor, 207/288-1234, www.basscottage. com, from $329), a grand 1885 building. Each has a boutique hotel vibe and a guest pantry. Some rooms have working fireplaces, whirlpool tubs, and/or private terraces with water views. Guests at both inns take breakfast at the Bass Cottage.

Completing the trio of inns sited in the Field is the **Yellow House Bed & Breakfast** (15 The Field, 207/288-5100, www. yellowhousemaine.com, from $289), a lovely 1872 summer cottage. The seven-room inn, moved to its current location in 1885, blends gentle ease with contemporary comforts. Enjoy breakfast on the inviting wraparound porch or in the parlor.

Hotels and Motels

If all you want is an air-conditioned room with a bed, **Robbins Motel** (396 Rte. 3, Bar Harbor, 207/288-4659, www.robbinsmotel. com, $69), an older property, has 30 small and unadorned (some might call them dismal)

Mount Desert Island on a Budget

At first glance, Mount Desert Island might seem an expensive place to visit, especially if you're not a fan of camping. Truth is, you can afford to visit the island even if your budget is tight.

- Once you've paid for your park pass, your recreation is free. There are no further fees to hike, canoe, bicycle, or swim, unless you need to rent equipment. If so, plan ahead and ask about any deals. Some sports outfitters offer a discount for advance reservations or multiday rentals. Some will allow you to rent a bike after a certain time and keep it for the next day, charging you for only one day. That allows you to get in an extra evening ride—ideal at the peak of summer when daylight lasts well into the evening.

- Outside the park, many of the recommended sights detailed here are free, as are most of the park ranger programs (check the schedule), including evening ones presented in the park's campgrounds. Free concerts and lectures are regularly presented at many locations around the island; check local newspapers or ask at information centers.

- You must eat, but you can keep prices down, even when dining out. For starters, opt for lodging with an in-room refrigerator if possible. Then stock up on breakfast, sandwich, and salad staples (milk, cereal, bread, luncheon meats and cheeses, vegetables, fresh fruit, etc.) at the supermarket. If you don't have a refrigerator, a cooler will do, but remember to keep it stocked with ice. (Collapsible coolers are available and easy to pack or carry on an airplane, or you can purchase an inexpensive Styrofoam one.) Even better is to have access to boiling water to make instant soups or ramen noodles, to which you can add all kinds of vegetables for a healthful meal. Immersion water heaters are inexpensive and small.

- If you want to dine out, lunch is almost always less expensive than dinner. For dinner, look for restaurants with early-bird specials; many places have very reasonable meals available before 6pm. Or consider combining your meal with evening entertainment at Reel Pizza. When you do dine out, take home any leftovers (assuming you have a refrigerator or cooler). Other inexpensive options are public suppers; look for notices on bulletin boards and in local newspapers. Perhaps you can't afford popovers at the Asticou in Northeast Harbor or the Jordan Pond House in the park, but you can enjoy them at the by-donation (no one checks how much you give) Community Kitchen daily breakfast in Southwest Harbor. And the Take-A-Break Café at the College of the Atlantic is open to the public for cafeteria-style fare that's always inexpensive and healthful, with vegan and vegetarian options.

- As for lodging, in general the farther you get from the key sights or town centers, the less it will cost. Look for accommodations within an easy walk of the Island Explorer bus so you won't have to drive (or perhaps even bring) a car. If you're staying for a week or longer, your best move is to find a cottage rental. (Hint: Prices for many rentals drop the week before Labor Day.) Another option is to consider a camping cabin. These rustic shelters generally do not have any plumbing—you'll have to walk to a shared bathhouse—but they are clean and dry and have real beds; some even provide linens or minimal cooking facilities. What you sacrifice in privacy is more than offset by the folks you'll meet from around the world.

- Ditch the car and use the free Island Explorer bus to get around. Not only does doing so save you money on gasoline and avoid parking hassles, but—big bonus points—it benefits the environment.

- And finally, wherever you go, whatever you do, always ask about any applicable discounts: automobile clubs, seniors, military, family rates, and so forth.

pine-paneled guest rooms with queen beds. There is no charm and it's not quiet, but it's cheap and clean. Off-season rates are as low as $40. Also available is a one-bedroom apartment with a full kitchen for $79.

The **Sunnyside Motel & Cottages** (1441 Rte. 3, Bar Harbor, 207/288-3602, www.sunnysidecottages.com, rooms from $75, cottages from $119) isn't fancy, but it's clean and woos families with amenities that include an outdoor pool, play area, and a Laundromat. Choose from motel rooms and one- or two-bedroom cottages.

The **Belle Isle Motel** (910 Rte. 3, Bar Harbor, 207/288-5726, www.belleislemotel.com, $99-129), a vintage mom-and-pop roadside motel, delivers clean and affordable lodgings. On the premises are a heated pool, playground, picnic area, and guest laundry. Dogs are welcome for $15/night.

Also on the lower end of the budgetary scale, the **Edenbrook Motel** (96 Eden St./ Rte. 3, Bar Harbor, 207/288-4975 or 800/323-7819, www.edenbrookmotelbh.com, $159-199) comprises four vintage motel buildings tiered up a hillside. Some rooms on the upper levels have panoramic views of Frenchman Bay. New owners in 2018 began updating the rooms, so rates are creeping upward. It's across from the College of the Atlantic, about 1.5 miles from Acadia's main entrance, and an easy 1-mile walk from downtown.

On the edge of downtown, across from the College of the Atlantic, are two adjacent sister properties tiered up a hillside: **Wonder View Inn & Suites** (50 Eden St., Bar Harbor, 207/288-3358, www.wonderviewinn.com, from $135) and the **Bluenose Hotel** (90 Eden St., Bar Harbor, 207/288-3348 or 800/445-4077, www.barharborhotel.com, from $240). The pet-friendly ($20/pet/night) Wonder View comprises four older motel buildings on 14 acres of estate-like grounds with grassy lawns and mature shade trees, an outdoor pool, and a restaurant. The estate was the home of famed mystery writer Mary Roberts Rinehart, who coined the phrase "The butler did it." Guest rooms vary widely, and rates reflect both style of accommodation and views. The Bluenose comprises two buildings, called Mizzentop and Stenna Nordica. Almost all of Mizzentop's rooms and suites are spacious and have fabulous views and balconies; some also have fireplaces. Stenna Nordica guest rooms, accessed from outdoor corridors, are more modest. Also here are a spa, fitness center, indoor and outdoor pools, and a lounge with live music every evening. Both properties need updating, but they're clean and fine, if you're not persnickety.

On the edge of town, the **Cromwell Harbor Motel** (359 Main St., Bar Harbor, 207/288-3201 or 800/544-3201, www.cromwellharbor.com, from $165) comprises four buildings set back from the road on nicely landscaped grounds with a heated outdoor pool.

The family-owned ★ **Highbrook Motel** (94 Eden St./Rte. 3, Bar Harbor, 207/288-3591 or 800/338-9688, www.highbrookmotel.com, from $225) comprises two buildings across from the College of the Atlantic and within walking distance of downtown. The upper building is pricier, but offers more privacy. Rates include a grab-and-go continental breakfast.

One of the town's best-known, most visible, and best-situated hotels is the **Bar Harbor Inn** (1 Newport Dr., Bar Harbor, 207/288-3351 or 800/248-3351, www.barharborinn.com, from $300), a sprawling complex on eight acres overlooking the harbor and islands. The 153 rooms and suites vary considerably in style, from traditional inn to motel, and are in three different buildings. Continental breakfast is included, and special packages, with meals and activities, are available—an advantage if you have children. The kids will appreciate the heated outdoor pool; adults might enjoy the full-service spa. Also under the same management and ownership (https://withamhotels.com) is the family-oriented **Acadia Inn** (98 Eden St., Bar Harbor, 207/288-3500, www.acadiainn.com, from $239), located between the park entrance and downtown Bar Harbor. A hot-and-cold breakfast buffet is included.

The appropriately named **Harborside Hotel & Marina** (55 West St., Bar Harbor, 207/288-5033 or 800/238-5033, www.theharborsidehotel.com, from $400) fronts on the water in downtown Bar Harbor. Most of the guest rooms, studios, and suites, all updated in 2019, have a water view and a semiprivate balcony. Some have large outdoor hot tubs. The resort fee allows access to the beautifully restored Bar Harbor Club, with a full-service spa, fitness center, tennis courts, and oceanfront heated pool. Also on the premises are a second outdoor pool, a good casual Italian restaurant, a pier, and a marina. Sharing use of those facilities is a sister property, the **West Street Hotel** (50 West St., 877/905-4498, www.theweststreethotel.com, from $400), a tony spot with a rooftop pool (ages 18 and older only) overlooking downtown, the harbor, islands, and the ocean. Rooms have a nautical vibe, and those on the West Street side have harbor-view balconies.

Seasonal Rentals

Contact **L. S. Robinson Co.** (337 Main St., Southwest Harbor, 207/244-5563, www.lsrobinson.com) or **Maine Island Properties** (Mount Desert, 207/244-4308, www.maineislandproperties.com) for listings of houses and cottages available by the week or month. In July-August, rates run $700-7,000 per week or more, plus tax and deposit. Both agencies handle rentals in all parts of Mount Desert. (If you decide to stay, they also have residential listings.) The Bar Harbor Chamber of Commerce's annual guide also has listings of cottages—some private, others that are part of cottage colonies.

Camping and Glamping

Mount Desert Island's private campgrounds are located at the northern end of the island, down its center, and in the southwest corner. Most are also on the routes of the free Island Explorer bus service, making it easy and economical—and preferable—to leave your car or RV at your campsite and avoid the parking problems between late June and Columbus Day. The Thompson Island and Hulls Cove Visitors Centers have listings of private campgrounds.

Family owned and operated, **Bar Harbor Campground** (409 Rte. 3, Bar Harbor, 207/288-5185, www.thebarharborcampground.com, $35-50) caters to families and offers a heated pool, a recreation hall, and a play area. It doesn't accept advance reservations, nor does it take credit cards. Many of the 300 sites have ocean views. Hookups are available.

The Baker family has operated **Hadley's Point Campground** (33 Hadley Point Rd., Bar Harbor, 207/288-4808, www.hadleyspoint.com, May 15-mid-Oct., $32-50) since 1969. Tent sites are nicely spaced in the woods and have a sense of privacy; big-rig sites, located in fields, are tight. Camping cabins ($90) are furnished with one queen and two twin beds and a bathroom with metered shower; pets are permitted for $10 per night. Facilities include a laundry, a heated pool, shuffleboard courts, horseshoes, and a playground. A public saltwater beach with a boat launch is within walking distance. The campground is eight miles from Bar Harbor.

Woods of Eden Glampground (12 Seabury Dr., Bar Harbor, 207/664-3332, www.woodsofeden.com, from $200) shelters guests in six safari-style tents spread out on 24 wooded acres. Each has a kitchenette, en suite bathroom with shower, and sleeps four to six; one tent is ADA accessible.

Terramor Outdoor Resort (1453 Rte. 102, Bar Harbor, 207/288-7500, https://terramoroutdoorresort.com, from $350) accommodates guests in five different safari-style tent options varying in size and amenities. All have electricity and European-style bedding; most have en suite bathrooms. Pets are welcome ($50/pet/stay). In addition to the 64 tents, the 60-acre wooded property features a pool, games lawn, and a fabulous main lodge with bar and restaurant.

INFORMATION AND SERVICES

The **Bar Harbor Chamber of Commerce** (1201 Bar Harbor Rd./Rte. 3, Trenton, 207/288-5103, www.barharbormaine.com) is open daily in summer. The chamber's **downtown branch** (2 Cottage St., Bar Harbor, 8am-4pm daily) is open year-round.

If you're traveling with kids, have them check out the *Kids' Guide to MDI* (https://cfournier1.wixsite.com/mysite) written by third-graders at Conners Emerson School in 2015-16.

Find **public restrooms** at the park visitors centers and in downtown Bar Harbor in Agamont Park, Harbor Place at the town pier, adjacent to the Village Green, and on the School Street side of the athletic field.

GETTING THERE AND AROUND

Bar Harbor is about 20 miles or 30-45 minutes, depending on traffic, via Route 3 from Ellsworth; about 45 miles or 75 minutes via Routes 1A and 3 from Bangor; and about 275 miles or five hours via Routes 195 and 3 from Boston. It's about 12 miles or 20 minutes via Routes 233 and 198 and 20 miles or 35 minutes via Route 3 to Northeast Harbor.

All **Island Explorer bus** routes begin and end at the Village Green downtown. Route 8/Trenton connects the airport with the downtown.

Bar Harbor has **metered parking,** with payment either at individual meters or at a kiosk. Rates for street and lot parking vary from $1.50-2/hour (quarters, credit card, or Park Mobile app), depending upon location.

Ferry

Although Winter Harbor is 43 miles or 1.15 hours from Bar Harbor by car, it's only about 7 miles by water. The summer schedule for the **Bar Harbor Ferry** (207/288-2984, www.barharborferry.com, round-trip $28 adults, $20 children) is coordinated with the Island Explorer bus's summertime Schoodic route, so you can board the ferry in Bar Harbor, pick up the bus at the dock in Winter Harbor, and be shuttled along the Schoodic Loop. Stop where you like for a picnic or a hike, and then board a later bus. Take the last bus back to the ferry and return to Bar Harbor. It makes for a super car-free excursion. It operates at least four times daily mid-June-mid-October.

Northeast and Seal Harbors

Ever since the late 19th century, the upper crust from Philadelphia has been summering in and around Northeast Harbor. Sure, they also show up in other parts of Maine, but it's hard not to notice the preponderance of Pennsylvania license plates surrounding Northeast Harbor's elegant "cottages" during mid-July-mid-August. In the last decade or so, growing numbers from Washington DC, New York, and Texas have joined the Pennsylvanians.

Even though Northeast Harbor is a well-known name with special cachet, it isn't even an official township; it's a zip-coded village within the town of Mount Desert (pop. 2,053), which collects the breathtaking property taxes and doles out the municipal services.

The attractive boutiques in Northeast Harbor's small downtown cater to a casually posh clientele, and the well-protected harbor attracts a tony crowd of yachties.

Except for three spectacular gardens and two specialized museums, not much here is geared to budget-sensitive visitors—but there's no charge for admiring the scenery.

Although all of Mount Desert Island is seasonal, Northeast Harbor is especially so, and it has a tiny and decreasing year-round population. Many businesses don't open until early July and close in early September.

SIGHTS

★ Somes Sound

As you head toward Northeast Harbor on Route 198 from the northern end of Mount Desert Island, you'll begin seeing cliff-lined Somes Sound, on your right. The glacier-sculpted fjard (not as deep or as steeply walled as a fjord) juts five miles into the interior of Mount Desert Island from its mouth between Northeast Harbor and Southwest Harbor. Watch for the right-hand turn for Sargent Drive (no RVs allowed), and follow the lovely, granite-lined route along the east side of the sound. Halfway along, a marker explains the geology of this spectacular natural inlet. There aren't many pullouts en route, and traffic can be fairly thick in midsummer, but don't miss it. **Suminsby Park,** located off Sargent Drive, 400 feet from Route 3, is a fine place for a picnic. The park has rocky shore access, a hand-carry boat launch, picnic tables, grills, and a pit toilet. An ideal way to appreciate Somes Sound is from the water—sign up for an excursion out of Northeast Harbor or Southwest Harbor.

★ Gardens

If you have the slightest interest in gardens, allow time for Northeast Harbor's two marvelous public gardens, both operated by the nonprofit **Mount Desert Land and Garden Preserve** (207/276-3727, www.gardenpreserve.org).

ASTICOU AZALEA GARDEN AND THUYA GARDEN

One of Maine's best spring showcases is the **Asticou Azalea Garden,** a 2.3-acre pocket where about 70 varieties of azaleas, rhododendrons, and laurels—many from the classic Reef Point garden of famed landscape designer Beatrix Farrand—burst into bloom. When Charles K. Savage, beloved former innkeeper of the Asticou Inn, learned the Reef Point garden was being undone in 1956, he went into high gear to find funding and managed to rescue the azaleas and provide them with the gorgeous setting they have today,

across the road and around the corner from the inn. Serenity is the key—with a Japanese sand garden that's mesmerizing in any season, stone lanterns, granite outcrops, pink-gravel paths, and a tranquil pond. Try to visit early in the season and early in the morning to savor the effect. Blossoming occurs May-August, but the prime time for azaleas is roughly mid-May-mid-June.

The garden is on Route 198, at the northern edge of Northeast Harbor, immediately north of the junction with Peabody Drive (Rte. 3). Watch for a tiny sign on the left (if you're coming from the north), marking access to the parking area. A small box suggests a $5 donation, and another box contains a garden guide ($2). Pets are not allowed in the garden. Take Island Explorer Route 5 (Jordan Pond) or Route 6 (Brown Mountain) and request a stop. Note: The Asticou Stream Trail, a lovely meander through fields and woods and down to the shoreline, connects the garden to the town. Look for a small signpost across from the Route 3 entrance to the garden.

Behind a carved wooden gate on a forested hillside not far from Asticou lies **Thuya Garden** (7am-7pm daily), also designed by Charles K. Savage as a semiformal English herbaceous garden, inspired by Beatrix Farrand and interpreted for coastal Maine. Special features of this enchanted garden are perennial borders and sculpted shrubbery. On a misty summer day, when few visitors appear, the colors are brilliant. Adjacent to the garden is **Thuya Lodge** (207/276-5130, 10am-4:30pm daily late June-Labor Day), former summer cottage of Joseph Curtis, donor of this awesome park. The lodge has an extensive botanical and horticultural library and quiet rooms for reading. A collection box next to the front gate requests a $5 donation per adult. To reach Thuya, continue on Route 3 beyond Asticou Azalea Garden and watch for the Asticou Terraces parking area (no RVs; two-hour limit) on the right. Cross the road and climb the Asticou Terraces Trail (0.4 mile) to the garden. Allow time to hang out at the three lookouts en route. Alternatively, drive 0.2 mile

beyond the Route 3 parking area, watching for a minuscule Thuya Garden sign on the left. Go 0.5 mile up the steep, narrow, and curving driveway to the parking area (but walking up reaps more rewards). Or take Island Explorer Route 5 (Jordan Pond) and request a stop.

Note: It's possible to connect Asticou and Thuya Gardens by walking the Asticou Hill Trail, which follows an old road, or hiking the moderately difficult (lots of exposed roots) Eliot Mountain Trail. The Asticou Hill Trail road across from the Asticou Inn provides access to both; it's a private road, but foot traffic has right-of-way.

ABBY ALDRICH ROCKEFELLER GARDEN

The **Abby Aldrich Rockefeller Garden** (207/276-3330 in season, www.gardenpreserve.org, by reservation only, mid-July-early Sept., $15), located in Seal Harbor, was created between 1926 and 1935, when the Rockefellers turned to renowned designer Beatrix Farrand to create a garden using treasures they'd brought back from Asia. The enclosed garden is a knockout, accented with English floral beds, Korean tombstone figures, a moon gate, woodland and water gardens, and even yellow roof tiles from Beijing. You can also stroll to the terrace of what was the Eyrie, the former Rockefeller summer home, removed in 1963. The garden is only open from mid-July to early September, and admission is limited and reservations are required; check the website for current details, and make plans well in advance. A garden guide with map is provided, but you're free to explore at your own pace. Although gorgeous anytime, the garden comes into peak bloom during the first two weeks of August. Hint: Most visitors arrive right at the session's start. Avoid the crowds by showing up a little later.

1: Asticou Azalea Garden **2:** tea and popovers with dreamy views at the Asticou Inn **3:** Abby Aldrich Rockefeller Garden

Petite Plaisance

On Northeast Harbor's quiet South Shore Road, **Petite Plaisance** (35 South Shore Rd., Northeast Harbor, 207/276-3940, www.petiteplaisanceconservationfund.org, Tues.-Sat. June 15-Aug. 31, donation) is a special-interest museum commemorating noted Belgian-born author and college professor Marguerite Yourcenar (pen name of Marguerite de Crayencour), the first woman elected to the prestigious Académie Française. From 1950 to 1987, Petite Plaisance was her home, and it's hard to believe she's no longer here; her intriguing possessions and presence fill the two-story house, of particular interest to Yourcenar devotees. In 2014 the French Ministry of Culture added Petite Plaisance to its registry of illustrious houses. Free hour-long tours of the 1st floor are given, by advance appointment only. Tours are offered in French or English, depending on visitors' preferences; French-speaking visitors often make pilgrimages here. No children under 12 are allowed. Call at least a day ahead, between 9am and 4pm, to schedule an appointment. Tours are free, but donations are much appreciated. Yourcenar admirers should request directions to Brookside Cemetery in Somesville, seven miles away, where she is buried.

Great Harbor Maritime Museum

Annual exhibits focusing on the maritime heritage of the Mount Desert Island area are held in the small, eclectic **Great Harbor Maritime Museum** (124 Main St., Northeast Harbor, 207/276-5262, 10am-5pm Tues.-Sat. late June-Labor Day, donation), housed in the old village fire station and municipal building. ("Great Harbor" refers to the Somes Sound area—Northeast, Southwest, and Seal Harbors, as well as the Cranberry Isles.) Yachting, coastal trade, and fishing receive special emphasis. Look for the canvas rowing canoe, built in Veazie, Maine, between 1917 and 1920; it's the only one of its kind known to exist today.

RECREATION

Hardy folks can test the cold Atlantic waters at the small saltwater beach at the head of the harbor at **Seal Harbor Beach** (Island Explorer Route 5/Jordan Pond).

Hiking

Mount Desert Land & Garden Preserve oversees nearly 1,700 acres between Seal Harbor and Northeast Harbor, including carriage roads open to pedestrians or horses but not bicycles, 10 hiking trails, Asticou, Thuya, and Abby Aldrich Rockefeller Gardens, and Little Long Pond, which allows swimming at designated points. Thank David and Peggy Rockefeller for preserving this beautiful chunk of land that borders but is separate from the national park. The trail network connects to the Brown Mountain Gatehouse and Jordan Pond House. You can download a trail map from www.gardenpreserve.org.

LONG POND CARRIAGE ROAD TRAIL

Distance: 3.4 miles round-trip
Duration: 2 hours
Elevation gain: Minimal
Effort: Easy
Trailhead: South end of Long Pond, west of Seal Harbor. From Bar Harbor, take the Island Explorer bus Route 5/Jordan Pond and get off at Seal Harbor Beach. Walk west a very short distance to Little Long Pond and enter the carriage roads. Or drive from Bar Harbor either on the Park Loop Road (the two-way section) or on Route 3 via Otter Creek, and park in a small lot on the north side of Route 3 at the bottom of Little Long Pond.

This loop—part of the 12 miles of carriage roads closed to bikes but open for hiking—is easy, a "walk in the woods" kind of experience. If you do it late in the day, use insect repellent. Be forewarned that dogs are allowed off leash here, so it doubles as an unofficial dog park.

The pond is officially named Long Pond, but it's known as **Little Long Pond** to distinguish it from the far larger Long Pond on the west side of the island. Head north, on the east shore of the pond, to signpost 28. Bear left toward signpost 24 and the lovely Cobblestone Bridge, then start heading west and south, meandering to signpost 32. Turn south (left) to signpost 33, where you'll bear left toward signpost 34 and back to Route 3. You can also do the loop in a clockwise direction, but counterclockwise gets you near the pond right at the start. If you're using the bus, flag it down or walk back to the Seal Harbor Beach stop.

HARBOR BROOK TRAIL

Distance: 3.4 miles out and back
Duration: 2.5 hours
Elevation gain: 124 feet
Effort: Easy
Trailhead: Off Peabody Drive/Route 3, approximately midway between Bracy Cove and Thuya Drive.

Don't expect big views from this quiet trail, but rather an enchanting mosey through mossy woodlands as it parallels Little Harbor Brook. En route, it crosses the Richard Trail, which leads to Thuya Garden. You can turn around and retrace your steps when the trail ends at the park's Jordan Pond Path (turn right and continue to the Jordan Pond House).

Option: Make it a moderate 4-mile hike that includes summiting 458-foot Eliot Mountain by turning left at the end of the trail and looping back to the trailhead via the Asticou Ridge, Charles Savage, and Richard Trails.

Bicycling

Island Bike Rental (102 Main St., Northeast Harbor, 207/266-5611) shares space with Shirt Off Your Back, a laundry service tucked down a stairway next door to the National Bank of Bar Harbor. Rentals are around $21 half day, $25 full day.

Golf

The 18-hole **Northeast Harbor Golf Club** (15 Golf Club Rd., 207/276-5335, www.nehgc.com) is open to visitors. The first nine, designed by Arthur Lockwood, opened in 1919; the second nine, designed by Herbert Strong, opened in 1925.

Northeast Harbor Trails

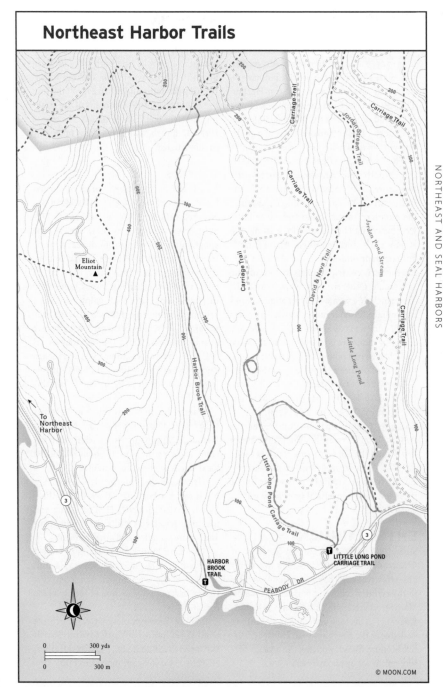

Carriage Trail

Carriage Trail

Carriage Trail

Carriage Trail

Jordan Stream Trail

Carriage Trail

David & Neva Trail

Jordan Pond Stream

Little Long Pond

Carriage Trail

Eliot
Mountain ▲

Harbor Brook Trail

To
Northeast
Harbor

Little Long Pond Carriage Trail

HARBOR
BROOK
TRAIL
🅃

LITTTLE LONG POND
CARRIAGE TRAIL
🅃

PEABODY DR.

3

3

0   300 yds

0   300 m

© MOON.COM

EXCURSION BOATS

Northeast Harbor is the starting point for a couple of boat services headed for the **Cranberry Isles;** other boats and ferries, which are slightly less expensive but have no narration, depart from Southwest Harbor. The vessels leave from the commercial floats at the end of the concrete Municipal Pier on Sea Street. Fares are provided here as a guide, but will fluctuate with fuel prices.

The 75-foot *Sea Princess* (207/276-5352, https://barharborcruises.com) carries visitors as well as an Acadia National Park naturalist on a 2.75-hour morning trip around the mouth of Somes Sound and out to Little Cranberry Island (Islesford) for a 50-minute stopover. The boat leaves Northeast Harbor at 10am daily mid-May-mid-October. A narrated afternoon trip departs at 1pm on the same route. Other trips operate, but not daily. These include a scenic 1.5-hour Somes Sound cruise and a 1.5-hour sunset cruise. Fees range $27-32 adults, $17-19 ages 5-12, $7-9 under age 5. Reservations are advisable for all trips, although even that provides no guarantee, since the cruises require a 15-passenger minimum.

Downeast Friendship Sloop Charters (Northeast Harbor Municipal Marina, 41 Harbor Dr., 207/266-5210, www.downeastfriendshipsloop.com) operates two traditional Friendship sloops, the *Helen Brooks* and the *Linda*. Private charters range $275-425, covering up to six passengers; shared trips are $85 per person for about three hours. A sunset sail is a lovely way to end a day.

ENTERTAINMENT

Since 1964 the **Mount Desert Festival of Chamber Music** (207/266-2550, www.mt-desertfestival.org) has presented concerts in the century-old Neighborhood House on Main Street at 8:15pm Tuesday mid-July-mid-August. Tickets ($30 general admission) are available at the Neighborhood House box office Monday-Tuesday during the concert season, online, or by phone reservation.

SHOPPING

Upscale shops, galleries, and boutiques with clothing, artworks, housewares, antiques, and antiquarian books line both sides of Main Street in Northeast Harbor, making for intriguing browsing and expensive buying (but be sure to check the sale rooms of the clothing shops for bona fide bargains). The season is short, though, with some shops open only in July-August.

Galleries

You'll enter another world at **Shaw Contemporary Jewelry** (100 Main St., Northeast Harbor, 207/276-5000 or 877/276-5001, www.shawjewelry.com). Besides the spectacular silver and gold beach-stone jewelry created by Rhode Island School of Design alumnus Sam Shaw, the work of more than 100 other jewelers is exquisitely displayed. There are also sculptures, Asian art, and rotating art exhibits. It all leads back toward a lovely, light-filled garden. Prices are in the stratosphere, but appropriately so. As one well-dressed customer was overheard saying to her companion: "If I had only one jewelry store to go to in my entire life, this would be it."

Wander behind Shaw's to find **Artemis Gallery** (1 Old Firehouse Ln., Northeast Harbor, 207/276-3001, www.artemisgallerybh.com), showing the work of about two dozen local artists in changing exhibitions.

Lisa Hall Studio (head of Main St., Northeast Harbor, 207/276-5900, www.lisa-halljewelry.com) carries Hall's seaglass and gemstone jewelry as well as luxurious soaps and lotions, candles, and other fun items.

A seasonal branch of Bar Harbor's **Island Artisans** (119 Main St., Northeast Harbor, 207/276-4045, www.islandartisans.com) carries an exceptional selection of locally made fine crafts.

Browse through magnificent bronze wildlife sculptures at **Christopher Smith Galleries** (125B Main St., Northeast Harbor, 207/276-3343, www.smithbronze.com).

Gifts and Clothing

The tony shops in Northeast Harbor are worth a visit and maybe even a major splurge. You'll find plenty of pink and lime green; Lilly Pulitzer is big here.

Early and late in the season, the summer crowd shops at **The Kimball Shop & Boutique** (135 Main St., Northeast Harbor, 207/276-3300, www.kimballshop.com) to stock up on wedding and Christmas gifts. It's all very tasteful.

FOOD

Hours listed are for peak season, early July-early September. If you're visiting at other times, call ahead, as most restaurants are open fewer days and shorter hours during slower periods.

Quick Bites

In the **Pine Tree Market** (121 Main St., Northeast Harbor, 207/276-3335, 8am-8pm Mon.-Sat., 9am-8pm Sun.), you'll find gourmet goodies, a huge wine selection, a resident butcher, fresh fish, a deli, homemade breads, pastries, sandwiches, and salads. The market offers free delivery to homes and boats.

Pop into **Milk & Honey Kitchen** (3 Old Firehouse Ln., Northeast Harbor, 207/276-4003, http://milkandhoneykitchen.com, 8am-4pm daily, $7-10) for especially good made-to-order sandwiches (10am-2pm), along with soups, salads, and sweets. Find it tucked behind Shaw Contemporary Jewelry.

Breakfast pastries, prepared sandwiches, soups and salads, and dinners-to-go are all available at **123 Main** (123 Main St., Northeast Harbor, 207/276-4166, www.123neh.com, 9am-3pm daily).

From June well into October, the **Northeast Harbor Farmers Market** sets up each Thursday, 9am-noon, across from the Kimball Terrace Inn on Huntington Road.

Family Favorites

The homemade doughnuts are reason enough to visit the **Colonel's Restaurant and Bakery** (143 Main St., Northeast Harbor, 207/276-5147, www.colonelsrestaurant.com,

8am-9pm daily), but tucked behind the bakery is a full-service restaurant, serving everything from burgers to prime rib, as well as the usual seafood musts ($10-25). Its kids' menu and casual atmosphere draws families, so sometimes it's boisterous inside. There's also a deck out back. The separate bar area often is the quietest spot with the fastest service.

Casual Dining

Nonguests are welcome at the **Asticou Inn** (Rte. 3, 207/276-3344 or 800/258-3373, www.asticou.com, 11:30am-8pm daily). Go for lunch or popovers ($8-20), or dinner ($14-36), when the menu ranges from pub favorites to New American with international accents. When the weather cooperates, the best seats are on the porch with serene views over Northeast Harbor.

Lobster

Drink in the views over Somes Sound whether dining inside or outside at **Abel's Lobster Pound** (12 Abels Ln., Mount Desert, 207/261-8221, www.abelslobstermdi.com), open for lunch and dinner; call for current schedule. Wood-fired steamed lobster is the specialty, but there's enough variety here to keep everyone happy.

ACCOMMODATIONS

Inns

For more than 100 years, the genteel **Asticou Inn** (Rte. 3, Northeast Harbor, 207/276-3344 or 800/258-3373, www.asticou.com, from $250) has catered to the whims and weddings of Northeast Harbor's well-heeled summer rusticators. She's an elegant, if faded, old gal that seems right out of a 1950s Hollywood romance: Hardwood floors are topped with Asian and braided rugs, rooms are papered with floral or plaid wallpapers, and gauzy ruffled curtains blow in the breeze. It's all delightfully old-fashioned, and most guests would have it no other way. But it's not for everybody. The inn tops a lawn that slopes down to the yacht-filled harbor, and cocktails and lunch are served daily on the porch overlooking the heated pool, clay tennis court, and water. Accommodations are spread out between the main inn, three cottages, and four funky Topsiders, which seem inspired by the old *Jetsons* TV show. The nicest rooms and suites face the harbor. The inn's restaurant serves breakfast, lunch, and dinner daily. Try to plan a late-May or early-June visit; you're practically on top of the Asticou Azalea Garden, Thuya Garden is a short walk away (or hike via the Eliot Mountain Trail), and the rates are lowest. Asticou is a popular wedding venue, so if you're looking for a quiet weekend, check the inn's event schedule before booking a room.

Three miles from Northeast Harbor, in equally tony Seal Harbor, is a true bargain, the **Lighthouse Inn and Restaurant** (12 Main St./Rte. 3, Seal Harbor, 207/276-3958, www.lighthouseinnandrestaurant.com, $85-105). Sure, the two guest rooms and one suite are dated and dowdy, but at these prices, who cares? Downstairs is a restaurant (11am-8pm daily) with equally reasonable prices. It's a short walk to Seal Harbor.

Bed-and-Breakfasts

The **Colonel's Suites** (143 Main St., Northeast Harbor, 207/288-4775, www.colonelssuites.com, from $199), above the bakery/restaurant of the same name, provide comfortable accommodations with modern amenities. Rates, in season, include a full breakfast in the restaurant.

In 1888, architect Fred Savage designed the two Shingle-style buildings that make up the three-story **Harbourside Inn** (Main St., Northeast Harbor, 207/276-3272, www.harboursideinn.com, mid-June-mid-Sept., from $210). The owners preserved the old-fashioned feel by decorating the 11 spacious guest rooms and three suites with antiques. Most rooms have working fireplaces; some have kitchenettes. A light continental

breakfast is served. Trails to Norumbega Mountain and Upper Hadlock Pond leave from the back of the property.

Motels

Although it's overdue for an overhaul, you can't beat the location of the **Kimball Terrace Inn** (10 Huntington Rd., Northeast Harbor, 207/276-3383 or 800/454-6225, www.kimballterraceinn.com, from $199). The three-story motel faces the harbor, and every guest room has a patio or private balcony (ask for a harbor-facing room). Bring binoculars for yacht-spotting. The motel has an outdoor pool and a restaurant. It's a short walk from Northeast Harbor's downtown. Like the Asticou, it's a popular wedding venue. Some rooms are pet friendly ($25/day).

INFORMATION AND SERVICES

The harbor-front information bureau of the **Mount Desert Chamber of Commerce** (18 Harbor Rd., Northeast Harbor, 207/276-5040, www.mountdesertchamber.org) covers the villages of Somesville, Northeast Harbor, Seal Harbor, Otter Creek, Pretty Marsh, Hall Quarry, and Beech Hill.

Find **public restrooms** at the end of the building housing the Great Harbor Maritime Museum, in the town office on Sea Street, and at the harbor.

GETTING THERE AND AROUND

Northeast Harbor is about 12 miles or 20 minutes via Routes 233 and 198 or 20 miles/35 minutes via Route 3 from Bar Harbor. It's about 13 miles or 25 minutes to Southwest Harbor.

Northeast Harbor is served by Route 5 (Jordan Pond) and Route 6 (Brown Mountain) of the Island Explorer bus system.

Southwest Harbor and Vicinity

Southwest Harbor (pop. 1,764) is the hub of Mount Desert Island's "quiet side." In summer, its tiny downtown district is probably the busiest spot on the whole western side of the island (west of Somes Sound), but that's not saying a great deal. "Southwest" has the feel of a settled community, a year-round flavor that Bar Harbor sometimes lacks. And it competes with the best in the scenery department. The Southwest Harbor area serves as a very convenient base for exploring Acadia National Park, as well as the island's less-crowded villages and offshore Swans Island, Frenchboro, and the Cranberry Isles.

The quirky nature of the island's four town boundaries creates complications in trying to categorize various island segments. Officially, the town of Southwest Harbor includes only the villages of **Manset** and **Seawall**, but nearby is the precious hamlet of **Somesville**. The Somesville National Historic District, with its distinctive arched white footbridge, is especially appealing, but traffic gets congested here along Route 102, so rather than just rubbernecking, plan to stop and walk around.

SIGHTS

★ Wendell Gilley Museum

In the center of Southwest Harbor, the **Wendell Gilley Museum** (Herrick Rd. and Rte. 102, Southwest Harbor, 207/244-7555, www.wendellgilleymuseum.org, 10am-5pm Tues.-Sat. July-Aug., 10am-4pm Tues.-Sat. June and Sept.-Oct., $5 adults, $2 ages 5-12) was established in 1981 to display the lifework of local woodcarver Wendell Gilley (1904-1983), a onetime plumber who had gained a national reputation for his carvings by the time of his death. The museum houses more than 200 of his realistic bird specimens carved over more than 50 years. Summer exhibits also feature other wildlife artists. Many days, a local artist gives woodcarving demonstrations, and members of the local carving club often can be seen whittling away. The gift shop carries an ornithological potpourri, including books, binoculars, and carving tools. Kids over age eight appreciate this more than younger ones. Carving workshops, from two-hour intros to multiday classes on specific birds, are offered most weekdays during the summer.

Somesville Historical Museum and Gardens

The tiny **Somesville Historical Museum and Gardens** (Rte. 102, Somesville, 207/276-9323, www.mdihistory.org, 10am-4pm daily late June-late Aug., 10am-4pm Sat.-Sun. Sept.-mid-Oct., donation) is adjacent to the gently curving white bridge in Somesville, so there's a good chance you're going to stop nearby, if just for a photo. In season, the heirloom garden, filled with flowering plants and herbs of the 19th and early 20th centuries, is beautiful. The one-room museum has local artifacts and memorabilia displayed in a themed exhibit that changes annually. You can purchase a walking-tour guide to Somesville in the museum. If you're especially interested in history, ask about the museum's programs, which include speakers, demonstrations, and workshops.

The Maine Granite Industry Historical Society Museum

Delve into the history of Maine granite at the **Maine Granite Industry Historical Society Museum** (62 Beech Hill Cross Rd., Mount Desert, 207/244-7299, www.mainegraniteindustry.org, 10am-4pm Tues.-Sun. Apr. 1-Nov. 30, winter by appt., donation). Founder and curator Steven Haynes oversees a collection comprising hundreds of tools, photographs, ledgers, books, and other artifacts related to quarry workers, blacksmiths, stonecutters, and stone carvers. Immigrants from countries including

Southwest Harbor and Tremont

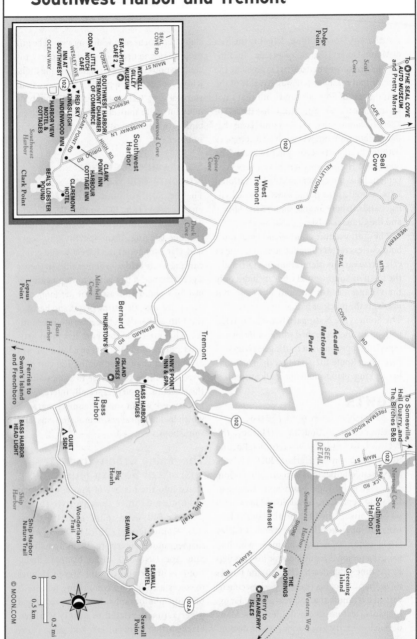

© MOON.COM

Italy, Finland, Sweden, Norway, and Portugal worked quarries in nine Maine counties, and the granite can still be seen in public buildings, including churches, courthouses, and libraries, as well as bridges throughout the country. Displays show the difference between granite from different quarries. Haynes is a wealth of information, and he loves to share his passion. He's often carving and polishing at the site.

RECREATION

Acadia National Park, of course, is the recreational focus throughout Mount Desert Island; on the island's western side, the main nonpark recreational activities are bike-, boat-, and picnic-related.

A broad swath of Acadia National Park cuts right through the center of this side of the island, and many of its hiking trails are far less congested than those elsewhere in the park. A connector trail from Southwest Harbor makes access to park trails easy. Seawall Campground, as well as the Wonderland and Ship Harbor Trails, lie within the town limits of Southwest Harbor.

At the **Southwest Harbor/Tremont Chamber of Commerce office** (329 Main St., Southwest Harbor, 207/244-9264 or 800/423-9264, www.acadiachamber.com), or at any of the area's stores, lodgings, and restaurants, pick up a copy of the *Trail Map/ Hiking Guide,* a very handy foldout map showing more than 20 hikes on the west side of Mount Desert Island. Trail descriptions include length, time required, and skill level (easy to strenuous).

Parks and Preserves
CHARLOTTE RHOADES PARK AND BUTTERFLY GARDEN
It's easy to miss the **Charlotte Rhoades Park and Butterfly Garden** (Rte. 102, Southwest Harbor, 207/244-9624, www. rhoadesbutterflygarden.org, 11am-7pm daily, $5 donation/family suggested), but that would be a mistake. This tiny seaside park was donated to the town in 1973, and the butterfly

garden with butterfly-inviting perennials, annuals, and shrubs, was established in 1998 to promote conservation education. About a dozen butterfly species have been sited here. A kiosk is stocked with butterfly observation sheets, and there's often a volunteer docent on duty on Thursday mornings. It's a lovely spot for a picnic. Check the website for info about garden tours. Time a visit with the annual butterfly release in July (reservations required). The park is on the water side of Route 102, between the Causeway Golf Club and the Seal Cove Road.

Bicycle Rentals
Southwest Cycle (370 Main St., Southwest Harbor, 207/244-5856, www.southwestcycle. com, hours vary seasonally) will fix you up with maps and lots of good advice for three loops (10-30 miles) on the western side of Mount Desert. Rentals begin around $25 for a full day, with multiday discounts available. The shop also rents every imaginable accessory, from baby seats to tag-a-longs.

Golf
The ocean-hugging nine-hole **Causeway Club** (Fernald Point Rd., 207/244-3780) is more challenging than it looks.

Deep-Sea Fishing
Go fishing with **Acadia Deep Sea Fishing Tours** (Beal's Wharf, Clark Point Rd., Southwest Harbor, 207/244-5385, www.acadiafishingtours.com, half day $69 adults, $49 ages 5-12) aboard the 43-foot *Vagabond,* and you might return with a lobster. The boat goes 8-20 miles offshore for mackerel, bluefish, codfish, and more. All equipment is included; dress warmly and come prepared with seasickness medications. Non-fishing passengers pay $10 less.

Boat Rentals and Lessons
Mansell Boat Rental Co. (135 Shore Rd., Manset, 207/244-5625, www. mansellboatrentals.com, hours vary seasonally), next to Hinckley, rents sailboats and

powerboats by the day or week, including a keel day-sailor or a 17-foot Boston Whaler for $295 per day. Also available are private sailing lessons: $295 for a two- to three-hour sail lesson cruise for one or two, which includes rigging and unrigging the boat.

Sea Kayaking

On the outskirts of Southwest Harbor's downtown is **Maine State Kayak** (254 Main St., Southwest Harbor, 207/244-9500, www.mainestatekayak.com, hours vary seasonally). Staffed with experienced, environmentally sensitive kayakers (all are Registered Maine Guides), the company offers two- to four-hour guided trips ($55-75 pp). Most popular is the four-hour Wildlife Excursion. Maine State Kayak also offers stand-up paddleboarding with its partner **Acadia SUP.** Options include a two-hour lake session or ocean trip ($60 including instructor and gear), and a 75-minute yoga class ($25).

Calm-Water Paddling

Just west of Somesville (take Pretty Marsh Rd.) and across the road from Long Pond, **National Park Canoe & Kayak Rental** (145 Pretty Marsh Rd./Rte. 102, Mount Desert, 207/244-5854, www.nationalparkcanoerental. com, mid-May-mid-Oct.) makes canoeing and kayaking a snap. Just rent the boat, carry it across the road to Pond's End, and launch it. Be sure to pack a picnic. Rates range $32-42 for a three-hour canoe, kayak, or paddleboard rental. A do-it-yourself sunset canoe or kayak tour (5pm-sunset) is $22 per person. The late fee is $10 per half hour. Reservations are essential in July-August.

If you've brought your own canoe or kayak, launch it at Pond's End. It's four miles to the south end of the lake. If the wind kicks up, skirt the shore; if it really kicks up from the north, don't paddle too far down the lake, because you'll have a difficult time getting back.

Another option is to launch your canoe on the quieter, cliff-lined southern end of the lake, much of which is in the national park. To find the put-in, take the Seal Cove Road (on the east end of downtown Southwest Harbor). Go right on Long Cove Road to the small parking area at the end near the pumping station. You can also put in from the Long Pond Fire Road, off Route 102 in Pretty Marsh.

Almost the entire west side of **Long Pond** is Acadia National Park property, so plan to picnic and swim along here; tuck into the sheltered area west of Southern Neck, a crooked finger of land that points northward from the western shore. Stay clear of private property on the east side of the lake.

EXCURSION BOATS

Southwest Harbor is the starting point for a couple of boat services headed for the Cranberry Isles. As always, rates will fluctuate with fuel prices.

Sail Acadia (Dysert's Great Harbor Marina, 11 Apple Ln., Southwest Harbor, 207/266-5210, www.downeastfriendshipsloop. com) is the umbrella for Downeast Friendship Sloop Charters and Quietside Cruises. The former sails the *Alice E.,* built in 1899 and the oldest working Friendship Sloop sailing today. Private charters start at $425 for a two- to three-hour sail, covering up to six passengers and including an appetizer and soft drinks; shared trips are $85 per person for two hours, $75 per person for three hours. Quietside offers scenic Somes Sound cruises that include baiting and hauling a lobster trap and visiting a seal colony ($40 adults, $25 ages 3-11) aboard the *Elizabeth T.,* a wooden lobster boat; private charter is $295, covering up to six passengers.

ENTERTAINMENT
Acadia Repertory Theatre

Somesville is home to the **Acadia Repertory Theatre** (Rte. 102, Somesville, 207/244-7260, www.acadiarep.com, $26 adults, $22 seniors, students, and military, $13 under age 16), which has been providing first-rate professional summer stock on the stage of Somesville's antique Masonic Hall since 1973. Classic plays by Oscar Wilde, Neil Simon, and even Molière have been staples, as has the annual Agatha Christie mystery. Performances in the 148-seat hall run at 8:15pm Tuesday-Sunday late June-late August, with 2pm matinees on the last Sunday of each play's run. Special children's plays are performed at 10:30am Wednesdays and Saturdays in July and August. Tickets for children's theater programs are $9 adults, $6 children.

Lecture and Concert Series

During July and August, the Claremont Hotel (22 Claremont Rd., Southwest Harbor, 207/244-5036 or 800/244-5036, www. theclaremonthotel.com) sponsors a free weekly lecture series, with noted experts, at 8:15pm on Thursday evenings. Past topics have ranged from the Art of the Maine Coast to Cameo Fever: From Catherine the Great to Scarlett O'Hara. It also offers a Saturday evening concert series ($15), with music ranging from jazz to classical.

EVENTS

During July and August, the noon Wednesday Pie Sale at the Somesville Union Meeting House (1132 Main St., Mt. Desert) is always a sellout.

In early August, the annual Claremont Croquet Classic, held on the grounds of the classic Claremont Hotel (22 Claremont Rd., Southwest Harbor), is open to all ages.

October brings Acadia's Oktoberfest (207/244-9264, www.acadiachamber.com), a weekend celebration with wine, beer, food, and music.

The Acadia Night Sky Festival (www. acadianightskyfestival.com), in September, includes lectures, movies, sky-viewing opportunities, and other activities.

SHOPPING

The best shopping locale on this side of the island is Southwest Harbor. Mind you, there aren't lots of shops, but the selection is interesting.

Fine art of the 19th and early 20th centuries, most depicting Maine and Mount Desert Island, is the specialty at Clark Point Gallery

(46 Clark Point Rd., Southwest Harbor, 207/244-0920). Cornerstone Gallery (322 Main St., Southwest Harbor, 207/244-5918) carries original works by local artists and artisans. Southwest Harbor Artisans (360 Main St., Southwest Harbor, no phone) is a cooperative effort operated by Maine artisans. Under the Dogwood Tree (326 Main St., Southwest Harbor, 207/244-3089) carries fun books, clothing, fabric, accessories, and intriguing doodads.

You can stop in at the Hinckley Ship'Store (130 Shore Rd., Southwest Harbor, 207/244-7100 or 800/446-2553, www. hinckleyshipstore.com) and pick up books, charts, and all sorts of Hinckley-logo gear. The Hinckley Company, a name of stellar repute since the 1930s, is one of the nation's premier boatbuilders. There are no tours of the Hinckley complex, but most yachters can't resist the urge to look in at the yard.

FOOD

Restaurant days and hours change frequently, so always call ahead to confirm.

Quick Bites

For wine, cheese, and gourmet goodies, pop into Sawyer's Specialties (353 Main St., Southwest Harbor, 207/244-3317, 10am-6pm Mon.-Sat.). For reasonably priced, all-hours takeout fare including pizzas, fried fare, salads, sandwiches, and more, head into Gott's Store (111 Bass Harbor Rd., Southwest Harbor, 207/244-3431, 3:30am-9pm daily Mon.-Fri., 5am-8pm Sat.-Sun.).

Here's a breakfast you can feel good about: Common Good Café (19 Clark Point Rd., Southwest Harbor, 207/479-5313, www. commongoodsoupkitchen.org, 7:30am-11:30am Tues.-Sun., donation) offers a self-serve buffet comprising hot popovers, slow-simmered steel-cut oatmeal, tea, and coffee, along with accompaniments including maple syrup and plain and flavored butters. Outdoor seating only, so if it's raining, it's closed. The volunteer-run program raises funds for the Common Good Soup Kitchen

Community, which distributes free soup to those who cannot make it to the café, offers a winter community meal, and oversees a winter clothing program, among other things. Be as generous as you can in your donation; just one popover with tea is about $12 at the Jordan Pond House, while here you can eat as many as you like. If you're on a tight budget, just give what you can. Every penny is appreciated. You might also consider picking up a package of the popover mix.

Island Bound Treats (302 Main St., Southwest Harbor, 207/266-3253, 11am-4pm Tues.-Sat.) makes scrumptious triple-berry, strawberry rhubarb, and blueberry pies.

Some of the island's most creative sandwiches and pizza toppings emerge from **Little Notch Cafe** (340 Main St., Southwest Harbor, 207/244-3357, hours vary seasonally, $9-20), next to the library in Southwest Harbor's downtown. Also available are Little Notch Bakery's famed breads, a couple of pasta choices, and homemade soups, stews, and chowders.

Treat yourself to mid-day small plates or pre-dinner cocktails overlooking Somes Sound at **Batson Fish Camp** at the Claremont Hotel (22 Claremont Rd., Southwest Harbor, 207/244-5036 or 800/244-5036). The menu emphasizes seafood with options such as fish and chips, oysters, and, of course, a lobster roll.

Yes, the cookies and bars that Maureen McDonald bakes at **Manset Little Farm** (281 Rte. 102A, Manset, 207/244-7013) are pricey at $4 each, but they're big and scratch-made from premium and organic ingredients. Trust me, after one bite, you'll be wishing you'd purchased more.

College of the Atlantic students run **Beech Hill Farm** (171 Beech Hill Rd., Mount Desert, 207/244-5204, 9am-4pm Tues.-Sat.), a 73-acre property with Maine Organic Farmers and Gardeners Association-certified organic gardens. Also here are acres of heirloom apple trees as well as forestland. Visit the farm stand for fresh produce as well as other organic or natural foods including cheeses and baked goods; the breakfast sandwiches earn raves.

Family Favorites

Good chowders, sandwiches, fried clams, lobster rolls, and even pizza are served at the cozy **Quietside Cafe** (11 Seal Cove Rd., Southwest Harbor, 207/244-9444, 11am-9pm daily, $6-18), with seating indoors and outside. Do save room for Frances's sky-high homemade blueberry and key lime pies.

Café Dry Dock (357 Main St., Southwest Harbor, 207/244-5842, www.cafedrydockinn.com, 11am-9:30pm daily, $12-30) earns kudos for longevity—it's been here for more than 30 years—as well as its reliably good food and service. Just skip the fries, which are baked. Dine inside or on the deck. There's usually live music on Wednesday evenings.

★ **Eat-a-Pita / Cafe 2** (326 Main St., Southwest Harbor, 207/244-4344, www.eatapitasouthwestharbor.com, 8am-4pm and 5pm-9pm daily), a casual, order-at-the-counter restaurant serving breakfast and lunch, morphs into a full-service restaurant ($14-28) at night. The dining room, furnished with old oak tables and chairs, has a funky, artsy 'tude; there's also patio seating outside and an outdoor bar (think pink flamingos). Start the day with a Greek or Acapulco omelet. Lunch emphasizes delicious pita sandwiches, burgers, paninis, and salads (call in advance for takeout); dinner choices include salads, light meals, a half-dozen pastas, and entrées. This is my usual choice for to-go sandwiches to enjoy while hiking in the park.

Casual Dining

Good food, good coffee, and good wine complement the Mediterranean-influenced menu at **Sips** (4 Clark Point Rd., Southwest Harbor, 207/244-4550, www.sipsmdi.com, 11am-8:30pm Mon.-Tues., 7am-8:30pm Wed.-Sat., 7am-noon Sun.), a congenial place. Small- and large-plate and tapas-style choices range

1: paddling on Long Pond **2:** Beal's Lobster Pier
3: Acadia Yurts **4:** the Claremont Hotel

$8-30; the risottos are especially good. A children's menu is available.

New American pub-style fare is the specialty at Coda (18 Village Green Way, Southwest Harbor, 207/244-8133, www.codasouthwestharbor.com, from 5pm Tues.-Sat., $14-28), where everything is made from scratch. There's often live entertainment.

Red sky at night, diners' delight: Gold walls, artwork, wood floors, and a giant hearth set a chic tone for ★ Red Sky (14 Clark Point Rd., Southwest Harbor, 207/244-0476, www.redskyrestaurant.com, 11:30am-2pm and 5pm-8pm Wed.-Sun., $24-38), one of the island's tonier restaurants. The creative fare emphasizes fresh seafood, hand-cut meats, and local organic produce; there's always a vegetarian choice. In 2020, the restaurant added outdoor seating in its private backyard, where picnic-style lunches also are available, weather permitting.

Gaze over Somes Sound and watch the sun set behind Cadillac Mountain while dining at Little Fern Restaurant at the Claremont Hotel (22 Claremont Rd., Southwest Harbor, 207/244-5036 or 800/244-5036). The menu adds a creative touch to classic Maine ingredients and dishes. It's open daily for breakfast, lunch, and dinner; vegan and gluten-free options are always available.

Lobster

Eat, drink, and be messy is the slogan at Beal's Lobster Pier (182 Clark Point Rd., Southwest Harbor, 207/244-3202, www.bealslobster.com, 11am-9pm daily). Go for the lobster, but if you're traveling with landlubbers, there are burgers, fried fish, salads, sandwiches, and even veggie burgers on the menu. There's also a kids' menu. Both sheltered and outdoor seating is available on the wharf.

Vintage burger-joint-style takeout meets lobster shack at Charlotte's Legendary Lobster Pound (465 Seawall Rd./Rte. 102A, Southwest Harbor, 207/244-8021, www.charlotteslegendarylobsters.com, 11am-8:30pm daily), an order-at-the-window, eat-on-picnic-tables spot that earns raves for its lobster and lobster rolls, but there's plenty more on the menu.

ACCOMMODATIONS

As the Asticou Inn is to Northeast Harbor, the Claremont is to Southwest Harbor. On the other end of the lodging scale, there are several commercial campgrounds in this part of the island, plus an Acadia National Park campground. Rates listed are for peak season.

Inns

If you're pining for the "old Maine" with updated amenities, stay at the Claremont Hotel (22 Claremont Rd., Southwest Harbor, 207/244-5036 or 800/244-5036, www.theclaremonthotel.com). This elegant, oceanfront, 1881 grande dame, dressed in mustard-yellow clapboard, occupies a spectacular six-acre hilltop setting overlooking Somes Sound. A new owner in 2020 promised to keep the historic charm while adding air-conditioning and flat screen TVs to all rooms and upgrading the bedding and decor. Guest rooms are split between the main inn and two smaller ones, the Clark House and Phillips House. Also on the premises are ocean-view and woodland-view cottages, a bar, two restaurants, and a confectionary. New for the 2021 season are an outdoor pool and multiple decks for taking in the views. Guests have access to croquet courts, a clay tennis court, one-speed cruiser bikes, golf carts, a dinner boat, spa services, and a family game room. The most popular time here is the first week in August, during the annual Claremont Croquet Classic. Children are welcome. Rates begin around $300.

Bed-and-Breakfasts

Most of Southwest Harbor's bed-and-breakfasts are clustered downtown, along Main Street and the Clark Point Road.

Built in 1884, the mansard-roofed Victorian Inn at Southwest (371 Main St./Rte. 102, Southwest Harbor, 207/244-3835, www.innatsouthwest.com, from $165) has 13 dormers and a wraparound wicker-furnished veranda. Seven 2nd- and 3rd-floor guest rooms—named for Maine lighthouses and full of character—are decorated with a mix of contemporary and antique furnishings. Breakfast and afternoon sweets are included.

Comfortable and spacious rooms, many with water views, welcome guests to the **Clark Point Inn** (109 Clark Point Rd., Southwest Harbor, 207/2440-9828, www.clarkpointinn. com, from $169). The location is steps from the ferry dock and an easy walk to downtown. A multicourse breakfast and evening sweets are provided. It's open year-round.

The elegant Queen Anne **Kingsleigh Inn 1904** (373 Main St., Southwest Harbor, 207/244-5302, www.kingsleighinn.com, from $195) has eight rooms, some with private harbor-facing decks, on three floors. The best splurge is the turret suite, with a fireplace, private deck, and a telescope trained on the harbor. Breakfast is a three-course affair, served on the water-view porch, weather permitting. Afternoon refreshments are served.

The linden-blossom fragrance can be intoxicating in summer at the **Lindenwood Inn** (118 Clark Point Rd., Southwest Harbor, 207/244-5335 or 800/307-5335, www.lindenwoodinn.com, from $189). The inn's 15 guest rooms, split between two buildings, and poolside bungalow are decorated in a sophisticated yet comfortable style. After you hike Acadia's trails, the heated pool and hot tub are especially welcome, and after that, perhaps enjoy a drink from the full bar. Some guest rooms have harbor views.

Comfortable, spacious rooms, many with water views, welcome guests to the **Clark Point Inn** (109 Clark Point Rd., Southwest Harbor, 207/2440-9828, www.clarkpointinn. com, $169-249). The location is steps from the ferry dock and an easy walk to downtown. A multicourse breakfast and evening sweets are provided. It's open year-round.

Set on a corner, well back from Clark Point Road, is ★ **Harbour Cottage Inn** (9 Dirigo Rd., Southwest Harbor, 207/244-5738 or 888/843-3022, www.harbourcottageinn. com, from $239). Built in 1870 as the annex

for the island's first hotel, it's now a lovely bed-and-breakfast with eight guest rooms and three suites decorated in a colorful and fun cottage style. Some guest rooms have jetted baths and/or fireplaces. Rates include a multicourse breakfast.

Motels and Cottages

Smack on the harbor and just a two-minute walk from downtown is the appropriately named **Harbor View Motel & Cottages** (11 Ocean Way, Southwest Harbor, 207/244-5031, www.harborviewmotelandcottages. com, $100-250). The family-owned complex comprises motel rooms spread out in two one-story buildings (ask for a renovated unit) and a newer three-story structure fronting the harbor. Also on the premises are housekeeping cottages and an apartment. A meager continental breakfast is served to motel guests July to early September. Pets are welcome in some units ($10/day or $60/week).

Directly across from the famed seawall and adjacent to the park, the **Seawall Motel** (566 Seawall Rd./Rte. 102A, Southwest Harbor, 207/244-9250 or 800/248-9250, www. seawallmotel.com, $140) is a no-surprises two-story motel (upstairs guest rooms have the best views). Kids 12 and younger stay free, and there's a laundry. The location is primo for bird-watchers. A hearty continental breakfast buffet is included. Also on the premises are three townhouse-style two-bedroom Oceanside Luxury Suites (from $2,400/week) with full kitchens and living areas.

Smack downtown, **Café Dry Dock Inn** (357 Main St., Southwest Harbor, 207/244-5842, www.cafedrydockinn.com, $149-295) has accommodations ranging from smallish guestrooms to a two-bedroom suite with full kitchen. Rooms are simply decorated, with white linens, contemporary accents, hardwood floors, and earth-toned walls.

In Manset, adjacent to the Hinckley Yacht complex and with jaw-dropping views down Somes Sound, is **The Moorings** (133 Shore Rd., Manset, 207/244-5523, www.mooringsinn.com, $150-270). The rustic oceanfront complex, under fourth-generation ownership, is part motel, part cottage rental, and part inn. It's tired, and soundproofing is minimal; what you're paying for here are the harbor-front location and views. Bikes, canoes, and kayaks are available from Mansell Boat Rental, which is on the premises. Dogs are a possibility.

Cottage Rentals

L. S. Robinson Co. (337 Main St., Southwest Harbor, 207/244-5563, www.lsrobinson. com) has an extensive list of cottage rentals in the area. The Southwest Harbor/Tremont Chamber of Commerce (329 Main St., Southwest Harbor, 207/244-9264 or 800/423-9264, www.acadiachamber.com) also keeps a helpful listing of privately owned homes and cottages available for rent.

Camping and Glamping

Acadia National Park's Seawall Campground is on this side of the island.

Built on the site of an old quarry, on a hillside descending to rocky frontage on Somes Sound, **Somes Sound View Campground** (86 Hall Quarry Rd., Mount Desert, 207/244-3890, off-season 207/244-7452, www.ssvc. info, late May-mid-Oct., $30-70) is among the smallest campgrounds on the island, with about 60 sites, most geared to tents and vans. Rustic camping cabins and glamping tents are $70-90 per night. Facilities include hot showers (if you're camping on the lowest levels it's a good hike up to the bathhouse), a heated pool, a boat launch, kayak, canoe, and paddleboat rentals, and a fishing dock. You can swim in the sound from a rocky beach. Leashed pets are allowed at campsites. Mooring rentals available. It's two miles south and east of Somesville and a mile east of Route 102.

The **Smuggler's Den Campground** (Rte. 102, Southwest Harbor, 207/244-3944, www.smugglersdencampground.com, $45-85) is a midsized, pet-friendly campground between Echo Lake and downtown Southwest Harbor. Trails access back roads to Echo Lake (1.25 miles) and Long Pond (1 mile) as well as

25 miles of Acadia National Park trails. Big-rig sites are grouped in the top third, pop-ups and small campers are in the middle third, and tenting sites are in the lower third and in the woods rimming the large recreation field. Also available are cabins ($130-200/night; $700-1475/week) ranging from rustic to deluxe with kitchen and bath and rental RVs ($1,650/week). Facilities include a laundry, free hot showers, Wi-Fi, a heated pool and kiddie pool, and a four-acre recreation field with horseshoe pits, half-court basketball, and lawn games.

On the eastern edge of Somesville, just off Route 198 at the head of Somes Sound, the ★ **Mount Desert Campground** (516 Somes Sound Dr./Rte. 198, Somesville, 207/244-3710, www.mountdesertcampground.com, $39-76) is centrally located for visiting Bar Harbor, Acadia, and the whole western side of Mount Desert Island. The campground has 152 wooded tent sites, about 45 on the water, spread out on 58 acres. Reservations are essential in midsummer—one-week minimum for waterfront sites, three days for off-water sites in July and August. (Book a year ahead for waterfront sites.) This popular and low-key campground gets high marks for maintenance, noise control, and convenient tent platforms. Another plus is the Gathering Place, where campers can relax, play games, use free Wi-Fi, and purchase coffee and fresh-baked treats or ice cream. No pets are allowed July-early September, and no trailers over 20 feet are permitted. Kayak, canoe, and stand-up paddleboard rentals are available.

Every stayed in a yurt or tiny house? You can at **Acadia Yurts** (200 Seal Cove Rd., Southwest Harbor, 207/669-2059, www.acadiayurts.com). Peppering the wooded property are six well-equipped, 24-foot studio yurts and one 30-foot one-bedroom yurt (from $1,100/week mid-June-late Sept., from $185/night with 3-night min. off-season). Also available are tiny houses (3-night min., from $150/night or $975/week mid-June-early Sept., from $130 off-season). The on-site wellness center offers a float tank, infrared sauna, and yoga studio.

INFORMATION AND SERVICES

The **Southwest Harbor/Tremont Chamber of Commerce** (329 Main St., Southwest Harbor, 207/244-9264 or 800/423-9264, www.acadiachamber.com) stocks brochures, maps, menus, and other local info.

In downtown Southwest Harbor, **public restrooms** are at the southern end of the parking lot behind the Main Street park and near the fire station. There are portable toilets at the town docks.

GETTING THERE AND AROUND

Southwest Harbor is about 13 miles or 25 minutes via Routes 198 and 102 from Northeast Harbor. It's about 14 miles or 25 minutes to Bar Harbor and about 3 miles via Route 102 to Tremont.

Southwest Harbor is serviced by Route 7/ Southwest Harbor of the Island Explorer bus system.

Tremont: Bass Harbor, Bernard, and Seal Cove

The "quiet side" of the island becomes even quieter as you round the southwestern edge into **Tremont** (pop. 1,563), which includes the villages of **Bernard; Bass Harbor,** home of Bass Harbor Head Light and ferry services to offshore islands; and **Seal Cove.** Tremont occupies the southwestern corner of Mount Desert Island. It's about as far as you can get from Bar Harbor, but Island Explorer Route No. 7/Southwest Harbor comes through regularly.

Be sure to visit these small villages. Views are fabulous, the pace is slow, and you'll feel as if you've stumbled upon "the real Maine."

SIGHTS

Country Store Museum

Stepping inside the former general store that's now headquarters for the **Tremont Historical Society** (Shore Rd., Bass Harbor, 207/244-9753, www.tremontmainehistory.us, 1pm-4pm Mon., Wed., Fri. July-mid-Oct.) is like stepping into the 1800s. Displays highlight the local heritage. If you're lucky, seventh-generation islander Muriel Davisson might be on duty and regale you with stories about her aunt, author Ruth Moore. You can buy copies of Moore's books here—good reads all. The museum is across from the Seafood Ketch.

The Seal Cove Auto Museum

The late Richard C. Paine Jr.'s Brass Era (1895-1917) car collection, one of the largest in the country, is nicely displayed and identified in the **Seal Cove Auto Museum** (1414 Tremont Rd./Rte. 102, Seal Cove, 207/244-9242, www.sealcoveautomuseum.org, 11am-5pm daily May-Oct., $10 adults, $8 seniors, free ages 17 and younger). All vehicles are in as-found condition; this ranges from fresh-from-the-barn to meticulously restored. It's easy for kids of any age to spend an hour here, reminiscing or fantasizing. Among the highlights are a 1913 Peugeot with mahogany skiff body; a 1915 F.R.P., the only one in existence; an original 1903 Ford Model A, the first car commercially produced by the Ford Motor Co.; and a 1909 Ford Model T "Tin Lizzie," from the first year of production. The oldest car in the collection is an 1899 DeDion-Bouton, one of the earliest cars produced in the world. The museum is about six miles southwest of Somesville. Or, if you're coming from Southwest Harbor, take Route 102 north to Seal Cove Road (partly unpaved) west to the other side of Route 102 (it makes a giant loop) and go north about 1.5 miles. The museum is not on the Island Explorer route.

Harding Wharf Lighthouse

Drive to the end of the road, and you can't miss the faux lighthouse at Harding Wharf. The Murphy family, who lived in what's now called Centennial House across the road, built the attached fishing shack in 1891. They sold it to Charles Harding in 1927, and it remained in the family until Charles's brother Clarence sold it to Nancy and Irving Silverman in 1981. Later that year, the Silvermans attached their colorful collection of 29 historical wooden lobster buoys to the seaward side of the shack.

RECREATION
Sea Kayaking

If you have your own boat, consider putting in at either the park's Pretty Marsh picnic area, off Route 102 in Pretty Marsh, or at the public boat launch at the end of Bartlett's Landing Road, off Indian Point Road near the Route 102 end. From either put-in, you can paddle around privately owned Bartlett Island. For a longer trip, head north along the shoreline past Black and Green Islands, both privately owned, to Alley Island, which is open for day access.

EXCURSION BOATS
★ Island Cruises

High praise goes to Island Cruises (Little Island Marine, Shore Rd., Bass Harbor, 207/244-5785, www.bassharborcruises.com), owned and operated by Captain Eli Strauss, for its narrated 3.5-hour lunch cruise to Frenchboro. The 49-passenger *R. L. Gott* departs at 11am daily during the summer. Eli was born navigating these waters, and his experience shows not only in his boat handling but also in his narration. Expect to pick up lots of local heritage and lore about once-thriving and now abandoned granite-quarrying and fishing communities, the sardine industry, and lobstering; and to see seals, cormorants,

guillemots, and often eagles. Eli also hauls a trap or two and explains lobstering. He earns major points for maneuvering the boat so that passengers on both sides get an up-close view of key sights. The trip allows enough time on Frenchboro for lunch. You could bring a picnic, but it's a treat to have lunch at Lunt's, where the menu ranges from hot dogs to lobster. Afterward, stroll through the village and visit the small museum, before returning through the sprinkling of islands along the 8.3-mile route.

It's an excellent, enthralling tour for all ages. Round-trip cost is $40 adults, $25 kids. Make reservations; if the weather looks iffy, call ahead to confirm. Most of the trip is in sheltered water, but rough seas can put the kibosh on it. Island Cruises also does a two-hour afternoon nature cruise among the islands that covers the same topics but spends a bit more time at seal ledges and other spots ($40 adults, $25 kids). On either trip, don't forget to bring binoculars. You'll find the Island Cruises dock by following signs to the Swans Island ferry and turning right at the sign shortly before the state ferry dock.

Acadia Charter Co.

Enjoy a custom, private cruise with a naturalist aboard the handsome *Vera Lee*, a Bunker & Ellis wooden lobster yacht, operated by Acadia Charter Co. (207/479-9082, www.acadiachartercompany.com); from $720 for four hours, plus $300 captain's fee and fuel. The 36-foot-long boat can carry six passengers.

SHOPPING

Linda Fernandez Handknits (Bernard Rd., Bernard, 207/244-7224) has beautiful handknit sweaters, mittens, hats, socks, Christmas stockings, and embroidered pillowcases, all crafted by the talented Fernandez family. The kids' lobster sweaters are especially cute.

Potters Lisbeth Faulkner and Ed Davis can often be seen working in their studio at Seal Cove Pottery & Gallery (Kelleytown Rd., Seal Cove, 207/244-3602, www.

sealcovepottery.com). In addition to their functional hand-thrown or hand-built pottery, they exhibit Davis's paintings as well as crafts by other island artisans.

FOOD

Call to confirm restaurant hours, especially when traveling early or late in the season.

Sure, there's seating inside the harbor-hugging **Seafood Ketch Restaurant** (47 Shore Rd., Bass Harbor, 207/244-7463, www.seafoodketch.com, 11am-8pm daily), but aim for a table on the patio so you can watch the lobster boats go to and fro. There are a few "landlubber delights," but the menu favors fresh seafood dishes—including the baked lobster-seafood casserole, a recipe requested by *Gourmet* magazine. Most entrées run $22-30, but sandwiches and lighter fare are available. This is a prime family spot, with a kids' menu and gluten-free menus. In early summer, be sure to bring bug dope if sitting outside. Follow signs for the Swans Island ferry terminal.

Few restaurants have as idyllic a setting as ★ **Thurston's Lobster Pound** (9 Thurston Rd., Bernard, 207/244-7600, www.thurstonforlobster.com, noon-8pm Mon.-Sat., market rates), which overlooks lobster boat-filled Bass Harbor. The screened dining room practically sits in the water. Also on the menu: chowders, sandwiches, and terrific desserts. Read the directions at the entrance and order before you find a table on one of two levels. Thurston's also has a full bar, with a huge stone hearth, deck, and roll-up walls that allow as much or as little of the weather in as necessary. It's an extremely popular place to relax with a drink, overlooking the sigh-worthy harbor.

ACCOMMODATIONS
Inns and Cottages

Bass Harbor Cottages and Country Inn (95 Harbor Dr./Rte. 102A, Bass Harbor, 207/244-3460, www.bassharborcottages.com) fronts on Bass Harbor. Accommodations are basic but clean; there's no maid service. The sturdy white home has three guest rooms ($159-279). Also on the premises are a number of rustic cottages and suites (from $159/day, $1,599/week).

Each of the four spacious oceanview guest rooms at ★ **Ann's Point Inn** (79 Ann's Point Rd., Bass Harbor, 207/244-9595, www.annspointinn.com, from $355) has a king bed covered in luxurious linens, a gas fireplace, and all the amenities you might expect,

Thurston's Lobster Pound

including robes and slippers. The inn, sited on a private waterfront lot at the tip of Ann's Point, pampers guests with a hot tub and a sauna, plus afternoon sweets. Even better, the inn's green and sustainable amenities include solar-powered electricity and hot water and garden-fresh fare at breakfast. All this is on two acres with 690 feet of shorefront, from which you can watch eagles soar and lobster boats at work.

Camping

Acadia National Park's Seawall Campground is on this side of the island.

A budget-friendly option is the nicely wooded **Quietside Campground and Cabins** (397 Tremont Rd./Rte. 102, Tremont, 207/244-50566, www.quietsidecampground. com), with 35 sites accommodating tents ($33, platforms provided) and small RVs ($28) up to 22 feet, some with water and 30-amp electricity. It also has log camping cabins ($68-75) with heat, electricity, a microwave, and a small refrigerator but no plumbing, and rustic cabins ($63) with a propane lantern, a gas grill, and a screened porch. There are two bathhouses with free hot showers, one with a coin-op laundry. Quiet, well-behaved pets are allowed for $1 per night. The campground is off the beaten track, but the tenting sites are very private, and the location ensures quiet.

Just a 10-minute walk from Bass Harbor

Head Light is **Bass Harbor Campground** (342 Harbor Dr./Rte. 102A, Bass Harbor, 207/244-5857 or 800/327-5857, www.bassharbor.com), owned and operated by the Carsey family. The campground has RV sites ($43-62) with electricity, water, sewer, and cable TV as well as plenty of wooded tent sites ($33-37), some with platforms. Hot showers and Wi-Fi are included. There's a heated pool, a playground, and a self-service coin-op laundry. Also on-site are one- and two-room camping cabins ($73-99), without baths but with electricity, a small refrigerator, and an outdoor gas grill, and yurts ($84-99); bring your own sheets, towels, blankets, dishes, and cooking utensils. Quiet, leashed, well-behaved pets are welcome, but there is no tolerance for barking or other offenses.

INFORMATION AND SERVICES

There's a **public restroom** at the Swans Island ferry terminal.

GETTING THERE AND AROUND

Tremont is about 3 miles via Route 102 or 8 miles via Route 102A from Southwest Harbor. It's about 17 miles or 30 minutes to Bar Harbor.

Tremont and Bass Harbor are on Route 7/Southwest Harbor of the Island Explorer bus system.

Islands Near Mount Desert

Four ferry-serviced islands offshore of Mount Desert Island are ideal for day trips: Swans Island, Frenchboro, and Islesford and Great Cranberry, two neighboring Cranberry Isles that can be hopscotched in one day using the passenger ferry service.

Only 15 of Maine's offshore islands still support year-round populations, and these are 4 of them. An island day trip removes you from the region's hustle-bustle, limited

as that may be, and allows you the opportunity to meet the folks who summer or live and work here year-round. You'll escape crowds and encounter little, if any, traffic, and experience a taste of island life. These islands aren't for those who need commercial distractions. Although there are some worthy sights, the allure of an island is the overall experience: hobnobbing with locals and summerfolk on the ferry, wandering quiet roads, and perhaps enjoying a shore-front picnic.

Getting to an island, or two, is easy, but it does take some planning. Most excursion boats for the Cranberries depart from Northeast Harbor, although one line originates in Southwest Harbor. All carry bikes but no cars; the state car ferry for Swans Island departs from Bass Harbor, south of Southwest Harbor and part of the town of Tremont. The Maine State Ferry Service also operates the ferry to Long Island (referred to as Frenchboro, the name of the village on the island) from Bass Harbor, but for day trips the schedule requires careful planning.

★ CRANBERRY ISLES

The Cranberry Isles (pop. 141), south of Northeast and Seal Harbors, comprise **Great Cranberry, Little Cranberry** (called Islesford), **Sutton, Baker,** and **Bear Islands.** Islesford and Baker include property belonging to Acadia National Park.

Two commercial passenger ferries, one from Northeast Harbor and the other from Southwest Harbor, to-and-fro between their home ports, stopping at Great Cranberry and Islesford twice on every trip. You can visit one or both on one ticket. The schedule, along with a shuttle service on Great Cranberry, makes it easy to visit both in one day. Bring a bike to explore the narrow, mostly level roads, or simply wander on foot, but remember to respect private property. Unless you've asked for and received permission, do not cut across private land to reach the shore.

The Cranberry name has been attributed to 18th-century loyalist governor Francis Bernard, who received these islands along with all of Mount Desert Island as a king's grant in 1762. Cranberry bogs, now long gone, on the two largest islands evidently caught his attention. Permanent European settlers were here in the 1760s, and there was even steamboat service by the 1820s.

Lobstering and other marine businesses are the commercial mainstays, boosted in summer by the various visitor-related pursuits. Artists and writers come for a week, a month, or longer.

Note: There are no inns on either island, only rental houses. Plan ahead for meals, as food options are limited.

Great Cranberry

Largest of the islands is Great Cranberry, with a year-round population of about 45 that swells to around 400 in the summer. You can easily explore this island's highlights in a couple of hours. The Main Road extends the length of the island, about two miles, with a few pleasant viewpoints along the way. It's an easy walk or bicycle ride, with some gentle hills and very little traffic; do follow the rules of the road, though. If you bring your dog, it must be kept leashed.

SIGHTS

It's about a 15-minute walk on the Main Road to **Cranberry House,** home to the **Preble-Marr Historical Museum** (207/244-7800, www.gcihs.org, 10am-4pm daily mid-June-mid-Oct., free) and a café, an arts center, and free Wi-Fi. The volunteer-operated museum is a pleasure to visit, with well-informed staffers who radiate enthusiasm. One museum exhibit commemorates *Hitty, Her First Hundred Years,* the 1930 Newbery Medal-winning novel by Rachel Field, a one-time island summer resident. (Her home, not open to the public, was the Preble House, on the right between the ferry dock and the museum, with lilac bushes in front and a large pine in the right rear corner). The arts center presents movies, lectures, concerts, workshops, and other activities and events. The take-out café, with seating on the deck, serves sandwiches, lobster rolls, salads, and sweets. Better yet, get lunch to go and wander down the mile-long **Cranberry House Trail** behind the museum to the sand beach on Whistler Cove. The easy trail moseys through an evergreen forest with a green moss floor to a rock beach; bring insect repellent.

Day Trip to Frenchboro, Long Island

Since Maine has more Long Islands than anyone cares to count, most of them have other labels for easy identification. Here's a case in point—a Long Island known universally as Frenchboro, the name of the village that wraps around Lunts Harbor. The year-round population hovers around 60. Frenchboro is an especially quiet place, where islanders live as islanders always have—making a living from the sea and being proud of it. For more on that, read *Hauling by Hand,* a fascinating, well-researched book published in 1999 by eighth-generation islander Dean Lunt.

In 1999, when roughly half of the island (914 acres, including 5.5 miles of shorefront) went up for sale by a private owner, an incredible fundraising effort collected nearly $3 million, allowing purchase of the land in 2000 by the Maine Coast Heritage Trust. Some of the funding helped restore the village's church and one-room schoolhouse. Since then, thanks to a gift from David Rockefeller, the preserve expanded to include Rich's Head, adding 192 acres and three miles of shoreline. Visitors now have access to 13.5 miles of rustic hiking trails, most unmarked, lacing 1,159 acres—more than 80 percent of the island, including about 8.2 miles of shoreline. You can download an island map from Maine Coast Heritage Trust (www.mcht.org). No camping or fires are permitted.

Frenchboro is a delightful day trip. A good way to get a sense of the place is to take the 3.5-hour lunch cruise run by captain Ian Strauss of Island Cruises (Little Island Marine, Shore Rd., Bass Harbor, 207/244-5785, www.bassharborcruises.com). For an even longer day trip, take the passenger ferry *R. L. Gott* during its weekly run for the Maine State Ferry Service. Each Friday, early April-late October, the *R. L. Gott* departs Bass Harbor at 8am, arriving in Frenchboro at 9am. The return trip to Bass Harbor is at 6pm, allowing nine hours on the island. The Maine State Ferry Service (207/244-3254, daily recorded info 800/491-4883, http://maine.gov/mdot/ferry/frenchboro) vessel *Captain Henry Lee* travels to Frenchboro on other days, but these trips usually don't allow time on the island.

When you go, take a picnic with you, or stop at Lunt's Dockside Deli (207/334-2902, 11am-2pm daily), open only in July and August. It's a very casual establishment—order at the window, grab a picnic table, and wait for your name to be called. Lobster and fish chowder are the specialties, but the menu offers sandwiches, hot dogs, and even vegetable wraps. Prices are low, the view is wonderful, and you might even get to watch lobsters being unloaded from a boat.

The Frenchboro Historical Society Museum (207/334-2924, www.frenchboro.lib.me.us, free), just up from the dock, has interesting old tools, other local artifacts, and a small gift shop with mostly island-made goods. It's usually open afternoons Memorial Day-Labor Day. The island's network of easy and not-so-easy maintained trails wind through the woods and along the shore; some can be squishy, and some are along boulder-strewn beachfront. All are rustic, and most are unmarked, so proceed carefully. In the center of the island is a beaver pond. There's a restroom above the Dockside Deli and two others near the museum.

Every year since 1961, on the second Saturday of August, Frenchboro hosts its annual Lobster Festival (www.frenchboro-dinner.org), a midday meal comprising lobster, chicken salad, hot dogs, coleslaw, homemade pies, and more, served rain or shine, with proceeds benefiting a local cause. Islanders and hundreds of visitors gather in the village for the occasion, which also includes live music, the All the Road We Got footrace (almost 5K), and other activities. The Maine State Ferry makes a special run that day.

FOOD

Pick up picnic fixings or order sandwiches, burgers, lobster rolls, or whatever else is on the day's menu at the Great Cranberry General Store (12 Cranberry Rd., 207/244-0622), home to the take-out Seawich Café, located adjacent to the ferry dock. There are a few tables inside and on the deck. It's a great spot to catch up on the island gossip and watch the comings and goings on the ferries.

Hitty's Café (207/244-7845, 10am-4pm daily, $10-20), at the Cranberry House, serves soups, salads, and sandwiches, with seating inside or on the porch and lawn. It's also an Internet hot spot.

SERVICES
Public restrooms are located midway between the store and the shore and at the Cranberry House.

Little Cranberry (Islesford)
The second-largest island is Little Cranberry, locally known as Islesford.

You'll arrive at the Town Dock, one of three adjacent docks; the others are the Fishermen's Wharf and the Islesford Dock. Just off the dock is the Islesford Historical Museum, operated by the park service.

PARKS AND PRESERVES
Wind and tide have created the rocky berm that defines Gilley Beach, a cobbled expanse on Islesford's south shore. To get there from the Town Dock, follow Main Street, which morphs into Gilley Beach Road, to the end, where a 100-foot right-of-way provides access.

From the Town Dock, follow Main Street to the first right on Maypole Point Road (also known as Sand Beach Rd.), and continue for about a half mile. Just beyond the cemetery and before the pavement ends, you'll find Hadlock Park on the water. It's a tiny park, but it has easy-on-the-eyes views to Great Cranberry, Sutton, and Mount Desert Islands.

SHOPPING
Islesford is an artsy place.

The Islesford Dock Gallery (on the dock, 207/244-7494, http://islesforddock. com) shows the works of about 18 artists in four rooms.

Islesford Pottery (on the dock, 207/244-9108, www.islesford.com/idcartmb.html) is Marian Baker's summertime ceramic studio. A teacher at Maine College of Art in Portland, Marian makes particularly appealing functional pieces, and she carries the work of other potters as well. If you're lucky, she'll have a pot on the wheel. She also sells a handy map of the island ($1), with profits given to charity. Street

and road signs are scarce on the island, but the map at least provides orientation.

Winter's Work (on the dock, 207/610-0021, www.winterswork.com) is a tiny, one-room gallery with an eclectic selection of works—and fudge!—by primarily island and Maine artists and authors, including Ashley Bryan.

A five-minute walk from the waterfront will bring you to Islesford Artists (Mosswood Rd., www.islesfordartists.com, 10am-5pm daily July-Aug., 10am-4pm Mon.-Fri. or by appointment May-June and Sept.-Oct.), an excellent gallery specializing in works by Maine island artists. Run by Danny and Katy Fernald, the gallery is several blocks from the harbor, but there's a sign, and Marian Baker's map will get you here. Or just ask—the islanders are always helpful.

Islesford is home to internationally renowned artist, writer, poet, children's book illustrator, and humanitarian Ashley Bryan (b. 1923). The Ashley Bryan Center (413-687-2762, www.ashleybryancenter.org), created in 2013, aims to "preserve, celebrate, and share broadly" the artist's work through programs and exhibits. The center's Storyteller Pavilion (Hadlock Rd., 10am-4pm daily daily) houses Bryan's magnificent sea glass panels, inspired by medieval stained glass windows and comprising sea glass assembled with papier-mâché in images depicting the life of Christ. Also on view are some of his puppets and other creations. Ask locally about current programs.

FOOD
On the wharf nearest the museum is The Islesford Dock (207/244-7494, http://islesforddock.com, 11am-3pm and 5pm-9pm Tues.-Sat. and 10am-3pm and 5pm-9pm Sun. July-Aug., closed Mon. and Tues. in Sept., $12-32), which hangs over the water. Dinner entrees may include grilled rib eye, shrimp curry, or a seafood stew; a kids' menu is available at lunch and dinner. Prices are moderate, the food is excellent, and the views across to Acadia's mountains are incredible.

Reservations are wise in midsummer, especially for a sunset table. Sunday brunch is served 10am-2pm. Water taxis are available to return to Northeast Harbor after dinner and a night boat is often available to ferry visitors to Northeast Harbor.

SERVICES

You'll find **restrooms** on the dock.

For **cottage rentals,** see www.islesford. com.

Getting There and Around

Walking or pedaling are the best ways to explore these islands, but there's also usually a summer golf-cart-style shuttle operating on Great Cranberry (free, donations appreciated). Do call to confirm current ferry schedules, as online versions aren't always accurate.

Beal and Bunker (207/244-3575) provides year-round mail and passenger boat service to the Cranberries from Northeast Harbor. The schedule makes it possible to do both islands in one day. The summer season, with more frequent trips, runs late June-Labor Day. The boats make a variety of stops on the three-island route (including Sutton in summer), so be patient as they make the circuit. It's a people-watching treat. If you just did a round-trip and stayed aboard, the loop would take about 1.5 hours. Round-trip tickets (covering the whole loop, including intra-island trips if you want to visit both Great Cranberry and Islesford) are $32 adults, $16 ages 3-11, free under age 3. Bicycles are $8 round-trip. The off-season schedule operates early May-mid-June and early September-mid-October; the winter schedule runs mid-October-April. In winter, the boat company advises phoning ahead on what Mainers quaintly call "weather days."

The **Cranberry Cove Ferry** (upper town dock, Clark Point Rd., Southwest Harbor, 207/244-5882, cell 207/460-1981, www. downeastwindjammer.com, $32 adult, $22 child, $8/bicycle) operates a summertime service to the Cranberries mid-May-mid-October. The ferry route begins at the upper town dock (Clark Point Rd.) in Southwest

Harbor and makes stops in Manset and Great Cranberry before reaching Islesford an hour later and reversing the itinerary; it's two hours total if you stay on the boat. (Stops at Sutton can be arranged.) In summer (July-Aug.) there are five trips daily; four in spring and fall.

SWANS ISLAND

Six miles off Mount Desert Island lies scenic, roughly 7,000-acre Swans Island (www. swansisland.org), named after Colonel James Swan, who bought it and two dozen other islands as an investment in 1786. As with the Cranberries, fishing is the year-round way of life here, with lobstering being the primary occupation. In summer, the population practically triples with the arrival of artists, writers, and other seasonal visitors. The island has no campsites, few public restrooms, and only a handful of guest rooms. Visitors who want to spend more than a day tend to rent cottages by the week.

You'll need either a bicycle or a car to get around, as the ferry docks at the island's northeast corner and the village center is on the other. Should you choose to bring a car, it's wise to make reservations for the ferry, especially for the return trip. Bicycling is a good way to get around, but be forewarned that the roads are narrow, lacking shoulders, and hilly in spots. It's wise to pull over when the rush of cars off an incoming ferry passes.

If you can be flexible, wait for a clear day and then pack a picnic and catch the first ferry (7:30am) from Bass Harbor. At the ferry office in Bass Harbor, request a Swans Island map. Keep an eye on your watch so you don't miss the last ferry (4:30pm) back to Bass Harbor.

Sights

Just 100 yards from the ferry terminal is the **Swans Island Lobster & Marine Museum** (Ferry Rd., 207/526-4423 or 207/526-4282, 11am-3pm Mon.-Fri., June-late Sept.), a labor of love created by brothers Ted and Galen Turner. They've collected artifacts from the island's rich fishing heritage, and are full of stories and lore. Admission is free, but donations are appreciated. While here, ask for directions to the nearby Life Along the Shore ecology exhibit. Delve into more of the island's history at Swan's Island Library (451 Atlantic Rd., 207/526-4330), which has exhibits.

Lighthouse Park/Hockamock Head Light (207/526-4025, www.burntcoatharbor-light.com), officially called Burnt Coat Harbor Light, in Lighthouse Park, is on the island's west side. The distinctive square lighthouse, built in 1872 and now automated, sits on a rocky promontory overlooking Burnt Coat Harbor, Harbor Island, lobster boat traffic, and crashing surf. Visitors can view art and history exhibits in the keeper's house, climb the light tower (call for current days and hours), and admire the oil house and bell house from the exterior. A short ADA-accessible trail makes it easy for anyone to appreciate the gorgeous views from the headland summit.

Hiking

Looping around Hockamock Head are 1.8 miles of moderate, signed hiking trails, including a short ADA-accessible one, and two beaches. Park at the lighthouse, and pick up a trail map at the information kiosk. The Long Point Beach Trail, accessible from the lower parking area, passes through a spruce forest and traverses a bog bridge before climbing to the lighthouse. A 200-foot ADA-accessible path continues to the summit. From here, you can see Marshall Island, Merchant's Row, and Isle au Haut from the summit. Continue looping back to the parking area through the forest. Access the Burying Point Trail from the middle section of the parking area. It drops steeply to a clearing; keep left and follow the bank to Burying Point Beach. The return loops back through the forest, with a spur to the lighthouse complex. While hiking, keep an eye out for bald eagles, as there are nine known nesting pairs on the island. An accessible vault toilet is available.

Swimming

Ask for directions to one of three prime island swimming spots: Carrying Place Beach and Fine Sand Beach (both saltwater) or Quarry Pond (freshwater). Carrying Place Beach is easiest to reach by car. Fine Sand Beach is on the west side of Toothacher Cove; you'll have to navigate about a mile of unpaved road to get there, and then hoof about 10 minutes down a rough trail through the woods, but it's worth the trouble. Be prepared for chilly water, however. Quarry Pond is in Minturn, on the opposite side of Burnt Coat Harbor from the lighthouse. Follow the one-way loop around, and you'll see it on your right as you're rounding the far side of the loop.

Events

A Swans Island summer highlight is the Sweet Chariot Music Festival (www.sweetchari-otmusicfestival.com), a three-night midweek extravaganza in early August. Windjammers arrive from Camden and Rockland, enthusiasts show up on their private boats, and the island's Oddfellows Hall is standing room only for three evenings of folk singing, storytelling, and impromptu high jinks. About 3:30pm the first two days, musicians go from boat to boat in Burnt Coat Harbor, entertaining with sea chanteys. Along the route from harbor to concert, enterprising local kids peddle lemonade, homemade brownies, and kitschy craft items. It's all very festive but definitely a "boat thing," not very convenient for anyone without water transport.

Food

Dining choices are few. TIMS Takeout (40 North Rd., 207/526-4410, www.tims-swans-island.com, 10am-5pm daily, $5-20) and TIMS The Island Market & Supply (207/526-4043) are the places to go for everything, from burgers to pizza. There are usually a few take-out shops operating on the island each summer.

Accommodations

If you want to stay over, don't expect to find a bed on the island during the festival unless you know someone. Other times, there's The Harbor Watch Inn (111 Minturn Rd.,

The Maine Sea Coast Mission

The Maine Sea Coast Mission's *Sunbeam V*

Remote islands and other isolated communities along Maine's rugged coastline may still have a church, but few have a full-time minister; fewer yet have a health-care provider. Yet these communities aren't entirely shut off from either preaching or medical assistance.

Since 1905, the **Maine Sea Coast Mission** (207/288-5097, www.seacoastmission.org), a nondenominational, nonprofit organization rooted in a Christian ministry, has offered a lifeline to these communities. The mission, based in Bar Harbor, serves nearly 2,800 people on eight different islands, including Frenchboro, the Cranberries, Swans, and Isle au Haut, as well as others living in remote coastal locations on the mainland. Its numerous much-needed services include a Christmas program; in-school, after-school, and summer school programs; emergency financial assistance; food assistance; a thrift shop; ministers for island and coastal communities; scholarships; and health services.

Many of these services are delivered via the mission's *Sunbeam V,* a 75-foot diesel boat that has no limitations on when it can travel and few on where it can travel. In winter, it even serves as an icebreaker, clearing harbors and protecting boats from ice damage. During your travels in the Acadia region, you might see the *Sunbeam V* homeported in Northeast Harbor or on its rounds.

A nurse and a minister usually travel on the ship. The minister may conduct services on the island or on the boat, which also functions as a gathering place for fellowship, meals, and meetings. The minister also reaches out to those in need and those who are marginalized or ill, and often helps with island funerals. Onboard telemedicine equipment enables the nurse to provide much-needed health care, including screening clinics for diabetes, cholesterol, and prostate and skin cancer; flu and pneumonia vaccines; and tetanus shots.

The mission welcomes donations and volunteers. You can make a difference.

207/526-4563, www.swansisland.com, $1125-165). Two of the motel's refurbished four spacious and clean guest rooms have kitchen facilities. Two have water views; all have Wi-Fi.

Another possibility is the waterfront

Carter House (207/266-0958 or 207/526-4198, $95), which has views over the Mill Pond and out to the harbor. Breakfast is included, and guests have kitchen privileges. Islander Nancy Carter is a great source of info about the island.

Getting There and Around

Swans Island is a six-mile, 40-minute trip on the state-operated car ferry *Captain Henry Lee,* operated by the **Maine State Ferry Service** (207/244-3254, daily recorded info 800/491-4883, http://maine.gov/mdot/ferry/swansisland). The ferry makes up to six round-trips a day, the first from Bass Harbor at 7:30am Monday-Saturday and at 9am Sunday, and the last from Swans Island at 4:30pm. Round-trip fares are around $17.50 adults, $6.25 ages 6-17; bikes are $16.50 adults, $11.25 children; cars are $38.50. Only four reservations are accepted for vehicles; be in line at least 15 minutes before departure or you risk forfeiting your space.

To reach the Bass Harbor ferry terminal on Mount Desert Island, follow the distinctive blue signs, marked "Swans Island Ferry," along Routes 102 and 102A.

Southwest Cycle (370 Main St., Southwest Harbor, 207/244-5856 or 800/649-5856, www.southwestcycle.com, year-round) rents bikes by the day and week. It also has ferry schedules and Swans Island maps. For the early-morning ferry, you'll have to pick up bikes the day before; be sure to reserve them if you're doing this in July-August.

Schoodic Peninsula

Slightly more than 3,437 of Acadia National

Park's acres are on the mainland Schoodic Peninsula—the rest are all on islands, including Mount Desert. World-class scenery and the relative lack of congestion, even at the height of summer, make Schoodic a special Acadia destination.

The Schoodic Peninsula is just one of several "fingers" of land that point seaward as part of eastern Hancock County and western Washington County. Sneak around to the eastern side of Frenchman Bay to see this region from a whole new perspective. One hour from Acadia National Park's visitors center, you'll find Acadia's mountains silhouetted against the sunset, the surf slamming onto Schoodic Point, and the peace of a calmer lifestyle.

Highlights

Look for ★ to find recommended sights, activities, dining, and lodging.

★ **Schoodic Point:** Surf crashes against slabs of pink granite on the remote tip of the Schoodic Peninsula (page 143).

★ **Schoodic Loop:** Drive or bike around the tip of the peninsula and enjoy world-class scenery (page 144).

★ **Schoodic Head Loop:** Although you can drive almost to the summit, it's far more rewarding—and peaceful—to hike it (page 147).

★ **Donnell Pond Public Reserved Land:** A treasure for outdoors enthusiasts, this reserve includes mountains to hike and ponds to paddle and fish, plus sandy beaches and backwoods campsites (page 152).

★ **Petit Manan Point:** Birds, birds, birds, as well as easy hiking with great views are your rewards for visiting this part of the Maine Coastal Islands National Wildlife Refuge (page 158).

★ **Hancock and Sullivan Gallery Tour:** Talented artists and artisans are plentiful here. Visiting their off-the-beaten-path shops and studios is a perfect way to explore the region and score some great souvenirs (page 169).

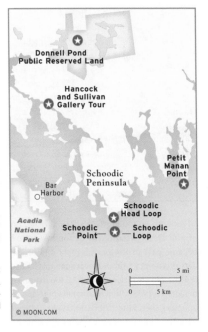

Schoodic Peninsula

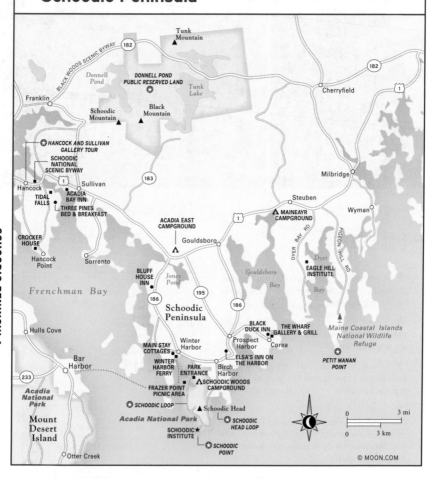

As with so much of Acadia's acreage on Mount Desert Island, the Schoodic section became part of the park largely due to the deft diplomacy and perseverance of George B. Dorr. No obstacle ever seemed too daunting to Dorr. In 1928, when the owners objected to donating their land to a national park tagged with the Lafayette name (geopolitics of the time being involved), Dorr even managed to obtain congressional approval for the 1929 name change to Acadia National Park—and Schoodic was part of the deal.

This section of Acadia National Park isn't as awe-inspiring as that on Mount Desert, but it's no less powerful. Even though it's on the mainland, it feels more remote, and the landscape has a raw edge, with too-frequent fog shrouding the stunted and scraggly spruce

---

Previous: a view from Schoodic section of Acadia National Park; Schoodic Peninsula; Corea Harbor.

clinging to its pink granite shores. The additions of the Schoodic Woods Campground, a parking lot, and a welcome center have increased Schoodic's popularity, but it remains pretty quiet here.

While you're this far east, explore a couple other natural treasures: the Petit Manan and Corea Heath sections of the Maine Coastal Islands National Wildlife Refuge, spectacular spots for bird-watching; and the Donnell Pond Public Reserved Land, an inland trove of lakes and peaks that lures hikers and anglers. Although beyond any traditional definition of the Acadia region, they're well worth discovering. Better yet, you can loop them together via two scenic byways, one national and one state.

PLANNING YOUR TIME

While most visitors still arrive by car or RV, the Island Explorer bus service's Schoodic Route operates between late June and Labor Day and connects with ferry service from Bar Harbor. If you want to tour beyond the bus

and ferry routes, you'll need a car. There's much to see: Besides the jaw-dropping scenery, the region's calling cards are outdoor recreation and shopping the artists' and artisans' studios tucked here and there.

The biggest attractions here are the spectacular vignettes and vistas—of offshore lighthouses, distant mountains, close-in islands, and unchanged villages. Check out each small and large finger of land: Hancock Point, Sorrento, and Winter Harbor's Grindstone Neck. Circle the Gouldsboro Peninsula, including Prospect Harbor, and detour to Corea. Meander down the Petit Manan Peninsula to the Maine Coastal Islands National Wildlife Refuge. If you still have enough time, head inland and follow Route 182, a designated scenic highway noodling between Hancock and Cherryfield, making it a point to visit the Donnell Pond Public Reserved Land. En route, be sure to dip in and out of at least some of the artisan's studios and galleries that dot the byways. Accomplish all this and you'll have a fine sense of place.

Schoodic Section of Acadia National Park

The Schoodic section of Acadia National Park has an entirely different feel from the main part of the park on Mount Desert. It's much smaller, far less busy, and feels more rugged, wild, and remote. It provides fewer recreational opportunities, but it's magnificent and well worth visiting. Here you'll find rare stands of jack pine and maritime shrubland communities. It's also an important breeding, nesting, and stopover for migratory songbirds.

Although still far less visited than the Mount Desert Island section of the park, Schoodic is gaining in popularity. If you can, aim for an early-morning or late-afternoon visit.

SIGHTS

★ Schoodic Point

The highlight of this part of the park is Schoodic Point, with vistas that seemingly stretch all the way to Spain. The point is at the end of a two-way spur off the Schoodic Loop Road. Although crowds gather at the height of summer, especially when the surf is raging, the tiered parking lot seldom fills up. Check local newspapers for the time of high tide and try to arrive here then; the word *awesome* is overused, but it certainly describes Schoodic

Point's surf performance on the rugged pink granite. The setting sun makes it even more brilliant. This area is open 6am-10pm only. There are restrooms near the parking lot.

If you've brought children, keep them well back from the water; a rogue wave can sweep them off the rocks all too easily, which has happened. Picnics are great here (make sure you bring a bag for litter), and so are the tide pools at mid-tide and low tide. Birding is spectacular during spring and fall migrations.

And on the subject of birds, you'll see a sign here: Do Not Feed Gulls or Other Wildlife. Heed it—but even if you *don't* feed the gulls, they can threaten your lunch if you're having a picnic here. They'll swoop down shamelessly and snatch it away before you even realize they've spotted you. From extensive practice with unsuspecting visitors, they've become adept at thievery.

★ Schoodic Loop

The major sights of Acadia's Schoodic section lie along the six-mile one-way road that meanders counterclockwise around the tip of the Schoodic Peninsula. You'll discover official and unofficial picnic areas, hiking trailheads, offshore lighthouses, a welcome center with exhibits, and turnouts with scenic vistas. From this side of Frenchman Bay, the views of Mount Desert Island's summits are gorgeous, rising beyond islands sprinkled here and there. Although also named the Park Loop Road, this route is best referred to as the Schoodic Loop, to distinguish it from the one on Mount Desert Island. Begin at the **Schoodic Woods Campground Welcome Center,** where you can pick up information and leave your car to explore via bicycle or the Island Explorer bus.

While a car may seem the most convenient way to see the sights, you'll actually be better served looping via bicycle (rentals available at the ferry dock or near the park entry road) or by riding the bus. This section of the park is gaining in popularity, and the increase in cars is straining the designated parking areas along the loop. Once you're on the one-way

section, parking is only allowed in designated pull-offs and parking lots, and these often are filled. With a bike, you can stop where and when you want. The bus picks up at non-designated stops, if you flag it down. If you do drive, be especially vigilant around bicyclists; many families include young or novice cyclers. Note: Neither RVs nor trailers are allowed on the loop beyond the campground.

The first landmark is **Frazer Point Picnic Area,** with lovely vistas, picnic tables, and wheelchair-accessible restrooms. Other spots are fine for picnics, but this is the only official one. The area takes its name from Thomas Frazer, a free African American and the first recorded nonnative resident of Winter Harbor, who operated a saltworks here and was listed in the 1790 census.

From the picnic area, the road becomes one-way; no parking is allowed in the right lane. There are periodic pullouts, but these generally hold only two or three cars. Despite the fact that this is far from the busiest section of Acadia, it can still be frustrating not to be able to find a space in the summer months. The best advice is to stay in the area and do this loop early in the morning or later in the afternoon or via bicycle. The late September–early October foliage is gorgeous, but traffic does increase then. While you're driving, if you see a viewpoint you like with room to pull off, stop; it's a long way around to return.

Drive roughly 1.5 miles from the picnic area to **Raven's Head,** an unmarked, Thunder Hole-type cliff with sheer drops to the churning surf below and fabulous views. There are no fences, and the cliffs are eroded, so it's not a good place for little ones. The trail is unsigned, but there's a small pullout on the left side of the road opposite it. Be extremely careful here, stay on the path (the environment is very fragile and erosion is a major problem), and stay well away from the cliff's edge.

At 2.2 miles past the picnic area, watch for a narrow, unpaved road on the left, across from an open beach vista. It winds for one mile (keep left at the fork) up to a tiny

Lighthouses

The best known of the Acadia region's coastal beacons is Bass Harbor Head Light, part of Acadia National Park. Perched high on a promontory overlooking the entrance to Bass Harbor, it flashes a distinctive red beacon, automated since 1974. To visit the light, take Route 102 to the bottom (southern end) of Mount Desert Island, then take Route 102A and watch for signs. The setting is spectacular, and the grounds are accessible during daylight hours. Be sure to descend the stairs toward the shore and view the 26-foot tower from below.

Roughly from north to south (strictly speaking, though, it's east to west), here are some of the other still-operating lighthouses in the Acadia region. All are automated; most are accessible only by boat. None of the light towers are accessible to the public. Four lights in this area—Winter Harbor, Blue Hill, Dyce's Head, and Pumpkin Island—are no longer used as navigational beacons, although their towers still stand. Here are some of the more likely ones you may come across in the region.

Prospect Harbor Light

- On a clear day, you can spot Petit Manan Light from the tip of Petit Manan Point, on the mainland Petit Manan section of the Maine Coastal Islands National Wildlife Refuge. Built in 1817 and rebuilt in 1855, it rises 119 feet from its base. It's located 3.5 miles offshore, directly south of Milbridge. Some excursion boats cruise by the island, which is also home to puffins.

- Prospect Harbor Light, established in 1850, rebuilt in 1891, and automated in 1951, sits on the tip of Prospect Point. It can be viewed across the harbor from Route 186, or you can drive to the gate for a closer look.

- Clearly visible (on a clear day, that is) from Acadia's Park Loop Road, Egg Rock Light was built in 1875 on bleak, barren Egg Rock, protecting the entrance to Frenchman Bay. The squat, square keeper's house, topped by a square light tower, resembles no other Maine lighthouse. The light, now under the aegis of the Maine Coastal Islands National Wildlife Refuge, was automated in 1976.

- The Cranberry Isles mail boat out of Northeast Harbor passes dramatically located Bear Island Light on its daily rounds. Located on Acadia National Park land at the entrance to Northeast Harbor, the light tower and its keeper's house are privately leased in exchange for upkeep. There's no public access to the island. The automated light has been a privately maintained navigational aid since 1989. The present tower was built in 1889.

- Baker Island Light, built in 1828 during John Quincy Adams's presidency and rebuilt in 1855, is accessible only by boat, and then via a boardwalk. The brick tower rises 43 feet. Most of the 123-acre island, one of the five Cranberry Isles, is part of Acadia National Park. Charles W. Eliot, president of Harvard University 1869-1909 and one of the prime movers behind the establishment of the park, shone a small spotlight on Baker Island when he published a sympathetic short memoir of a 19th-century Baker Island farmer and fisherman. Entitled *John Gilley, One of the Forgotten Millions,* and reprinted in 1989 by Bar Harbor's Acadia Press, it's a must-read—a poignant story of a hardscrabble pioneering life.

Educating for the Future

The Schoodic section of Acadia National Park is well on the way to becoming a world-class center for the study of science and nature, thanks to a history of benefactors dating back to the early 19th century. Maine native and Wall Street tycoon John G. Moore once owned most of Schoodic Point. In 1927, George Dorr persuaded Moore's heirs to donate the land to the Hancock County Trustees of Public Reservations, with the stipulation that the land be used as a public park and for the "promotion of biological and other scientific research." Seven years later, more than 2,000 acres of the peninsula were donated to Acadia National Park.

The timing was perfect. John D. Rockefeller Jr. was then working with the National Park Service to construct the Park Loop Road on Mount Desert Island. The U.S. Naval Radio Station on Otter Point was in the way, so Rockefeller, working with Dorr, helped the National Park Service work with the U.S. Navy to relocate the station to Schoodic Point. Six buildings were constructed. Most noteworthy is Rockefeller Hall, a French Norman Revival-style mansion designed by New York architect Grosvenor Atterbury, who used a similar design for the park's carriage road gatehouses on Mount Desert Island.

In 1935, the U.S. Naval Radio Station at Schoodic Point was commissioned, and by the late 20th century, the 100-acre campus comprised more than 35 buildings and was home to 350 U.S. Navy employees. When the station closed in 2002, the land was returned to the park for use as a research and education center.

It took 10 years and millions of dollars to transform the former base. The campus now offers housing and dining facilities for individual researchers, groups, and conferences, as well as classrooms, laboratories, and a modern 124-seat auditorium. A renovated Rockefeller Hall, listed in the National Register of Historic Places, now serves as Schoodic's welcome center, with exhibits highlighting Schoodic's ecology and history, the former navy base's radio and cryptologic operations, and current research programs. Credit for the renovations goes to local benefactor Edith Robb Dixon, who donated $1 million in the name of her late husband, Fitz Eugene Dixon Jr.

Schoodic Institute at Acadia National Park (207/288-1310, www.schoodicinstitute. org) is the nonprofit that partners with Acadia to manage the campus and advance science and education in Acadia and across the National Park system. Schoodic Institute connects education with research, while managers at Acadia National Park rely on the research to restore Acadia's ecosystems and improve their resiliency in the face of rapid environmental changes.

Schoodic Institute offers education and research programs aimed not only at scientists and researchers but also at students and teachers. It also hosts programs for the general public, such as guided birding tours. The institute also hosts Acadia National Park's artist-in-residence program and works with the park to present programs, lectures, special events, and ranger-led activities; check the online calendar for current offerings. Among these are "bio blitzes," in which teams of specialists and volunteers research the park's plant and animal species in minute detail. In 2013-2014, a two-year blitz focused on beetles found more than 100 species never previously identified in the park. In 2015, the blitz collected approximately 300 species of wasps, bees, and ants. Preliminary results from 2016 blitz recorded 249 species of butterflies and moths.

parking circle, from which you can follow the trail (signposted Schoodic Trails) to the open ledges on 440-foot **Schoodic Head.** From the circle, there's already a glimpse of the view, but it gets much better. If you bear right at the road fork, you'll come to a grassy parking area with access to the Alder Trail (over to the Blueberry Hill parking lot) and the Schoodic Head Trail. That said, don't use this parking area as a hiking base; leave it for those who don't have the time, inclination, or ability to tackle the trails.

Continue on the Schoodic Loop Road and hang a right onto a short, two-way spur to **Schoodic Point.** On your right is the **Schoodic Institute** campus (207/288-1310, www.schoodicinstitute.org), on the site of a former top-secret U.S. Navy base that became part of the park in 2002. At the entrance is a small info center (with ADA-accessible restroom), staffed by volunteers and park rangers. Continue up the road to the restored **Rockefeller Welcome Center** (10am-4pm daily late May-mid-Oct., 10am-4pm Mon.-Fri. mid-Oct.-late May). Inside are exhibits highlighting Schoodic's ecology and history, the former navy base's radio and cryptologic operations, and current research programs. The Schoodic Institute also offers ranger-led activities, lectures by researchers or nationally known experts addressing environmental topics related to the park and its surroundings, and other programs and events. Check the online calendar for current opportunities.

After touring the campus, continue out to **Schoodic Point,** the highlight of the drive, with surf crashing onto big slabs of pink granite. Be extremely cautious here; chances of rescue are slim if a rogue wave sweeps someone offshore. In peak season, you may have to make a loop or two of the parking lot to score a space. Alternatively, park at the Schoodic Institute and walk 0.4 mile to the point.

From Schoodic Point, return to the Loop Road. Look to the right and you'll see Little Moose Island, which can be accessed at low tide. Be careful, though, not to get stranded here—ask at the info center for safe crossing times. Continue about one mile past the Schoodic Point/Loop Road intersection to the **Blueberry Hill** parking area, a moorlike setting where the low growth allows almost 180-degree views of the bay and islands. There are a few trails in this area—all eventually converging on **Schoodic Head,** the highest point on the peninsula. (Don't confuse this with Schoodic Mountain, which is well north of here.) Across and up the road a bit (a pullout on the right side holds about three cars) is the trailhead for the 180-foot-high **Anvil headland.**

As you continue along this stretch of road, keep your eyes peeled for eagles soaring above. There's a nest on the northern end of Rolling Island; you can see it with binoculars from some of the roadside pullouts.

From Blueberry Hill, continue 1.2 miles to a pullout for the East Trail, the shortest and most direct route to Schoodic Head. From here, it's about another mile to the park exit, in Wonsqueak Harbor. It's another two miles to the intersection with Route 186 in Birch Harbor.

HIKING
Schoodic Section of Acadia National Park

An 8.1-mile network of hiking trails laces the Schoodic section of the park. Serious hikers should park at the campground welcome center and begin there. The Blueberry Hill parking area is most convenient for most other trails, but this lot can fill. Consider parking at the welcome center and taking the bus to the trailhead. Hikers, walkers, and bicyclists should purchase the 50¢ trail system map at the center.

★ SCHOODIC HEAD LOOP

Distance: 2.4 miles round-trip
Duration: Varies with route; 1-2 hours
Elevation gain: 440 feet
Effort: Moderate, some steep sections
Trailhead: Blueberry Hill parking area, Schoodic Loop

The Schoodic Head Loop comprises three connecting trails, and it can be hiked clockwise or counterclockwise from the trailhead. If time is tight, choose just one trail to hike. The clockwise route begins with the easiest terrain and ends with a downhill scramble over a steep and rocky hillside. It's tough on the knees, and you have to be very careful with your footing in this direction. If you hike it counterclockwise, beginning with the Anvil Trail, you'll get the toughest terrain out of the way first.

You can access the loop at various points, but the most parking is at the Blueberry Hill parking area. The easy one-mile Alder Trail, which is especially popular for birding, departs from just south of the parking lot entrance and connects through the woods and some marshy areas to the unmarked Ranger

Schoodic Section of Acadia National Park

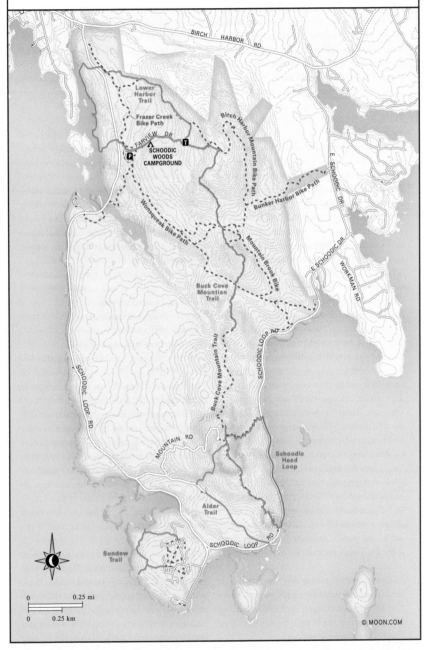

BIRCH HARBOR RD

Lower Harbor Trail

Frazer Creek Bike Path

FARVIEW DR

SCHOODIC WOODS CAMPGROUND

Birch Harbor Mountain Bike Path

Bunker Harbor Bike Path

Womarqueak Bike Path

Mountain Brook Bike

E SCHOODIC DR

E SCHOODIC DR

WORKMAN RD

Buck Cova Mountain Trail

Buck Cove Mountain Trail

SCHOODIC LOOP RD

SCHOODIC LOOP RD

MOUNTAIN RD

Schoodic Head Loop

Alder Trail

SCHOODIC LOOP RD

Sundew Trail

0   0.25 mi
0   0.25 km

© MOON.COM

Cabin Road; head left for about 50 yards and watch for the Schoodic Head Trail marker.

The moderate Schoodic Head Trail climbs for 0.3 mile, beginning in the woods and emerging onto ledges as it nears the summit. The views are expansive and well worth any effort.

The 1.1-mile Anvil Trail descends over moderate terrain with a few steep sections. A highlight here is the Anvil promontory, a rocky knoll. Whichever way you choose to hike, be extremely careful on the Anvil Trail, as the terrain is rugged, with lots of roots and loose rocks.

A fourth trail, the 0.5-mile East Trail, descends from the summit and emerges on the Schoodic Loop Road about one mile beyond the Blueberry Hill parking area. This is the shortest, steepest, and most direct route to the summit and can be hiked independently or looped in with the other trails.

BUCK COVE MOUNTAIN TRAIL
Distance: 2.2-4.2 miles, one-way
Duration: 2-4.5 hours
Elevation gain: 440 feet
Effort: Moderate to difficult
Trailhead: Schoodic Woods Campground
From the day-use parking area, walk up the campground road to the group area to find the trailhead. The blue-blazed trail winds through cedar groves and spruce and jack pine woodlands, crosses bike paths, threads wetlands, and passes cliffs and even a cave.

From the trailhead, it's 2.2 miles to Buck Cove Mountain's 224-foot summit. From there the trail continues another mile and ascends the north face of Schoodic Head, where it connects with the Schoodic Head trails. It's another mile to the Blueberry Hill parking area, a total of 4.2 miles one-way; you can return via the Island Explorer bus. Or consider doing it in the opposite direction: Take the bus to Blueberry Hill, and get the steepest hiking done early and arrive back at your car.

LOWER HARBOR TRAIL
Distance: 1.5 miles one way

Duration: 1-1.5 hours
Elevation gain: Minimal
Effort: Easy
Trailhead: Park at the welcome center and walk down the access road. The trailhead is across the main road. Alternatively, you can create a loop by accessing the trail from the bike path system.
From the trailhead, follow the path northwest along the shoreline and through pine forests. Keep an eye out for birds along the way. When you reach the end, return the way you came.

SUNDEW TRAIL
Distance: 1 mile each way including spurs
Duration: 1-2 hours
Elevation gain: Minimal
Effort: Easy
Trailhead: To find it, take the Schoodic Loop Road, turn right to Schoodic Point, right again at the Schoodic Institute campus and stay straight on Acadia Drive. Follow signs to Moore Auditorium and park. Look for the trail sign at the back of the parking lot.
Sundew is an easy and wonderful family walk through dense woodlands. It has spurs that access pink granite shores offering great views. Don't tell too many others, but this is an excellent spot for watching the sunset, just make sure to bring a flashlight for the hike back. There's a good chance you'll have the trail to yourself, as it's not as well known as Schoodic's other trails.

There are two trailheads for Sundew. The other trailhead is by the picnic pavilion behind the Commons. You can hike this out and back or make it a loop by walking through campus from one trailhead to the other.

BICYCLING
If you have a bike, try to pedal the Schoodic Loop Road early or late in the day—especially if you're doing a family outing in which everyone clusters together. It's a lovely bike route, but the shoulders on this peninsula are soft and sandy and not great for bikes. Keep to the right and use the road, not the shoulders. Leave your car at the Schoodic Woods Campground welcome center and do a counterclockwise loop through the park using the

new nonmotorized paths to complete the roughly eight-mile trip without venturing onto Route 186. If you are arriving by ferry and want to avoid pedaling between the village and park, take the Island Explorer bus to the campground and begin there. It's a fine day trip. Do purchase a Schoodic Trail System Map (50¢) at the campground welcome center.

Many of the park's 8.3 miles of signed bike paths are steep and winding, but panoramic views reward your efforts.

Sea Schoodic Kayak and Bike (8 Duck Pond Rd., Winter Harbor, 833/724-6634, www.seaschoodic.com) rents bicycles (from $30/day adult, $25 child bike). It's wise to make advance reservations.

ENTERTAINMENT AND EVENTS
Ranger Programs
Ranger-led programs in the Schoodic section of the park include guided bird walks, naturalist walks, and hikes. There are also evening campground programs and special offerings for children such as a story hour, touch tank, and a junior naturalist program. Check the park calendar for current offerings.

Schoodic Institute
The Schoodic Institute (Schoodic Point, 207/288-1310, www.schoodicinstitute.org) offers lectures, usually by researchers or nationally known experts, addressing environmental topics related to the park and its surroundings. It also offers other programs and events, including ranger-led activities. Check the online calendar for current opportunities.

ACCOMMODATIONS AND CAMPING
Visitors attending a program at the Schoodic Institute (Schoodic Point, 207/288-1310, www.schoodicinstitute.org) are eligible to stay in accommodations on its grounds. These include a bunkhouse, duplex suites, cabins, and apartments, with rates ranging $60-160, as well as a few handsomely renovated apartments in Rockefeller Hall, from $250.

Acadia National Park's 90-site ★ Schoodic Woods Campground (Park Loop Rd., Schoodic Peninsula, 877/444-6777 or 518/885-3639 international, www.recreation.gov, credit or debit card required, $22-40) is sited on an approximately 1,400-acre property over which Acadia National Park holds a conservation easement. It's located about a mile south of Route 186, north of the Frazer Point Picnic Area. Sites include remote walk-in tenting, drive-in tenting, and RV sites with water and electricity. There are no showers, but ask about availability locally. There is also a welcome center and an amphitheater with National Park Service programming. Hiking trails connect it to Schoodic Head, and nonmotorized paths link the east and west sides of the peninsula.

INFORMATION
Information about Acadia National Park on the Schoodic Peninsula is available at the welcome center at the Schoodic Woods Campground and Rockefeller Welcome Center on the Schoodic Institute campus, both on the Schoodic Loop, but neither operates as a full-blown visitors center.

On Mount Desert Island, info is available at the park's Hulls Cove Visitors Center.

To plan ahead, see the Acadia website (www.nps.gov/acad), where you can download a Schoodic map. To see the Island Explorer bus schedule for Schoodic as well as all of Mount Desert Island, visit www.exploreacadia.com.

GETTING THERE AND AROUND
The Schoodic Section of Acadia National Park is about 26 miles via Routes 1 and 186 from Ellsworth. It's about 20 miles or 30 minutes to Milbridge, on the Down East Coast.

1: Schoodic section in Acadia National Park
2: bicycling Acadia's Schoodic section
3: the welcome center at Schoodic Woods Campground 4: Sundew Trail

Car

From Ellsworth, stay north (keep left) on Route 1 from where it splits with Route 3. Continue north on Route 1 for about 16 miles, through Hancock and Sullivan, until you reach Gouldsboro. From Route 1 in Gouldsboro, the park entrance is eight miles. Take Route 186 south to Winter Harbor. Drive through town, heading east, then turn right at the park entrance sign.

To reach the park boundary from Bar Harbor, take Route 3 north to the head of Mount Desert Island, then across Mount Desert Narrows to Trenton. The usual route is to continue to a congested intersection at the edge of Ellsworth, where you'll pick up Route 1 north (turn right) and continue as above. But you can avoid some of the traffic congestion on Route 3 in Trenton by ducking east via Route 204 toward Lamoine and its state park, and then back up to Route 1 via Mud Creek Road.

Passenger Ferries

Although Winter Harbor is about 43 miles or about 75 minutes from Bar Harbor by car, it's only about 7 miles by water.

The Bar Harbor Ferry (207/288-2984, www.barharborferry.com, round-trip $28 adults, $20 children, $6 bicycle) operates at least four times daily mid-June-late September between the Bar Harbor Inn Pier (7 Newport Dr., Bar Harbor) and the Schoodic Marine Center (88 Sargent St., Winter Harbor), and coordinates with the Island Explorer (www.exploreacadia.com) bus's summertime Schoodic route, Route 8. The ferry doesn't carry e-bikes. Pets are welcome.

The ferry's summer schedule is coordinated with the Island Explorer bus's summertime Schoodic route, so you can board the ferry in Bar Harbor, pick up the bus at the dock in Winter Harbor, and be shuttled along the Schoodic Loop. Stop where you like for a picnic or a hike, and then board a later bus. Take the last bus back to the ferry and return to Bar Harbor. It makes for a super car-free excursion.

Bus

The free Island Explorer (www.exploreacadia.com) bus Route 8 covers the lower part of the peninsula, from Winter Harbor through Prospect Harbor and including the Schoodic section of the park. The bus operates roughly every half hour 8:30am-5pm late June-August, and hourly in the spring and fall. The Island Explorer bus connects with the ferries from Bar Harbor, making it possible to explore this section of the park while staying on Mount Desert Island, without driving all the way around to reach it. It's an efficient and environmentally friendly way to go.

Schoodic Parks and Preserves

Acadia National Park is why you're here, of course, but the region also has many parks and preserves where you can slip away with little company. Birders, especially, won't want to miss Petit National Point, a division of the Maine Coastal Islands National Wildlife Reserve that specializes in restoring seabird populations. The Donnell Pond Public Reserved Land comprises coastal lakes and mountains that offer exceptional hiking, paddling, fishing, and camping. Hike here for sweeping views over Mount Desert Island and Frenchman Bay. And the very active Frenchman Bay Conservancy, a local land trust, has preserved numerous lands offering hiking and coastal access.

★ DONNELL POND PUBLIC RESERVED LAND

More than 15,000 acres of remote forests, ponds, lakes, and mountains have been

Donnell Pond Public Reserved Land

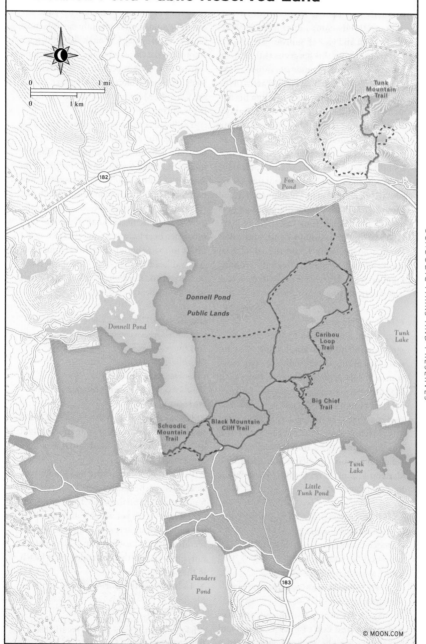

© MOON.COM

preserved for public access in Donnell Pond Public Reserved Land (Maine Bureau of Parks and Lands, 207/827-1818, www.parksandlands.com, hours vary seasonally), north and east of Sullivan. Developers had their eyes on this gorgeous real estate in the 1980s, but preservationists rallied to the cause. Outright purchase of 7,316 acres in the Spring River Lake area came through the far-sighted Land for Maine's Future program. Now the reserve includes five peaks taller than 900 feet, a 1,940-acre wetland, and 35 miles of freshwater shoreline, making it especially rich for bird-watchers. Hikers can climb Schoodic, Black, Caribou, and Tunk Mountains for expansive views taking in Frenchman Bay and Mount Desert Island; paddlers and anglers have Donnell Pond, Tunk Lake, Spring River Lake, Long Pond, Round Pond, and Little Pond, among others. Route 182, an official scenic highway, snakes through the Donnell Pond preserve. Hunting is permitted, so take special care during hunting season.

Hiking

Why would a guidebook focused on Acadia send you inland for hiking? Views! The rewards for hiking these peaks are open ledge summits delivering panoramic views over island-studded Frenchman Bay, the rounded peaks of Mount Desert Island, and the Down East coastline. The hiking isn't easy here, but it isn't technical, and the options are varied. The interconnecting trail system takes in Schoodic Mountain, Black Mountain, and Caribou Mountain on Donnell Pond Public Reserved Land.

SCHOODIC MOUNTAIN

Distance: 2.8 miles round-trip
Duration: 2 hours
Elevation gain: 800 feet
Effort: Moderate to difficult
Trailhead: Schoodic Beach Parking Area, off Route 183, Franklin

To make a day of it, pack a picnic and take a swimsuit (and don't forget a camera and binoculars for the summit views). On a brilliantly clear day, you'll see Baxter State Park's Katahdin, Maine's western mountains, the peaks of Acadia National Park, and the ocean beyond. And in late July-early August, blueberries are abundant on the summit. Such rewards make this is a popular hike, so don't expect to be alone, especially on fall weekends when the foliage colors are spectacular. Follow the Schoodic Mountain Loop clockwise, heading west from the trailhead.

Trailheads can be accessed by either boat or vehicle. To reach the vehicle-access trailhead for Schoodic Mountain from Route 1 in East Sullivan, drive 4.5 miles northeast on Route 183 (Tunk Lake Rd.). Cross the Down East Sunrise Trail, a former railroad bed, and turn left at the Donnell Pond sign onto the gravel Schoodic Beach Road. Go about 0.25 mile, then bear left at the fork, continuing 2.3 miles to the Schoodic Beach Parking Area and trailhead for Schoodic Mountain, Black Mountain, and Caribou Mountain, and a trail to Schoodic Beach.

BLACK MOUNTAIN CLIFFS LOOP

Distance: 3 miles round-trip
Duration: 2 hours
Elevation gain: 800 feet
Effort: Moderate to difficult
Trailhead: Schoodic Beach Parking Area, off Route 183, Franklin

This trail accesses the western side of Black Mountain. The reward for your efforts might be a refreshing swim in Donnell Pond, so come prepared.

Pass through the parking lot boulder barricade, follow the beach access trail, and look for the trailhead on the right. The trail climbs for 1.2 miles until you reach a junction. Bear left and continue across the cliffs before descending to the beach for an additional 1.3 miles. It's a 0.5-mile return along the beach to the parking area.

To link with the Caribou Loop Trail, go

1: biking and walking paths 2: trail sign 3: hiking Schoodic Mountain in the Donnell Pond Public Reserved Land

1

2

WINTER HBR.

FRAZER PT.
SCHOODIC PT.
BUNKER'S HBR.
WONSQUEAK HBR.

3

straight at the junction and continue 0.6 mile to the Black Mountain summit, which offers 360-degree views.

Follow the directions for the Schoodic Mountain Trail to the Schoodic Beach Parking Area trailhead.

BIG CHIEF TRAIL

Distance: 2.2 miles round-trip
Duration: 2 hours
Elevation gain: 800 feet
Effort: Moderate to difficult
Trailhead: Black Mountain Rd., off Route 183, Franklin

The Big Chief trail takes hikers up the southern slope of Black Mountain. Follow the directions for the Schoodic Mountain Trail to the Schoodic Beach parking lot, but keep right at the fork for Black Mountain Road and continue 2.2 miles to the parking area. The trailhead is just beyond and across the road.

From the trailhead, the path climbs steadily for 0.6 mile through the woods on Donnell Pond Public Reserved Land, leveling out a bit before you reach bald ledges. Follow the signs to continue to the true summit by taking the loop trail around Wizard Pond (which may seem more like Wizard Puddle). The forest in this area is thought to be one of the state's few stands of unlogged, old growth forest. Views take in the forested lands and nearby lakes and peaks, and they extend out to Acadia's peaks.

You can piggyback this hike with Schoodic Mountain, using that trailhead as a base for both climbs. Another possibility is to add Caribou Mountain to this hike. That loop exceeds seven miles, making a full day of hiking.

CARIBOU LOOP TRAIL

Distance: Minimum 7 miles round-trip
Duration: 6-8 hours
Elevation gain: 900 feet
Effort: Difficult to strenuous
Trailhead: Off Route 182, T10 SD, an unorganized township east of Franklin

When you're ready for an all-day hike, consider this backcountry beauty connecting Black and Caribou Mountains. The loop itself is 6.1 miles, but accessing it from the trailhead adds another 0.9 mile each way on the Caribou Mountain Trail. You can also create your own distance, as this loop links to the Schoodic Mountain and Big Chief trailheads.

Find the trailhead on the Dynamite Brook Road, approximately 0.5 mile off Route 182. Follow the path as it steadily climbs Black Mountain. When the trail splits, veer left to reach the summit of Caribou Mountain. Continue along the trail until you start your descent on the east side of the mountain, back toward the fork in the trail. When you reach the fork, bear left, continuing your descent and retracing your steps back to the trailhead.

TUNK MOUNTAIN

Distance: 4.4 miles round-trip
Duration: 4 hours
Elevation gain: 900 feet
Effort: Difficult to strenuous
Trailhead: Off Route 182, T10 SD, an unorganized township east of Franklin

A parking area with a restroom provides access to Tunk Mountain, a locally popular hike that takes in several remote ponds en route to the bald summit. Be sure to take plenty of water and pack a lunch or energy snacks.

From the trailhead, follow the path 0.5 mile until you reach Hidden Ponds Loop. Turn right, onto the loop trail, following it for 1 mile, passing Salmon and Little Long Ponds, before rejoining the main Tunk Mountain trail. Turn right onto the Tunk Mountain trail and continue along the path. Not far beyond the junction with the Hidden Pond trail, the Tunk Mountain trail becomes steep, with stone steps and a set of iron rungs in one spot to assist hikers. (If the weather is marginal, limit your hike to the lower trail.) Another 0.2 mile of trail atop the mountain ridge leads to an overlook on Nature Conservancy property with views to the north of sprawling forests and the Narraguagus River watershed. When you're ready, return the way you came.

Paddling

The Donnell Pond Public Reserved Land's major water bodies are **Donnell Pond** (big enough by most gauges to be called a lake) along with **Tunk Lake** (considered one of Maine's cleanest lakes), **Spring River Lake,** and **Long Pond;** all are accessible for boats (even, alas, powerboats). In early August, Round Mountain, rising a few hundred feet from Long Pond's eastern shore, is a great spot for gathering blueberries and huckleberries.

To reach the boat launch for Donnell Pond from Route 1 in Sullivan, take Route 200 north to Route 182. Turn right and go about 1.5 miles to a right turn just before Swan Brook. Turn and go not quite two miles to the put-in; the road is poor in spots but adequate for a regular vehicle. The Narrows, where you'll put in, is lined with summer cottages ("camps" in the Maine vernacular); keep paddling east to the more open part of the lake.

Continue on Route 182 to find the boat launches for Tunk Lake and Spring River Lake (hand-carry only). Canoeists and kayakers can access Tunk Stream from Spring River Lake.

Swimming

Two beach areas on Donnell Pond are popular for swimming: **Schoodic Beach** and **Redman's Beach.** Both have picnic tables, fire rings, and pit toilets. It's a 0.5-mile hike to Schoodic Beach from the parking lot. Redman's Beach is only accessible by boat. Other pocket beaches are also accessible by boat or via roadside pullouts.

A sand beach on a remote freshwater pond is the reward for a 0.25-mile hike into the Frenchman Bay Conservancy's **Little Tunk Pond Preserve.** From Route 1 in Sullivan, take Route 183 about five miles, then look for the parking area on the left. Just east of that is the **Spring River Lake Beach Day Use Area,** with parking and toilets.

Fishing

It's no surprise that the Donnell Pond Public Reserved Land is a favorite among anglers. Landlocked salmon can be found in Donnell Pond, Tunk Lake, and Spring River Lake. Lake trout (togue) are found in Tunk Lake. For brown trout, cast your line in Long Pond.

Open-water season in Hancock County and adjacent Washington County is April 1-September 30, but after August 16, you must use artificial lures in brooks, rivers, and streams. Check with local wardens for information regarding catch limits and other regulations for specific bodies of water, or call the **Maine Department of Fish and Wildlife** (207/288-8000, www.state.me.us/ifw). A copy of the rules and regulations for Hancock County can be downloaded from the website.

Maine residents younger than 16 and non-residents younger than 12 do not need licenses. Freshwater fishing licenses can be purchased online or at many stores and most town offices. Maine residents pay $25 for the season. Nonresident freshwater licenses for ages 16 and older are $64 for the season, $11 for one day (24 hours), $23 for three days (72 hours), $43 for seven days, and $47 for 15 days. A Maine saltwater recreational fishing registration is required for anyone over the age of 16 and can be added at no extra charge when purchasing a freshwater license. It is required to have your license with you when fishing, whether in fresh- or saltwater.

Camping

A handful of authorized primitive campsites can be found on the Donnell Pond Public Reserved land at **Tunk Lake** (southwestern corner) and **Donnell Pond** (at Schoodic Beach and Redman's Beach), all accessible on foot or by boat. Each has a table, a fire ring, and a nearby pit toilet. Many of the sites are on the lakefront. All are first come, first served with no fees or permits required; they are snapped up quickly on midsummer weekends. You can camp elsewhere within this public land, except in day-use areas, but fires are not permitted at unofficial sites.

★ PETIT MANAN POINT
Maine Coastal Islands National Wildlife Refuge

Restoring and managing colonies of nesting seabirds is the focus of the **Maine Coastal Islands National Wildlife Refuge,** which spans 250 coastal miles and comprises 61 offshore islands and four mainland parcels totaling more than 8,230 acres spread out in five refuges. Occupying a 2,195-acre peninsula in Steuben with 10 miles of rocky shoreline and three offshore islands is the refuge's outstandingly scenic **Petit Manan Point Division** (Pigeon Hill Rd., Steuben, 207/546-2124, www.fws.gov/refuge/maine_coastal_islands, sunrise-sunset daily year-round). The remote location means it sees only about 15,000 visitors per year, and most of those are likely birders, as more than 300 different bird species have been sighted here. Among the other natural highlights are stands of jack pine, coastal raised peatlands, blueberry barrens, freshwater and saltwater marshes, granite shores, and cobble beaches. Note: There is no visitors center.

The moderately easy, 4-mile round-trip Birch Point Trail and the slightly more difficult, 1.8-mile round-trip Hollingsworth Trail loop provide splendid views and opportunities to spot wildlife along the shore and in the fields, forests, and marshlands. The Hollingsworth Trail, leading to the shoreline, is better of the two. This is foggy territory, but on clear days you can see the 123-foot lighthouse on Petit Manan Island, 2.5 miles offshore (for a closer look at the puffin colony there, book a trip on an excursion boat from Milbridge). The Birch Point Trail heads through blueberry fields to Dyer Bay and loops by the waterfront, with much of the trail passing through woods. Family-friendly interpretive signage explains flora and fauna along the route.

If you arrive in August, help yourself to blueberries. Cross-country skiing is permitted in winter.

GETTING THERE

From Route 1, on the east side of Steuben, take Pigeon Hill Road. Six miles down is the first parking lot, for the Birch Point Trail; another 0.5 mile takes you to the parking area for the Hollingsworth Trail. Space is limited.

Pigeon Hill

En route to the Petit Manan Point Division of the Maine Coastal Islands National Wildlife Refuge, you'll pass the trailhead for **Pigeon Hill,** a moderate hike that reaps views taking in Cadillac Mountain, Petit Manan Light, and the island-studded Bold Coast. The 317-foot summit is the highest point on Washington County's coastline. Since acquiring this 170-acre preserve, **Downeast Coastal Conservancy** (207/255-4500, www.downeastcoastalconservancy.org) has enhanced the original trail and added new ones. It now has 1.8 miles of linked trails to the summit ledges; the shortest route, 0.8 mile round-trip, ascends steeply but swiftly. For the best views on the descent, take the Summit Loop and Silver Mine Trails; the latter passes an abandoned silver mine (not much to see but a pile of rocks). This is a primo spot for spying hawks as well as migratory birds, such as spruce grouse, ruffed grouse, dark-eyed juncos, and bald eagles.

GETTING THERE

From Route 1, on the east side of Steuben, take Pigeon Hill Road 4.5 miles. The trailhead is on the western side of the road.

FRENCHMAN BAY CONSERVANCY

The very active **Frenchman Bay Conservancy** (FBC, 207/422-2328, www.frenchmanbay.org) manages more than 8,000 acres of conserved lands with more than 25 miles of trails. The conservancy publishes the free *Short Hikes* map, available locally, which provides directions to several of these. Trail maps can also be downloaded from the website.

Tidal Falls Preserve, Hancock

FBC's eight-acre Tidal Falls Preserve overlooks Frenchman Bay's only reversing falls (roiling water when the tide turns). The best time to view the falls is two hours before or after low tide. Bring a picnic to enjoy on a table overlooking the falls and ledges where seals often slumber. It's an idyllic spot. A concert series takes place here on Monday evenings during the summer; bring a picnic or opt for the food cart. No dogs are permitted.

GETTING THERE

From Route 1 in Hancock, take East Side Road 0.7 miles to Tidal Falls Road. Turn left and drive to the end.

Northern Corea Heath Trail, Gouldsboro

The 600-acre Northern Corea Heath is spectacular property, with divergent ecosystems including bogs, ledges, and mixed-wood forest. *Heath* is a local word for peatland or bog, and this one is a rare coastal plateau bog, distinguished because it rises above the surrounding landscape. Natural features include pitcher plants, sphagnum mosses, rare vascular plants, and jack pines. It's a fabulous place for bird-watching, too, and the preserve borders a section of the Maine Coastal Islands National Wildlife Refuge. A one-mile trail loops through the preserve. Trail access is signed on Corea Road, 1.9 miles from the Route 195 intersection.

GETTING THERE

From Route 186 in Prospect Harbor, take Route 195/Corea Road 1.9 miles and look for the sign and parking lot on the left.

Taft Point Preserve, Gouldsboro

Roughly 1.75 miles of trails network this 68-acre preserve comprising woodlands and waterfront. You'll find two loops, the 0.5-mile Jones Cove Trail and the 0.75-mile Flanders Bay Trail. The half-mile Beach Trail, which follows the shorefront for a third of a mile, connects the two. If you only have time for one loop, opt for the Jones Trail and continue on the Beach Trail for 0.22 mile to the shorefront. The reward: gorgeous views of Acadia's rounded peaks, Stave Island, Calf Island, Schieffelen Point, and Schoodic Mountain.

GETTING THERE

From Route 1, take the southern section of Route 186 and follow it 1.1 miles to Taft Point

Tidal Falls Preserve

Road on your right. Continue on Taft Point Road for 0.4 mile, and then keep right when the road splits. There's parking for six cars. Beyond here, the road is private.

Baker Hill and Long Ledges, Sullivan

These two adjoining preserves offer 376 acres laced with roughly six miles of trails. If you only have an hour or so and want big rewards for minimal effort, hoof it up Baker Hill. Stick to the main trail for the quickest trip. Trails pass through fir trees and over ledges before a short ascent to an overlook with views over Frenchman Bay. If you have time to linger, the Boundary Trail connects to two of eight trails on Long Ledges, making it possible to loop through that 4-mile moderatenetwork. Highlights in this preserve include the overgrown ruins of an old granite quarry, a small pond, and vernal pools.

If you have two cars and are up for a full day's adventure, consider the **Schoodic Connector Trail,** a 6.5-mile hike from the Baker Hill trailhead to the summit of Schoodic Mountain, in the Donnell Pond preserve; add another 1.4 miles to descend to the Schoodic Mountain trailhead, for a nearly 8-mile hike.

GETTING THERE

From Route 1 in Sullivan, take Punkinville Road and drive 0.2 miles to signed parking lot on the left; continue 0.4 miles to find the Long Ledges parking lot and trailhead.

Tucker Mountain, Sullivan

If you only have time for a short hike and prefer a workout, opt for the steep, 1-mile round-trip Tucker Mountain Trail. The reward: Views over Frenchman Bay to Mount Desert Island from the open summit.

GETTING THERE

Park in the Long Cove rest area on the waterside of Route 1, where there's a vault toilet and picnic tables. Cross Route 1, to an old road, and look right for the blue diamond trail signs.

Little Tunk Pond, Sullivan

It's an easy .25-mile walk into this undeveloped pond, with a nice sand beach. Great spot for a post-hike swim or a lazy family afternoon.

GETTING THERE

From Route 1, take Rte. 183/Tunk Lake Rd. north 4.7 miles. About .25 miles after the Donnell Pond Public Reserve Land sing, you'll see the FBC Preserve sign and parking lot on your left.

GOULDSBORO
Maine Coastal Islands National Wildlife Refuge

In addition to the Petit Manan Point Division, the Petit Manan National Wildlife Refuge also encompasses the 623-acre Gouldsboro Bay Division; the 1,028-acre Sawyer's Marsh Division, in Milbridge; and the 431-acre Corea Heath Division, home to one of Maine's most significant peatlands.

SOUTHERN COREA HEATH TRAIL

Here's a welcome find for anyone with mobility issues or pushing a stroller. The Southern Corea Heath Trail is an easy, 0.4-mile round-trip, wheelchair-accessible gravel trail to an observation platform with a panoramic view of the coastal plateau bog, also known as a peatland or heath.

From the intersection with Route 186 in Prospect Harbor, follow Route 195, Corea Road, 2.6 miles to the refuge parking area on the right.

SALT MARSH TRAIL

Observe waterfowl, shorebirds, and eagles on this moderate, 1.6-mile round-trip hike through conifers to two observation platforms overlooking a salt marsh on Gouldsboro Bay's West Bay.

From Route 1, take the Chicken Mill Pond Road to Fletcher Wood Road and drive 0.2 mile, continuing straight 0.1 mile when the main road veers right.

Schoodic Communities

You won't find chain restaurants or accommodations in the villages peppering the Schoodic region, but you will find a genuine slice of Down East, Maine, along with inviting shops and galleries. The towns and villages salting the region—Winter Harbor (pop. 516); Gouldsboro (pop. 1,737), including the not-to-be-missed villages of Birch Harbor, Corea, and Prospect Harbor; Hancock (pop. 2,394); Sullivan (pop. 1,236); and Sorrento (pop. 274)—seem suspended in time. They are quiet and rural, with lobster fishing still an economic anchor.

WINTER HARBOR

Winter Harbor is known best as the gateway to Schoodic. It shares the area with an old-money, low-profile, Philadelphia-linked summer colony on exclusive Grindstone Neck. Only a few clues hint at the colony's presence, strung along the western side of the harbor. Winter Harbor's summer highlight is the annual Lobster Festival, the second Saturday in August. The gala daylong event includes a parade, live entertainment, games, and more crustaceans than you could ever consume.

Recreation
SWIMMING AND PADDLING

The best freshwater swimming and calmwater paddling in the area is at **Jones Beach** (sunrise-sunset daily), a community-owned recreation area on Jones Pond in West Gouldsboro. Here you'll find restrooms, a nice playground, picnic facilities, a boat launch, a swim area with a float, and a small beach. The beach is located at the end of Recreation Road, off Route 195, which is 0.3 mile south of Route 1. No unleashed pets are permitted.

Sea Schoodic Kayak and Bike (8 Duck Pond Rd., Winter Harbor, 833/724-6634, www.seaschoodic.com, hours vary seasonally) has rental fresh-water kayaks stashed on Jones

Pond (from $45 double, $35 single). The shop also provides directions, PFDs, and paddles.

GOLF
Play the nine-hole **Grindstone Neck Golf Course** (Grindstone Ave., Winter Harbor, 207/963-7760, www.grindstonegolf.com, May-Oct., $33-45 for 9 holes, $20 twilight) just for the dynamite scenery—water views from every hole—or for a glimpse of the exclusive late-19th-century summer enclave. Established in 1891, the public course attracts a tony crowd; 150-yard markers are cute little birdhouses.

Boat Excursions
Cruise aboard the 40-foot *Tricia Clark* to Petit Manan Island, home to Petit Manan Light, and view puffins, seals, and other seabirds with **Acadia Puffin Cruise** (88 Sargent St., Winter Harbor, 207/598-7900, https://acadiapuffincruise.com). The three-hour cruise costs $75 adults, $45 ages 6-12, and $20 age 5 and younger. Complimentary snacks, water, and binoculars are available on board.

Entertainment and Events
SCHOODIC ARTS FOR ALL
Concerts, art classes, coffeehouses, workshops, and related activities are presented year-round by the energetic **Schoodic Arts for All** (207/963-2569, www.schoodicarts.org), a volunteer organization. Many activities are held at historic Hammond Hall in downtown Winter Harbor. A summer series presents monthly concerts on Friday evenings May-October.

The **Schoodic Arts Festival** takes place over two weeks in early August and is jam-packed with daily workshops and nightly performances for all ages. Call for a schedule, and register early for any program that you don't want to miss.

WINTER HARBOR LOBSTER FESTIVAL

Winter Harbor's biggest wingding is the annual Lobster Festival, on the second Saturday in August. The gala daylong event includes a parade, live entertainment, lobster boat races (a serious competition, with 13 classes determined by size and power), a crafts fair, games, and lots and lots of crustaceans. For more information, visit www.acadia-schoodic.org.

Shopping

You can find just about anything at the **Winter Harbor 5 & 10** (349 Main St., Winter Harbor, 207/963-7927, www.winterharbor5and10.com). It's the genuine article, an old-fashioned five-and-dime that's somehow still surviving in the age of Walmart.

Handmade and practical goods and gifts make it a delight to browse tiny **Nib & Thible** (355 Main St., Winter Harbor).

In the village center is **Artisans & Antiques** (357 Main St., Winter Harbor, 207/963-2400), a 15-member group shop with a nice mix of craftwork and treasures.

Works by contemporary Maine artists, including noted painters and sculptors, are exhibited in rotating shows at **Littlefield Gallery** (145 Main St., Winter Harbor, 207/963-6005, www.littlefieldgallery.com). Works are displayed both in a purpose-built gallery and in the house, as well as a few in the yard.

Prospect Harbor Soap Co. (4 Duck Pond Rd. at Rte. 186, Winter Harbor, 207/963-7598, www.prospectharborsoapco.com) maintains an outlet where you can purchase lotions, handmade soaps, and other skin-care products.

Food

QUICK BITES

J. M. Gerrish (352 Main St., Winter Harbor, 207/963-7000, 8am-3pm Wed.-Sun) has had its ups and downs, but locals are confident that the century-old store is now back in local, reliable hands. Open for breakfast and lunch, it also has a classic ice cream counter along with a small penny candy section.

Stock up on gourmet goodies at **Grindstone Neck of Maine** (311 Newman St./Rte. 186, Winter Harbor, 207/963-7347 or 866/831-8734, www.grindstoneneck.com, hours vary seasonally), just north of downtown Winter Harbor, which earns high marks for its smoked salmon, spreads and pâtés, and smoked cheeses, all made without preservatives or artificial ingredients. Also available are fresh fish, wine, and frozen foods for campers.

Market Day, the retail shop for Raven's Nest Farm, is located at the Cook's Corner, the intersection of Route 186 and Main Street. You'll find farm-fresh fare with an Italian accent, including pastas and baked goods like doughnuts.

Pick up veggies, meats, eggs, cheeses, and handcrafted fiber products as well as jams, preserves, and baked goods at the **Winter Harbor Farmers Market** (Newman St., Winter Harbor, 9am-noon Tues. late June-early Sept.).

FAMILY FAVORITES

The best place for grub and gossip in Winter Harbor is **Chase's Restaurant** (193 Main St., Winter Harbor, 207/963-7171, 7am-8pm Tues.-Sun., $10-28), a seasoned but updated, no-frills booth-and-counter operation turning out down-home American fare and decent seafood. Kids' meals run $7-8.

CASUAL DINING

Chef Mike Poirier and baker Alice Letcher's ★ **Salt Box** (10 Newman St., Winter Harbor, 207/422-9900, http://saltboxmaine.com, from 5pm Tues.-Sun. late May-early Oct. and noon-3pm Fri.-Sun. July-Aug., $20-36), in a contemporary building overlooking the harbor, has earned a following. The decor is open and upscale, the creative New American fare is sophisticated yet approachable and focused on fresh seasonal ingredients, and the service is excellent.

LOBSTER AND SEAFOOD

The **Fisherman's Galley** (7 Newman St./ Rte. 186, Winter Harbor, 207/963-5585, www. fishermansgalleymaine.com, 4pm-9pm Mon.- Sat. late June-early Sept., $6-26) is a cool, rustic, earth-friendly lobster and seafood spot, with options for landlubbers and a full bar with Maine craft beers on tap. Guests order at the counter, and the food is delivered to their tables. The menu makes it easy to cobble together a meal that fits your appetite and budget. Dine inside, outside under a tent, or get a lobster boil in a bucket to go.

Out front of Fisherman's Galley is **Nui's** (11am-3pm Mon.-Sat.), a food cart serving meat-packed lobster rolls and gourmet hot dogs (from $3).

The Lobstore (258 Newman St./Rte. 186, Winter Harbor, 207/963-8600, www.thelobstore.net, 11am-6pm daily) is more than a seafood market. Pick up fresh fish and prepared foods for your campsite or kitchen, or opt for a lobster roll, chowder, lobster cooked to order, and even sushi.

Accommodations

Roger and Pearl Barto, whose family roots in this region go back five generations, have four rental accommodations on their Henry Cove oceanfront property, ★ **Main Stay Cottages** (66 Sargent St., Winter Harbor, 207/963-2601, www.mainstaycottages-rvpark. com, $100-135). Most unusual is the small, one-bedroom Boat House, which has stood since the 1880s. It hangs over the harbor, with views to Mark Island Light, and you can hear the water gurgling below at high tide (but it is cramped, be forewarned). Other options include a very comfortable efficiency cottage, a one-bedroom cottage, a 2nd-floor suite with a private entrance, and a four-bedroom house ($150-250/night). All have big decks and fabulous views over the lobster boat-filled harbor; watch for the eagles that frequently soar overhead. Main Stay is on the Island Explorer bus route and just steps from where the Bar Harbor Ferries dock.

The Bartos, owners of **Main Stay Cottages and RV Park** (66 Sargent St., Winter Harbor, 207/963-2601, www. mainstaycottages-rvpark.com, $49), have a 10-site campground overlooking Henry Cove. It's designed for self-contained RVs, as there are no restrooms or showers on-site; sewer, water, electric, and Wi-Fi are available.

Library

Find the **Winter Harbor Public Library** (18 Chapel Ln., Winter Harbor, 207/963-7556, www.winterharbor.lib.me.us) in the 1888 beach-stone and fieldstone Channing Chapel.

Getting There and Around

Winter Harbor is about 26 miles via Routes 1 and 186 from Ellsworth. It's about 20 miles or 30 minutes to Milbridge, on the Down East Coast.

CAR

From Ellsworth, stay north (keep left) on Route 1 from where it splits with Route 3. Continue north on Route 1 for about 16 miles, through Hancock and Sullivan, until you reach Gouldsboro. From Route 1 in Gouldsboro, the park entrance is eight miles via Route 186 south through Winter Harbor.

To reach the town from Bar Harbor, take Route 3 north to the head of Mount Desert Island, then across Mount Desert Narrows to Trenton. The usual route is to continue to a congested intersection at the edge of Ellsworth, where you'll pick up Route 1 north (turn right) and continue as above. But you can avoid some of the traffic congestion on Route 3 in Trenton by ducking east via Route 204 toward Lamoine and its state park, and then back up to Route 1 via the Mud Creek Road.

PASSENGER FERRY

Although Winter Harbor is roughly 43 miles or 1.15 hours from Bar Harbor by car, it's only about 7 miles by water. The summer schedule for the **Bar Harbor Ferry**

(207/288-2984, www.barharborferry.com, round-trip $28 adults, $20 children) is coordinated with the Island Explorer bus's summertime Schoodic route, so you can board the ferry in Bar Harbor, pick up the bus at the dock in Winter Harbor, and be shuttled along the Schoodic Loop. Stop where you like for a picnic or a hike, and then board a later bus. Take the last bus back to the ferry and return to Bar Harbor. It makes for a super car-free excursion. The ferry operates at least four times daily mid-June-mid-October.

BUS

The free **Island Explorer** (www.exploreacadia.com) bus Route 8 covers the lower part of the peninsula, from Winter Harbor through Prospect Harbor, late June-August. The bus circulates roughly once an hour, with a schedule that coordinates with the ferry.

GOULDSBORO

Gouldsboro—including the not-to-be-missed villages of Birch Harbor, Corea, and Prospect Harbor—earned its own minor fame from Louise Dickinson Rich's 1958 book *The Peninsula*, a tribute to her summers on Corea's Cranberry Point, "a place that has stood still in time." Since 1958, change has crept into Corea, but not so as you'd notice. It's still the same quintessential lobster-fishing community, perfect for photo ops.

Boat Excursions

Join Corea native Captain Dan Rogers aboard the F/V *Bottom Line* for a two-hour **Catch Your Lobster Tour** (39 Francis Pound Rd., Corea, 207/546-0556, https://lobster.tours, $100 adults, $50 age 10 and younger). On the cruise from Corea Harbor to Petit Manan Light, you'll likely see seals and Atlantic puffins as well as help haul lobster traps. Each paying guest goes home with one lobster. Tours run twice daily, Monday-Saturday, and have a maximum of six passengers.

Shopping
ART, ANTIQUES, AND BOOKS

The folk-art funk begins on the exterior of the **Salty Dog Gallery/Hurdy Gurdy Man Antiques** (173 Main St., Prospect Harbor, 207/963-7575), a twofold find. The lower level is filled with fun folk-art vintage goods. Upstairs, owner Dean Kotula displays his fine art: documentary-style photographic prints.

Visiting the **U.S. Bells Foundry & Watering Cove Studios** (56 W. Bay Rd./Rte. 186, Prospect Harbor, 207/963-7184, www.usbells.com) is a treat for the ears, as browsers try out the many varieties of cast bronze bells made in the adjacent foundry by Richard Fisher. If you're lucky, he may have time to explain the process—particularly intriguing for children, and a distraction from their instinctive urge to test every bell in the shop. The store also carries works by other members of this talented family. These include quilts, wood-fired stoneware and porcelain, woodworking pieces and furniture, and photos. U.S. Bells is 0.25 mile up the hill from Prospect Harbor's post office.

The nifty **Chapter Two** (611 Corea Rd., Corea, 207/963-7269, www.chaptertwocorea.com) is home to Spurling House Gallery, Corea Rug Hooking Company, and Accumulated Books Gallery. Spread out in two buildings is a nice selection of used and antiquarian books, fine crafts, and hand-hooked rugs. Yarn, rug-hooking supplies, and lessons are available.

Down the first dirt lane after the Corea post office is the **Corea Wharf Gallery** (13 Gibbs Ln., Corea, 207/963-2633, www.coreawharfgallery.com). Inside a humble wharf-top fishing shack are displayed historic photographs of Corea, taken in the 1940s-1960s by Louise Z. Young, born in Corea in 1919. She was a friend of painter Marsden Hartley, and took many candid photographs of him around the area. Young also worked with noted photographer Berenice Abbott. Also here are artifacts from Corea's history, especially ones connected to fishing. The gallery doubles as a food stand selling lobster, lobster rolls, hot dogs, and ice cream.

Food

QUICK BITES

For scrumptious baked goods and sandwiches, pop into **Flour Girls Bakery** (501 Main St., Birch Harbor, 207/963-5941, 7am-2pm Mon.-Fri.). Another tasty lunch option is **Gyp'sea Chix** (404 Main St., Birch Harbor, 207/812-0198, 11:30am-2:30pm Tues.-Sun.).

At 150-acre certified-organic **Darthia Farm** (51 Darthia Farm Rd., Gouldsboro, 207/963-7771, www.darthiafarm.com), the **Farm Store** (8am-5pm Mon.-Fri., 8am-noon Sat. June-Sept.) sells fresh produce as well as herbal salves and vinegars, hand-spun hand-dyed yarn, and other products.

German and Italian presses, Portuguese corks, and Maine fruit all contribute to the creation of Bob and Kathe Bartlett's award-winning dinner and dessert wines at **Bartlett Maine Estate Winery** (175 Chicken Mill Pond Rd., Gouldsboro, 207/546-2408, www.bartlettwinery.com, 10am-5pm Mon.-Sat. June-Oct., or by appointment), just north of the Schoodic Peninsula. Founded in 1982, the winery produces more than 20,000 gallons annually in a handsome wood-and-stone building designed by the Bartletts. Not ones to rest on their many laurels, in 2008 the Bartletts introduced grape wines, and more recently, the **Spirits of Maine Distillery** (do try the Rusticator Rum). There are no tours, but you're welcome to sample for a small tasting fee. Reserve wines—the dry blueberry is excellent—and others of limited vintage are sold only on-site. A sculpture garden patio makes a nice spot to relax. Bartlett's is 0.5 mile south of Route 1 in Gouldsboro.

INTERNATIONAL

Downeast Mexican Takeout (22 Old Rte. 1, Gouldsboro, 207/963-4043, 11am-7pm Tues.-Sun., $3-10) doesn't look like much, but it turns out excellent, made-to-order homemade Michoacan fare. Patience is key here, as it takes a while to prepare, especially if

there are other orders in the queue. Seating is limited a few picnic tables outside and in a screened shelter.

FAMILY FAVORITES

Shoot pool, play darts or horseshoes, watch the game on TV, sip a cold drink, and savor a burger or fried seafood at the family-friendly ★ **The Pickled Wrinkle** (9 E. Schoodic Dr., at the intersection with Rte. 186, Birch Harbor, 207/963-7916, www.thepickledwrinkle.com, 11am-9pm daily, $9-23). Don't be fooled by the humble appearance; the owners know their way around the kitchen and opt for local and organic whenever possible. That said, the overall atmosphere is more tavern than restaurant. There's often live music, and Thursday jazz afternoons always draw a crowd. The Friday-night all-you-can-eat haddock fry is a deal.

CASUAL DINING

Ask locally about **Bunker's Wharf** (260 East Schoodic Dr., Birch Harbor) overlooking postcard-perfect Wonsqueak Harbor.

LOBSTER AND SEAFOOD

You'd be hard-pressed to find a better place to enjoy a lobster than the ★ **Wharf Gallery & Grill** (13 Gibbs Ln., Corea, 207/963-8888, www.corealunch.com, 11am-4pm daily), an eat-on-the-wharf lobster shack overlooking dreamy, lobster boat-filled Corea Harbor. The menu includes lobster rolls, lobster grilled cheese (trust me, try it), crab claws, oysters, hot dogs, sausages, and ice cream. Owner Joe Young is a sixth-generation lobsterman and a descendant of Corea's original settlers. Images taken by his aunt, photographer Louise Z. Young, are displayed in the shed gallery. Ask Joe to share a few stories about his aunt and the family's relationship with painter Marsden Hartley; he's a great storyteller.

Accommodations

INNS AND BED-AND-BREAKFASTS

Sited on a bluff with sweeping views over Frenchman Bay, the **Bluff House Inn** (57

Bluff House Rd., Gouldsboro, 207/963-7805, www.bluffinn.com, year-round, $95-185) offers guest rooms in a 1980s post-and-beam lodge, a two-bedroom apartment, and one-room cabins. Verandas wrap around the 1st and 2nd floors of the lodge, so bring binoculars for sighting ospreys and bald eagles. Settle by one of two stone fireplaces or grab a seat by the window. Lodge rooms are a bit dated, but new owners plan updates. Breakfast is expanded continental. Pet-friendly rooms are available for an extra $15/stay.

Watch lobster boats unload their catch at the dock opposite ★ **Elsa's Inn on the Harbor** (179 Main St., Prospect Harbor, 207/963-7571, www.elsasinn.com, $140-175), with views overlooking the harbor and beyond to a lighthouse. Every room has an ocean view, and a few have separate entrances. Innkeepers Scott and Cherrie Markwood pamper their guests with nice linens, down duvets, and afternoon refreshments. A hearty hot breakfast is served either indoors in the dining room or outside on the porch or patio. After a day of exploring, settle into a rocker on the veranda and gaze over the boat-filled harbor out to Prospect Harbor Light. One room is ADA-accessible; two are pet friendly.

Black Duck Inn on Corea Harbor (Crowley Island Rd., Corea, 207/963-2689, www.blackduckme.com, May-mid-Oct., from $200) has four handsomely decorated guest rooms that can be rented individually or as suites, as well as plenty of common space. Innkeepers Will and Rae Mathewson also operate a gallery at the inn and are the founders of a nonprofit dedicated to music and arts education. Small pets are a possibility.

Camping

The primitive, commercial, self-serve, backcountry-style **Acadia East Campground** (547 Rte. 1, Gouldsboro, 833/246-2267, www.acadiaeastcampground.com, $30) opened in 2018 with 6 tent sites on 8.8 wooded acres and plans to expand to 30 sites. You must bring your own water and take out all trash. There's a vault toilet. Each site has a fire ring and picnic table. It's dog friendly.

INFORMATION

Schoodic Chamber of Commerce (207/963-7658, https://schoodicchamber.com).

Library

Check out the **Dorcas Library** (Rte. 186, Prospect Harbor, 207/963-4027, www.dorcas.lib.me.us).

Getting There and Around

Gouldsboro is about 18 miles via Route 1 from Ellsworth. The town straddles Route 1 and includes the upper and eastern portions of the Schoodic Peninsula. Route 186 loops the peninsula, but Route 195 provides the fastest access from Route 1 to Prospect Harbor. From Prospect Harbor it's about 2 miles to Birch Harbor via Route 186 or about 3 miles to Corea via Route 195. From Prospect Harbor, it's about 4 miles or 10 minutes to Winter Harbor via Route 186 or about 10 miles or 15 minutes to Steuben or 15 miles or 20 minutes to Milbridge via Routes 186 and 1.

The free **Island Explorer** (www.exploreacadia.com), Route 8, covers the lower part of the peninsula, connecting Winter Harbor and the ferries to the Schoodic section of Acadia, Birch Harbor, and Prospect Harbor, from late June through August. You'll need a car or bicycle to explore Corea or other parts of Gouldsboro.

HANCOCK, SULLIVAN, AND SORRENTO

Between Ellsworth and Gouldsboro, the villages of Hancock, Sullivan, and Sorrento straddle Route 1, which ties the region together and provides inviting glimpses and vistas of Frenchman Bay and glacial-sculpted mountains of Mount Desert Island. Venture down the ocean-side back roads and you'll discover an old-timey summer colony at Hancock Point, complete with a library, post

---

1: Corea Harbor 2: the Wharf Gallery & Grill

office, yacht club, and tennis courts. Meander inland and you'll be rewarded with artisans' studios, especially in Sullivan, and easily accessed ponds and lakes and mountain trailheads along the byway.

In its heyday, Sullivan was a center for shipbuilding and quarrying. Interpretative signage at two roadside pullouts, one before the bridge and another next to the former Dunbar's Store, provide information on the area's heritage, flora, and fauna. The town also has the distinction of being where two Nazi spies, William Colepaugh and Erich Gimpel, landed in the dark of a snowy November night in 1944, dropped off by the submarine *U-1230*.

Tiny Sorrento isn't really much more than a classic summer colony, and that's all the reason you need for a leisurely drive down the peninsula. It has tennis courts, a yacht club, a nine-hole golf course edging the ocean, and what's left of a swimming pool, created in 1913 by damming a cove just above the village. If you fall for the place, try to find a copy of *Sorrento, A Well-Kept Secret,* by Catherine O'Clair Herson, published in 1995 for the town's centennial. It's filled with historical photos and stories.

Recreation
DOWN EAST SUNRISE TRAIL
Hike, mountain bike, snowshoe, cross-country ski, or ride an ATV, snowmobile, or even a horse on the Down East Sunrise Trail (www.sunrisetrail.org). The gravel-surfaced trail, a joint effort by the Maine Department of Transportation and Maine Department of Conservation, stretches 85 miles along a rehabilitated discontinued railroad bed between Washington Junction, in Hancock, and Ayers Junction, south of Calais. Maps, available to download from the website, show trailheads, highlights, and parking lots along the route. The 30-mile section between Washington Junction and Cherryfield roughly follows the Down East coastline of the Schoodic region. Additional access points include Franklin and Sullivan; see the map for details and directions.

The seven-mile Franklin Crossing to Tunk Lake Road section edges Schoodic Bog and the southwest corner of the Donnell Pond Public Reserved Land and offers fine views of Schoodic Mountain. There's limited parking on both ends: the Franklin Crossing intersection with Route 182 and the Tunk Lake Road intersection on Route 183.

OUTFITTERS AND TRIPS
Antonio Blasi is a Master Maine Sea Kayak and Recreational Guide whose **Hancock Point Kayak Tours** (58 Point Rd., Hancock, 207/266-4449, http://schoodicmaineguide. com) offers guided paddles on Frenchman Bay or on an area lake. A three-hour bay paddle, including all equipment, safety, and paddling demonstrations, and usually an island break, is $45/seat double kayak, $55 single kayak. A 1.5-hour lake tour is $55 pp single or double or $75 for two adults and one small child. Overnight kayak camping trips are $150 pp.

Do-it-yourselfers may also rent a canoe or kayak from **Water's Edge Canoe & Kayak Rentals** (222 Franklin Rd., Franklin, 207/460-6350 or 207/460-7734). Canoe rentals are $25 for one day, $65 for three days, or $125 per week; single kayaks are $30, $80, or $150; double kayaks are $40, $100, or $200. Although the location is at the water's edge on Hog Bay, it's tidal, so it's advisable to take the craft elsewhere; delivery is possible. Credit cards are not accepted.

Entertainment and Events
PIERRE MONTEUX SCHOOL
The **Pierre Monteux School for Conductors and Orchestra Musicians** (Rte. 1, Hancock, 207/422-3280, www.monteuxschool.org), a prestigious summer program founded in 1943, has achieved international renown for training dozens of national and international classical musicians. It presents two well-attended concert series late June-July. The Wednesday series (5pm, $15 adults) features chamber music; the Sunday concerts (5pm, $25 adults, $5 students) feature

symphonies. An annual free family concert usually is held in early to mid-July. All concerts are held in the school's Forest Studio; payment is accepted via cash or check only. At both series, kids younger than 18 are admitted for free with an adult.

MONDAY MUSIC AT TIDAL FALLS

On Monday evenings in July-August, weather permitting, the **Frenchman Bay Conservancy** (207/422-2328, www.frenchmanbay.org) presents a concert series at its Tidal Falls Preserve. Pack a picnic supper or purchase one from the food cart. Music might include jazz, steel pan drums, ukuleles, or an orchestra.

Shopping

★ HANCOCK AND SULLIVAN GALLERY TOUR

From Route 1 take Eastside Road, just before the Hancock-Sullivan Bridge, and drive 1.6 miles south to the Wray family's **Gull Rock Pottery** (103 Gull Rock Rd., Hancock, 207/422-3990, www.gullrockpottery.com). Torj and Kurt Wray created this gallery, which daughter-in-law Akemi now runs. She's continued crafting their wheel-thrown, hand-painted, dishwasher-safe pottery decorated with cobalt blue and white Japanese-style motifs, but has added some of her own designs. Complementing the indoor gallery is an outdoor, oceanfront sculpture gallery with views to Mount Desert Island.

Cross the Hancock-Sullivan Bridge, then take your first left off Route 1 onto Taunton Drive to find the next four galleries, beginning with Dan Farrenkopf's and Phid Lawless's **Lunaform** (66 Cedar Ln., Sullivan, 207/422-0923, www.lunaform.com), set amid beautifully landscaped grounds surrounding an old quarry. At first glance, it appears that many of the wonderfully aesthetic garden ornaments created here are hand-turned pottery, when in fact they're hand-turned steel-reinforced concrete. Take the first right off Taunton Drive onto Track Road, proceed 0.5 mile, then turn left onto Cedar Lane.

Return to Taunton Drive and take the next right onto Quarry Road, then left on Whales Back Road, a rough dirt lane, to find granite sculptor Obadiah Bourne Buell's **Stone Designs Studio and Granite Garden Gallery** (124 Whales Back Rd., Sullivan, 207/422-3111, www.stonedesignsmaine.com). Bourne displays his home accents and garden features in a self-serve gallery adjacent to a quarry and in the surrounding gardens. This really is a magical spot, and if you time it right, you might be able to see the sculptor at work.

Continue on South Bay Road (note that it becomes dirt for a roughly 0.5-mile section) and turn left, heading north, when it meets Route 200/Hog Bay Road. Almost immediately on your left is Charles and Susanne Grosjean's **Hog Bay Pottery** (245 Hog Bay Rd./Rte. 200, Franklin, 207/565-2282, www.hogbay.com), in operation since 1974. Inside the casual, laid-back showroom are Charles's functional, nature-themed pottery and Susanne's stunning handwoven wool rugs. Pottery seconds are often available.

Continue south. Just before the intersection with U.S. 1 is a double hit. Artist Paul Breeden, best known for the remarkable illustrations, calligraphy, and maps he's done for *National Geographic*, Time-Life Books, and other national and international publications, displays and sells his paintings at the **Spring Woods Gallery and Willowbrook Garden** (19 Willowbrook Ln., Sullivan, 207/422-3007, www.springwoodsgallery.com or www.willowbrookgarden.com). Also filling the handsome modern gallery space are paintings by Ann Breeden. Be sure to allow time to meander through the shady sculpture garden, where there's even a playhouse for kids.

Food

QUICK BITES

Maine Coast Smokehouse (1545 U.S. 1, Hancock, 207/422-0028, www.mainecoastsmokehouse.com, hours vary seasonally), produces excellent smoked seafood and also carries Maine-made products. Big interior windows allow visitors to see into the production facility and watch the action.

Pick up groceries, beverages, and premade or made-to-order fare at the **Dunbar Store** (1983 Rte. 1, Sullivan, 207/422-0280, 7am-7pm Mon.-Sat., 8am-4pm Sun.).

INTERNATIONAL

Have a hankering for Korean? Sonye Carroll and family serve bibimbap, bulgogi, barbecued ribs, and kimchee, along with top-notch crabmeat rolls, as well as burgers and dogs, homemade doughnuts, and Gifford's ice cream at the seasonal **YU Takeout** (674 Rte. 1, Hancock, 207/412-0944, 11am-8pm daily, $8-20).

FAMILY FAVORITES

Don't be put off by "Wilbur," the lobster sculpture outside **Ruth & Wimpy's Kitchen** (792 Rte. 1, Hancock, 207/422-3723, www. ruthandwimpys.com, 3pm-8pm Mon.-Sat., $10-28). You'll probably see a crowd as well. This family-fare standby serves hefty sandwiches, lobster, pizza, pasta, and steak. Antique license plates and collections of miniature cars and trucks accent the interior.

CASUAL DINING

The gastropub menu at **Ironbound** (1513 U.S. 1, Hancock, 207/422-3395, www.ironbound-inn.com, from 5pm Tues.-Sun. mid-June-mid-Oct., $10-30) ranges from burgers and salads to ribs and ribeye, making it easy to please everyone. A huge brick hearth adorned with copper pots anchors one end of the main dining room. The atmosphere is casual, with wood floors and undressed tables. The fare complements the setting, with ingredients sourced locally whenever possible. Play bocce on the lawn while enjoying the outside bar, The Bounder.

The unpretentious dining rooms at the ★ **Crocker House Country Inn** (967 Point Rd., Hancock Point, 207/422-6806, www. crockerhouse.com, 5:30pm-9pm daily late May-mid-Oct., 5:30pm-8:30pm Fri.-Sun. Apr. and Nov.-Dec., $34-40) provide a setting for well-prepared European fare crafted from fresh and local ingredients; reservations are essential, as this is one of the area's most consistent and popular dining spots.

Another dependable dining experience is **Chipper's** (1239 U.S. 1, Hancock, 207/422-8238, www.chippersrestaurant.com, 5pm-9pm Wed.-Sat.). Owner Chipper Butterwick opened his popular restaurant in 1995 and expanded the simple cape-style building in 2010, adding a pub. The restaurant's wide-ranging menu includes rack of lamb and filet mignon, but the emphasis is on seafood; the crab cakes earn rave reviews. Entrées include a sampling of tasty haddock chowder and a salad, but save room for the homemade ice cream for dessert. Entrées are in the $18-35 range, but some appetizer-salad combos provide budget options, and lighter fare ($6-15) is available in the pub.

LOBSTER AND SEAFOOD

Tracey's Seafood (2719 Rte. 1, Sullivan, 207/422-9072, 11am-8pm daily, $5-20) doesn't look like much from the road, but don't be fooled. The Tracey family harvests the clams, catches the lobsters, shucks, picks, and dishes out ultra-fresh lobster, chowders, and fried seafood. There's a takeout window and picnic tables on the lawn as well as a dining room with table service. Portions are big, prices are low—$4 burgers, two-fer lobster rolls (usually around $12-18, but I've seen them as low as $10), and weekend fish fries and clam fries with free seconds. Don't miss the homemade pies. For inside dining, BYOB.

Accommodations

INNS AND BED-AND-BREAKFASTS

Sustainable living is the focus of the peaceful ★ **Three Pines Bed and Breakfast** (274 East Side Rd., Hancock, 207/460-7595, www.threepinesbandb.com, year-round, $125), fronting Sullivan Harbor, just below the Reversing Falls. This quiet, off-the-grid,

1: Three Pines Bed and Breakfast **2:** Crocker House Country Inn

40-acre oceanfront property is home to ducks, rare-breed chickens, and wool-producing sheep as well as a kitchen garden, berry bushes, and an orchard with apple and peach trees. Photovoltaic cells provide electricity, water is solar heated, and appliances are primarily propane powered. Two inviting guest rooms have private entrances and water views. A full vegetarian breakfast (with fresh eggs from the farm) is served. A tandem kayak and a canoe are available. You can walk or pedal along an abandoned railway line, and you can launch a canoe or kayak from the yard. Children and pets require advance arrangements.

Follow Hancock Point Road 4.8 miles south of Route 1 to the three-story, gray-blue **Crocker House Country Inn** (967 Point Rd., Hancock, 207/422-6806, www.crockerhouse.com, $125-180), Rich and Liz Malaby's antidote to Bar Harbor's summer traffic. Built as a summer hotel in 1884, the inn underwent rehabbing a century later, but it retains a delightfully old-fashioned air despite offering contemporary conveniences. Breakfast is included. A few bicycles are available, and clay tennis courts are nearby. If you're arriving by boat, request a mooring. The inn's dining room, open nightly for dinner in season, is a draw in itself. Some rooms are pet friendly.

Although ★ **Ironbound** (1513 U.S. 1, Hancock, 207/422-3395 www.ironboundinn.com, $175-195), a four-room inn located above the restaurant of the same name, is right on Route 1, when you're on the garden-view balconies, or on the lawn out back, you're oblivious to any traffic. Rooms are bright and airy (some allow pets for an extra $20), and guests have use of a comfy sitting area downstairs, adjacent to the restaurant. Rates include continental breakfast. Guests can arrange for a private lobster boat tour. The inn adjoins Crabtree Neck Conservation Trust lands, laced with trails and a pond.

About 12 miles east of Ellsworth is the oceanfront **Acadia Bay Inn** (12 Miramar Ave., Sullivan Harbor, 207/422-0127, www. acadiabayinn.com, $199-289), a Shingle-style inn with wraparound porch and extensive balconies. Out front are the peaks of Mount Desert across Frenchman Bay. This updated 1889 summer home evokes the easy elegance of days gone by. The inn has a private beach, but the water is terminally chilly. A full breakfast is included.

COTTAGES

Flanders Bay Cabins (2673 Rte. 1, Sullivan, 443/299-9821, www.flandersbay.com) has three one-bedroom ($715/week) and three two-bedroom ($835/week) unfussy, rustic cabins; a three-bedroom chalet ($1,210/week), and a three-bedroom shorefront house ($1,925/week). All are on or near the waterfront and have fabulous views. Some units are pet-friendly ($35/stay) with advance planning. Bring your own linens and towels or rent them.

The views to Mount Desert are dreamy from **Edgewater Cabins** (25 Benvenuto Ave., Sullivan, 207/422-6414 May 15-Oct. 15, 603/472-8644 rest of year, www.edgewatercabins.com, $595-995/week), a colony of seven housekeeping cottages on a spit of land jutting into Frenchman Bay. The well-tended four-acre property has both sunrise and sunset water views, big trees for shade, and lawns rolling to the shorefront. Stays of at least three nights ($95-175/night) are possible, when there's availability. Also offered are boat tours of Frenchman Bay aboard the *Edgewater II* (from $45 pp for two hours).

CAMPING

Fronting on Flanders Bay, **Acadia Seashore Camping & Cabins** (2695 Rte. 1, Sullivan, 207/422-0130, www.acadiaseashorecamping.com, $35-46 tent, $46 small camper, $46-50 RV) doesn't offer much privacy, but it makes up for that with its views across the water to Mount Desert Island.

INFORMATION

Schoodic Chamber of Commerce (207/963-7658, https://schoodicchamber.com).

Scenic Byways and Trails

The Schoodic region boasts not one but two designated scenic byways: the **Schoodic National Scenic Byway,** which wraps around the peninsula, and the **Blackwoods Scenic Byway,** an inland blue highway cutting through the Donnell Pond Public Reserved Land. If time permits, drive at least one of these routes. Ideally, you'd do both, because the scenery differs greatly. The best option is to connect the two via Route 1, creating a loop that includes lakes and forests, mountains and fields, ocean and rocky coast. If you have only one day to explore this region, this route takes in the best of it. In early to mid-October, when the fall foliage is at its peak, the vistas are especially stunning.

The 29-mile Schoodic National Scenic Byway stretches from Hancock on Route 1 to Gouldsboro and then south on Route 186 and around the Schoodic Peninsula, ending in Prospect Harbor. A detailed guide is available at www.schoodicbyway.org. Along the route are seven outdoor **Kids Quest** sites designed to engage families in the region's history, culture, and ecology. A detailed guide is available at www.schoodicbyway.org. Other information is available at www.byways.org.

The 12.5-mile **Blackwoods Scenic Byway** meanders along Route 182 inland of Route 1, from Franklin to Cherryfield. It slices through the Donnell Pond Public Reserved Lands, edges lakes and mountains, and passes through small villages. You'll find access to trailheads and boat launches at Donnell Pond and Tunk Lake. Blueberry barrens, which turn crimson in autumn, can be seen on the rolling hills around Franklin and Cherryfield. Although Cherryfield is beyond the Schoodic region, it's a beautiful town to visit, filled with stately Victorian homes. It's also the self-proclaimed wild blueberry capital of the world. Maps and information are available at www. blackwoodsbyway.org.

Also running through the Acadia region is the **Downeast Fisheries Trail** (www.downeastfisheriestrail.org), which follows Maine's coastline from Penobscot Bay to Cobscook Bay. The mapped trail comprises 45 sites celebrating Maine's marine resources. Marked sites, including roughly two dozen in the Acadia region, allow you to delve into Maine's fishing and maritime heritage by visiting fish hatcheries, aquaculture facilities, active fishing harbors, processing plants, working wharves and piers, and related historic sites. You can request a printed copy of the map by calling 207/581-1435.

Library

The inviting octagonal **Hancock Point Library** (Hancock Point Rd., Hancock Point, 207/422-6400, summer only) was formed in 1899. More than a library, it's a center for village activities. Check the bulletin boards by the entrance to find out what's happening when.

Getting There and Around

Gouldsboro is about 18 miles via Route 1 from Ellsworth. The town straddles Route 1 and includes the upper and eastern portions of the Schoodic Peninsula. Route 186 loops the peninsula, but Route 195 provides the fastest access from Route 1 to Prospect Harbor. From Prospect Harbor it's about 2 miles to Birch Harbor via Route 186 or about 3 miles to Corea via Route 195. From Prospect Harbor, it's about 4 miles or 10 minutes to Winter Harbor via Route 186 or about 10 miles or 15 minutes to Steuben or 15 miles or 20 minutes to Milbridge via Routes 186 and 1.

The free **Island Explorer** (www.exploreacadia.com) bus Route 8 covers the lower part of the peninsula, connecting Winter Harbor and the ferry to the Schoodic section of Acadia, Birch Harbor, and Prospect Harbor, from late June through August. You'll need a car to explore Corea or other parts of Gouldsboro.

STEUBEN, MILBRIDGE, AND FRANKLIN

Continue northeast beyond the Schoodic Peninsula, and you'll arrive in Steuben, on the far side of Gouldsboro Bay. Not that you'll notice; frankly, there's little here to mark its presence on Route 1, and only a small village if you venture off it, although that's changing as the land is carved up by developers (the number of Land for Sale signs is frightening). Only a small sign indicates that the Petit Manan section of the Maine Coastal Islands National Wildlife Refuge awaits those who turn down Pigeon Hill Road.

If you want to see this part of the coast from the sea, especially Petit Manan lighthouse and its puffin colony, you have to venture up to Milbridge. Although not truly part of the Acadia region by any definition, it's the closest port with lighthouse-sighting, bird-watching, or scenic nature cruises. If you're camping in Steuben, it's also the closest option for food, with a supermarket and a few restaurants.

From Milbridge, you can loop back to Hancock along Route 182, the Blackwoods Scenic Byway, which moseys through the Donnell Pond Public Land Reserve, with access to ponds, lakes, and trailheads. En route is the vest-pocket village of Franklin. It's a beautiful route, especially in autumn, when the leaves are brilliant and the blueberry barrens in Cherryfield and Franklin are crimson.

Paddling

Well off the beaten path is **Dyer Harbor** in Steuben. Take Dyer Bay Road off Route 1, then go left on Pinkham Bay Bridge Road. Just before the bridge is a boat launch for small craft. It's a fine spot to launch a kayak for a coastal paddle in relatively protected waters.

Robertson Sea Tours and Adventures

Captain Jamie Robertson's **Robertson Sea Tours and Adventures** (Milbridge Marina, Fickett's Point Rd., 207/483-6110 or 207/461-7439, www.robertsonseatours.com, May 15-Oct. 1) offers cruises from the Milbridge Marina aboard the *Kandi Leigh* or the *Susan*

Jane, a pair of classic Maine lobster boats. Options include bird-watching (puffins and seabirds), whale-watching, lighthouse-viewing, lobstering, and a full-day combo. Prices range $60-250 adults, $45-185 children for the 2-6-hour cruises. Boat minimums may apply.

Entertainment and Events

EAGLE HILL SUMMER LECTURES

The **Eagle Hill Institute** (59 Eagle Hill Rd., Steuben, 207/546-2821, www.eaglehill.us) presents advanced natural history seminars and scientific illustration workshops and publishes peer-reviewed scientific journals. It also sponsors various opportunities to meet and mingle with scientists and others. If you're especially interested in natural history and the arts, the institute offers longer programs as well. The institute is located four miles off Route 1. Take Dyer Bay Road off Route 1, bearing left at the fork on Mogador Road, for a total of 3.6 miles, and then go left on Schooner Point Road and right on Eagle Hill Road. Programs take place in the dining hall lecture room.

Free public **lectures,** by recognized experts on often fascinating topics, are offered two or three times each week. Subjects have included Maine Poets and the Natural World; Lichens After Death: The Lichens of Graveyards; Bees of Maine Gardens; and A Maine Man to be Proud of: Joshua Lawrence Chamberlain. Guests are invited to arrive early to hike the institute's 2.5-mile network of easy to moderate trails (pick up a trail map in the office) or to peruse the library, which offers 8,000 books on natural history science and 1,000 books about art history. An onsite restaurant may be open for dinner on program nights.

Shopping

Arthur Smith (Rogers Point Rd., Steuben, 207/546-3462) is the real thing when it comes to chainsaw carvings. He's an extremely talented folk artist who looks at a piece of wood and sees an animal in it. His carvings of great blue herons, eagles, wolves, porcupines, flamingos, and other creatures are incredibly detailed, and his wife, Marie, paints them in lifelike colors. Don't expect a fancy studio; much of the work can be viewed roadside.

Also in Steuben, but on the other end of the spectrum, is **Ray Carbone** (460 Pigeon Hill Rd., Steuben, 207/546-2170, www.ray-carbonesculptor.com, 10am-4pm Thurs.-Sat. or appt.), whose masterful wood, stone, and bronze sculptures and fine furniture are definitely worth stopping to see and perhaps buy. Don't miss the granite sculptures and birdbaths in the garden.

Food
QUICK BITES
Thank the migrant community who arrive here in summer to pick blueberries for ★ **Vazquez Mexican Takeout** (38 Main St., Milbridge, 207/546-2219, 10am-7pm Mon.-Fri., $4-12). What began as a food truck serving authentic Mexican fare to blueberry pickers has evolved into a family-operated permanent seasonal takeout spot, with picnic tables on a covered patio and on the lawn. The food is excellent, the portions are generous, and the Mexican fare is delicious and authentic, with house-made tortillas and salsas.

Fire & Dough Wood Fired Pizza (164 Main St., Milbridge, 207/546-8116, www.fireanddoughdowneast.com, 11:30am-7pm Wed.-Sun., $7-10), a mobile kitchen, offers 10-inch pizzas; outdoor seating only.

Sure, you can get the usual burgers and fried foods at **The Meadow's Takeout** (1000 Rte. 1, Steuben, 207/546-3434, 11:30am-7:30pm Thurs.-Sat., noon-7pm Sun., $10-21), but it also serves Portuguese fare. Despite the name, there's indoor seating, too.

Ray's Meat Market (69 Dyers Bay Rd., Steuben, 207/546-7097, 6am-6pm Tues.-Sat., 8am-5pm Sun.) is full-service butcher shop and convenience store that also offers sandwiches, prepared foods, and baked goods.

FAMILY FAVORITES
Cheery waiters serve big portions of home-cooked fare at **44 Degrees North** (17 Main St., Milbridge, 207/546-4440, www.44-degrees-north.com, 11am-7:30pm Mon.-Sat., $10-30). The front room is family oriented, with booths, tables, and cheerful decor. The back room doubles as a bar and has a big-screen TV. As is typical in this part of Maine, there's a case full of mouthwatering desserts. Most heartier entrée choices are less than $17.

Milbridge House (20 Main St., 207/544-4454, www.milbridgehouse.com, 6am-2pm Thurs.-Sun., $6-20) serves home-style comfort food for breakfast and lunch.

Camping
Town-owned **McClellan Park** (Wayman Rd., Milbridge, 207/542-2422, $10/site), a gift to the town in 1925 from George B. McClellan, son of a Civil War general, has 14 primitive wooded campsites, each with picnic table and fire ring. The 10-acre ocean-front park, sited on Tom Leighton Point at the mouth of Narraguagus Bay, has a picnic area and excellent views of undeveloped islands.

Since 1958, the Ayr family has welcomed campers at its quiet, well-off-the-beaten-path property on Joy Cove. With a convenient location 15 minutes from Petit Manan National Wildlife Refuge and 20 minutes from Schoodic Point, **Mainayr Campground** (321 Village Rd., Steuben, 207/546-2690, www.mainayr.com, late May-mid-Oct., $30-33) has 35 mostly wooded tenting and RV sites (5 with full hookups). Also on the premises are a playground, a laundry, a beach for tidal swimming, clamming flats, a grassy launch area for kayaks and canoes, a camp store, berries for picking, and fresh lobsters.

Information
Info on the area is available from the **Milbridge Area Merchants Association** (https://narraguagusbay.org).

Getting There and Around

From Ellsworth, it's about 9 miles or 15 minutes to Hancock or about 11 miles or 15 minutes to Sullivan via Route 1. From Ellsworth to Sorrento is about 17 miles or 25 minutes via Routes 1 and 185. From Sullivan, it's about 15 miles or 20 minutes to Winter Harbor via Routes 1 and 186; about 17 miles or 25 minutes to Corea via Routes 1 and 195; and about 16 miles or 20 minutes to Steuben or about 21 miles or 25 minutes to Milbridge via Route 1.

From Ellsworth, it's about 12 miles or 20 minutes to Franklin via Routes 1 and 182/Blackwoods Scenic Byway. From Franklin, it's about 22.5 miles or 30 minutes to Milbridge via Routes 182/Blackwoods Scenic Byway and Route 1.

Blue Hill Peninsula

The Blue Hill Peninsula, once dubbed "the Fertile Crescent," is unique. Few other Maine locales harbor such a concentration of artisans, musicians, and on-their-feet retirees juxtaposed with topflight wooden-boat builders, lobstermen, and umpteenth-generation Mainers. Perhaps surprisingly, the mix seems to work.

The peninsula dangles into Penobscot Bay, anchored by the towns of Bucksport to the west and Ellsworth to the east and tethered via bridge to Deer Isle at its tip. It comprises several enclaves with markedly distinctive personalities—artsy Blue Hill, historic Castine, quiet Orland, boaty Brooklin, rural Brooksville, and sedate Sedgwick—all stitched together by a network of narrow, winding country highways and byways. Thanks to the mapmaker-challenging coastline and a handful

Highlights

Look for ★ to find recommended sights, activities, dining, and lodging.

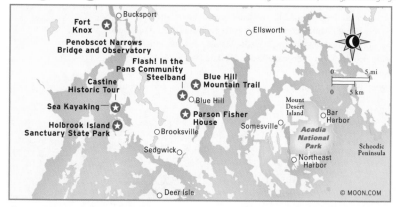

★ **Fort Knox:** A good restoration, frequent events, and secret passages make this late-19th-century fort one of Maine's best (page 180).

★ **Penobscot Narrows Bridge and Observatory:** On a clear day, the views from the 447-foot-high tower, one of only three bridge observatories in the world, extend from Katahdin to Cadillac Mountain (page 181).

★ **Castine Historic Tour:** A turbulent history detailed on signs throughout town makes Castine an irresistible place to tour on foot or by bike (page 186).

★ **Sea Kayaking:** Hook up with "Kayak Karen" in Castine for a tour (page 189).

★ **Parson Fisher House:** More than just another historic house, the Parson Fisher House is a remarkable testimony to one man's ingenuity (page 193).

★ **Blue Hill Mountain Trail:** It's a relatively easy hike to the summit of Blue Hill Mountain, which has fabulous 360-degree views (page 194).

★ **Flash! In the Pans Community Steelband:** Close your eyes and you might think you're on a Caribbean island when you hear this phenomenal steel-pan band (page 196).

★ **Holbrook Island Sanctuary State Park:** Varied hiking trails and great birding are the rewards for finding this off-the-beaten-path preserve (page 202).

Blue Hill Peninsula

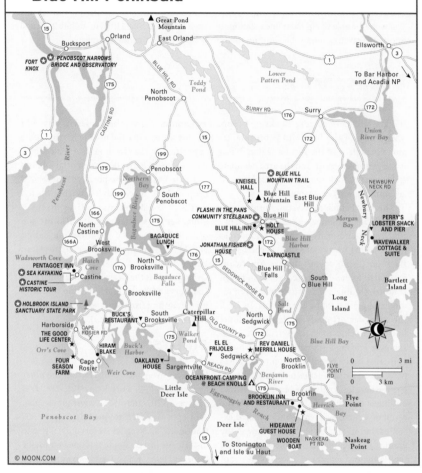

of freshwater ponds and rivers, there's a view of water around nearly every bend.

You can watch the sun set from atop Blue Hill Mountain; tour the home of the fascinating Jonathan Fisher; stroll through the charming village of Castine; visit tiny Brooklin, the self-proclaimed wooden boat-building capital of the world; and browse top-notch studios and galleries salted throughout the peninsula.

Mosey even more off the beaten path to Cape Rosier and visit the homestead of back-to-the-landers Helen and Scott Nearing; tour the nearby Four Season Farm, where organic guru Eliot Coleman sets the trend; and hike the underutilized trails of the Holbrook Island Sanctuary. Venture a bit inland of Route 1 and you'll find lovely lakes for paddling and swimming and another hill to hike.

Previous: Castine's main street; Castine's waterfront; The Sow's Ear Winery in Brooksville.

PLANNING YOUR TIME

To truly enjoy this region, you'll want to spend at least 2-3 days leisurely exploring here, as you won't be able to zip from one location to another. Traveling along the winding roads, discovering galleries and country stores, and lodging at traditional inns are all part of the experience. Arts fans will want to concentrate their efforts in Blue Hill. For architecture and history buffs, Castine is a must.

Bucksport Area

It's a stretch to consider Bucksport (pop. 4,924) part of the Blue Hill Peninsula, let alone include it in the Acadia region, but it is the gateway to it all, and the area has some sights worth a look-see and reasonably priced accommodations and campsites.

The new Penobscot Narrows Bridge provides an elegant entry to Bucksport, a long-time rough-and-ready river port and former papermaking town that's slowly gentrifying. Bucksport is no upstart. Native Americans gravitated to these Penobscot River shores in summer, finding a rich source of salmon for food and grasses for basket making. In 1763, the area was officially settled by Colonel Jonathan Buck, a Massachusetts Bay Colony surveyor who modestly named it "Buckstown" and organized a booming shipping business here. His remains are interred in a local cemetery, where his tombstone bears the distinct outline of a woman's leg; this is allegedly the result of a curse by a witch Buck ordered executed, but in fact it's probably a flaw in the granite. The monument is across Route 1 from the Hannaford supermarket, on the corner of Hinks Street.

Just south of town, at the bend in the Penobscot River, Verona Island (pop. 544) is best known as the mile-long link between Prospect and Bucksport. Prospect is home to the Penobscot Narrows Bridge and Observatory and Fort Knox, guarding the mouth of the Penobscot River. Just before you cross the bridge from Verona to Bucksport, hang a left, then a quick right to a small municipal park with a boat launch and broad views of Bucksport Harbor (and the old paper mill). Admiral Robert Peary's arctic exploration vessel, the *Roosevelt,* was built on this site in 1905 and used in his final 1908 expedition to the North Pole. A scale model can be viewed in the Buck Memorial Library.

Route 1 east of Bucksport leads to **Orland** (pop. 2,225), whose idyllic setting on the banks of the Narramissic River makes it a magnet for shutterbugs. It's also the site of a unique service organization called H.O.M.E. (Homeworkers Organized for More Employment). **East Orland** (officially part of Orland) claims the Craig Brook National Fish Hatchery and Great Pond Mountain (you can't miss it, jutting from the landscape on the left as you drive east on Route 1).

SIGHTS
★ Fort Knox

Looming over Bucksport Harbor, the *other* **Fort Knox** (740 Fort Knox Rd./Rte. 174, Prospect, 207/469-6553, www.maine.gov, 9am-6pm May-Oct., to 7pm July-Aug., $4.50-6.50 adults, $2.50 ages 5-11 fort only) is a state historic site just off Route 1. Named for Major General Henry Knox, George Washington's first secretary of war, the sprawling granite fort was begun in 1844. Built to protect the upper Penobscot River from attack, it was never finished and never saw battle. Still, it was, as guide Kathy Williamson says, "very well thought out and planned, and that may have been its best defense." Begin your visit at the Visitor and Education Center, operated by the Friends of Fort Knox, a nonprofit group that has partnered with the state to preserve and interpret the fort. Guided tours are sometimes available. The fort's distinguishing features include two complete Rodman cannons. Wear rubberized shoes and bring a flashlight to explore the underground passages; you can set the kids loose. The fort hosts Civil War reenactments several times each summer as well as a Medieval Tournament, a paranormal-psychic fair, and other events (check the website). The Halloween Fright at the Fort is a ghoulish event for the brave. The grounds are accessible all year. Bring a picnic; views over the river to Bucksport are fabulous.

★ Penobscot Narrows Bridge and Observatory

On a clear day, do not miss the **Penobscot Narrows Bridge and Observatory** (9am-7pm daily July-Aug., 9am-6pm daily May-June and Sept.-Oct., $7-9 adults, $5 ages 5-11, includes fort admission), accessible via Fort Knox. The three-deck observatory caps the bridge's 447-foot-high west tower, with the observatory's top floor sited at 420 feet above the Penobscot River. It's one of only three such structures in the world, and the only one in the United States. You'll zip up in an elevator, and when the doors open, you're facing a wall of glass—it's a bit of a shocker, and downright terrifying for anyone with a serious fear of heights. Ascend two more flights (an elevator is available) and you're in the glass-walled observatory; the views on a clear day extend from Katahdin to Mount Desert Island. Even when it's hazy, it's still a neat experience.

Alamo Theatre

The 1916 **Alamo Theatre** (85 Main St., Bucksport, 207/469-0924 or 800/639-1636, event line 207/469-6910, www.oldfilm.org, 9am-4pm Mon.-Fri. year-round) shows not only contemporary films but also indie and local ones. Before each feature, it screens archival shorts about New England produced or revived by the unique **Northeast Historic Film,** which is headquartered here. NHF has more than 10 million feet of film in its archives, including rarities. Celebrities ranging from Ken Burns to Oprah Winfrey have requested footage for projects. Stop in, survey the restoration, visit the displays (donation requested), and browse the Alamo Theatre Store for antique postcards, T-shirts, toys, and reasonably priced videos on ice harvesting, lumberjacks, maple sugaring, and other traditional New England topics.

H.O.M.E.

Adjacent to the flashing light on Route 1 in Orland, **H.O.M.E.** (Homeworkers Organized for More Employment, 207/469-7961) is tough

Fort Knox and the Penobscot Narrows Bridge and Observatory

to categorize. Linked with the international Emmaus Movement founded by a French priest, H.O.M.E. was started in 1970 by Lucy Poulin and two nuns at a nearby convent. The quasi-religious organization shelters refugees and the homeless, operates a soup kitchen and a car-repair service, runs a day-care center, and teaches work skills in a variety of hands-on cooperative programs. Seventy percent of its income comes from sales of crafts, produce, and services. At the Route 1 **store** (Rte. 1 and Upper Falls Rd., 9am-4:30pm daily), you can buy handmade quilts, organic produce, maple syrup, and jams—and support a worthwhile effort. You may also tour the craft workshops on the property.

Bucksport Waterfront Walkway

Stroll the one-mile paved walkway from the Bucksport-Verona Bridge to Webber Docks. Along the way are historical markers, picnic tables, a gazebo, restrooms, and expansive views of the harbor and Fort Knox.

RECREATION
Hiking
GREAT POND MOUNTAIN TRAIL

Distance: 2.3 miles round-trip
Duration: 2 hours
Elevation gain: 639 feet
Effort: Easy to moderate
Trailhead: 0.9 mile north of Craig Brook National Fish Hatchery at 70 Don Fish Rd., Orland

Great Pond Mountain's biggest asset is its 1,038-foot summit, with 360-degree views and lots of space for panoramic picnics. On a clear day, Baxter State Park's Katahdin is visible from Great Pond Mountain's north side. In autumn, watch for migrating hawks. Access to the mountain is via gated private property beginning about one mile north of the hatchery parking area. Roadside parking is available near the trailhead, but during fall foliage season, you may need to park at the hatchery. Pick up a brochure from the box at the trailhead, stay on the trail, and respect the surrounding private property. The mountain is

part of the 4,500-acre Great Pond Mountain Wildlands, maintained by the **Great Pond Mountain Conservation Trust** (207/469-7190, www.greatpondtrust.org).

From the trailhead, follow the Great Pond Mountain Trail 0.3 mile until you reach the intersection with the Connector trail. Continue along the Stuart Gross Trail as it winds its way up the mountain, gradually gaining elevation. Admire wildflowers along the way. When you've taken in the view at the summit, return the way you came, enjoying the easier descent.

Great Pond Mountain Wildlands

Encompassing two parcels of land and roughly 4,500 acres, the Great Pond Mountain Wildlands is a jewel. Acquired by the **Great Pond Mountain Conservation Trust** (207/469-7190, www.greatpondtrust.org) in 2005 after a decade of negotiation, the Wildlands comprises two sections. The larger parcel surrounds Hothole Valley, including Hothole Brook, prized for its trout, and shoreline on Hothole Pond. The smaller tract includes two miles of frontage on the Dead River (not to be confused with the Dead River of rafting fame in northwestern Maine) and reaches up Great Pond Mountain and down to the ominously named Hellbottom Swamp. The land is rich with wildlife: black bears, moose, bobcats, and deer, to name just a few species; plus, with the pond, swamp, and river, it's ideal for bird-watching. The 14 miles of woods roads lacing the land are open for walking, mountain biking, and snowshoeing, and the waterways invite fishing and paddling. Avoid the area during hunting season. Snowmobiling is permitted; ATVs are banned. Access to the Dead River tract is from the Craig Brook National Fish Hatchery; follow Don Fish Road to the Dead River Gate and Dead River Trail. The South Gate to Hothole Pond Tract is on Route 1 just southwest of Route 176. There's a parking lot at the gate, or, when it's open, you can drive in along Valley Road about 2.5 miles to another parking area.

Great Pond Mountain Trail

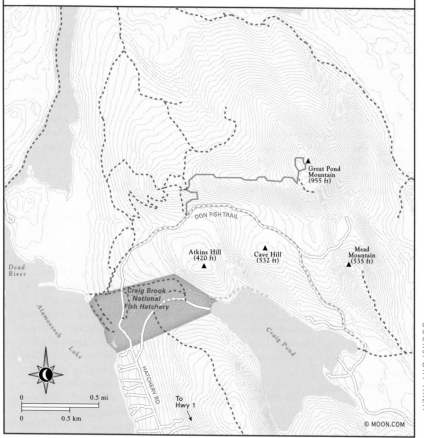

Great Pond Mountain
(955 ft)

DON FISH TRAIL

Atkins Hill
(420 ft)

Cave Hill
(532 ft)

Mead
Mountain
(535 ft)

Dead
River

Craig Brook
National
Fish Hatchery

Alamoosook Lake

Craig Pond

HATCHERY RD.

To
Hwy 1

0   0.5 mi

0   0.5 km

© MOON.COM

Craig Brook National Fish Hatchery

For a day of hiking, picnicking, swimming, canoeing, and a bit of natural history, pack a lunch and head for 135-acre **Craig Brook National Fish Hatchery** (306 Hatchery Rd., East Orland, 207/469-7300, www.fws. gov/northeast/craigbrook), on Alamoosook Lake. Turn off Route 1 six miles east of Bucksport and continue 1.4 miles north to the parking area. The **visitors center** (8am-3pm daily, free) offers interactive displays on Atlantic salmon (don't miss the downstairs viewing area), displays of fly-fishing artifacts and memorabilia, maps, and a restroom. The grounds are accessible 6am-sunset daily year-round. Established in 1889, this U.S. Fish and Wildlife Service hatchery raises sea-run Atlantic salmon for stocking seven Maine rivers. The birch-lined shorefront has picnic tables, a boat launch, an Atlantic salmon display pool, additional parking, and a spectacular cross-lake view. Watch for eagles, ospreys, and loons.

Canoeing

If you've brought a canoe, **Silver Lake,** just two miles north of downtown Bucksport, is a beautiful place for a paddle. There's no development along its shores, and the bird-watching is excellent. Swimming is not allowed and is punishable by a $500 fine; this is Bucksport's reservoir. To get to the public launch, take Route 15 north off U.S. 1. Go 0.5 mile and turn right onto McDonald Road, which becomes Silver Lake Road, and follow it 2.1 miles to the launch site.

SHOPPING

Locals come just as much for the coffee and conversation as the selection of new and used reads at **BookStacks** (71 Main St., Bucksport, 207/469-8992).

Stubborn Cow Glass (55 Main St., Bucksport, 207/433-7505), a working stained glass studio and gallery, sells gorgeous works in all sizes.

FOOD

Carrier's Mainely Lobster (corner of Rtes. 1 and 46, Bucksport, 207/469-1011, www.carriersmainelylobster.com, 11am-8pm daily, $5-25) doesn't look like much, but it's owned by a fishing family and one of the best local spots for lobster and fried seafood. There's an indoor dining room out back as well as picnic tables.

The area's other top spot, roughly 100 yards up the road, is **Crosby's Drive-In and Dairy Bar** (30 Rte. 46, Bucksport, 207/469-3640, 10:30am-8pm daily, $5-25), which has been dishing out burgers, dogs, fried seafood, and ice cream since 1938.

Now here's something different: **Friars' Brewhouse Tap Room** (84 Main St., Bucksport, 207/702-9156, 11:30am-2pm Tues.-Thurs., 11:30am-7pm Fri.-Sat., $8-16) is run by two Franciscan friars who brew Belgian-style craft beer, bake bread and treats, and serve a light menu (sandwiches, cheese/charcuterie plates, lobster rolls, flatbreads, etc.) in a diner-esque space with religious accents.

Walk down the alley next to the Dairy Port to find **Verona Wine and Design** (77 Main St., Bucksport, 207/745-0731, www.

veronawineanddesign.com, 4pm-9pm Wed.-Sat., $7-19), a wine and tapas restaurant with seating indoors as well as on a private patio out back. Make a meal from shareable dishes, sandwiches, appetizers, and desserts.

MacLeod's (63 Main St., Bucksport, 207/469-3963, http://macleodsrestaurant.com, from 4pm Wed.-Sat., $10-25) is Bucksport's most popular and enduring restaurant. Some tables in the pleasant dining room have glimpses of the river and Fort Knox. The wide-ranging American menu has choices for all tastes and budgets. Reservations are wise for Saturday nights.

ACCOMMODATIONS
Inns

If only the six simple guest rooms at the old-timey **Alamoosook Lakeside Inn** (off Route 1, Orland, 207/469-6393 or 866/459-6393, www.alamoosooklakesideinn.com, year-round, $165) actually overlooked the lake, it would be the perfect rustic lakeside lodge. The property is gorgeous, and the location is well suited for exploring the area. All guest rooms, decorated in a country style, have windows and doors opening onto a long, enclosed sun-porch overlooking the lake (so if the curtains are open, other guests passing by can see into your room). The lodge has 1,300 feet of lakefront and is great for wildlife-watching and fishing (especially for bass, trout, salmon, and pickerel), and guests may use the inn's canoes and kayaks. Paddle across the lake to the fish hatchery for a hike up Great Pond Mountain. If the weather doesn't cooperate, retreat to the basement rec room, with games, a fireplace, a library, and even a kitchenette. Two rooms are pet friendly ($15/night). Note: The inn often hosts events.

In downtown Bucksport, the four-story, 40-room **Fort Knox Park Inn** (64 Main St., Bucksport, 207/469-3113, www.fortknoxparkinn.com, $120-150) is right at the harbor's edge. A light continental breakfast is included. Be sure to request a water view, preferably on an upper floor, or you'll be facing a parking lot.

Motels

On the edge of downtown and set back from Route 1, the **Bucksport Motor Inn** (70 Rte. 1, Bucksport, 207/469-3111, www.bucksportmotorinn.com, $119) is a family-owned, vintage 1956 motel that's being updated; be sure to ask for one of the renovated rooms. Perks include refrigerators and microwaves. Some rooms are dog friendly ($20/stay).

Camping

The rivers, lakes, and ponds between Bucksport and Ellsworth make the area especially appealing for camping, and sites tend to be cheaper than in the Bar Harbor area. Six miles east of Bucksport, on the shores of 10-mile-long Toddy Pond, which reaches 100 feet in depth in some places, is **Balsam Cove Campground** (286 Back Ridge Rd., East Orland, 207/469-7771, www.balsamcove.com, late May-late Sept., $30-60), which leans toward bigger RVs. Facilities on the 50 acres include 60 wooded waterfront or water-view tent and RV sites, rental cabins ($80-90), on-site rental RVs ($120-130), a dump station, a store, laundry, free showers and Wi-Fi, boat rentals, and freshwater swimming. Dogs are welcome on camping sites for $2 per night. During July and August, especially on weekends, reservations are wise.

INFORMATION AND SERVICES

In Bucksport, **public restrooms** next to the town dock (behind the Bucksport Historical Society) are open spring-fall. Restrooms are open year-round in the Gateway gas station (at the Route 1 traffic light next to the Bucksport bridge) and in the Bucksport Municipal Office (Main St., Mon.-Fri.).

GETTING THERE AND AROUND

Bucksport is about 20 miles or 35 minutes via Route 15 from Bangor. It's about 17 miles or 25 minutes via Routes 1 and 15 to Blue Hill, about 22 miles or 30 minutes via Route 1 to Ellsworth, and about 18 miles or 30 minutes via Routes 175 and 166 to Castine.

Castine

Castine (pop. 1,366) is a gem—a serene New England village with a tumultuous past. It tips a cape, surrounded by water on three sides, including the entrance to the Penobscot River, which made it a strategic defense point. Once beset by geopolitical squabbles, saluting the flags of three different nations (France, Britain, and the Netherlands), its only crises now are local political skirmishes. This is an unusual community, a National Register of Historic Places enclave that many people never find. Today a major presence is Maine Maritime Academy, yet Castine remains the quietest college town imaginable. Students in search of a party school won't find it here; naval engineering is serious business.

Visitors will discover a year-round community with a busy waterfront, an easy-to-conquer layout, wooded trails on the outskirts of town, an astonishing collection of splendid Georgian and Federalist architecture, and water views nearly every which way you turn. If you're staying in Blue Hill or even Bar Harbor, spend a day here. Or book a room in one of the town's lovely inns, and use Castine as a base for exploring here and beyond. Either way, you won't regret it.

HISTORY

Originally known as Fort Pentagouet, Castine received its current name courtesy of Jean-Vincent d'Abbadie, Baron de St-Castin. A young French nobleman manqué who married a Wabanaki princess named Pidiwamiska, d'Abbadie ran the town in the second half of

Maine Maritime Academy

The state's only merchant-marine college—one of only seven in the nation—occupies 35 acres in the middle of Castine. Founded in 1941, the Maine Maritime Academy awards undergraduate and graduate degrees in such areas as marine engineering, ocean studies, and marina management, preparing a student body of about 850 men and women for careers as ship captains, naval architects, and marine engineers.

The academy owns a fleet of 60 vessels, including the historic gaff-rigged research schooner *Bowdoin*, flagship of Arctic explorer Admiral Donald MacMillan, and the 499-foot training vessel *State of Maine*, usually berthed down the hill at the waterfront. The *Bowdoin*, the Official Vessel of the State of Maine, is a National Historic Landmark. In 1996-1997, the *State of Maine*, formerly the U.S. Navy hydrographic survey ship vessel *Tanner*, underwent a $12 million conversion for use by the academy. It is still subject to deployment, and in 2005 the school quickly had to find alternate beds for first-year students using the ship as a dormitory when it was called into service in support of rescue and rebuilding efforts after Hurricane Katrina in New Orleans.

Weekday **tours of the campus** can be arranged through the admissions office (207/326-2206 or 800/227-8465 outside Maine, www.mainemaritime.edu). Campus highlights include the three-story Nutting Memorial Library, in Platz Hall; the Henry A. Scheel Room, a cozy oasis in Leavitt Hall containing memorabilia from late naval architect Henry Scheel and his wife, Jeanne; and the well-stocked bookstore (Curtis Hall, 207/326-9333).

the 17th century before his eventual return to France.

A century later, in 1779, occupying British troops and their reinforcements scared off potential American seaborne attackers (including Col. Paul Revere), who turned tail up the Penobscot River and ended up scuttling their more than 40-vessel fleet—a humiliation known as the Penobscot Expedition and still regarded as one of the worst naval defeats for the United States.

When the boundaries for Maine were finally set in 1820, with the St. Croix River marking the east rather than the Penobscot River, the last British Loyalists departed, some floating their homes north to St. Andrews in New Brunswick, Canada, where a few still can be seen today. For a while, peace and prosperity became the bywords for Castine—with lively commerce in fish and salt—but it all collapsed during the California gold rush and the Civil War trade embargo, leaving the town down on its luck.

Of the many historical landmarks scattered around town, one of the most intriguing must be the sign on "Wind Mill Hill," at the junction of Route 166 and State Street:

On Hatch's Hill there stands a mill. Old Higgins he doth tend it. And every time he grinds a grist, he has to stop and mend it.

In smaller print, just below the rhyme, comes the drama:

Here two British soldiers were shot for desertion.

Castine has quite a history indeed.

SIGHTS

★ Castine Historic Tour

To appreciate Castine fully, you need to arm yourself with the Castine Merchants Association's visitors brochure-map (all businesses and lodgings in town have copies) and follow the numbers on bike or on foot. With no stops, walking the route takes less than an hour, but you'll want to read dozens of historical plaques, peek into public buildings, shoot some photos, and perhaps even do some shopping.

The **Wilson Museum** (107 Perkins St., 207/326-8545, www.wilsonmuseum.org, 10am-5pm Mon.-Fri., 2pm-5pm Sat.-Sun. late May-late Sept., free), a cabinet of curiosities founded in 1921, contains an intriguingly eclectic and well-presented two-story collection of prehistoric artifacts, ship models, dioramas, baskets, tools, and minerals assembled over a lifetime by John Howard Wilson, a geologist-anthropologist who first visited Castine in 1891 (and died in 1936). Among the exhibits are Balinese masks, ancient oil lamps, cuneiform tablets, Zulu artifacts, pre-Inca pottery, and assorted local findings. It's well worth visiting.

Next door is the late 18th-century John Perkins House, moved to Perkins Street from Court Street in 1969 and restored with period furnishings. It's open in July and August for guided tours (on the hour, 2pm-5pm Sun. and Wed., $5).

Across the street and open the same days and hours as the Perkins House are the Village Blacksmith and the Woodshop, both with free demonstrations (usually Wed and Sun. July-Aug.).

At the end of Battle Avenue stands the 19th-century Dyce Head Lighthouse, no longer operating; the keeper's house is owned by the town. Alongside is a public path (signposted Enter at Your Own Risk) leading via a wooden staircase to a tiny patch of rocky shoreline and the beacon that has replaced the lighthouse.

The highest point in town is Fort George, site of a 1779 British fortification. Nowadays, little remains except grassy earthworks, but there are interpretive displays and picnic tables.

Main Street, descending toward the water, is a feast for historic architecture fans. Artist Fitz Hugh Lane and author Mary McCarthy once lived in elegant houses along the elm-lined street (both are identified on the map, but neither building is open to the public). On Court Street between Main and Green Streets stands turn-of-the-20th-century Emerson Hall, site of Castine's municipal offices.

Across Court Street, Witherle Memorial Library, a handsome early-19th-century building on the site of the 18th-century town jail, looks out on the Town Common. Also facing the Common are the Adams and Abbott Schools, the former still an elementary school. The Abbott School (10am-4pm Mon.-Sat., 1pm-4pm Sun. July-early Sept., reduced schedule spring and fall, donation), built in 1859, has been carefully restored for use as a museum and headquarters for the Castine Historical Society (207/326-4118, www.castinehistoricalsociety.org). A big draw at the volunteer-run museum is the 24-foot-long Bicentennial Quilt, assembled for Castine's 200th anniversary in 1996. The historical society, founded in 1966, organizes lectures, exhibits, and special events (some free) in various places around town.

On the outskirts of town, across the narrow neck between Wadsworth Cove and Hatch's Cove, stretches a rather overgrown canal (signposted British Canal), which was scooped out by the occupying British during the War of 1812. Effectively severing land access to the town of Castine, the Brits thus raised havoc, collected local revenues for eight months, and then departed for Halifax with enough funds to establish Dalhousie College, now Dalhousie University. Wear waterproof boots to walk the canal route; the best time to go is at low tide.

If a waterfront picnic sounds appealing, settle in on the grassy earthworks along the harbor front at Fort Madison, site of an 1808 garrison (then Fort Porter) near the corner of Perkins and Madockawando Streets. The views from here are fabulous, and it's accessible all year. A set of stairs leads down to the rocky waterfront.

Tours

The Castine Historical Society (17 School St., 207/326-4118, www.castinehistoricalsociety.org) offers free guided walking tours in July and August; call for schedule. Private tours may be available; call for details.

Or, opt for a 60- to 90-minute tour aboard Scarlet, a five-passenger, street-legal golf cart operated by the nonprofit Castine Touring Company (207/801-1122, https://castine-touring-company.business.site, $10 pp). It operates 10am-5pm daily during the summer season, departing from the Town Dock. Proceeds benefit local civic projects.

RECREATION
Witherle Woods

The 185-acre **Witherle Woods,** owned by Maine Coast Heritage Trust (www.mcht.org), is a popular walking area with a 4.2-mile maze of trails and old woods roads leading to the water. Many Revolutionary War-era relics have been found here; if you see any, do not remove them. Access to the preserve is via a dirt road off Battle Avenue, between the water district property (at the end of the wire fence) and the Manor's exit driveway, and diagonally across from La Tour Street. You can download a map from the website.

TOP EXPERIENCE

★ Sea Kayaking

Castine Kayak Adventures (17 Sea St., 207/866-3506, www.castinekayak.com) is spearheaded by Maine Guide Karen Francoeur, or "Kayak Karen," as she's known locally. All skill levels are accommodated, but Karen is particularly adept with beginners, delivering wise advice from beginning to end. Three-hour half-day trips are $55; six-hour full-day tours are around $110 and include lunch. Sunset tours, 2.5 hours, are $55; the sunrise tour includes a light breakfast for $55. Bioluminescent Night Paddle tours, under the stars (weather permitting), run about 2.5-3 hours and are $65 per person. If you have your own boat, call Karen; she knows these waters. She offers instruction for all levels as well as a Maine Sea Kayak Guide course.

Bicycling

Castine Kayak Adventures (17 Sea St., 207/866-3506, www.castinekayak.com) rents bicycles for $20/day or $100/week.

Swimming

Backshore Beach, a crescent of sand and gravel on Wadsworth Cove Road (turn off

---

1: Abbott School, Castine Historical Society
2: schooner *Bowdoin* at the Maine Maritime Academy 3: kayaking around Castine

Battle Ave. at the Castine Golf Club), is a favorite saltwater swimming spot, with views across the bay to Stockton Springs. Be forewarned, though, that ocean swimming in this part of Maine is not for the timid. The best time to try it is on the incoming tide, after the sun has had time to heat up the mud. At mid- to high tide, it's also the best place to put in a sea kayak.

Golf

The nine-hole **Castine Golf Club** (200 Battle Ave., 207/326-8844, www.castinegolf-club.com) dates to 1897, when the first tee required a drive from a 30-step-high mound. Willie Park Jr. redesigned it in 1921.

Boat Excursions

Guildive Cruises (207/701-1421, www.castinecruises.com) offers two different ways to enjoy Castine from the water. The *Guildive,* constructed in 1934 and captained by Kate Kana and Zander Parker, offers two-hour sails, departing up to three times daily from the Castine Public Wharf, for $50. Sunset sails, which include a light appetizer, are $55. *Lil' Toot* offers two excursions by reservation: one to Holbrook Island providing about 3.5 hours to enjoy the parklands and the other a 1.5-hour harbor tour ($120 for two people, $35 each additional person).

ENTERTAINMENT AND EVENTS

See what's on the calendar for the Castine Arts Association (www.castinearts.org). Possibilities for live music include **Danny Murphy's Pub** (on the wharf, tucked underneath the bank and facing the parking area and harbor) and Jazz Tuesdays at the **Pentagoet Inn.**

The **Castine Town Band** often performs free concerts on the common; check www.castine.org for its schedule.

A different band performs on the Town Dock every Wednesday evening for free **Waterfront Wednesdays.**

The **Wilson Museum** (107 Perkins St.,

207/326-8545, www.wilsonmuseum.org) frequently schedules concerts, lectures, and demonstrations.

The Trinitarian Church often brings in high-caliber musical entertainment.

Castine sponsors the intellectual side of the early-August Wooden Boat Regatta. The Castine Yacht Club brings in a who's who of big-name sail-related designers and racers for this annual lecture series. Other events include on-the-dock boat tours and limited sailing opportunities.

Gardening fans should ask about kitchen and garden tours, which occur every few years.

SHOPPING

Gallery B (5 Main St., 213/839-0851, www.gallerybgallery.com) shows fine art and sculpture. The Compass Rose Bookstore (3 Main St., 207/326-5034) specializes in maritime history, coastal Maine-based authors, and environmental history, and doubles as a coffee bar. Oil paintings by local artists Joshua and Susan Adam are on view at Adam Gallery (7 Main St., 207/326-8272). Mary Margarets Mercantile (207/326-5102, www.marymargaretsmercantile.com), brimming with eclectic items from clothing and gifts to housewares and yarn, occupies the first floor of the Castine Emporium (15 Main St.); Analog Attic (207/326-5102), selling vinyl records, classic video games, and retro equipment, is on the second floor.

FOOD

Quick Bites

The Castine Farmers Market takes place on the Town Common 9am-11:30am Thursdays.

Luscious baked goods fill the counter of Castine Variety (5 Main St., 207/326-9920, 7am-8pm daily, $6-22), a restored former general store. The menu blends classic American fare with Hawaiian and Southeast Asian flavors, a nod to the owner's background. BYOB.

MarKels (26 Water St., 207/326-9510, www.markelsbakehouse.com, 7am-3pm daily), a higgledy-piggledy eatery of three

rooms and a deck at the end of an alleyway tucked between Main and Water Streets, is a delicious find for breakfast, lunch, or sweets. Stop here for coffee, juices, pastries, interesting snacks and salads, homemade soups, specials, and delicious sandwiches.

The Captain's Catch (Town Dock, 207/460-4212, 11am-4pm daily), a waterfront take-out stand, is an excellent bet for summer classics such as lobster and crab rolls, burgers, and haddock sandwiches. You can't beat the location or the view, and much of the menu is locally sourced and made from scratch.

Casual Dining

Jazz music plays softly and dinner is by candlelight at the ★ Pentagöet Inn (26 Main St., 207/326-8616 or 800/845-1701, www.pentagoet.com, from 6pm Tues.-Sat., $18-34). In fine weather, you can dine on the porch. Choices vary from roasted *loup de mer* to slow-cooked lamb shank, or simply make a meal of small plates and starters, such as crab cakes and a salad. Don't miss the lobster bouillabaisse or the chocolate *budino,* a scrumptious warm Italian pudding that melts in your mouth (a must for chocoholics). Enjoy live jazz on the porch 5pm-8pm Tuesdays in July and August. Don't miss the Baron's Pub, if only to peek in at the portrait collection.

ACCOMMODATIONS

Inns

Castine is not the place to come if you require in-room phones, air-conditioning, or fancy bathrooms. The pace is relaxed and the accommodations reflect the easy elegance of a bygone era.

The three-story Queen Anne-style ★ Pentagöet Inn (26 Main St., 207/326-8616 or 800/845-1701, www.pentagoet.com, May-late Oct., $149-349) is the perfect Maine summer inn, right down to the lace curtains billowing in the breeze, the soft floral wallpapers, and the intriguing curiosities that

1: downtown Castine 2: Pentagöet Inn

accent but don't clutter the guest rooms. Innkeepers Jack Burke, previously with the U.S. Foreign Service, and Julie Van de Graaf, a pastry chef, took over the century-old inn in 2000 and have given it new life, upgrading rooms and furnishing them with Victorian antiques, adding handsome gardens, and carving out a niche as a dining destination. The inn's 16 guest rooms are spread between the main house and the adjoining, pet-friendly, renovated 1791 Federal-style Perkins House. A hot buffet breakfast, afternoon refreshments, and evening hors d'oeuvres are provided. Borrow one of the inn's bikes and explore town or simply walk—the Main Street location is convenient to everything Castine offers.

The venerable **Castine Inn** (41 Main St., 207/326-4365, www.castineinn.com, $130-235) has 19 second- and third-floor guest rooms and suites; some have water views; a few are air-conditioned; some have detached private baths. Public space includes a formal living room as well as a wraparound porch overlooking the gardens. Breakfast ($9 guests, $10 public) is served in the dining room, which features a wraparound mural of Castine.

INFORMATION AND SERVICES

Castine has no local information office, but all businesses and lodgings in town have copies of the Castine Merchants Association's visitors brochure-map. For additional information, go to the **Castine Town Office** (Emerson Hall, 67 Court St., 207/326-4502, www.castine.me.us, 8am-3:30pm Mon.-Fri.). Find **public restrooms** by the dock, at the foot of Main Street.

Penobscot Bay Press (https://penobscotbaypress.com), which publishes a collection of local newspapers, also maintains an excellent website, with listings for area businesses as well as articles highlighting area happenings.

GETTING THERE AND AROUND

Castine is about 16 miles or 25 minutes via Routes 1, 175, and 166 from Bucksport. It's about 20 miles or 30 minutes via Routes 166, 199, 175, and 177 to Blue Hill.

Blue Hill

Twelve miles south of Route 1 is the hub of the peninsula, Blue Hill (pop. 2,686), exuding charm from its handsome old homes to its waterfront setting to the shops, restaurants, and galleries that boost its appeal.

Eons back, Native American summer folk gave the name Awanadjo ("small, hazy mountain") to the mini-mountain that looms over the town and draws the eye for miles around. The first permanent settlers arrived in the late 18th century, after the French and Indian War, and established mills and shipyards. More than 100 ships were built here between Blue Hill's incorporation in 1789 and 1882—bringing prosperity to the entire peninsula.

Critical to the town's early expansion was its first clergyman, Jonathan Fisher, a remarkable fellow who has been likened to Leonardo da Vinci. In 1803, Fisher founded Blue Hill Academy (predecessor of today's George Stevens Academy), then built his home (now a museum), and eventually left an immense legacy of inventions, paintings, engravings, and poetry.

Throughout the 19th century and into the 20th, Blue Hill's granite industry boomed. Scratch the Brooklyn Bridge and the New York Stock Exchange and you'll find granite from Blue Hill's quarries. Around 1879, the discovery of gold and silver brought a flurry of interest, but little came of it. Copper was also found here, but quantities of it, too, were limited.

At the height of industrial prosperity, tourism took hold, attracting steamboat-borne summer boarders. Many succumbed to the scenery, bought land, and built waterfront summer homes. Thank these summer folk and their offspring for the fact that music has long been a big deal in Blue Hill. The Kneisel Hall Chamber Music School, established in the late 19th century, continues to rank high among the nation's summer music colonies. New York City's Blue Hill Troupe, devoted to Gilbert and Sullivan operettas, was named for the longtime summer home of the troupe's founders.

Scoot over to neighboring **Surry** (pop. 1,466) for an oceanfront lobster shack with views over Mount Desert Island followed by to-die-for ice cream.

SIGHTS
★ Parson Fisher House

Named for a brilliant Renaissance man who arrived in Blue Hill in 1794, the **Parson Fisher House** (44 Mines Rd./Rte. 15/176, 207/374-2459, www.jonathanfisherhouse. org, 1pm-4pm Wed.-Sat. early July-late Aug., 1pm-4pm Fri.-Sat. to mid-Oct., $5) immerses visitors in period furnishings and Jonathan Fisher lore. And Fisher's feats are breathtaking: He was a Harvard-educated preacher who also managed to be an accomplished painter, poet, mathematician, naturalist, linguist, inventor, cabinetmaker, farmer, architect, and printmaker. In his spare time, he fathered nine children. Fisher also pitched in to help build the yellow house on Tenney Hill, which served as the Congregational church parsonage. Now it contains intriguing items created by Fisher, memorabilia that volunteer tour guides delight in explaining, including a camera obscura. Don't miss it.

Historic Houses

A few of Blue Hill's elegant houses have been converted to museums, inns, restaurants, and even some offices and shops, so you can see them from the inside out. To appreciate the private residences, you'll want to walk, bike, or drive around town. You can download a self-tour map created by local students from https://bluehillhistory.org/self-tour/.

In downtown Blue Hill, a few steps off Main Street, stands the **Holt House** (3 Water St., www.bluehillhistory.org, 1pm-4pm Tues. and Fri., 11am-2pm Sat. July-mid-Sept., $3 adults, free under age 13), home of the Blue Hill Historical Society. Built in 1815 by Jeremiah Holt, the Federal-style building contains restored stenciling, period decor, and masses of memorabilia contributed by local residents. In the carriage house are even more goodies, including old tools, a sleigh, carriages, and more.

Walk or drive up Union Street (Rte. 177), past George Stevens Academy, and wander **The Old Cemetery,** established in 1794. If gnarled trees and ancient headstones intrigue you, there aren't many good-size Maine cemeteries older than this one.

Bagaduce Music

One of Maine's more unusual institutions is the **Bagaduce Music** (49 South St., 207/374-5454, www.bagaducemusic.org, 10am-4pm Mon.-Fri. or by appointment), where you can borrow from a collection of more than 3000,000 titles. Somehow this seems appropriate for a community that's a magnet for music lovers. Annual membership is $25 ($15 for students 18 and younger); fees range $1-4 per piece. Check the library's site for information about performances in its 100-seat hall.

Scenic Route

Parker Point Road (turn off Rte. 15 at the Blue Hill Public Library) takes you from Blue Hill to Blue Hill Falls the back way, with vistas en route toward Acadia National Park. For more serene views, drive the length of **Newbury Neck**, off Route 172 in Surry; you might even bookend the drive with a lobster dinner at the tip followed by an ice cream back in downtown Surry.

Blue Hill

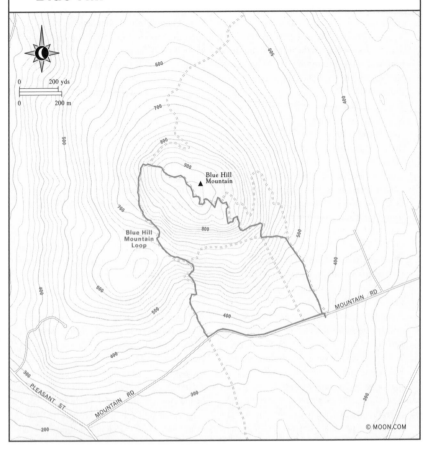

RECREATION
Hiking
★ BLUE HILL MOUNTAIN TRAIL

Distance: 1.8 miles round-trip

Duration: 1.5 miles

Elevation gain: 567 feet

Effort: Easy to moderate

Trailhead: Take Route 15 (Pleasant St.) to Mountain Road and follow it 0.8 mile to the trailhead (on the left) and the small parking area (on the right). Alternatively, you can walk (uphill) the mile from the village to reach the trailhead.

"Mountain" seems a fancy label for a 934-footer, yet Blue Hill Mountain stands alone, visible from Camden and even beyond. On a clear day, head for the summit and take in the wraparound view encompassing Penobscot Bay, the hills of Mount Desert, and the Camden Hills. In mid-June the lupines along the way are breathtaking; in fall the colors are spectacular, with reddened blueberry barrens added to the variegated foliage. Go early in the day; it's a popular, easy-to-moderate hike.

From the Mountain Road Trailhead, take the Osgood Trail. Follow it northwest until it curves southeast, then follow the path to reach the summit. Enjoy the spectacular views. When you're ready, return the way you came.

Another option is the easier Becton Trail, departing from the Turkey Farm Road trailhead (0.6 mi. north off Rte. 172). Follow the trail 2 miles to the summit then return the same way.

Parks and Preserves
BLUE HILL HERITAGE TRUST
Blue Hill Heritage Trust (157 Hinckley Ridge Rd., 207/374-5118, www.bluehillheritagetrust.org, 8:30am-5pm Mon.-Fri.) works hard at preserving the region's landscape. Trail maps for all sites can be downloaded from the website. It also presents a Walks and Talks series, with offerings such as a mushroom walk and talk, a full-moon hike up Blue Hill Mountain, and farm tours. Many include talks by knowledgeable folks on complementary topics. The trust publishes *Hiking Trails & Public Access Points of the Greater Blue Hill Peninsula*, a 60-page booklet with details about trails, boat launches, swimming spots, and preserves.

BLUE HILL TOWN PARK
At the end of Water Street is a small park with a terrific view, along with a small pebble beach, picnic tables, a portable toilet, and a playground.

Outfitters
The **Activity Shop** (139 Mines Rd., 207/374-3600, www.theactivityshop.com) rents bicycles for $125/week and canoes, kayaks, and paddleboards for $125-245/week, including delivery on the peninsula.

Boat Excursions
Join captain Linda Greenlaw, of *Perfect Storm* fame, for the **Perfect Tour** (207/479-3000, https://theperfecttour.com) aboard the *Earnest*. Operating from Perry's Lobster Shack in Surry, Greenlaw offers two- to eight-hour custom charters beginning at $600 for two hours. Options include Catch Your Dinner: Lobster Fishing 101, Cocktail Cruise, Sunset Cruise, and Floating Picnic, in addition to fishing, bird-watching, and wildlife-watching.

BLUE HILL FALLS
A favorite spot for experienced kayakers and canoeists is Blue Hill Falls, which churns

Hike Blue Hill for splendid views.

with white water when the tide turns. Check for times of high and low tide. Roadside parking is illegal, but the law is too often ignored. The Route 175 bridge is narrow, and cars often stop suddenly as they come over the hill, so be particularly cautious here.

ENTERTAINMENT AND EVENTS

Variety and serendipity are the keys here. Check local calendar listings and tune in to **radio station WERU** (89.9 and 102.9 FM, www.weru.org), the peninsula's own community radio; there might be announcements of concerts by local resident pianist Paul Sullivan or the Bagaduce Chorale, or maybe a contra dance. **George Stevens Academy** has a free Tuesday evening lecture series in July-August.

The October **Foliage Food & Wine Festival** has workshops, lectures, music, and plentiful dining opportunities.

Live Music and Theater
★ **FLASH! IN THE PANS COMMUNITY STEELBAND**

If you're a fan of steel band music, the **Flash! In the Pans Community Steelband** (207/374-2172, www.flashinthepans.org) usually performs somewhere on the peninsula 7:30pm-9pm Monday mid-June-early September. Local papers carry the summer schedule for the nearly three-dozen-member band, which deserves its devoted following. Admission is usually a small donation to benefit a local cause.

KNEISEL HALL CHAMBER MUSIC SCHOOL

Since 1922, chamber-music students have been spending summers perfecting their skills and demonstrating their prowess at the **Kneisel Hall Chamber Music School** (Pleasant St./Rte. 15, 207/374-2811, www.kneisel.org). Festival concerts by faculty and guest artists run Friday evenings and Sunday afternoons late June-late August. The concert schedule is published in the spring, and reserved-seating tickets ($35 inside, $25 on the porch outside, nonrefundable) can be ordered online or by phone. Other opportunities to hear the students and faculty exist, including young-artist concerts, children's concerts, open rehearsals, and more. Kneisel Hall is about 0.5 mile from the center of town.

BLUE HILL CONCERT ASSOCIATION

The volunteer **Blue Hill Concert Association** (207/326-4666, www.bluehillconcertassociation.org) presents professional chamber music concerts January-March at the First Congregational Church (22 Tenney Hill Rd.). Recommended donation is $30.

NEW SURRY THEATRE

The **New Surry Theatre** (918 Union St., 207/200-4720, www.newsurrytheatre.org) stages musicals and classics each summer.

SURRY ARTS: AT THE BARN

Home to the former Surry Opera Company, the Surry Concert Barn is being revitalized by **Surry Arts: At The Barn** (8 Cross Rd., Surry, 207/669-9216, http://surryartsandevents.com), which presents a wide range of performances, from flamenco guitar to jazz, classical to blues.

Lectures

The **Shaw Institute** (55 Main St., 207/374-2135, www.shawinstitute.org), a nonprofit scientific research organization focused on chemical exposure and climate change, sponsors an evening lecture series.

Festivals and Events

WERU's annual **Full Circle Fair** is usually held in mid-August at the Blue Hill Fairgrounds (Rte. 172, north of downtown Blue Hill). Expect world music, good food, crafts, and socially and environmentally progressive talks. On Labor Day weekend, the **Blue Hill Fair** (Blue Hill Fairgrounds, Rte. 172, 207/374-9976) is one of the state's best agricultural fairs. Both the **Foliage, Food**

Gallery Hopping in Blue Hill

Perhaps it's Blue Hill's location near the renowned Haystack Mountain School of Crafts. Perhaps it's the way the light plays off the rolling countryside and onto the twisting coastline. Perhaps it's the inspirational landscape. Whatever the reason, numerous artists and artisans call Blue Hill home, and top-notch galleries are abundant. Here's a sampler.

One mile north of downtown, **Rackliffe Pottery** (132 Ellsworth Rd./Rte. 172, Blue Hill, 207/374-2297, www.rackliffepottery.com), in its fourth generation of family ownership and noted for its vivid blue wares, has been producing lead-free pottery from clay sourced on the property since 1969.

Smack downtown, don't miss **Jud Hartmann** (79 Main St. at Rte. 15, Blue Hill, 207/461-530, www.judhartmanngallery.com). The spacious, well-lighted gallery carries Hartmann's limited-edition bronze sculptures of the woodland Native Americans of the Northeast. Hartmann often can be seen working on his next model in the gallery—a real treat. He's a wealth of information about his subjects, and he loves sharing the mesmerizing stories he's uncovered during his meticulous research.

The **Liros Gallery** (14 Parker Point Rd., Blue Hill, 207/374-5370, www.lirosgallery.com) has been dealing in Russian icons since the mid-1960s. Prices are high, but the icons are fascinating. The gallery also carries Currier & Ives prints, antique maps, and 19th-century British and American paintings. Just up the street is the **Cynthia Winings Gallery** (24 Parker Point Rd., Blue Hill, 917/204-4001, www.cynthiawiningsgallery.com), which shows contemporary works by local artists. From here it's a short walk to **Blue Hill Bay Gallery** (Main St., Blue Hill, 207/374-5773, www.bluehillbaygallery.com), which represents contemporary artists in various media.

Also on Main Street are two other fun, artsy gallery-shops. **Handworks Gallery** (48 Main St., Blue Hill, 207/374-5613, www.handworksgallery.org) sells a range of fun, funky, utilitarian, and fine-art crafts, including jewelry, furniture, rugs, wall hangings, and clothing, by more than 50 Maine artists and craftspeople.

About two miles from downtown is another don't-miss: **Mark Bell Pottery** (289 Rte. 15, Blue Hill, 207/374-5881, www.markbellpottery.com), in a tiny building signaled only by a small roadside sign, is the home of exquisite, award-winning porcelain by the eponymous potter. It's easy to understand why his wares have been displayed at the Smithsonian Institution's Craft Show as well as at other juried shows across the country. The delicacy of each vase, bowl, or piece is astonishing, and the glazes are gorgeous. Twice each summer he has kiln openings—must-go events for collectors and fans.

BLUE HILL PENINSULA
BLUE HILL

& Wine Festival and **Word. Blue Hill Literary Arts Festival** take place in October.

SHOPPING

Independent shops line Blue Hill's main and spill over onto the side streets.

Blue Hill Books (26 Pleasant St./Rte. 15, 207/374-5632, www.bluehillbooks.com) is a wonderful independent bookstore that hosts a series of talks by authors during the summer.

Three Wishes (28 Water St., 207/374-5400) offers an eclectic mix of women's clothing along with home and gift items.

Games and toys for all ages fill **Out on a Whimsey Toys** (50 Main St., 207/388-3911).

MAE Blue Hill (49 Main St., 207/374-2506) carries splurge-worthy housewares and clothing.

You're all but guaranteed to find the perfect Maine something, such as a book, pillow, chocolates, or a tote, for that hard-to-buy-for someone at **The Meadow of Blue Hill** (140 Maine St., 207/374-3785).

Browse clothing, home goods, jewelry, and gifty items at **MOYO Boutique** (27 Water St., 207/374-9101).

FOOD

Quick Bites

Picnic fare and pizza are available at Merrill & Hinckley (11 Union St., 207/374-2821, 6am-9pm Mon.-Sat., 8am-8pm Sun.), a quirky, 150-year-old family-owned grocery and general store.

The Blue Hill Wine Shop (138 Main St., 207/374-2161, www.bluehillwineshop.com, 10am-5:30pm Mon.-Sat.), tucked into a converted horse barn, carries more than 1,000 wines, plus teas, coffees, breads, and cheeses. Wine tastings and music nights pepper the calendar.

Peninsula Provisions (5 Maine St., 207/374-5621, 8am-5pm Mon.-Fri., 8am-3pm Sat.) shares its space with a florist and sells coffee, ice cream, baked goods, and chocolates. Don't miss the Art Box, a vending machine with $10 works by 10 local artists—a perfect gift for someone back home.

I think Pug Nuts (1276 Surry Rd., Surry, 207/412-0086, hours vary seasonally) is a contender for world's best ice cream and gelato, with intriguing flavors such as birch beer, rosewater, and lavender and honey, as well as the usual favorites.

The Blue Hill Co-Op and Café (70 South St., 207/374-2165, http://bluehill.coop, 7am-7pm Mon.-Sat., 8am-6pm Sun.) sells organic and natural foods. Breakfast items, sandwiches, salads, and soups are available in the café.

DeepWater Brewing Co. (33 Tenney Hill Rd., 207/374-2441, 4:30pm-8pm Tues.-Sun., $13-18) serves pub-style fare. Dine inside or out. Ask about tours of the solar-powered brewery, located in a beautifully renovated historic barn behind the pub.

Local gardeners, farmers, and craftspeople peddle their wares at the Blue Hill Farmers Market (9am-11:30am Sat. late May-early Oct.). It's a particularly enduring market, well worth a visit. Demonstrations by area chefs and artists are often on the agenda. Find it at the Blue Hill Fairgrounds, unless it's fair week, during which it moves to the Blue Hill Congregational Church.

Family Favorites

Marlintini's Grill (83 Mines St./Rte. 15, 207/374-2500, www.marlintinisgrill.com, 11am-9:30pm daily, $10-20) is half-sports bar and half-restaurant. You can sit in either, but the bar side can get raucous. Best bet: the screened-in porch. The American and tavern fare menu includes nightly home-style specials, and there's also a kids' menu. The portions are big, the service is good, and the food is decent.

Just south of town is Barncastle (125 South St., 207/374-2300, www.barncastle.me, noon-8pm Tues.-Sat., entrées $9-16), serving a creative selection of wood-fired pizzas in three sizes as well as sandwiches, calzones, salads, and entrees such as spanakopita and ribs in a lovely Shingle-style cottage. There are vegetarian options. Expect to wait for a table; this is one popular spot.

Siam Sky (8 Mill St., 207/374-7157, www.siamskyrestaurant.com, 11:30am-2:30pm and 4-9pm daily) serves excellent Thai food, with dining inside and on a streamside porch.

Casual Dining

For breakfast or lunch, tuck into Sandy's Blue Hill Café (40 Main St., 207/374-5550, http://sandysbluehillcafe.com, 8am-3pm Thurs.-Mon., $14-24), which also roasts its own coffee beans. Check online for info about dinner concerts.

Fine Dining

For a lovely dinner by candlelight, make reservations at ★ Arborvine (33 Upper Tenney Hill/Main St., 207/374-2119, www.arborvine.com, 5:30pm-8pm Tues.-Sun., entrées $28-35), a conscientiously renovated, two-century-old Cape-style house with four dining areas, each with a different feel and understated decor. Chef-owner John Hikade and his wife, Beth, prepare American entrées such as crispy roasted duckling and roasted rack of lamb. Their mantra has been fresh and local for more than 30 years.

1: Pug Nuts 2: Perry's Lobster Shack

Seafood

For lobster, fried fish, and the area's best lobster roll, head to **The Fish Net** (163 Main St., 207/374-5240, 11am-8pm Wed.-Mon.), an inexpensive, mostly take-out joint on the eastern end of town.

It's not easy to find ★ **Perry's Lobster Shack** (1076 Newbury Neck Rd., Surry, 207/667-1955, noon-7pm daily), but it's worth the effort for a classic lobster-shack experience. This traditional Maine lobster shack is about five miles down Newbury Neck, just after the Causeway Place beach. Expect lobster, lobster and crab rolls, corn, chips, mussels, and clams. From the pier-top picnic tables, you're overlooking the water with Mount Desert Island as a backdrop. Unlike most lobster shacks, this one has table service and a children's menu. No credit cards. Perry's also has a food truck that you may see around the region.

ACCOMMODATIONS
Inns and Bed-and-Breakfasts

What's old is new at **Barncastle** (125 South St., 207/374-2330, www.barn-castle.com, $145-195), a late-19th-century Shingle-style cottage that's listed in the National Register of Historic Places. It opens to a two-story foyer with a split stairway and balcony. Rooms and suites open off the balcony. All are spacious, minimally decorated, and offer contemporary amenities, including a fridge and a microwave. Rates include a continental breakfast. The downstairs tavern serves pizza, salads, and sandwiches; noise can be a factor.

★ **The Blue Hill Inn** (Union St./Rte. 177, 207/374-2844 or 800/826-7415, www.bluehillinn.com, from $195) is the epitome of a classic country inn. Built as a private residence in 1830 and converted to an inn in 1841, the antiques-filled inn is just steps from Main Street's shops and restaurants. Ten guest rooms and a suite have real chandeliers, four-poster beds, down comforters, fancy linens, and braided and Oriental rugs. Rear rooms overlook the extensive cutting garden, with chairs and a hammock. A three-course breakfast is served in the elegant dining room. Afternoon refreshments with sweets appear in the living room daily, and superb hors d'oeuvres are served 6pm-7pm in two elegant parlors or the garden. Also available are two year-round, pet-friendly suites (from $295) with cooking facilities in the contemporary Cape House.

Glamping

Under Canvas Acadia (702 Surry Rd., Surry, 207/512-4265, www.undercanvas.com/camps/acadia, from $359), opened in May 2021, offers 64 tents in seven styles to accommodate couples, friends, and families. All have en suite bathrooms. The property, with 1,200 feet of shoreline edging Union River Bay, is about a 35-minute drive from the park. Facilities include a waterfront, communal dining and gathering space. Facilities include a communal dining and gathering space on the waterfront.

Long-Term Rentals

Weekly or longer-term rentals can pay off if you have a large family or are planning a group vacation. The Blue Hill Peninsula has lots of rental cottages, camps, and houses, but the trick is to plan well ahead. This is a popular area in summer, and many renters sign up for the following year before they leave town. For information, contact Sandy Douvarjo of **Peninsula Property Rentals** (15 Main St., Blue Hill, 207/374-2428, www.peninsulapropertyrentals.com).

The **Wavewalker Cottage and Suite** (28 Wavewalker Ln., Surry, 207/667-5767, www.wavewalkerbedandbreakfast.com) has a jaw-dropping location near the tip of Newbury Neck. It sits on 20 private acres with 1,000 feet of shorefront as well as woods and blueberry fields. Choose from a suite ($200) with kitchenette and private entrance or a separate two-bedroom-plus-loft cottage ($1,800/week in season, from $250/night off season with a three-night minimum).

INFORMATION AND SERVICES

The **Blue Hill Peninsula Chamber of Commerce** (207/374-3242, www.bluehillpeninsula.org) is the best source for information on Blue Hill and the surrounding area.

Penobscot Bay Press (https://penobscotbaypress.com), which publishes a collection of local newspapers, also maintains an excellent website, with listings for area businesses as well as articles highlighting area happenings (http://baycommunityregister.com).

At the **Blue Hill Public Library** (5 Parker Point Rd., 207/374-5515, www.bluehill.lib.me.us), ask to see the suit of armor, which *may* have belonged to Magellan. The library sponsors a summer lecture series.

Public restrooms are in the Blue Hill Town Hall (Main St.), Blue Hill Public Library (Main St.), and Blue Hill Memorial Hospital (Water St.).

GETTING THERE AND AROUND

Blue Hill is about 17 miles or 25 minutes via Routes 1 and 15 from Bucksport and about 20 miles or 30 minutes via Routes 166, 199, 175, and 177 from Castine. It's about 14 miles or 20 minutes via Route 172 to Ellsworth, and about 11 miles or 15 minutes via Route 15 to Buck's Harbor in Brooksville.

Brooklin, Brooksville, and Sedgwick

I'm going to let you in on a secret—a part of Maine that seems right out of a time warp, a place with general stores and family farms, where family roots go back generations and summer rusticators have returned for decades. Nestled near the bottom of the Blue Hill Peninsula and surrounded by Castine, Blue Hill, and Deer Isle, this often-missed area offers superb hiking, kayaking, and sailing, plus historic homes and unique shops, studios, lodgings, and personalities.

The best-known town is **Brooklin** (pop. 824), thanks to two magazines: *The New Yorker* and *WoodenBoat*. Wordsmiths extraordinaire E. B. and Katharine White "dropped out" to Brooklin in the 1930s and forever afterward dispatched their splendid material for *The New Yorker* from here. (The Whites' former home, a handsome colonial not open to the public, is on Route 175 in North Brooklin, 6.5 miles from the Blue Hill Falls bridge.) In 1977, *WoodenBoat* magazine moved its headquarters to Brooklin, where its 60-acre shore-side estate attracts builders and dreamers from all over the globe.

Nearby **Brooksville** (pop. 934) drew the late Helen and Scott Nearing, whose book *Living the Good Life* made them role models for back-to-the-landers. Their Harborside compound on **Cape Rosier** now verges on must-see status. **Buck's Harbor,** a section of Brooksville, is the setting for *One Morning in Maine,* one of Robert McCloskey's beloved children's books.

Incorporated in 1789, the oldest of the three towns is **Sedgwick** (pop. 1,196), which once included all of Brooklin and part of Brooksville. Now wedged between Brooklin and Brooksville, it includes the hamlet of **Sargentville,** the Caterpillar Hill scenic overlook, and a well-preserved complex of historic buildings. The influx of pilgrims—many of them artists bent on capturing the spirit that has proved so enticing to creative types—continues in this area.

You can easily spend a day moseying the twisting highways and byways looping though this region. Look at the route numbers, which double on many roads, and it's possible to think you're driving north, south, east, and west simultaneously, which also explains how you can watch the sun both rise and set over the Atlantic. It's easy to get turned around, so keep your *Maine Atlas & Gazetteer* or other detailed map handy.

BROOKSVILLE

Sights

THE GOOD LIFE CENTER

Forest Farm, home of the late Helen and Scott Nearing, is now the site of the **Good Life Center** (372 Harborside Rd., Harborside, 207/326-8211, www.goodlife.org). Advocates of simple living and authors of 10 books on the subject, the Nearings created a trust to perpetuate their farm and philosophy. Resident stewards lead **tours** (usually 1pm-5pm Thurs.-Mon. mid-June-early Sept., Sat.-Sun. early Sept.-mid-Oct., $10 donation). Ask about the schedule for the traditional Monday-night meetings (7pm), featuring free programs by gardeners, philosophers, musicians, and other guest speakers. Occasional work parties, workshops, and conferences are also on the docket. From Route 176 in Brooksville, take Cape Rosier Road and go 8 miles, passing Holbrook Island Sanctuary. At the Grange Hall, turn right and follow the road 1.9 miles to the end. Turn left onto Harborside Road and continue 1.8 miles to Forest Farm, across from Orrs Cove.

FOUR SEASON FARM

About a mile beyond the Nearings' place is **Four Season Farm** (609 Weir Cove Rd., Harborside, 207/326-4455, http://fourseasonfarm.com), the lush organic farm owned and operated by internationally renowned gardeners Eliot Coleman and Barbara Damrosch. Both have written numerous books and articles and starred in TV gardening shows. The experimental market garden, a model for small-scale sustainable agriculture, operates year-round. Visitors are welcome to drive in and around the farm; a farm stand operates on Saturdays; call for hours.

LOCAL HISTORY

The **Brooksville Historical Society Museum** (150 Coastal Rd./Rte. 176, Brooksville, www.brooksvillehistoricalsociety.org, 1pm-4pm Wed. and Sun. July-Aug.) houses a collection of nautical doodads, farming implements, blacksmith tools, and quilts

in a converted boathouse. The museum is restoring a local farmhouse for more exhibits.

SCENIC ROUTES

Get way, way off the beaten path with a loop around **Cape Rosier,** the westernmost arm of the town of Brooksville. The Cape Rosier loop takes in Holbrook Island Sanctuary, Goose Falls, the hamlet of Harborside, and plenty of water and island views. Note that some roads are unpaved, but they usually are well maintained. Cape Rosier's roads are poorly marked, perhaps deliberately, so keep your DeLorme atlas handy.

Recreation

★ HOLBROOK ISLAND SANCTUARY

In the early 1970s, foresighted benefactor Anita Harris donated to the state 1,230 acres in Brooksville that would become the **Holbrook Island Sanctuary** (207/326-4012, www.parksandlands.com, free). From Route 176, between West Brooksville and South Brooksville, head west on Cape Rosier Road, following brown-and-white signs for the sanctuary. Trail maps and bird checklists are available in boxes at trailheads or at park headquarters. The easy Backshore Trail (about 30 minutes) starts here, or go back a mile and climb the steep-ish trail to **Backwoods Mountain** for the best vistas. Other attractions include shorefront picnic tables and grills, four old cemeteries, super bird-watching during spring and fall migrations, a pebble beach, and a stone beach. Leashed pets are permitted, but no bikes are allowed on the trails, and camping is not permitted. The park is officially open May 15-October 15, but the access road and parking areas are plowed in winter for cross-country skiers.

BICYCLING

Bicycling in this area is for confident, experienced cyclists. The roads are particularly narrow and winding, with poor shoulders. The best bet for casual pedal pushers is the area around **Cape Rosier,** where traffic is light.

BEACH

Find town-owned Bakeman Beach, a sand-and-gravel swath, hugging the Weir Cove Rd., southeast of Four Season Farm on Cape Rosier.

PICNICKING

You can take a picnic to the Bagaduce Ferry Landing, in West Brooksville off Route 176, where there are picnic tables and cross-river vistas toward Castine. Another good spot is Holbrook Island Sanctuary on Cape Rosier.

Bagaduce Theatre

Bagaduce Theatre (176 Mills Point Rd., Brooksville, 207/801-1536, www.bagaducetheatre.com) presents plays starring Equity actors from May into September.

Shopping

Most of these businesses are small, owner-operated shops, which means they're often catch-as-catch-can.

ANTIQUES

When you need a slate sink, a claw-foot tub, brass fixtures, or a Palladian window, Architectural Antiquities (52 Indian Point Ln., Harborside, 207/326-4938, www.arch-antiquities.com), on Cape Rosier, is just the ticket—a restorer's delight. Prices are reasonable for what you get, and they'll ship your purchases. It's open all year by appointment; ask for directions when you call.

TEXTILES

Amelia Poole handcrafts one-of-a-kind scarves, clothing, and art from all-natural and sustainable textiles—including cotton, silk and linen—dyed with plant-sourced colors at Ecouture Textile Studio (30 Bagaduce Rd., Brooksville, 339/832-2930, http://ecouturetextilestudio.com). She also conducts one-day workshops. Sharing the space is Makers' Market (30 Bagaduce Rd., Brooksville, 207/812-3703) showing an especially fine selection of mostly locally crafted works.

Food

QUICK BITES

In North Brooksville, where Route 175/176 crosses the Bagaduce River, stands the Bagaduce Lunch (145 Franks Flat, Penobscot, 11am-7pm Thurs.-Tues.), a take-out shack named an "American Classic" by the James Beard Foundation in 2008. Owners Judy and Mike Astbury buy local fish and clams. Check the tide calendar and go when the tide is changing; order fried clams, settle in at a picnic table, and watch the reversing falls. If you're lucky, you might sight an eagle, osprey, or seal.

You often can find Tinder Hearth's (1452 Coastal Rd., Brooksville, 207/326-8381, http://tinderhearth.com) organic, wood-fired, European-style breads and croissants in local shops and at farmers markets, but you can buy them right at the bakery on Tuesday and Friday. Pastries are baked Tuesday-Saturday. On some evenings, Tinder Hearth bakes thin-crust pizzas, usually 5pm-8pm; reservations are required, so call for the current schedule and menu. It's on the western side of Route 176 north of the Cape Rosier Road. It's not well marked, so keep an eye out for the Open sign.

Lunch is the specialty at Buck's Harbor Market (6 Cornfield Hill Rd., South Brooksville, 207/326-8683, www.bucksharbormarket.com, 8am-6pm daily), a low-key, marginally gentrified general store popular with yachties in summer. Pick up sandwiches, cheeses, prepared foods, breads, and treats for a Holbrook Island adventure.

Three varieties of English-style hard cider are the specialty at The Sow's Ear Winery (Rte. 176 at Herrick Rd., Brooksville, 207/326-4649, no credit cards), a minuscule operation in a funky two-story shingled shack. Winemaker Tom Hoey also produces sulfite-free blueberry, chokecherry, and rhubarb wines, all of which you can sample. Ask to see his cellar. Lining the walls in the tiny tasting room/shop are books, also for sale, that concentrate on architecture and history, with specialty areas highlighting Gothic arches and Russian history, but including plenty of other esoteric topics.

CASUAL DINING

Behind Buck's Harbor Market is ★ **Buck's Restaurant** (6 Cornfield Hill Rd., Brooksville, 207/326-8688, 5:30pm-8:30pm Mon.-Sat., $20-28), where guests dine at white-clothed tables inside or on a screened porch. Chef Jonathan Chase's American menu reflects what's locally available and changes frequently. Service is excellent.

The **Oakland House Dining Room** (435 Herrick Rd., Brooksville, 207/359-8521, www.oaklandhouse.com, 7:30am-10am and from 5:30pm Tues.-Sat., 7:30am-10am, 11am-2pm, and from 5:30pm Sun., $12-38), serves farm-to-table, American breakfasts, dinners, and Sunday brunch in a lovely porch-style room.

Accommodations

COTTAGE COLONIES

The fourth generation manages the **Hiram Blake Camp** (220 Weir Cove Rd., Harborside, 207/326-4951, www.hiramblake. com, Memorial Day-late Sept., no credit cards), but other generations pitch in and help with gardening, lobstering, maintenance, and kibitzing. Fifteen one- to six-bedroom cottages line the shore of this 100-acre property, which has been in family hands since before the Revolutionary War. The camp itself dates from 1916. Don't bother bringing reading material: The dining room has ingenious ceiling niches lined with countless books. Guests also have the use of rowboats, and kayak rentals are available. Home-cooked breakfasts and dinners are served family-style; lobster is always available at an additional charge. Much of the fare is grown in the expansive gardens. Other facilities include a dock, a recreation room, a pebble beach, and an outdoor chapel. There's a one-week minimum (beginning Sat. or Sun.) from late June through August, when cottages go for $1,300-4,000 per week (including breakfast, dinner, and linens). Off-season rates (no meals or linens, but cottages have cooking facilities) are $850-2,900 per week. Pets are welcome.

The ninth generation is operating ★ **Oakland House Seaside Inn & Cottages** (435 Herrick Rd., Brooksville, 207/359-8521, www.oaklandhouse.com, from $170). Much of this rolling, wooded land fronting on Eggemoggin Reach was part of an original grant from King George III way back in 1765. Eight nicely furnished and well-equipped one- and two-bedroom cottages are tucked along the shoreline and in the trees, and 10 newly renovated rooms and two-bedroom suites are in the main inn. Other pluses are trails threading through the woods and providing access to viewpoints and a pocket beach. An on-site restaurant offers breakfast and dinner. Rental canoes, kayaks, paddleboards, bikes, and fishing gear are available; sailboat and powerboat excursions are offered; and horseback riding and tennis can be arranged. Two cottages are dog friendly ($25/night).

GUEST HOUSE

Sited on the lovely Oakland House Seaside Resort grounds is **Acorn Guesthouse** (435 Herrick Rd., Brooksville, 207/359-8521, www.mainehostel.com, $60-99), offering a mix of dorm-style, private, and semiprivate rooms. Living spaces, bathrooms, and the kitchen are shared. Linens and towels are provided.

Information and Services

The best source of information about the region is the **Blue Hill Peninsula Chamber of Commerce** (207/374-2281, www.bluehillpeninsula.org).

Penobscot Bay Press (https://penobscotbaypress.com), which publishes a collection of local newspapers, also maintains an excellent website, with listings for area businesses as well as articles highlighting area happenings.

Check out **Free Public Library** (1 Town House Rd./Rte. 176, Brooksville, 207/326-4560).

1: Buck's Harbor Market and Buck's Restaurant
2: Oakland House Dining Room

Getting There and Around

Buck's Harbor, Brooksville, is about 8 miles or 15 minutes from Blue Hill via Routes 15, 175, and 176. From Buck's Harbor, it's about 8 miles or 15 minutes to Harborside on Cape Rosier via Route 176 to the Cape Rosier Road or about 9 miles or 15 minutes to Sedgwick.

SEDGWICK

Sights

HISTORICAL SIGHTS

Now used as the museum and headquarters of the Sedgwick-Brooklin Historical Society, the 1795 **Reverend Daniel Merrill House** (Rte. 172, Sedgwick, 2pm-4pm Sun. July-Aug. donation) was the parsonage for Sedgwick's first permanent minister. Inside the house are period furnishings, old photos, toys, and tools; a few steps away are a restored 1874 schoolhouse, an 1821 cattle pound (for corralling wandering bovines), and a hearse barn. Pick up a brochure during open hours and guide yourself around the buildings and grounds. The **Sedgwick Historic District,** crowning Town House Hill, comprises the Merrill House and its outbuildings, plus the imposing 1794 Town House and the 23-acre Rural Cemetery (the oldest headstone dates from 1798) across Route 172.

Recreation

PARKS AND PRESERVES

Just south and below the Caterpillar Hill scenic overlook, take the Cooper Farm Road to find two preserves, one for an easy to moderate hike and the other for a swim or paddle. The Blue Hill Heritage Trust's **Cooper Farm at Caterpillar Hill** offers a three-loop trail network winding through blueberry barrens and woods. The entire outer loop is 1.5 miles round-trip, but you can shorten or lengthen the route via the cross trails. In late July and August you can help yourself to the blueberries.

Afterward, continue a bit farther along the Cooper Farm Road to Landing Road, which leads to the **Sedgwick/Brooksville Town Landing** on Walker Pond. You'll find docks and floats, picnic tables, and a small sand beach with shallow water. It's a fine place to picnic, swim, paddle, or launch a small boat.

Shopping

Most of these businesses are small, owner-operated shops, which means they're often catch-as-catch-can.

BOOKS

Don't miss the "world's smallest bookstore," Bill Henderson's **Pushcart Press Bookstore** (380 Christy Hill, Sedgwick, 207/266-2531). It's a trove of literary fiction both used (paperbacks $2, hardbacks $5) and new, including editions of the *Pushcart Prize: Best of the Small Presses* annual series. Sales help support Pushcart fellowships.

Food

MEXICAN FUSION

★ **El El Frijoles** (41 Caterpillar Rd./Rte. 15, Sargentville, 207/359-2486, www.elelfrijoles. com, 11am-8pm Wed.-Sat., $6-16)—that's *L. L. Beans* to you gringos—gets raves for its made-from-scratch California-style empanadas, burritos, and tacos, many of which have a Maine accent. Try the spicy lobster burritos or a daily special, such as ranchero shrimp tacos or lobster quesadillas. Dine in the screen house or on picnic tables on the lawn; there's a play area for children.

QUICK BITES

Family-run **Strong Brewing Company** (7 Rope Ferry Rd., Sedgwick, 207/359-8722, http://strongbrewing.com, noon-7pm Tues.-Sat.) is open for tastings; the **Gott Lunch Food Truck** (207/479-3982, $7-14) operates here Wed.-Sat. Find it at the intersection of Routes 15 and 176.

Information and Services

The best source of information about the region is the **Blue Hill Peninsula Chamber of Commerce** (207/374-2281, www.bluehill-peninsula.org).

Scenic Drives

Caterpillar Hill's scenic vista

No one seems to know how Caterpillar Hill got its name, but its reputation comes from a panoramic vista of water, hills, and blueberry barrens—with a couple of convenient picnic tables where you can stop for lunch, photos, or a ringside view of sunset and fall foliage. From the 350-foot elevation, the views take in Walker Pond, Eggemoggin Reach, Deer Isle, Swans Island, and even the Camden Hills. The signposted rest area is on Route 175/15; watch out for the blind curve when you pull off the road.

Between Sargentville and Sedgwick, Route 175 offers elevated views of Eggemoggin Reach, with shore access to the Benjamin River just before you reach Sedgwick village.

Get way, way off the beaten path with a loop around Cape Rosier, the westernmost arm of the town of Brooksville. The Cape Rosier loop takes in Holbrook Island Sanctuary, Goose Falls, the hamlet of Harborside, and plenty of water and island views. Note that some roads are unpaved, but they usually are well maintained.

Penobscot Bay Press (https://penobscot-baypress.com), which publishes a collection of local newspapers, also maintains an excellent website, with listings for area businesses as well as articles highlighting area happenings.

Check out Sedgwick Village Library (Main St., Sedgwick, 207/359-2177).

Getting There and Around

Sedgwick is about 8 miles or 15 minutes via Route 175 from Brooksville. It's about 5 miles or 10 minutes to Brooklin via Route 175 or 10 miles or 15 minutes to Blue Hill via Route 172.

BROOKLIN
Sights
WOODENBOAT PUBLICATIONS

On Naskeag Point Road, 1.2 miles from Route 175 in downtown Brooklin, a small sign marks the turn to the world headquarters of *WoodenBoat* (Naskeag Point Rd., Brooklin, 207/359-4651, www.woodenboat.com). Buy magazines, books, clothing, and all manner of nautical merchandise at the handsome store, stroll the grounds, or sign up for one of the dozens of one- and two-week spring, summer, and fall courses in seamanship, navigation, boatbuilding, sailmaking, marine carving, and more; tuition varies by course and duration. Special courses are geared to kids, women, pros, and all-thumbs neophytes. The camaraderie is legendary, and so is the cuisine. School visiting hours are 8am-5pm Monday-Saturday June-October.

SCENIC ROUTES

Naskeag Point Road begins off Route 175 in "downtown" Brooklin, heads down the peninsula for 3.7 miles past the entrance to *WoodenBoat* Publications, and ends at a small shingle beach (limited parking) on Eggemoggin Reach. Here you'll find picnic tables, a boat launch, a seasonal toilet, and a marker commemorating the 1778 battle of Naskeag, when British sailors came ashore from the sloop *Gage,* burned several buildings, and were run off by a ragtag band of local settlers. Cape Rosier's roads are poorly marked, perhaps deliberately, so keep your DeLorme atlas handy.

Recreation

HIKING AND BIRD-WATCHING

Maine Coast Heritage Trust's 138-acre **Harriman Point Preserve** comprises woodlands, wetlands, salt marshes, and a bog, as well as shell and gravel beaches. A one-mile trail leads to a fork. Keep left for a quarter mile to a point on Allen Cove. If you look westward, you might spy the former home of E. B. White, author of the children's classics *Stuart Little* and *Charlotte's Web.* Retrace your steps and take the other spur 0.25 mile to a beach and views across Blue Hill Bay to Mount Desert Island. Bird-watchers flock here during spring and fall migrations, but it's a fine spot any time of year to explore the varied habitats, watch for wildlife, and enjoy the scenery. To get to the preserve, take Route 175 to Harriman Point Road. Go 0.5 mile on Harriman Point Road to the parking lot on

the right, and cross the street to find the trailhead.

BICYCLING

Bicycling in this area is for confident, experienced cyclists. The roads are particularly narrow and winding, with poor shoulders. The best bet for casual pedal pushers is **Naskeag Point Road.**

Shopping

GALLERIES

Virginia G. Sarsfield handcrafts paper products, including custom lampshades, calligraphy papers, books, and lamps, at **Handmade Papers** (113 Reach Rd., Brooklin, 207/359-8345, www.handmadepapersonline.com).

It's worth the mosey out to Flye Point to find **Flye Point Sculpture & Art Gallery** (436 Flye Point Rd., Brooklin, 207/610-0350), where Peter Stremlau displays fine works in varied media by Maine-based and Maine-inspired artists. Wander through gardens and woodlands accented with sculptures. More sculptures, as well as paintings and accordion books, are inside the gallery. The waterfront location is spectacular.

GIFTS

Leaf and Anna (12 Reach Rd., 207/359-5030), in Brooklin village, is a browser's delight filled with garden and kitchen must-haves, items for boats, and books.

Food

LOCAL FLAVORS

The **Brooklin General Store** (4 Reach Rd., junction of Rte. 175 and Naskeag Point Rd., Brooklin, 207/359-8359, 8am-6pm Mon.-Fri., 9am-6pm Sat.-Sun.), dating from 1866 but completely rebuilt in 2017, carries groceries, beer and wine, newspapers, and local chatter as well as sandwiches, breakfast treats, baked goods, and pizza.

1: Pushcart Press Bookstore **2:** Battle of Naskeag memorial **3:** *WoodenBoat* Publications headquarters

1

2

3

E. B. White: Some Writer

Every child since the mid-1940s has heard of E. B. White—author of the memorable *Stuart Little*, *Charlotte's Web*, and *Trumpet of the Swan*—and every college kid for decades has been reminded to consult his or her copy of *The Elements of Style*. But how many realize that White and his wife, Katharine, were living not in the big city but in the hamlet of North Brooklin, Maine? It was Brooklin that inspired Charlotte and Wilbur and Stuart, and it was Brooklin where the Whites lived very full, creative lives.

Abandoning their desks at *The New Yorker* in 1938, Elwyn Brooks White and Katharine S. White bought an idyllic saltwater farm on the Blue Hill Peninsula and moved here with their young son, Joel, who became a noted naval architect and yacht builder in Brooklin before his death in 1997. Andy (as E. B. had been dubbed since his college days at Cornell) produced 20 books, countless essays and letters to editors, and hundreds (maybe thousands?) of "newsbreaks"— those wry clipping-and-commentary items sprinkled through each issue of *The New Yorker*. Katharine continued wielding her pencil as the magazine's standout children's-book editor, donating many of her review copies to Brooklin's Friends Memorial Library, one of her favorite causes. (The library also has two original Garth Williams drawings from *Stuart Little*, courtesy of E. B., and a lovely garden dedicated to the Whites.) Katharine's book, *Onward and Upward in the Garden*, a collection of her *New Yorker* gardening pieces, was published in 1979, two years after her death.

Later in life, E. B. sagely addressed the young readers of his three award-winning children's books:

> Are my stories true, you ask? No, they are imaginary tales, containing fantastic characters and events. In real life, a family doesn't have a child who looks like a mouse; in real life, a spider doesn't spin words in her web. In real life, a swan doesn't blow a trumpet. But real life is only one kind of life—there is also the life of the imagination. And although my stories are imaginary, I like to think that there is some truth in them, too—truth about the way people and animals feel and think and act.

E. B. White died on October 1, 1985, at the age of 86. He and Katharine and Joel left large footprints on this earth, but perhaps nowhere more so than in Brooklin.

CASUAL DINING

Fresh farm-to-table fare is served at the **Brooklin Inn Restaurant** (Rte. 175, Brooklin, 207/359-2777, www.thebrooklininn. com, 5pm-7:30pm Wed.-Sat. $15-30).

Accommodations
BED-AND-BREAKFASTS

It's an easy walk to the village center from the **Maine Hideaway Guest House** (19 Naskeag Point Rd., Brooklin, 207/610-2244, www.themainehideaway.com, $115-135), a nicely renovated and updated 1874 Victorian with contemporary decor. Rates include breakfast. Some rooms share baths. Other onsite accommodations include an apartment and a two-story suite ($165).

New owners in 2019 have updated and renovated the **Brooklin Inn** (Rte. 175, Brooklin, 207/359-2777, www.thebrooklininn.com, $145-175), which offers four handsome guestrooms.

CAMPING

With 730 feet of waterfront on Eggemoggin Reach and 16 wooded acres, **Oceanfront Camping @ Reach Knolls** (666 Reach Rd., Brooklin, 207/359-5555, www.reachknolls. com, $29 tent, $39 RV, no credit cards) is a no-frills campground with 32 wooded sites, some with water views. The camp office has free showers and potable water; there is no water at the sites. The campground can accommodate RVs up to 35 feet in length, and electricity is available. There are privies and a dump station. A path leads to the pebbly beach where you can launch a kayak.

Information and Services

The best source of information about the region is the Blue Hill Peninsula Chamber of Commerce (207/374-2281, www.bluehill-peninsula.org).

Penobscot Bay Press (https://penob-scotbaypress.com), which publishes a collection of local newspapers, also maintains an excellent website, with listings for area businesses as well as articles highlighting area happenings.

The Friends Memorial Library (Rte. 175, Brooklin, 207/359-2276) has the lovely Circle of Friends Garden, with benches and a brick patio. It's dedicated to the memory of long-time Brooklin residents E. B. and Katharine White.

Getting There and Around

Brooklin is about 5 miles or 10 minutes via Route 175 from Sedgwick. It's about 12 miles or 20 minutes to Blue Hill via Route 175 or about 18 miles or 30 minutes to Deer Isle Village via Routes 175 and 15.

Deer Isle and Isle au Haut

After weaving your way down the Blue Hill

Peninsula and crossing the soaring, oh-so-narrow bridge to Little Deer Isle, you've entered the realm of island living. Sure, bridges and causeways connect the points, but the farther down you drive, the more removed from civilization you'll feel. The pace slows; the population dwindles. Fishing and lobstering are the mainstays. Lobster boats rest near many homes, and trap fences edge properties. If your ultimate destination is the section of Acadia National Park on Isle au Haut, the drive down Deer Isle to Stonington serves to help disconnect you from the mainland. To reach the park's acreage on Isle au Haut, you'll board the Isle au Haut ferryboat for the trip down Merchant Row to the island. In summer, you can go directly to the park's Duck Harbor

Highlights

Look for ★ to find recommended sights, activities, dining, and lodging.

★ **Haystack Mountain School of Crafts:** This internationally renowned crafts school has an award-winning architectural design in a stunning setting (page 216).

★ **Nervous Nellie's:** Sculptor Peter Beerits's ever-expanding whimsical world captivates all ages, and it's free (page 217).

★ **Arts and Crafts Galleries:** Given the inspiring scenery, it's no surprise to find dozens of fabulously talented artisans on Deer Isle (page 219).

★ **Edgar Tennis Preserve:** Serene views and pleasant places to picnic are reasons enough to hike the easy trails here (page 221).

★ **Barred Island Preserve:** Bring binoculars to sight nesting eagles on the island (page 222).

★ **Sea Kayaking:** Paddle between the plentiful islands off Stonington and into hidden coves (page 223).

★ **Acadia National Park:** Isle au Haut's limited access makes this remote section of the park truly special. It's unlikely you'll have to share the trails—or the views—with more than a few other people (page 230).

© MOON.COM

Deer Isle

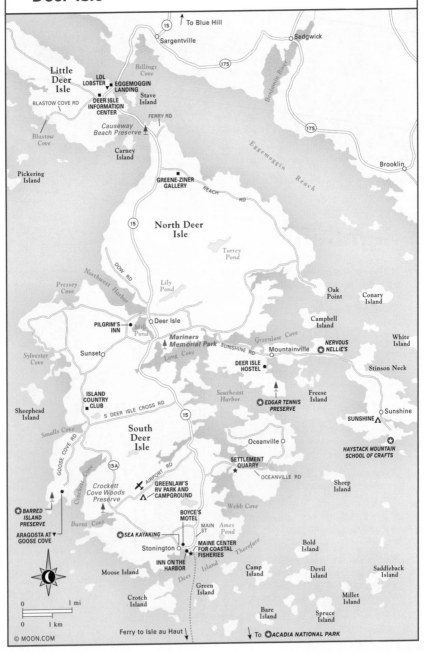

To Blue Hill
15
Sargentville
Sedgwick
175
Billings Cove
Little Deer Isle
LDL LOBSTER
EGGEMOGGIN LANDING
Stave Island
DEER ISLE INFORMATION CENTER
BLASTOW COVE RD
FERRY RD
175
Benjamin River
Causeway Beach Preserve
Blastow Cove
Carney Island
Eggemoggin Reach
Brooklin
Pickering Island
GREENE-ZINER GALLERY
REACH RD
North Deer Isle
15
Torrey Pond
Oak Point
Conary Island
DOW RD
Lily Pond
Pressey Cove
Northwest Harbor
Campbell Island
White Island
PILGRIM'S INN
Deer Isle
Mill Pond
Greenlaw Cove
Mariners Memorial Park
SUNSHINE RD
Mountainville
NERVOUS NELLIE'S
Stinson Neck
Sunset
Long Cove
DEER ISLE HOSTEL
Sylvester Cove
ISLAND COUNTRY CLUB
S DEER ISLE CROSS RD
Southeast Harbor
EDGAR TENNIS PRESERVE
Freese Island
Sunshine
SUNSHINE
Sheephead Island
Smalls Cove
South Deer Isle
15
Oceanville
HAYSTACK MOUNTAIN SCHOOL OF CRAFTS
GOOSE COVE RD
15A
SETTLEMENT QUARRY
OCEANVILLE RD
Sheep Island
Crockett Cove Woods Preserve
Crockett Cove
AIRPORT RD
GREENLAW'S RV PARK AND CAMPGROUND
Webb Cove
BARRED ISLAND PRESERVE
Burnt Cove
BOYCE'S MOTEL
MAIN ST
Ames Pond
ARAGOSTA AT GOOSE COVE
SEA KAYAKING
Stonington
MAINE CENTER FOR COASTAL FISHERIES
Bold Island
Saddleback Island
INN ON THE HARBOR
Moose Island
Deer Island
Camp Island
Devil Island
Crotch Island
Green Island
Millet Island
0   1 mi
0   1 km
Bare Island
Spruce Island
© MOON.COM
Ferry to Isle au Haut
To ACADIA NATIONAL PARK

Landing; in other months, it requires a hike through the woods.

Deer Isle and Isle au Haut are inexorably linked yet distinctly separate and very different. Both seduce visitors with their rugged independence and undeveloped landscapes. Deer Isle's main town of Stonington is a metropolis compared to Isle au Haut, with a population of about 1,200 versus fewer than 50. The sidewalks roll up relatively early in Stonington, but there's not much even in the way of pavement on Isle au Haut. Deer Isle has stepped tentatively into the 21st century; Isle au Haut remains pretty much in the 20th—and the early 20th at that. Electricity came to Isle au Haut in 1970, and telephone service soon followed—although cellular service is spotty at best.

In addition to fisherfolk, Deer Isle is a colony of artists and artisans in equal parts due to the inspiring scenery and the inspirational Haystack Mountain School of Crafts. Top-notch galleries and working studios are found throughout the island. It's also home to numerous small preserves, ideal for easy hiking and bird-watching, and its bevy of nearby islands beckon sea kayakers.

While dreamers and summer rusticators are plentiful, Stonington is first and foremost a working waterfront dominated by lobster and fishing boats and the remnants of once-active granite quarrying operations. It's also the jumping-off point for trips to Isle au Haut.

The biggest attraction on Isle au Haut is a remote section of Acadia National Park that's raw and rugged—beautiful, even breathtaking in parts. It's not as dramatic as the Mount Desert Island section, but it seduces visitors with its simplicity, peacefulness, and lack of cars. On the trails that hug the granite shoreline and climb the forested hills, perhaps more than in any other section of the park, you can truly feel removed from civilization.

PLANNING YOUR TIME

If you're coming to this region specifically to visit Acadia National Park on Isle au Haut, plan your visit to time with the Isle au Haut Company's boat service directly to the park (early June-mid-Sept.); otherwise it's nearly a 10-mile round-trip from the Town Dock to Duck Harbor and back. The park boat is first come, first served, so it's wise to be in line well before your intended departure. The park limits capacity to only 128 people, including campers, each day, although there's no real way to enforce that. Reservations for the park's primitive campground open in early April, and slots go quickly. Deer Isle and Little Deer Isle are primarily fishing communities with seasonal tourism centered primarily on touring galleries, sea kayaking, hiking the preserves, soaking in the small-town vibe, and savoring the island-dotted vistas. July and August are the busiest months—although the region is well off the usual tourist trail—with September being a lovely month to visit, although businesses have fewer open hours and some galleries close.

Previous: Robinson Point Light; statue in Stonington; Blue Hill-Deer Isle Bridge.

Deer Isle

"Deer Isle is like Avalon," wrote John Steinbeck in *Travels with Charley*. "It must disappear when you are not there." Deer Isle, the name of both the island and its midpoint town, has been romancing authors and artisans for decades, but it is unmistakably real to the quarry workers and fishermen who've been here for centuries. These longtimers are a sturdy lot, as even Steinbeck recognized: "I would hate to try to force them to do anything they didn't want to do."

Early-18th-century maps show no name for the island, but by the late 1800s nearly 100 families lived here, supporting themselves first by farming, then by fishing. In 1789, when Deer Isle was incorporated, 80 local sailing vessels were scouring the Gulf of Maine in pursuit of mackerel and cod, and Deer Isle men were circling the globe as yachting skippers and merchant seamen. At the same time, in the once-quiet village of Green's Landing (now called Stonington), the shipbuilding and granite industries boomed, spurring development, prosperity, and the kinds of rough high jinks typical of commercial ports the world over.

Green's Landing became the "big city" for an international crowd of quarry workers carving out the terrain on Deer Isle and nearby Crotch Island, the source of high-quality granite for Boston's Museum of Fine Arts, the Smithsonian Institution, a humongous fountain for John D. Rockefeller's New York estate, and less showy projects all along the Eastern Seaboard. The heyday is long past, but the industry did extend into the 20th century, including a contract for the pink granite at President John F. Kennedy's Arlington National Cemetery gravesite. Today, Crotch Island is the site of Maine's only operating island granite quarry.

Measuring about nine miles north to south (plus another three miles for Little Deer Isle), the island of Deer Isle today has a handful of hamlets (including **Sunshine, Sunset, Mountainville,** and **Oceanville**) and two towns—**Stonington** (pop. 1,043) and **Deer Isle** (pop. 1,975). Road access is via Route 15 on the Blue Hill Peninsula. A huge suspension bridge, built in 1939 over Eggemoggin Reach, links the Sargentville section of Sedgwick with Little Deer Isle; from there, a sinuous 0.4-mile causeway connects to the northern tip of Deer Isle.

Deer Isle is an artisans' enclave, anchored by the Haystack Mountain School of Crafts. Studios and galleries are plentiful, although many require noodling along back roads to find them. Stonington, a rough-and-tumble fishing port with an idyllic setting, is slowly being gentrified as more and more galleries and upscale shops open for the summer each season. Long-empty downtown buildings have recently been purchased, and locals are holding their collective breath hoping that any improvements don't change the town too much. Already, real estate prices and accompanying taxes have escalated way past the point where many a local fisherman can hope to purchase, and in some cases maintain, a home.

SIGHTS

Sightseeing on Deer Isle means exploring back roads, browsing the galleries, walking the trails, hanging out on the docks, and soaking in the ambience.

★ Haystack Mountain School of Crafts

The renowned **Haystack Mountain School of Crafts** (Sunshine Rd., Deer Isle, 207/348-2306, www.haystack-mtn.org) in Sunshine is open to the public on a limited basis, but if it fits into your schedule, go. Anyone can visit the school store and dining room or walk down the central stairs to the water; to see more of the campus, take a tour (1pm Wed., $5), which includes a video, viewing works on display, and the opportunity to visit some studios. Beyond that, there are slide programs, lectures, demonstrations, and concerts presented by faculty and visiting artists on varying weeknights early June-late August. Perhaps the best opportunities are the end-of-session auctions, held on Thursday nights every 2-3 weeks, when you can tour the studios for free before the evening auction. It's a great opportunity to buy craftwork at often very reasonable prices.

★ Nervous Nellie's

Part museum, part gallery, part jelly kitchen, and part tearoom, **Nervous Nellie's** (600 Sunshine Rd., Deer Isle, 800/777-6845, www. nervousnellies.com, 9am-5pm daily, free) is all that and more. Most visitors come to purchase the hand-produced jams and jellies and, perhaps, watch them being made. Once here, they discover sculptor Peter Beerits's "natural history museum of the imagination." Beerits, who has an MFA in sculpture, has built a fantasy world that's rooted in his boyhood and complements *The Nervous Nellie Story,* his comic-book-format illustrated series. "Years ago, I was primarily an artist who exhibited works in galleries. Now I'm primarily a museum curator," he says.

The buildings, fields, gardens, and woods are filled with interactive scenes and whimsical wood and metal sculptures Beerits has created from the flotsam and jetsam of everyday island life—farming implements, household furnishings, and industrial whatnots—what Beerits calls "good junk from the dump."

There's an interactive western town complete with a hotel, a Chinese laundry, a jail, a fortune-teller, a sheriff's office, blacksmith shop, and the Silver Dollar Saloon. Inside the saloon, Wild Bill Hickok is playing his last hand of cards, his back to a gunman sneaking through the back door. "Hickok made the mistake one time of sitting with his back to a door, not the wall," Beerits says, adding that the hand he holds, two aces and two eights, is now known as a dead man's hand in poker. It's that kind of detail that adds a touch of reality

to the scenes, and it's the opportunity to grab a seat at the table that engages visitors and keeps the cameras clicking. The West fades into the Mississippi Delta, where blues music draws visitors into Red's Lounge, where a pianist and guitarist crank out the blues, while a couple flirts in a corner booth.

Beerits moved the original Hardy's Store here. Like a living-history museum, it provides a glimpse into island life decades ago. No detail is overlooked, from the red hot dogs and buns in the steamer to the pickled eggs on the counter, from Neville Hardy at the register to the women seated out front eyeing the gas pump.

Many visitors take in these sights and then settle into the café for a snack, not realizing that there's much more to see. In the woods behind, King Arthur's knights in shining armor, some larger than life, guard and inhabit the Grail Castle. Continue down the path, and you'll arrive at a woodlands church, another of Beerits's projects.

You can easily spend an hour here, and there's no admission; wander freely. Beerits will gladly explain his creations, if he's available. He offers free insider tours at 1pm on select Sundays. The property is also home to **Nervous Nellie's Jams and Jellies,** known for outstanding, creative condiments. You can peek into the kitchen to see the jams being made. The self-serve **Mountainville Café,** open May-early October, offers tea, coffee, and scones—with, of course, delicious Nervous Nellie's products; sampling is encouraged. Stock up, because they're sold in only a few shops. Also sold is a small, well-chosen selection of Maine products. Really, trust me, you must visit this place.

Historic Houses and Museums

There's more to the 1830 **Salome Sellers House** (416 Sunset Rd./Rte. 15A, Sunset Village, 207/348-6400, www.dis-historicalsociety.org, 1pm-4pm Wed.-Fri. mid-June-mid-Sept., donation) than first meets the eye. A repository of local memorabilia, archives, and intriguing artifacts,

Getting Crafty

Internationally famed artisans—sculptors and papermakers, weavers and jewelers, potters and printmakers—become the faculty each summer for the unique **Haystack Mountain School of Crafts** (207/348-2306, www.haystack-mtn.org). Founded in 1950 by Mary Beasom Bishop (1885-1972) and a group of talented Maine artisans as a studio research and study program, Haystack has grown into one of the top craft schools in the country, and its campus is listed in the National Register of Historic Places.

Under the direction of beloved former director Francis Merritt, the school opened its first campus near Haystack Mountain, in Montville, Maine, in 1951. Ten years later, when the state unveiled plans to build a new highway (Rte. 3) that would bisect that campus, the school relocated to its present 40-acre oceanfront location at the end of the Sunshine Road in Deer Isle. It was a good move.

You would be hard-pressed to find a more artistically stimulating and architecturally stunning environment. Architect Edward Larrabee Barnes's award-winning campus perfectly complements its dramatic setting. The angular, cedar-shingled buildings are connected via walkways, teaching decks, and a central staircase that cascades like a waterfall down the wooded hillside to the rocky coast below. The visual impression is one of spruce and ledge, glass and wood, islands and water.

One thing that makes Haystack work is its diverse student body. Students of all abilities, from beginners through advanced professionals, come from around the globe for the 2-3-week summer sessions, taking weekday classes and enjoying round-the-clock studio access to follow their creative muses. In a recent year, students ranged in age from 18 to 75 and represented professions from retired teacher to physicist. What brings them all here, said former director Stuart Kestenbaum, is the "direct making experience." That experience draws not only those who make but also those who collect. For a collector of fine craft, he says, taking a class is a "great way to get insight into the making process; it gives a different relationship with the craft being collected." Each session also includes a range of craft. These may include blacksmithing, drawing, metals, wood, beads, clay, fiber, printmaking, glass, weaving, mixed media, paper, and baskets.

it's also the headquarters of the **Deer Isle-Stonington Historical Society.** Sellers, matriarch of an island family, was a direct descendant of *Mayflower* settlers. She lived to be 108, a lifetime spanning 1800-1908, earning the record for oldest recorded Maine resident. The house contains Sellers's furnishings, and in a small exhibit space in the rear is a fine exhibit of baskets made by Maine's Indigenous people. Behind the house are the archives, heritage gardens, and an exhibit hall filled with nautical artifacts. Enthusiastic volunteer guides, many of them island natives, bring all this to life. They love to provide tidbits about various items; seafarers' logs and ship models are particularly intriguing, and don't miss the 1920s peapod, the original lobster boat on the island. The house is just north of the Island Country Club and across from Eaton's Plumbing.

Close to the Stonington waterfront, the **Deer Isle Granite Museum** (51 Main St., Stonington, 207/367-6331, www.deerislegranitemuseum.org, noon-5pm Tues., Thurs., and Sat.-Sun. July-Aug.) was established to commemorate the centennial of the quarrying business hereabouts. The best feature of the small museum is a 15-foot-long working model of Crotch Island, center of the industry, as it appeared at the turn of the 20th century. Flatcars roll, boats glide, and derricks move—it all looks very real. Donations are welcome.

Another downtown Stonington attraction is a Lilliputian complex known as the **Miniature Village.** Beginning in 1947, the late Everett Knowlton created a series of replicas of local buildings and displayed them on granite blocks in his yard. Since his death, they've been restored and put on display each summer in town—along with a donation box to support the upkeep. The village is set up on East Main Street (Rte. 15), below Hoy Gallery.

Pumpkin Island Light

A fine view of Pumpkin Island Light can be had from the cul-de-sac at the end of the Eggemoggin Road on Little Deer Isle. If heading south on Route 15, bear right at the information booth after crossing the bridge and continue to the end.

Maine Center for Coastal Fisheries

The purpose of the Maine Center for Coastal Fisheries (13 Atlantic Ave., Stonington, 207/367-2708, https://coastalfisheries.org/) is "to energize and facilitate responsible community-based fishery management, collaborative marine science, and sustainable economic development to benefit the fishermen and the communities of Penobscot Bay and the Eastern Gulf of Maine." Bravo to that! At its Discovery Wharf (10am-4pm Sun.-Fri., free) are educational displays and interactive exhibits, including virtual reality experiences, a touch wall, and a touch tank highlighting Maine fisheries and the Gulf of Maine ecosystem. One of the driving forces behind the venture is Ted Ames, who won a $500,000 MacArthur Fellowship "genius grant" in 2005.

★ ARTS AND CRAFTS GALLERIES

Thanks to the presence and influence of Haystack Mountain School of Crafts, supertalented artists and artisans lurk in every corner of the island. Most galleries are tucked away on back roads, so watch for roadside signs. Many have studios open to the public where you can watch the artists at work.

LITTLE DEER ISLE

Blacksmith Douglas E. Wilson shows his creations at Wilson Forge (455 Eggemoggin Rd., 207/348-6871, www.wilsonforge.com)

DEER ISLE

The Greene-Ziner Gallery (73 Reach Rd., 207/348-2601, www.melissagreene.com) is a double treat. Melissa Greene turns out incredible painted and incised pottery—she's represented in the Smithsonian's Renwick Gallery—and Eric Ziner works magic in metal sculpture and furnishings. Your budget may not allow for one of Melissa's pots (in the four-digit range), but I guarantee you'll covet them. The gallery also displays the work of several other local artists. Also here is a farm stand with baked goods, produce, and more.

The Frederica Marshall Gallery (81 N. Deer Isle Rd., 207/348-2782, www.fredericamarshall.com) is a multifaceted find. Marshall is a master brush painter who delights in explaining Japanese sumi-e work and demonstrating the brushes that vary from a cat's whisker to four horsetails in size. She also has a classroom and offers workshops ranging from two hours to four days in length. Her husband, Herman Kidder, operates Kidder Forge on the same property. His knives forged from old tools are available in the gallery.

One of the island's premier galleries is Elena Kubler's The Turtle Gallery (61 N. Deer Isle Rd./Rte. 15, 207/348-9977, https://theturtlegallery.com), in a handsome space formerly known as the Old Centennial House Barn (owned by the late Haystack director Francis Merritt) and the adjacent farmhouse. Group and solo shows of contemporary paintings, prints, and crafts are hung upstairs and down in the barn; works by gallery artists are in the farmhouse; and there's usually sculpture in the gardens both in front and in back. It's just north of Deer Isle Village, across from the Shakespeare School.

In the village, Deer Isle Artists Association (5 Main St., 207/348-2330, www.deerisleartists.com) features two-week exhibits of paintings, prints, drawings, and photos by member artists.

Also downtown is Gallery Mozelle (42 Bridge St., 207/460-2329, www.gallerymozelle.com).

com), showing fine jewelry as well as works in varied media, including clay, fibers, and glass.

Even if you can't afford to buy, at least peek into **Devta Doolan** (3 Main St., 917/361-1861), a very high-end handcrafted jewelry studio.

The **Deer Isle Artisans Market** (207/348-6294, 10am-2om Thurs.) sets up in the Old Deer Isle Elementary School parking lot on Rte. 15.

Detour down Sunshine Road to visit **Peter Beerits Sculpture at Nervous Nellie's** (600 Sunshine Rd., 800/777-6845, www.nervousnellies.com), a world of whimsy that will entertain all ages. If the timing works, combine it with the Wednesday tour at Haystack.

Stonington

Cabinetmaker Geoffrey Warner features his work at **Geoffrey Warner Studio** (43 N. Main St., 207/367-6555, www.geoffreywarnerstudio.com). Warner mixes classic techniques with contemporary styles and Eastern, nature-based, and arts and crafts accents to create some unusual and rather striking pieces. He also crafts the budget-friendly ergonomic Owl stool and offers kits and workshops. Ask about studio tours.

The **gWatson Gallery** (68 Main St., 207/367-2900, www.gwatsongallery.com) represents a number of top-notch painters and printmakers. Occasionally it hosts live jazz.

J. McVeigh Jewelry (27 W. Main St., 207/348-3080, http://jmcveighjewelry.com) shows the works of more than 25 artisans.

Paintings, many in bold, bright colors, can be found at Jill Hoy's **Hoy Gallery** (80 Main St., 207/367-2368, www.jillhoy.com).

On the other end of Main Street, **Marlinespike Chandlery** (58 W. Main St., 207/348-2521, www.marlinespike.com) specializes in ropework, both practical and fancy.

1: one of many galleries in Deer Isle 2: Discovery Wharf 3: Haystack Mountain School of Crafts

RECREATION
Parks and Preserves

Foresighted benefactors have set aside precious acreage for respectful public use on Deer Isle. The Nature Conservancy (207/729-5181, www.nature.org) owns two properties: **Crockett Cove Woods Preserve** and **Barred Island Preserve.** The conscientious steward of other local properties is the **Island Heritage Trust** (420 Sunset Rd., Sunset, 207/348-2455, www.islandheritagetrust.org, 8am-4pm Mon.-Fri.). At the office you can pick up notecards, photos, T-shirts, and helpful maps and information on hiking trails and nature preserves. Proceeds benefit the Island Heritage Trust's efforts; donations are appreciated.

SETTLEMENT QUARRY

One of the easiest, shortest walks in the area leads to an impressive vista. It begins from the parking lot on Oceanville Road, a little less than one mile off Route 15 and marked by a carved granite sign. It's about a five-minute walk to the top of the old quarry, where the viewing platform (aka the "throne room") takes in the panorama—all the way to the Camden Hills on a good day. In early August, wild raspberries are an additional enticement. Three short loop trails lead into the surrounding woods from here. A map is available in the trailhead box.

★ EDGAR TENNIS PRESERVE

The 145-acre **Tennis Preserve** (sunrise-sunset daily), off Sunshine Road, has very limited parking, so don't try to squeeze in if there isn't room; schedule your visit for another hour or day. But do go, and bring at least a snack if not a full picnic to enjoy on one of the convenient rocky outcroppings (be sure to carry out what you carry in). Allow at least 90 minutes to enjoy the walking trails, one of which skirts Pickering Cove, providing sigh-producing views. Another trail leads to an old cemetery. Parts of the trails can be wet, so wear appropriate footwear. Bring binoculars for bird-watching. To find the preserve, take

Sunshine Road 2.5 miles to Tennis Road, and follow it to the preserve.

SHORE ACRES PRESERVE

The 38-acre preservecomprises old farmland, woodlands, clam flats, a salt marsh, and granite shorefront. Three walking trails connect in a 1.5-mile loop, with the Shore Trail section edging Greenlaw Cove. As you walk along the waterfront, look for the islands of Mount Desert rising in the distance and seals basking on offshore ledges. Do not walk across the salt marsh, and try to avoid stepping on beach plants. To find the preserve, take Sunshine Road 1.2 miles and then bear left at the fork onto Greenlaw District Road. The preserve's parking area is just shy of one mile down the road. Park only in the parking area, not on the paved road.

CROCKETT COVE WOODS PRESERVE

Donated to the Nature Conservancy by benevolent, eco-conscious local artist Emily Muir, 98-acre Crockett Cove Woods Preserve (sunrise-sunset daily year-round) is Deer Isle's natural gem—a coastal fog forest laden with lichens and mosses. Four interlinked walking trails cover the whole preserve, starting with a short nature trail. Pick up the helpful map-brochure at the registration box. Wear rubberized shoes or boots, and respect adjacent private property. From Deer Isle Village, take Route 15A to Sunset Village. Go 2.5 miles to Whitman Road, and then to Fire Lane 88.

★ BARRED ISLAND PRESERVE

Owned by the Nature Conservancy but managed by the Island Heritage Trust, Barred Island Preserve (www.islandheritagetrust. org, sunrise-sunset daily year-round) was donated by Carolyn Olmsted, grandniece of noted landscape architect Frederick Law Olmsted, who summered nearby. A former owner of adjacent Goose Cove Lodge donated an additional 48 acres of maritime boreal fog forest. A single walking trail, one mile long,

leads from the parking lot to a point. At low tide, and when eagles aren't nesting, you can continue out to Barred Island. Another trail skirts the shoreline of Goose Cove, before retreating inland and rejoining the main trail. From a high point on the main trail, you can see more than a dozen islands, many of which are protected from development, as well as Saddleback Ledge Light, 14 miles distant. To get to the preserve, follow Route 15A to Goose Cove Road and then continue to the parking area on the right. If it's full, return another day.

HOLT MILL POND PRESERVE

The Stonington Conservation Commission administers the town-owned Holt Mill Pond Preserve, where more than 47 bird species have been identified (bring binoculars). It comprises four habitats: upland spruce forest, lowland spruce-mixed forest, freshwater marsh, and saltwater marsh. A self-guided nature trail is accessible off Airport Road. Look for the Nature Trail sign just beyond the medical center. A detailed trail brochure, available at the trailhead kiosk, is accented with drawings by noted artist Siri Beckman.

AMES POND

Ames Pond is neither park nor preserve, but it might as well be. On a back road close to Stonington, it's a mandatory stop in July-August, when the pond wears a blanket of pink and white water lilies. From downtown Stonington, take Indian Point Road just under a mile east to the pond.

CAUSEWAY BEACH AND SCOTT'S LANDING

If you're itching to dip your toes into the water, stop by Causeway Beach along the causeway linking Little Deer Isle to Deer Isle. It's popular for swimming and is also a significant habitat for birds and other wildlife. On the other side of Route 15 is Scott's Landing, with more than 20 acres of fields, trails, and shorefront.

The Maine Island Trail

In the early 1980s, a "trail" of coastal Maine islands was only the germ of an idea. By the end of the millennium, the Maine Island Trail Association (MITA) counted some 4,000 members dedicated to conscientious (i.e., low- or no-impact) recreational use of more than 200 public and private islands and coastal sites along 375 miles of Maine coastline from the New Hampshire border to Canada. Access to the trail is only by private boat; the best choice is a sea kayak, to navigate shallow or rock-strewn coves.

The trail's publicly owned islands—supervised by the state Bureau of Public Lands—are open to anyone. The private islands are restricted to MITA members, who pay $45 per individual or $65 per family per year for the privilege (and, it's important to add, the responsibility). With the fee comes the Maine Island Trail Guidebook, providing directions and information for each of the islands, full MITA smartphone app access, a biannual newsletter, and local discounts. With membership comes the expectation of care and concern. "Low impact" means different things to different people, so MITA experienced acute growing pains when enthusiasm began leading to "tent sprawl."

To cope with and reverse the overuse, MITA has created an "adopt-an-island" program, in which volunteers become stewards for specific islands and keep track of their use and condition. MITA members are urged to pick up trash, use tent platforms where they exist, and continue elsewhere if an island has reached its assigned capacity (stipulated on a shoreline sign and/or in the guidebook).

Membership information is available from the Maine Island Trail Association (207/761-8225, www.mita.org).

ED WOODSUM PRESERVE AT MARSHALL ISLAND

The Maine Coast Heritage Trust (www.mcht.org) owns Marshall Island, the largest undeveloped island on the Eastern Seaboard. Since acquiring it in 2003, the trust has added 10 miles of hiking trails on three inter-connected loops. After exploring, picnic on Sand Cove Beach on the southeastern shore. For transportation, check with Bert & I (207/460-8679), which offers charter service. Primitive camping is available by reservation (207/729-7366) at designated sites; fires require a permit (207/827-1800).

MARINERS MEMORIAL PARK

Thank the Evergreen Garden Club for the 23-acre Mariners Memorial Park, comprising fields, woodlands, marsh, bog, and shorefront on Long Cove. Facilities include a launch for small boats and a picnic area. A mowed 0.5-mile path loops around the edge from the parking area. About midway is a memorial honoring those who lost their lives at sea. The lupines are gorgeous here in June.

Dogs must be leashed. The park's entrance is on the western end of the Sunshine Road, just off Route 15.

Guided Walks

The Island Heritage Trust (402 Sunset Rd., Sunset, 207/348-2455, www.islandheritagetrust.org), along with the Stonington and Deer Isle Conservation Commissions, sponsors a Walks and Talks series. See the website or call for information and reservations.

TOP EXPERIENCE

★ Sea Kayaking

The waters around Deer Isle, with lots of islets and protected coves, are extremely popular for sea kayaking, especially off Stonington.

If you sign up with the Maine Island Trail Association (207/761-8225, www.mita.org,), you'll receive a handy manual that steers you to more than a dozen islands in the Deer Isle archipelago where you can camp, hike, and picnic—eco-sensitively, please. Annual membership is $25/digital, $45/individual, $65/family.

Boat traffic can be a bit heavy at the height of summer, so to best appreciate the tranquility of this area, try this in September after the Labor Day holiday. Nights can be cool, but days are likely to be brilliant. Remember that this is a working harbor.

The six-mile paddle from Stonington to Isle au Haut is best left to experienced paddlers, especially since the local lobstermen refer to kayakers as "speed bumps."

OUTFITTERS AND GUIDED TRIPS

Driftwood Kayak (17 Hardy's Hill Rd., Deer Isle, 617/957-8802, www.driftwoodkayak.com) offers fully outfitted guided one- to three-day trips in the waters off Deer Isle from $210 per person.

Upwest & Downeast Sea Kayaking (37 Seabreeze Ave., Stonington, 207/664-8433 or 207/367-2725, https://upwestanddowneast.com) offers day trips ($130), evening trips ($60), and multiday (from $450/day for 2 people, fully outfitted) trips in the waters around Deer Isle. Private trips are available.

The **Activity Shop** (139 Mines Rd., Blue Hill, 207/374-3600, www.theactivityshop.com) rents bicycles for $125/week and canoes, kayaks, and paddleboards for $125-245/week. Delivery is available to Deer Isle.

Swimming

The island's only major freshwater swimming hole is the **Lily Pond,** northeast of Deer Isle Village. Just north of the Shakespeare School, turn into the Deer Run Apartments complex. Park and take the path to the pond, which has a shallow area for small children.

Golf and Tennis

About two miles south of Deer Isle Village, watch for the large sign on the left for the **Island Country Club** (Rte. 15A, Sunset, 207/348-2379, early June-late Sept.), a nine-hole public golf course that has been here since 1928. Also at the club are three Har-Tru

tennis courts. The club's cheeseburgers and salads are among the island's best bargain lunches.

EXCURSION BOATS

Isle au Haut Boat Company

The **Isle au Haut Boat Company** (27 Seabreeze Ave., Stonington, 207/367-5193 or 207/367-6516, www.isleauhaut.com) offers a number of scenic cruises. The narrated 1.25-hour Scenic Harbor Cruise ($24 adults, $12 under age 12), during which the crew hauls a string of lobster traps, departs Stonington at 2pm Monday-Saturday. Special puffin trips ($80 adults, $45 under age 12) and lighthouse tours ($75 adults, $45 under age 12) are available on a limited basis. A Crotch Island Quarry trip (limited schedule, $50 adults, $25 kids) includes a guided walking tour. Another option is to cruise over and back to Isle au Haut without stepping foot off the boat ($24 adults). Dockside parking is $12-14.

Sunset Bay Co.

Cruise through East Penobscot Bay aboard the mail boat *Katherine* (207/701-9316, www.eagleislandrentals.com, $50 adults, $36 under age 12), which departs the Deer Isle Yacht Club at 9:30am Monday-Saturday, for a two-hour excursion taking in Eagle, Butter, Barred, and Great Spruce Head Islands. Call for reservations, parking details, and to confirm the time.

Captain Steve's Boat Tours

Former Stonington harbormaster Captain Steve Johnson enjoys sharing Stonington Harbor's highlights aboard the *Bert & I* (207/460-8679 or 207/367-2991, http://deerislecabinwithboattours.com, $140/hour for 4-6 passengers). Options include Stonington Harbor, lighthouse, island, seal-watching, and sunset tours ranging 1-2 hours. Ask about his drop-off service to Green Island, where you can spend a few hours exploring, picnicking, and swimming in a freshwater quarry.

ENTERTAINMENT AND EVENTS

Stonington's National Historic Landmark, the 1912 **Opera House** (207/367-2788, www. operahousearts.org), is home to Opera House Arts, which hosts films, plays, lectures, concerts, family programs, and workshops year-round.

Bird-watchers flock to Deer Isle in mid-May for the annual **Wings, Waves & Woods Weekend** (www.deerisle.com).

Mid-July brings the **Stonington Lobsterboat Races** (207/348-2804), very popular competitions held in the harbor, with lots of possible vantage points. Stonington is one of the major locales in the lobster-boat race circuit.

The **Peninsula Potters Studio Tour and Sale** (www.peninsulapotters.com) is held in October, when more than a dozen potters from Blue Hill to Stonington welcome visitors.

Want to meet locals and learn more about the area? **Island Heritage Trust** (www. islandheritagetrust.org) sponsors a series of walks, talks, and tours late May-mid-September. For information and reservations, call 207/348-2455.

SHOPPING

The greatest concentration of shops is in Stonington, where galleries, clothing boutiques, and eclectic shops line Main Street.

In "downtown" Deer Isle Village, Candy and Jim Eaton now operate **The Periwinkle** (8 Main St., Deer Isle, 207/348-2256), stocking it with a fun mix of books, handcrafts, and niceties.

Prints & Reprints (31 Main St., Stonington, 207/367-5821) is filled with used and antiquarian books along with artwork and a bit of this and that.

Just beyond the Opera House, **Dockside Books & Gifts** (62 W. Main St., Stonington, 207/367-2652) carries just what its name promises, with a specialty in marine and Maine books. The rustic two-room shop has spectacular harbor views.

Find imported women's clothing from Nigerian, Tibetan, and Indian cottage industries; unique jewelry; and unusual notecards at **The Dry Dock** (24 Main St., Stonington, 207/367-5528).

The Nature Shop at Island Heritage Trust (420 Sunset Rd., Deer Isle, 207/348-2455) carries nature- and wildlife-related books, clothing, and other items.

FOOD

Options for dining are few, and restaurants suffer from a lack of consistency. Patience is more than a virtue here; it's a necessity.

Quick Bites

Coffee zealots praise **44 North Coffee** (70 Main St., Stonington, 207/348-3043, https://44northcoffee.com, 6:30am-5pm Mon.-Sat, 8am-2pm Sun.), a spacious café serving coffee and pastries. 44 North also operates a tiny shop out of its roastery (7 Main St., Deer Isle, 207/348-5208, 8am-2pm Mon.-Sat.), where you can grab a cuppa and a baked treat.

Burnt Cove Market (Rte. 15, Stonington, 207/367-2681, 6am-9pm daily) sells pizza, fried chicken, and sandwiches, plus beer and wine.

Stonington Ice Cream Company (66 Main St., Stonington, 207/367-2900, 11am-9pm daily) earns raves for its lobster rolls, but this takeout also serves sandwiches, salads, and soups in addition to Gifford's ice cream.

The **Fairway Café** (442 Sunset Rd., Deer Isle, 207/348-2379, www.islandcountryclub. net, 11am-2pm daily), located at the Island Country Club, is a good bet for a reasonably priced lunch.

The Island Community Center (6 Memorial Ln., just off School St., Stonington) is the locale for the lively **Stonington Farmers Market** (https://thestoningtonfarmersmarket.com, 10am-noon Fri. late May-late Sept.), with more than 50 vendors selling smoked and organic meats, fresh herbs and flowers, produce, gelato and yogurt, maple syrup, jams and jellies, fabulous breads and baked goods, chocolates, international foods, crafts, and so much more. Go early; items sell out quickly.

Local artisans sell hand-crafted works including jewelry, clothing, sculptures, and home goods at the **Deer Isle Artisans Market** (10am-2pm Thurs.) on Route 15 adjacent to the town office.

The **Deer Isle Night Market** takes place 4pm-6pm Tuesdays late May through November, when food vendors selling produce and other fresh foods set up at 11 Main Street.

Family Favorites

Fried seafood, lobsters, burgers, ice cream, and other usuals are available at **There's a Treat Takeout** (495 N. Deer Isle Rd./Rte. 15, Deer Isle, 207/348-9444, 11am-7pm daily), a popular and inexpensive family spot with picnic tables and a playground. Simple sandwiches, burgers, and hot dogs start at $4, while fried seafood baskets begin around $15.

Harbor Cafe (36 Main St., Stonington, 207/367-5099, 6am-8pm Mon.-Sat., 6am-2pm Sun., $7-25) is *the* place to go for breakfast (you can eavesdrop on the local fisherfolk if you're early enough), but it's also open for lunch and dinner. Food varies, as does the service; the best advice is to stick to the basics or go for the fish fry with free seconds on Friday nights.

The views are top-notch from the dining area at the harborside **Stonecutters Kitchen** (5 Atlantic Ave., Stonington, 207/367-2442, www.stonecutterskitchenme.com, 11am-8pm daily, $10-25), an order-at-the-counter deli offering sandwiches, fried fare, lobster, and good pizza. The entrance is through the **Harbor View Store** (207/367-2530, 4am-8pm Mon.-Sat., 7am-8pm Sun.), where you can pick up breakfast sandwiches in the wee hours.

Casual Dining

Gaze over lobster boats to-ing and fro-ing around spruce-and-granite-fringed islands from ★ **Acadia House Provisions** (27 Main St., Stonington, 207/367-2555, http://acadiahouseprovisions.com, 4:30pm-8:30pm Tues., 11:30am-1:30pm and 4:30pm-8:30pm Wed.-Sat., $15-28), a culinary bright spot fronting on the harbor in downtown Stonington. Chef Ryan McCaskey of Chicago's Acadia Restaurant (recipient of two Michelin stars) opened here in 2019, serving an American farm-to-table menu.

At ★ **Aragosta at Goose Cove** (300 Goose Cove Rd., Deer Isle, 207/348-6900, www.aragostamaine.com, 5pm-9pm Mon. and Thurs.-Fri., 10am-2pm and 5pm-9pm Sat.-Sun., $25-40, $85-125 tasting menu), every table in the bi-level dining room and outdoor deck offers a dreamy water view. The emphasis is on seafood, but Chef Devin Finigan's oft-changing New American menu draws from what's currently available from local farms, foragers, and fishers. Finigan, a 2020 James Beard Best Chef Northeast semifinalist, also makes her own charcuterie, salts, and ice cream.

Seafood and house-made pastas are the specialties at **Fin & Fern** (25 Seabreeze Ave., Stonington, 207/348-3111, http://finandfernme.com, 5pm-8pm Wed.-Sun., $15-25), which overlooks the ferry terminal. Chef-owner Andrew Chappel traveled the world as a private chef aboard private yachts before landing here. Parking can be a challenge.

Lobster and Seafood

LDI Lobster (202 Little Deer Isle Rd., Little Deer Isle, 207/348-2843, 11am-7pm Wed.-Sun.), a takeout, serves fresh lobster and seafood, along with options for landlubbers and kids. Enjoy it on a picnic table overlooking Eggemoggin Reach.

ACCOMMODATIONS
Inns and Bed-and-Breakfasts

The ★ **Inn on the Harbor** (45 Main St., Stonington, 207/367-2420 or 800/942-2420, www.innontheharbor.com, from $175) is exactly as its name proclaims—its expansive

1: Stonington waterfront 2: LDI Lobster 3: Pilgrim's Inn 4: Aragosta at Goose Cove

deck hangs right over the harbor. Although updated, the 1880s complex still has an air of unpretentiousness. Most of the 13 guest rooms and suites, each named after a windjammer, have fantastic harbor views and private or shared decks where you can keep an eye on lobster boats, small ferries, windjammers, and pleasure craft; binoculars are provided. Streetside rooms can be noisy at night. Two rooms are dog friendly ($25/stay, 50 lbs max.). Rates include a continental buffet.

★ **Pilgrim's Inn** (20 Main St., Deer Isle, 207/348-6615, www.pilgrimsinn.com, early May-mid-Oct., from $199) comprises a beautifully restored colonial building with 12 rooms and three newer, pet-friendly cottages. Thanks to its location between the harbor and peaceful Mill Pond, every room offers a water view. The inn, listed in the National Register of Historic Places, began life in 1793 as a boardinghouse named the Ark. Current owners Scott Hall and Nicole Neder are updating with a more contemporary vibe, without losing the historic feel. The grounds encourage relaxing, with gardens, paths mowed through a meadow, and chairs and a hammock for enjoying the views. Rates include a full breakfast.

★ **Aragosta at Goose Cove** (300 Goose Cove Rd., Deer Isle, 207/348-6900, www.aragostamaine.com, from $280) is a spectacular 21.9-acre oceanfront property with comfy, updated suites and cottages sprinkling the woodlands and ledges. Rates include access to the private beach as well as a full breakfast in the main lodge. The restaurant also serves dinner and brunch on weekends. It's adjacent to Barred Island Preserve.

Motels

Right in downtown Stonington, just across the street from the harbor, is **Boyce's Motel** (44 Main St., Stonington, 207/367-2421 or 800/224-2421, www.boycesmotel.com, year-round, $89-175). The 11 units have refrigerators; some have kitchens and living rooms, and one has two bedrooms. Across the street, Boyce's has a private harbor-front deck for its guests. Ask for rooms well back from Main Street to lessen street noise. Some rooms are pet friendly ($15/stay); restrictions apply.

Hostel and Bunkhouse

The rustic-bordering-on-primitive **Deer Isle Hostel** (65 Tennis Rd., Deer Isle, 207/348-2308, www.deerislehostel.com, $30-70, no credit cards), set near the Tennis Preserve, is overseen by owner Dennis Carter, a Surry native and local stoneworker and carpenter. The three-story, timber-frame building is completely off the grid, with a pump for water, an outhouse, outdoor hot water-can shower, and solar-powered lighting. Carter hand-cut the granite for the basement, and the timbers in the nail-free frame are hand-hewn from local blown-down spruce. He expects guests to work in the extensive organic gardens, using produce for shared meals prepared on a woodstove, the sole source of heat. The goal is sustainability, not profit. Communal dinners are available nightly—guests either help with preparation or make a $7-10 contribution. Accommodations include private and dorm rooms and huts. Bedding is provided; sleeping bags are not permitted.

Rustic Cottages

When you truly want to escape the trappings of civilization, make reservations for one of four rental cottages on **Eagle Island** (207/701-9316, www.eagleislandrentals.com) located in East Penobscot Bay, about 2.5 miles off Deer Isle. The private island is off the grid, and not all cottages have indoor plumbing, but it is a very special experience for those who don't mind roughing it with basic comforts. Rates range from $800/week for a cozy camp with outhouse and solar shower to $2,500/week for a six-bedroom former boarding home with indoor plumbing.

Camping

Greenlaw's RV Park & Campground (11 Greenlaw Park Rd, 207/200-1279, www.greenlawscampground.com, $43-65/day) is a small campground with large wooded and open sites ranging from primitive tent to full hookups for RVs. It's located just over a mile from Stonington Harbor.

INFORMATION AND SERVICES

The **Deer Isle-Stonington Chamber of Commerce** (207/348-6124, www. deerislemaine.com) has a summer information booth on a grassy triangle on Route 15 in Little Deer Isle, 0.25 mile after crossing the bridge from Sargentville (Sedgwick).

Find **public restrooms** at the Atlantic Avenue Hardware pier and the Stonington Town Hall on Main Street, Chase Emerson Library in Deer Isle Village, and behind the information booth on Little Deer Isle.

GETTING THERE AND AROUND

Deer Isle Village is about 12 miles or 25 minutes via Route 15 from Brooksville. Stonington is about six miles or 15 minutes via Route 15 from Deer Isle Village.

Isle au Haut

Eight miles off Stonington lies Isle au Haut. Approximately 3,200 acres, roughly half the island, belongs to Acadia National Park. Pronounced variously as "I'll-a-HO" or "I'LL-a-ho," the island has nearly 20 miles of hiking trails, excellent birding, and a tiny village. The most recent U.S. census counted the population as 73, but islanders say it hovers around 40 souls. Most of those who call Isle au Haut home year-round eke out a living from the sea. Each summer, the population temporarily swells with day-trippers, campers, and cottagers. Come autumn, it settles in to the measured pace of life on an offshore island.

Native American shell middens document 5,000 years of use. Samuel de Champlain, threading his way through this archipelago in 1604 and noting the island's prominent central ridge, named it Isle au Haut (High Island). Appropriately, the tallest peak (543 feet) is now named Mount Champlain.

Peletiah Barter, the island's first European settler, arrived in 1792 and his descendants still live and work here. Incorporated on its own in 1874, Isle au Haut earned a world record during World War I, when all residents were members of the Red Cross. Electricity came in 1970, and phone service in 1988.

More recent fame has come to the island thanks to island-based authors Linda Greenlaw, of *Perfect Storm* fame, who wrote *The Lobster Chronicles,* and more recently Kate Shaffer, of Black Dinah Chocolatiers, who shared her recipes along with island tales in *Desserted.* Although both books piqued interest in the island, Isle au Haut remains uncrowded and well off the beaten tourist track.

Most of the southern half of the six-mile-long island belongs to Acadia National Park, thanks to the wealthy summer visitors who began arriving in the 1880s. It was their heirs who, in the 1940s, donated valuable acreage to the federal government. Today, this offshore division of the national park has a well-managed 18-mile network of trails, a few lean-tos, several miles of paved and unpaved road, a lighthouse inn, and summertime passenger-ferry service to the park entrance. The National Park Service has a no-promote policy regarding Isle au Haut; unless you ask about it, you won't be told about it.

In the island's northern half are the private residences of fishing families and summer folk, a minuscule village (including a market, gift store, takeout shack, a gallery, library, school, and post office), and a five-mile stretch of paved road. The only vehicles on the island are owned by residents.

If spending the night on Isle au Haut sounds appealing (it is), you'll need to plan well ahead; it's no place for spur-of-the-moment sleepovers. (Even spontaneous day

Isle au Haut

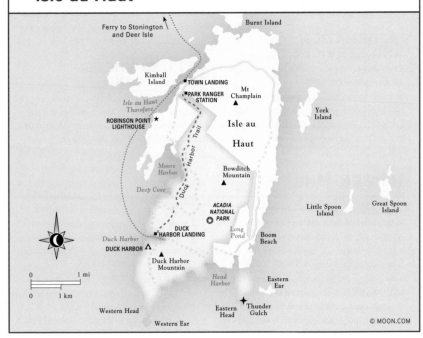

Ferry to Stonington
and Deer Isle

Burnt Island

Kimball
Island

■ TOWN LANDING

Mt
Champlain ▲

■ PARK RANGER
STATION

Isle au Haut
Thorofare

ROBINSON POINT ★
LIGHTHOUSE

York
Island

Isle au

Haut

Moore
Harbor

Bowditch
Mountain ▲

Deep Cove

Little Spoon
Island

Great Spoon
Island

ACADIA
NATIONAL
PARK

Long
Pond

Boom
Beach

Duck Harbor

■ DUCK
HARBOR LANDING

DUCK HARBOR ⛺

▲ Duck Harbor
Mountain

| 0 | 1 mi |
| 0 | 1 km |

Head
Harbor

Eastern
Ear

Western Head

Eastern
Head

Thunder
Gulch

Western Ear

© MOON.COM

trips aren't always possible.) The best part about staying on Isle au Haut is that you'll have much more than seven hours to enjoy this idyllic island.

Folk singer Gordon Bok penned the lyrics to *The Hills of Isle au Haut:*

The winters drive you crazy
And the fishin's hard and slow
You're a damn fool if you stay
But there's no better place to go

TOP EXPERIENCE

★ ACADIA NATIONAL PARK

Mention **Acadia National Park** and most people think of Bar Harbor and Mount Desert Island, where more than two million visitors arrive each year. The Isle au Haut section of the park sees about 5,000-7,500 day-use visitors annually, with an official daily cap of 128,

including a maximum of 30 camping at Duck Harbor. The limited boat service, the remoteness of the island, and the scarcity of campsites contribute to the low count, leaving the trails and views for only a few hardy souls. Isle au Haut provides perhaps the best opportunity in the park for low-density or solitary experiences. Consider it Acadia's backcountry. Park facilities are limited to a ranger station, maintenance facility, dock, and primitive campground.

Isle au Haut is rich in natural resources, with more than 700 species of plants. Three vascular plants—swarthy sedge, screwstem, and inkberry—are considered endangered or threatened in Maine, and a fourth, mountain sandwort, is of special concern. The island's diverse habitats range from bogs and small wetlands to ledges.

This section of the park not only is remote, but it also offers a rare opportunity to view an undeveloped shoreline, to experience solitude amid the glory of nature, and to ponder un-hindered Atlantic views.

About a third of a mile from the town landing, where the year-round mail boat and an excursion boat dock, is the **park ranger station** (207/335-5551), where you can pick up trail maps and park information—and use this end of the island's only public toilet. Do yourself a favor and plan ahead by download-ing Isle au Haut maps and information from the Acadia National Park website, www.nps.gov/acad/isle-au-haut.htm.

RECREATION
Hiking

Hiking on Acadia National Park trails is the major recreation on Isle au Haut. Even in the densest fog, you'll see valiant hikers heading out. A loop road circles the whole island; an unpaved section goes through the park, con-necting with the mostly paved nonpark sec-tion. Walking on it makes for an easy hike. Beyond the road, none of the park's 18 miles of trails could be labeled "easy": the footing is rocky, rooted, and often squishy. The park is committed to maintaining the primitive na-ture of the Isle au Haut trails, which means they're narrower, with few man-made en-hancements. But the views—of islets, distant hills, and ocean—make the effort worthwhile. Wear proper footwear and come prepared with water and food; there are no stores in the park.

A park ranger meets the boat that docks in Duck Harbor and provides a brief orientation for visitors. The biggest mistake most day-trippers make is overestimating how much terrain they can cover. It's wise to confer with the ranger about plans, especially if you're not an avid and experienced hiker. Be sure to top off water bottles at the pump. There's also a composting toilet available.

DUCK HARBOR TRAIL
Distance: 7.6 miles round-trip
Duration: 4 hours
Elevation gain: Minimal

Effort: Moderate
Trailhead: Park Ranger Station, north end of the island

The most-used park trail connects the town landing with Duck Harbor. You can either use this trail or follow the island road—mostly unpaved in this stretch—to get to the camp-ground when the summer ferry ends its Duck Harbor runs.

From the trailhead at the ranger station, follow the Duck Harbor Trail through the forest for 1.3 miles until the trail veers right. From there, the path continues another 3.3 miles through forest, passing the intersection with Bowditch Trail and crossing the Main Road, before it heads to the coastline. Enjoy the coastal views as you trek past Goss Beach. Follow the trail as it crosses over Main Road a second time and takes you up and down the hilly terrain. At the end of the trail is Duck Harbor. Return the way you came.

DUCK HARBOR MOUNTAIN TRAIL
Distance: 2.4 miles round-trip
Duration: 3-4 hours
Elevation gain: 300 feet
Effort: Strenuous
Trailhead: Western Head Road

Even though the summit is only 314 feet, this is the island's toughest trail. Still, it's worth the effort for the stunning, 360-degree views from the summit.

From the trailhead, follow Western Head Road south for 0.1 mile. When the trail splits, veer left to take Duck Harbor Mountain Trail. Scramble up the trail, which takes you over boulders, until you reach the summit of Duck Harbor Mountain. When you're done taking in the views, you can either return the way you came or continue along the Duck Harbor Trail until you reach Goat Trail. If you con-tinue on to Goat Trail, follow it until it con-nects with Western Head Road, which you can take northwest to get back to the trailhead.

WESTERN HEAD AND CLIFF TRAILS
Distance: 4 miles round-trip

Acadia National Park

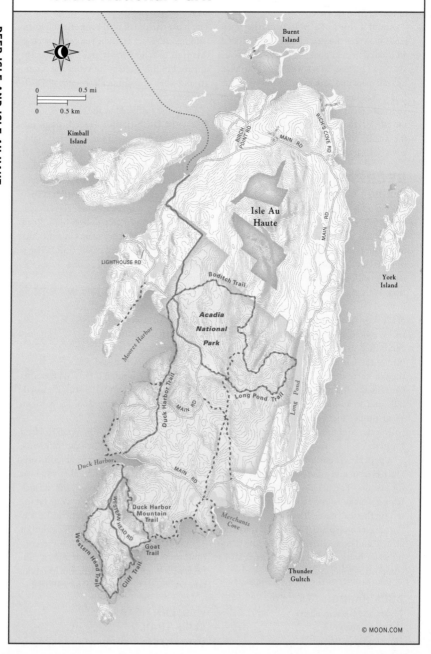

Burnt
Island

BIRCH POINT RD

MAIN RD

RICH'S COVE RD

MAIN RD

Kimball
Island

Isle Au
Haute

LIGHTHOUSE RD

Boditch Trail

York
Island

*Acadia
National
Park*

Long Pond Trail

Long Pond

Moores Harbor

Duck Harbor Trail

MAIN RD

Duck Harbor

MAIN RD

WESTERN HEAD RD

Duck Harbor
Mountain
Trail

Merchants
Cove

Western Head Trail

Cliff Trail

Goat
Trail

Thunder
Gultch

0   0.5 mi

0   0.5 km

© MOON.COM

Duration: 2 hours.
Elevation gain: 150 feet
Effort: Moderate
Trailhead: Western Head Road

For terrific shoreline scenery, take these two trails, at the island's southwestern corner, that form a nice loop around Western Head. The route follows the coastline, ascending to ridges and cliffs and descending to rocky beaches, with some forested sections. If the tide is out (and *only* if it's out), you can walk across the tidal flats to the quaintly named Western Ear for views back toward the island.

From the trailhead, follow the Western Head Road south 0.1 mile. When the trail splits, continue slightly right to stay on the Western Head Road. Continue 0.3 mile until it splits a second time, again veering right toward the coastline. Follow the trail along the coast, passing Western Head Mountain and then the turn off for the Cliff Trail.

If you wish to add another four miles (round-trip) to your hike, veer left at the intersection with the Cliff Trail to meet up with the challenging Duck Mountain Trail. If you wish to continue along the Western Head Road, follow the trail straight to trek through the forest and return to the trailhead.

LONG POND TRAIL

Distance: 3 miles one-way
Duration: 2 hours
Elevation gain: 150 feet
Effort: Strenuous
Trailhead: Main Road, western side of the island

This difficult loop hike crosses from the west to the east side of the island and passes Long Pond before climbing along the edges of Bowditch Mountain's summit. The trail intersects with the Median Ridge Trail and the Bowditch Trail.

From the Main Road, take the Long Pond Trail southeast through the woods, passing the turnoff for the Median Ridge Trail on your right. Continue on Long Pond Trail until you reach a ridge parallel to the Long Pond. From here, the trail veers west and then south, before heading north to meet up with

the Bowditch Trail. At the intersection with the Bowditch Trail, continue left to follow the Long Pond Trail back to the trailhead.

BOWDITCH TRAIL

Distance: 4 miles round-trip
Duration: 2-3 hours
Elevation gain: 350 feet
Effort: Moderate
Trailhead: Off Duck Harbor Trail, 1.5 miles from the ranger station

The Bowditch Trail passes through bogs, forests, and wet ledges as it climbs to the mountain's 405-foot summit, where it connects to the Median Ridge-Long Pond Trail. Varied terrain and good views make the effort worthwhile.

From the ranger station, follow the Duck Harbor Trail until it meets up with the Bowditch Trail. Veer left to take the Bowditch Trail until it intersects with the Long Pond Trail. At the intersection, veer right to take the Long Pond Trail south until you reach another intersection where you'll turn right to stay on the Long Pond Trail. From there, take the Long Pond Trail another 0.4 mile to reach the Main road, which you can follow northwest to find the start of the Bowditch Trail. From there, retrace your steps along the Duck Harbor Trail back to the ranger station.

WALKS AND UNMARKED HIKES

Befriend a local and ask for directions to **Seal Trap,** an easy trail to a postcard-worthy harbor on the island's west side. (The name, by the way, evolved from *Ciel Trappe,* which means Sky Trap and has nothing to do with seals). The unmarked trail crosses private property, so do ask locally whether you can hike it, and practice good trail etiquette. Another unmarked trail is **Mount Champlain,** a moderate hike up to the 543-foot summit, which provides few views because it's heavily forested. Access is on the north end of the island.

When the water is rough, **Boom Beach,** on the island's east side, is the place to be. As crashing waves roll in over the round rocks, they rumble, hence the boom. The stormier it

is, the wilder this spot becomes. It's an easy five-minute walk to the stone beach from the main road (the only road) along a spruce-lined path edged with moss- and lichen-covered rocks. Bring a picnic, but don't even consider swimming here. Boom Beach is approximately 0.25 mile north of Long Pond beach; look for a grassy pullout.

If you're traveling counterclockwise around the island, take the first road on the right just north of Head Harbor, when the road turns to tar (you'll see a bright yellow house just down the road); across from the log cabin in the field, follow the mowed path to the shore, then look for a sign for **Thunder Gulch.** Follow the trail through the woods and down the middle of Eastern Head. Tension seems to build as you walk through the woods, and then the trail emerges to open ocean views. Waves roll into a cleavage in the rock before erupting in a tower of spray. One islander describes it as a Zen-like place "where all your questions will be answered."

In Duck Harbor, park rangers suggest **Eben's Head** as a great trail for those visiting with young children. It's a short, easy loop skirting the coastline and taking in two cobble beaches that are ideal for beachcombing and splashing. An offshoot climbs a rocky knob guarding the entrance to Duck Harbor, a fine place for a picnic, but keep youngsters away from the edges. The trail is on the park map, and the ranger who meets the boat can provide directions.

Bird-Watching

Isle au Haut's offshore location makes it a popular stopover for migrating bats; shorebirds, including purple sandpipers; songbirds; and raptors, including bald eagles. It's also renowned as a wintering haven for harlequin ducks.

Bicycling

Pedaling is limited to the 12 or so miles of hilly roads: 5 miles paved, and 7 with loose gravel and ledges. While cycling is a way to get around, frankly, the terrain isn't exciting, fun, or view-worthy. Mountain bikes are not allowed on the park's hiking trails. You can rent a bike (about $25/day) for the island from the Isle au Haut Ferry Service. It costs $22 round-trip to bring your own bike aboard the Isle au Haut ferry. Both boats carry bikes *only* to the town landing, not to Duck Harbor.

Swimming

For freshwater swimming, head for **Long Pond,** a skinny, mile-long swimming hole running north-south on the east side of the island, abutting national park land. You can bike over there, clockwise along the road, almost five miles, from the town landing. Or bum a ride from an island resident. There's a minuscule beach-like area on the southern end with a picnic table and a float. If you're here only for the day, though, there's not enough time to do this *and* get in a long hike. Opt for the hiking—or do a short hike and then go for a swim (the shallowest part is at the southern tip).

ENTERTAINMENT AND EVENTS

Although Isle au Haut is pretty much a make-your-own-fun place, summer events usually include a Fourth of July parade, which all islanders participate in, so there are few spectators, and an island talent show in August. Look also for signs at the town landing dock about themed cook-offs, which might include such gourmet items as Spam.

If visiting with young children, there are swings and a cedar climbing gym at the **Isle au Haut School,** a one-room schoolhouse for children in grades K-8. The **Revere Memorial Library** (www.revere.lib.me.us) has an excellent children's room.

1: hiking in Isle au Haut's Acadia section 2: Duck Harbor Campground 3: Duck Harbor in Isle au Haut 4: the Isle au Haut Boat Company's excursion ferry

SHOPPING

One doesn't go to Isle au Haut to shop, but if you want to purchase books by island authors, Maine-made jewelry and gifts, or other souvenirs, Kendra Chubbuck's **Shore Shop Gifts** (1 Main Rd., 207/335-2244, www.maineshoreshopgifts.com) is well worth a visit. The shop is in the village, just north of the Town Dock **The Island Store** (207/335-5211, www.theislandstore.net), just north of the Town Dock, stocks essentials and a few splurge-worthy items.

FOOD

Isle au Haut is pretty much a BYO place—and for the most part, that includes BYO food.

Thanks to **The Island Store** (207/335-5211, www.theislandstore.net), barely a five-minute walk from the town landing, you won't starve. The summer inventory includes all the makings for a great picnic. On the other hand, food probably won't be your prime interest here—Isle au Haut is as pretty as it gets.

And then there's **The Maine Lobster Lady** (207/335-5141, www.mainelobsterlady.com, $14-22), Diana Santospago's seasonal takeout serving lobster in many forms, chowders, and fried seafood and whoopie pies as well as breakfast sandwiches, pies, milk shakes, ice cream, and iced coffee. Find her parked at the General Store. It's usually open 11am-6pm, Tuesday-Sunday, but call to confirm if you really want to experience this. There are picnic tables with umbrellas on the thoroughfare's edge.

ACCOMMODATIONS
Camping

Online reservations open April 1 at 10am for the five six-person lean-tos at ★ **Duck Harbor Campground** (207/335-5551, www.recreation.gov). The season runs May 15 to October 15; the fee is $20/night. The maximum stay is three nights and you can only stay once during each calendar year.

Unless you don't mind backpacking nearly five miles to reach the campground, try to plan your visit between mid-June and late September, when the mail boat makes a stop in Duck Harbor. It's wise to check with the **Isle au Haut Boat Company** (207/367-5193, www.isleauhaut.com) for the current ferry schedule before choosing dates for a lean-to reservation.

Note: Campers must carry all gear on and off the boat, which means navigating ramps and docks, and lean-to access is via a trail

a sailboat cruising by Acadia National Park on Isle au Haut

ascending rocky and rooted terrain. The distance from boat to campground is roughly 0.25 mile.

Trash policy is carry-in/carry-out, so pack a trash bag or two with your gear. Also bring a container for carting water from the campground pump, because it's 0.3 mile from the lean-tos. It's a 4-mile walk to the general store for food—when you could be off hiking the island's trails—so bring enough to cover your stay.

The three-sided lean-tos are big enough (8 by 12.5 feet, 8 feet high) to hold a small (two-person) tent, so bring one along if you prefer being fully enclosed. A tarp will also do the trick. (Also bring mosquito repellent—some years, the critters show up here en masse.) No camping is permitted outside of the lean-tos, and nothing can be attached to trees. If you're even tempted by the idea of trying to sneak off and backpack into the park for an overnight, forget it: The island is small and rangers, boat captains, and locals keep track of the comings and goings. Don't risk federal fines.

GETTING THERE
Isle au Haut Boat Company
The Isle au Haut Boat Company (Seabreeze Ave., Stonington, 207/367-5193, www.isleauhaut.com) generally operates five daily trips Monday-Saturday, plus two on Sunday from mid-June to early September. Other months, there are two or three trips Monday-Saturday. The best advice is to request a copy of the current schedule, covering dates, variables, fares, and extras.

Round-trips April-mid-October are $40 adults, $20 kids under age 12 (two bags per adult, one bag per child). Round-trip surcharges include bikes ($22) and kayaks/canoes ($46 minimum). Weather seldom affects the schedule, but be aware that heavy seas could cancel a trip.

There is twice-daily ferry service, early June-mid-September, from Stonington to Duck Harbor, at the edge of Isle au Haut's Acadia National Park campground. For a day trip, the schedule allows you about 4 hours on the island. No boats or bikes are allowed on this route, and no dogs are allowed in the campground. A ranger meets the boat in Duck Harbor and provides an orientation and campsite check-in. Before mid-June and after Labor Day, you'll be off-loaded at the Isle au Haut town landing, about 4.5 miles from Duck Harbor.

Ferries depart from the Isle au Haut Boat Company dock (Seabreeze Ave., off E. Main St. in downtown Stonington). Parking ($12-14) usually is available next to the ferry landing. Arrive at least an hour early to get all this settled so you don't miss the boat.

Ellsworth and Trenton

The punch line to an old Maine joke is "Ya cahn't get they-ah from he-ah." And the truth is, you can't get to Mount Desert Island without going through Ellsworth and Trenton.

While there are ways to skirt around a few of the worst traffic spots, both Ellsworth and Trenton have a few surprises that invite exploration. Historic homes, a grand theater, a delightful bird sanctuary, an inviting downtown, fun shops and galleries, and good dining options make Ellsworth worth more than a pit stop. Trenton, linked by a bridge to Mount Desert Island, is little more than a 6-7-mile strip of tourist-oriented businesses, but this stretch of road provides the first glimpses of the prize: the rounded peaks of Mount Desert Island.

Other pluses for the area include inexpensive lodging, an oceanfront

Highlights

Look for ★ to find recommended sights, activities, dining, and lodging.

★ **Woodlawn:** This treasure-filled Georgian mansion has gardens, carriage houses, and walking trails (page 241).

★ **Kisma Preserve:** Splurge on a behind-the-scenes tour of this preserve dedicated to conserving and protecting rescued and retired exotic animals (page 248).

★ **Flightseeing:** Get a proper introduction to Mount Desert Island by gliding with the hawks or getting a bird's-eye view from a small plane (page 249).

★ **The Great Maine Lumberjack Show:** A must for kids, this show demonstrates all the old-time logging skills (page 250).

Ellsworth and Trenton

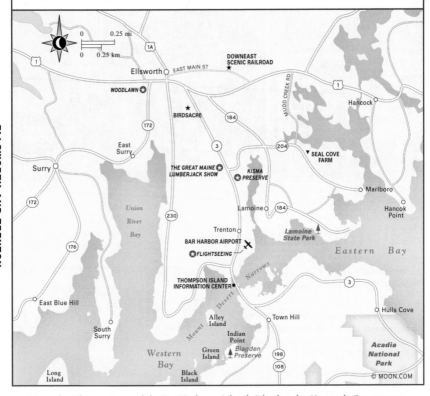

state park with camping, and the Bar Harbor Chamber of Commerce Information Center location on Route 3 in Trenton. If you're day-tripping to Mount Desert Island, you can leave your car here and hop aboard the free Island Explorer bus, eliminating driving and parking hassles.

PLANNING YOUR TIME

Most people pass right through Ellsworth and Trenton, never stopping to visit the handful of sights. Ellsworth is a thriving year-round community that doubles as a sub-urb for people employed on Mount Desert Island. It's also the Hancock County seat, the region's shopping hub, and home to the region's most traffic lights, although that's fewer than a half dozen. Don't expect to whiz through on Route 1, but unless there's a major accident or construction, it's not a major time suck. It's also the best spot to pick up necessities or even lunch before arriving on the island. Trenton is far more sea-sonal, but traffic often bogs down around the traffic lights and drivers rubbernecking the views. If you want to go car-free on Mount Desert Island, the Island Explorer's Route 1 bus services Trenton.

Previous: Marlboro Beach Park; Union River Lobster Pot; Grand Auditorium of Hancock County.

Ellsworth

Ellsworth (pop. 7,741), Hancock County's shire town, has mushroomed with the popularity of Acadia National Park, but you can still find handsome architectural remnants of the city's 19th-century lumbering heyday, which began shortly after its incorporation in 1800. Brigs, barks, and full-rigged ships—built in Ellsworth and captained by local fellows—loaded lumber here and carried it around the globe. Despite a ruinous 1855 fire that swept through downtown, the lumber trade thrived until late in the 19th century, along with factories and mills turning out shoes, bricks, boxes, and butter.

These days, Ellsworth is the region's shopping mecca. Antiques shops and small stores line Main Street, which doubles as Route 1 in the downtown section; supermarkets, strip malls, and big-box stores line Routes 1 and 3 between Ellsworth and Trenton.

Frankly, if you're here for Acadia, you'll likely just pass through Ellsworth, perhaps stopping for food or supplies, before continuing onto the island.

SIGHTS
★ Woodlawn

Very little has changed at Woodlawn (19 Black Horse Dr., Ellsworth, 207/667-8671, www.woodlawnmuseum.com, 10am-5pm Tues.-Sat., 1pm-4pm Sun. June-Sept., 1pm-4pm Tues.-Sun. May and Oct., $12 adults, $5 ages 5-12, grounds free) since George Nixon Black donated his home, also known as the Black Mansion, to the town in 1928. Completed in 1828, the Georgian house is a marvel of preservation—one of Maine's best—filled with Black family antiques and artifacts. House highlights include a circular staircase, rare books and artifacts, canopied beds, a barrel organ, and lots more. After taking an audio tour, plan to picnic on the manicured grounds, and then explore two sleigh-filled barns, the Memorial Garden,

and the two miles of mostly level trails in the woods up beyond the house. Consider timing a visit with one of the frequent events: On many Wednesday afternoons in July, August, and September, Afternoon High Tea ($25) is served in the garden (or in the carriage house if it's raining); reservations are required. On Tuesday afternoons 2pm-4pm, visitors can learn how to play nine-wicket golf croquet on the tournament-sized court ($10, includes equipment). On Route 172, watch for the small sign 0.25 mile southwest of U.S. 1, and turn into the winding uphill driveway.

Birdsacre

En route to Bar Harbor, watch carefully on the right for the sign that marks Birdsacre (289 High St./Rte. 3/Bar Harbor Rd., 207/667-8460, www.birdsacre.com, sunrise-sunset daily, donation), a 200-acre urban sanctuary. Wander the trails in this peaceful preserve, spotting wildflowers, birds, and well-labeled shrubs and trees, and you'll have trouble believing you're in prime tourist territory. One trail, a boardwalk loop through woods behind the nature center, is accessible for wheelchairs and strollers.

Noted ornithologist Cordelia Stanwood once lived in the 1850 Stanwood Homestead Museum (10am-4pm daily June-Sept., free) at the sanctuary entrance. Birdsacre is also a wildlife rehabilitation center, so expect to see all kinds of winged creatures, especially hawks and owls, in various stages of recuperation. Some will be returned to the wild, and others remain here for educational purposes. Stop by the Richmond Nature Center (10am-4pm daily June-Sept., volunteer dependent) for even more exhibits and gifts.

Downeast Scenic Railroad

The all-volunteer Downeast Rail Heritage Preservation Trust (8 Railroad Siding

Rd., Hancock, 866/449-7245, www. downeastscenicrail.org) has restored a 1948 diesel engine train and rehabilitated portions of the Calais Branch Line. Saturday-Sunday (late May-mid-Oct.) you can board the two vintage coaches, an open flatcar, or the caboose for a roughly 13-mile, 1.75-hour scenic excursion ($17 adults, $9 ages 3-12) to Ellsworth Falls and back. Work continues on the track to Green Lake, which will allow a 24-mile round-trip. If you're a train buff, ask about volunteer opportunities. From downtown Ellsworth, take Main Street northeast for 2.3 miles to Railroad Siding Road.

Telephone Museum

Discover life before cell phones at the **Telephone Museum** (166 Winkumpaugh Rd., 207/667-9491, www. thetelephonemuseum.org, 1pm-4pm Sat. July 1-Sept. 30 or by chance, $10 adults, $5 children), a hands-on museum with the East Coast's largest collection of old-fashioned switching systems. Find it 10 miles north of Ellsworth, 1 mile off Route 1A toward Bangor.

Ellsworth Historical Society Museum

Kids love the Old Hancock County Jail, now home to the **Ellsworth Historical Society Museum** (40 State St., www.ellsworthme.org/ ellshistory, 10am-3pm Thurs. and Sat. July-Aug., free). Built in 1886, the Queen Anne Revival building housed both the jail and the jail keeper's residence, an interesting combo. Even more interesting is that each of the cells is named—a more contemporary twist, as the monikers refer to local accommodations. The residence is filled with the whatnots of Ellsworth's history, a hodgepodge of antiques and artifacts. The decor reflects the Victorian period.

Green Lake National Fish Hatchery

Approximately one million Atlantic salmon smolts and fall parr are reared annually at the **Green Lake Fish Hatchery** (1 Hatchery Way/Rte. 180, 207/667-9531, www.fws.gov/ northeast/greenlake), which is open for self-guided tours (8am-4pm daily). The facility is located about 10 minutes north of downtown. Take Route 1A north to the junction with Route 179/180, then bear left on Route 180 and look for the sign on the left.

RECREATION
Hiking

Frenchman Bay Conservancy (207/422-2328, www.frenchmanbay.org) oversees the 13-acre **Indian Point Preserve.** The reward for following the footpath through the woods and across bog bridges to the Union River shorefront is a lovely view of the city. To find the preserve, drive south on Water Street, cross Card Brook, and at the top of the next hill, look for Tinker Farm Way on the right. The road to the preserve's parking lot angles off to the right.

Nature trails lace **Birdsacre** (289 Rte. 3/High St., 207/667-8460, www.birdsacre. com), a 200-acre sanctuary with three small ponds; one is accessible for wheelchairs and strollers. Two miles of mostly level trails can also be found behind the Black Mansion at **Woodlawn** (Surry Rd./Rte. 172, 207/667-8671, www.woodlawnmuseum.com).

Meander more than three miles of signed trails through 239 acres of woodlands to the rocky lakeshore in **Branch Lake Forest,** owned by the City of Ellsworth (207/667-2563). To find it, from downtown Ellsworth, take Route 1A 6.5 miles north to the signed access road on your left, and follow it for one mile to the parking lot.

Boat Launches

If you've brought your own boat, you can launch it into the Union River at the **Waterfront Park and Marina** on Water Street, which intersects Route 1 at the traffic light on the lower end of Main Street. Also here are picnic tables and Scoops, a

---

1: Woodlawn **2:** Morton's Moo **3:** Downtown Ellsworth's Rooster Brother **4:** the Stanwood Homestead Museum at Birdsacre

homemade ice cream kiosk. Another launch is on **Graham Lake,** just above the dam, on Route 180. To find it, take Route 1A north from downtown Ellsworth, then Route 180/179 to the split, then Route 180. Look for the boat launch sign on the right, just after the dam.

ENTERTAINMENT

Ellsworth has three free summer series. The **Ellsworth Concert Band** performs at 7pm Wednesday evening at Harbor Park, 410 Water Street. **Outdoor family movies** are shown at sunset Thursday at the Knowlton Playground on State Street (donations appreciated). **Concerts** are staged at Harbor Park at 6pm on Friday.

The carefully restored art deco **Grand Auditorium of Hancock County** (100 Main St., 207/667-9500, www.grandonline.org) is the year-round site of films, concerts, plays, and art exhibits.

SHOPPING

Ellsworth has an especially appealing downtown with a nice mix of independent shops.

Specialty Shops

Don't miss **Rooster Brother** (29 Main St./Rte. 1, 207/667-8675 or 800/866-0054, www.roosterbrother.com) for gourmet cookware, cards, and books on the main floor; coffee, tea, candy, cheeses, a huge array of exotic condiments, fresh breads, and other gourmet items on the lower level; and discounted merchandise on the 2nd floor, open seasonally. You can easily pick up all the fixings for a fancy picnic here.

John Edwards Market (158 Main St., 207/667-9377) is a twofold find: Upstairs is a natural-foods store, and downstairs is the terrific Wine Cellar Gallery, a year-round space showcasing Maine artists.

Just a block off Main Street and worth the detour is **Atlantic Art Glass** (25 Pine St., 207/664-0222), where you can watch Linda and Ken Perrin demonstrate glassblowing and buy their contemporary creations.

Brothers Dave and Don Herrington are the creative goldsmiths who design the jewelry sold at **Pyramid Studios** (10 State St., 207/667-3321, www.pyramid.ws).

Union River Book & Toy Co. (100 Main St., 207/667-6604, www.unionrivertoys.com) is filled with books, toys, games, puzzles, dolls, stuffed animals, puppets, and more to keep the kiddos happy should the weather turn gloomy.

Curiosities, plants, fossils, bones, and home accents make it fun to browse **The Rock & Art Shop** (163 Main St., 207/610-1300, www.therockandartshop.com).

Just south of downtown, at the corner of Court Street and Route 1, **Courthouse Gallery Fine Art** (6 Court St., 207/667-6611, www.courthousegallery.com) showcases works by some of Maine's top contemporary artists. Gallery owners Karin and Michael Wilkes have restored the 1834 Greek Revival courthouse, listed in the National Register of Historic Places. In addition to nine interior galleries, artwork is also shown in an adjacent historic building and in the sculpture park on the front lawn.

Antiques

You're unlikely to meet a single person who has left **Big Chicken Barn Books and Antiques** (1768 Bucksport Rd./Rte. 1, 207/667-7308, www.bigchickenbarn.com) without buying something. You'll find every kind of collectible on the vast 1st floor, courtesy of more than four dozen dealers. Climb the stairs for books, magazines, old music, and more. With free coffee, restrooms, and 21,000 square feet of floor space, this place is addictive. The Big Chicken is 11 miles east of Bucksport, 8.5 miles west of Ellsworth.

The 40-plus-dealer **Old Creamery Antique Mall** (13 Hancock St., 207/667-0522) fills 6,000 square feet on two jam-packed floors.

When the building housing **The Dream Catcher Antique and Collectibles** (107 Main St., 207/667-7886, www.dreamcatcherellsworth.com) was constructed in 1933, it first housed Harry C. Austin & Co., furniture dealers and funeral directors, an interesting combination. Now its three stories house more than 75 vendors selling everything from genuine antiques to shabby-chic pieces, estate jewelry, and Native American art.

Discount Shopping

Forgot to pack a fleece or sweater for cool evenings? Need a rain jacket or shorts? Wish you had a beach towel or a cooler? You'll find all that and more at the outlets and discount stores hugging the Route 3 strip in Ellsworth.

The **L. L. Bean Factory Store** (150 High St./Rte. 1, 207/667-7753) carries everything from clothing to sporting equipment, but don't expect a full range of sizes or designs. That said, I've never left empty-handed.

Across the road is **Reny's Department Store** (Ellsworth Shopping Center, 185 High St./Rte. 1, 207/667-5166, www.renys.com), a Maine-based discount operation with a "you never know what you'll find" philosophy. Trust me, you'll find something.

Marden's (461 High St./Rte. 3, 207/669-6036, www.mardenssurplus.com) is another Maine "bit of this, bit of that" enterprise with the catchy slogan "I shoulda bought it when I saw it." Good advice.

Sporting Goods

For an extensive sporting-gear inventory, plus advice on outdoors activities, stop in at **Cadillac Mountain Sports** (34 High St./Rte. 1, 207/667-7819).

FOOD

Quick Bites

If you're camping, you might want to stop at **Hannaford** (225 High St., 207/667-5300, www.hannaford.com, 7am-10pm daily), a full-service supermarket with a pharmacy (8am-8pm Mon.-Fri., 8am-6pm Sat., 8am-5pm Sun.) to pick up food and other must-haves.

Order breakfast anytime at **The Riverside Café** (151 Main St., 207/667-7220, 7am-2pm daily, $6-15). Lunch service begins at 11am. The café is named for its former location; it used to be down the street, overlooking the Union River.

Equally delicious are the home-style breakfasts at **Martha's Diner** (Reny's Plaza, 151 High St., 207/664-2495, http://marthasdiner. com, 6am-2pm Tues.-Fri., 6am-1pm Sat., 7am-1pm Sun., $4-8), where lunch is also served 11am-2pm Tuesday-Friday. Booths are red leatherette and Formica, and the waitresses likely will call you "doll." Cash only.

On the upper end of Main Street, **Flexit Café and Bakery** (192 Main St., 207/412-0484, https://flexitcafe.com, 7am-5pm daily) serves breakfast and lunch daily, with vegan and gluten-free options available. Most sandwiches and salads are $8-10.

Big flavors come out of tiny **86 This** (125 Main St., 207/610-1777, www.86thismaine. com, 11am-8pm Mon.-Fri., 11am-4pm Sat., $8-10), a wrap and burrito joint with seating. The flavors are rich, the portions are generous, and wraps are named after the owners' favorite indie bands. Get your food to go and walk the half block to the picnic tables on the library's shady lawn.

Jordan's Snack Bar (200 Down East Hwy./Rte. 1, 207/667-2174, www. jordanssnackbar.com, 11am-7pm Wed.-Mon.) has an almost cult following for its crabmeat rolls and fried clams. Wednesday cruise-ins (6pm-9pm) usually feature live entertainment and draw up to 50 vintage cars. Kids will love the game room and playground.

Ice cream doesn't get much finer than that sold at ★ **Morton's Moo** (9 School St., 207/266-9671, www.mortonsmoo.com, 11am-8pm daily), a family-run spot with a deservedly giant reputation for homemade Italian gelato and ice cream in creative flavors. It's half a block off Main Street behind Flexit.

You'll find fresh and prepared foods, breads, and more at the **Ellsworth Farmers Market** (190 Main St., www.ellsworthfarmersmarket.com, 9:30am-12:30pm Sunday).

The Lobster Experience

No visit to Maine can be considered complete without the experience of a "lobstah dinnah" at a lobster wharf, pound, or shack. Keep an eye on the weather, pick a sunny day, and head out.

If you're in the area before Memorial Day or after Labor Day, the options are not as varied—many such enterprises have a short season, although more and more are staying open at least through September.

There's nowhere to eat lobster within Acadia National Park (unless you're camping or picnicking and cook it yourself over a campfire), but Mount Desert Island and the surrounding region provide plenty of opportunities. Almost every restaurant, café, or bistro serves lobster in some form or other. But as you drive, bus, bike, or walk around, watch for the genuine article—the "real" lobster wharf. You want to eat outdoors, at a wooden picnic table, with a knockout view of boats and the sea. If you're camping, most lobster wharves will boil lobsters for you free or for a small fee. They'll wrap them in newspaper so they stay warm until you get back to your campsite. The best advice is to order them like pizza: Call ahead so they'll be ready when you show up for them.

At whatever place you choose, the drill is much the same, and the "dinners" are served anytime from 11am or noon onward (some places close as early as 4pm). First of all, dress very casually so you can manhandle the lobster without messing up decent clothes. If you want beer or wine, call ahead and ask if the place serves it; you may need to bring your own, since many such operations don't have beer-and-wine licenses, much less liquor licenses. In the evening, carry some insect repellent, in case mosquitoes crash the party.

A basic one-pound lobster and go-withs (coleslaw or potato salad, potato chips, and butter for dipping) should run $16-28, based on the seasonal lobster price; some shacks will include steamed clams too. Unfortunately, some places use margarine, which doesn't do lobster any favors. Don't skip dessert; many lobster shacks are known for their homemade pies.

It's not unusual to see lobster-wharf devotees carting picnic baskets with hors d'oeuvres, salads, and baguettes. I've even seen candles, champagne, tablecloths, and fresh flowers. Creativity abounds, but don't stray too far from the main attraction—the crustaceans.

Typically, you'll need to survey a chalkboard or whiteboard menu and step up to a window to order. You'll either give the person your name or get a number. A few places have staff to take your order or deliver your meal (and help you figure out how to eat it), but usually you'll head back to the window when your name or number is called. Don your plastic lobster bib and

Casual Dining

Decent pub fare is served at **Finn's Irish Pub** (156 Main St., 207/667-2808, 4pm-8pm Wed.-Sun., $8-15), and there's a kids' menu too.

Airline Brewing Company (153 Main St., 207/412-0045, www.abcmaine.beer, 11am-9pm daily, $8-13), a tasting room and cozy English pub, features Airline's tap and cask brews and ciders, along with well-prepared pub favorites.

Pair a brew from **Fogtown Brewing Company** (25 Pine St., 207/370-0845, www.fogtownbrewing.com, from 3pm Wed.-Sun.) with a sandwich or burger from the **Eat at Joe's** (207/266-6069, $10-18) food truck parked on site.

★ **Provender Kitchen & Bar** (112 Main St., 207/610-1480, www.eatprovender.com, 5pm-9pm Tues.-Sat., 9am-2pm Sun., $16-36) serves contemporary American fare in a historical setting complete with polished wood booths and soft lighting.

International

Mighty fine pizza is served at **Finelli Pizzeria** (12 Rte. 1, 207/664-0230, www.finellipizzeria.com, 11am-8pm daily, $7-20), a homey little spot where the pizza dough and focaccia are made fresh daily. The specialty is New begin the attack. If you're a neophyte, watch a pro at a nearby table. Some lobster wharves have "how-to" info printed on paper placemats. If you're really concerned (you needn't be), contact the Maine Lobster Promotion Council (www.mainelobsterpromo.com), which produces a brochure with detailed instructions. Don't worry about doing it wrong; you'll eventually get what you came for, and it'll be an experience to remember.

Here are six classic lobster experiences in Maine's Acadia region:

- **Bernard (Mount Desert Island):** Thurston's Lobster Pound (Steamboat Wharf Rd., Bernard, 207/244-7600, www.thurstonforlobster.com, 11am-9pm daily)

- **Southwest Harbor (Mount Desert Island):** Beal's Lobster Pier (182 Clark Point Rd., Southwest Harbor, 207/244-3202, www.bealslobster.com, 11am-9pm daily)

- **Deer Isle:** LDI Lobster (202 Little Deer Isle Rd., Little Deer Isle, 207/348-2843, 11am-7pm Wed.-Sun.)

- **Corea (Schoodic Peninsula):** Corea Wharf Gallery (13 Gibbs Ln, Corea, 207/963-2633, 11am-4pm daily)

- **Surry:** Perry's Lobster Shack and Pier (1076 Newbury Neck Rd., Surry, 207/667-1955, www.perryslobstershack.com, 10am-7pm daily)

- **Trenton:** Trenton Bridge Lobster Pound (Bar Harbor Rd./Rte. 3, Trenton, 207/667-2977, www.trentonbridgelobster.com, 8am-7:30pm Mon.-Sat.)

York-style thin-crust pizza, which is available by the pie or slab. Other options include calzones, pastas, subs, and salads.

Serendib (2 State St., 207/664-1030, www.serendibellsworth.com, hours vary seasonally, $12-18) serves authentic Indian-Sri Lankan cuisine prepared by owner Sanjeeva Abeyasekera, a native of Sri Lanka. Call for current hours.

Lobster

It's hard to say which is better—the serene views or the tasty lobster—at **Union River Lobster Pot** (8 South St., 207/667-5077, www.lobsterpot.com, 11:30am-7:30pm June-Oct.,

$15-24). It's tucked behind Rooster Brother, right on the banks of the Union River. The menu includes far more than lobster, with chicken, fish, meat, and pasta dishes, and a kids' menu is available. Remember to save room for pie, especially the blueberry.

INFORMATION AND SERVICES

It can be hard to spot the **Ellsworth Area Chamber of Commerce** (163 High St., 207/667-5584, www.ellsworthchamber.org) amid the malls and fast-food places lining High Street (Rte. 1). Watch for a small gray building topped by an Information Center sign (close to the road, on the right when heading toward Bar Harbor, just before Shaw's Plaza).

Public restrooms can be found in City Hall (City Hall Ave.) in downtown Ellsworth, open 24 hours daily, seven days a week; the library (46 State St.); the chamber of commerce; and the picnic area and boat launch (Water St.).

Libraries

Don't miss a chance to visit one of the state's loveliest libraries, the **Ellsworth Public Library** (46 State St., 207/667-6363, www. ellsworth.lib.me.us), listed in the National Register of Historic Places. George Nixon Black, grandson of the builder of the Woodlawn museum, donated the Federal-style building to the city in 1897.

GETTING THERE AND AROUND

Ellsworth is about 14 miles via Route 172 from Blue Hill. It's about 20 miles or 30-45 minutes, depending on traffic, to Bar Harbor and about 25 miles or 35 minutes via Routes 1 and 186 to Winter Harbor on the Schoodic Peninsula.

Road-wise, Ellsworth is the epicenter of Acadia. Route 1, the main thoroughfare along the coast, and Route 1A, which connects to Bangor, meet in downtown Ellsworth. Route 172 connects Ellsworth to the Blue Hill

Peninsula and on to Deer Isle, Stonington, and the mail boat to Isle au Haut. Route 1 continues north, providing access to the Schoodic Peninsula and a remote section of the park. Bar Harbor Road (Rte. 3), which funnels all traffic to Mount Desert Island, is often a summertime bottleneck. If you want to hit the region's highlights, by all means stay on Routes 1 and 3, but if your time is limited and your goal is maximum park time, consider these shortcuts.

If you're approaching from the south on Route 1 and your destination is Mount Desert Island, you can avoid downtown and the strip. When you cross the bridge in Ellsworth, turn right at the traffic light onto Route 230 (Water St.) and follow it about 6.5 miles, turning left onto Goose Cove Road, which rejoins Route 230. (You can stay on Route 230; it's just a longer route because it loops around the point.) Bear left on Route 230, then right at the intersection with Route 3. The causeway connecting to Mount Desert Island is less than a mile away.

If your destination is the Schoodic region, at the intersection of Route 1A and Route 1 (Main St.) in downtown Ellsworth, follow East Main Street and avoid the Route 1 strip. East Main Street morphs into Washington Junction Road and reconnects with Route 1 northeast of the Route 3 split for Mount Desert Island, avoiding the worst congestion.

Trenton

Unless you're arriving by boat, you can't get to Mount Desert Island without first going through Trenton (pop. 1,481), which straddles Route 3 from Ellsworth south. Stores, restaurants, motels, amusements, and gift shops line the six-mile strip, and some are worth at least a nod. If you're traveling with children, count on being begged to stop. Rural Lamoine (pop. 1,602) provides a reprieve. Few discover this peninsula-tipping town, with an oceanfront state park and

gorgeous views over Eastern and Frenchman Bays to Mount Desert Island.

SIGHTS
★ Kisma Preserve

I can't stress this enough: **Kisma Preserve** (446 Bar Harbor Rd./Rte. 3, 207/667-3244, www.kismapreserve.org, 10am-6pm daily mid-May-late fall) is not a zoo; it's a nonprofit educational facility, and everything revolves around preserving and protecting the animals, most of which are either rescues or retirees. Rules are strictly enforced—no running, loud voices, or disruptive behavior is permitted. The easiest way to view the animals is on a one-hour guided tour (about $20). Guides educate visitors about the biology of the animals, how they came to be here, and whether they'll be returned to the wild. For serious animal lovers, the preserve offers behind-the-scenes tours and close-ups; there are even options for camping in the preserve. It truly is a special place, home to more than 100 exotic and not-so-exotic creatures, with an emphasis on wolves and bears. Donations are essential to Kisma's survival, and yes, it's pricey, but so is feeding and caring for these animals.

★ Flightseeing

Two businesses provide options for getting an eagle's-eye view of the area. Both are based on the Route 3 side of Hancock County/Bar Harbor Airport, just north of Mount Desert Island.

Scenic Flights of Acadia (Bar Harbor Rd./Rte. 3, 207/667-6527, www.scenicflightsofacadia.com) offers low-level flightseeing services in the Mount Desert Island region. Flights range 15-75 minutes, with prices beginning around $50 per person with a two-passenger minimum.

Scenic Biplane and Glider Rides (968 Bar Harbor Rd./Rte. 3, 207/667-7627, www.acadiaairtours.com) lets you soar in silence with daily glider flights. The one- or two-passenger gliders are towed to an altitude of at least 2,500 feet and then released. An FAA-certified pilot guides the glider. Rates begin at $220 for a 25-minute flight for one or two. Other options include rides in an open-cockpit biplane and helicopter rides (from $75 pp). All flights are subject to an airport fee.

RECREATION
Lamoine State Park

Lamoine State Park (23 State Park Rd./Rte. 184, Lamoine, 207/667-4778, www.parksandlands.com, day use $6 nonresident adults,

$4 Maine resident adults, $1 ages 5-11) features a pebble beach and a picnic area with a spectacular view, a children's play area, and campsites. If you've brought your own boat, the park also provides a boat ramp for launching. Careful, though: the currents are strong here. Although the 55-acre park isn't officially open in winter, it's popular for cross-country skiing and snowshoeing. This is strictly do-it-yourself fun, as there are no marked trails.

Lamoine Beach and Bloomfield Park

Follow Route 184 to the end (about a mile beyond the park), and you'll arrive at **Lamoine Beach**, a town-owned sand swath with picnic tables, a boat launch, and spectacular views of Mount Desert Island. For freshwater swimming, try **Bloomfield Park** (on Bloomfield Park Rd., off Asa's Ln.), a town-owned park with picnic tables on Blunt's Pond. Both have toilets.

Thompson Island Picnic Area

Edging the ocean at Mount Desert Narrows is the **Thompson Island Picnic Area** (Rte. 3, Thompson Island, Trenton). It has picnic tables, fire grills, a water fountain, and restrooms. At low tide, you might see locals raking the mudflats for clams.

Paddling

Acadia 1 Watersports (1564 Shore Rd., Lamoine, 207/667-2963 or 888/786-0676, www.kayak1.com) rents solo sea kayaks for $45 per day or $155 per week; tandems are $55 per day or $215 per week; SUPs are $65 per day or $240 per week. For rentals over one day, delivery is free to Lamoine Beach and can be arranged throughout the Acadia region for a fuel fee. Be careful if paddling the Mount Desert Narrows, as the currents can be tricky.

Golf

Try to keep your eye on the ball rather than the views at the challenging 18-hole **Bar Harbor Golf Course** (Rte. 3 and Rte. 204, 207/667-7505, www.barharborgolfcourse.

com). Despite the name, it's not in the island community, nor even on the island.

ENTERTAINMENT

★ The Great Maine Lumberjack Show

Ace lumberjack "Timber" Tina Scheer has been competing around the world since she was seven, and she shows her prowess at the **Great Maine Lumberjack Show** (127 Bar Harbor Rd./Rte. 3, Trenton, 207/667-0067, www.mainelumberjack.com, 7pm daily mid-June-early Sept., 4pm Sat. and 2pm Sun. early Sept.-mid-Oct., $14 adults, $13 over age 62, $10 ages 4-11). During the 75-minute "Olympics of the Forest," you'll watch two teams compete in 12 events, including ax throwing, crosscut sawing, logrolling, speed climbing, and more. Some events are open to participation. If you want to learn skills, one-hour lessons for up to six participants are $60-75. Performances are held rain or shine. Seating is under a roof, but dress for the weather if it's inclement. The ticket office opens at 6pm. The venue is dog friendly.

FOOD

One of the best-known and longest-running (since 1956) lobster joints is **Trenton Bridge Lobster Pound** (Bar Harbor Rd./Rte. 3, Trenton, 207/667-2977, www.trentonbridgelobster.com, 11am-7:30pm Mon.-Sat. late May-mid-Oct.), on the right next to the bridge leading to Mount Desert Island. Watch for the "smoke signals"—steam billowing from the huge vats.

Mosey through Lamoine to **Seal Cove Farm** (202 Partridge Cove Rd./Rte. 204, Lamoine, 207/667-7127, www.mainegoatcheese.com), a working goat farm best known for its handcrafted artisan cheeses. Adjacent to the small post-and-beam farm stand is an outdoor wood-burning oven (noon-7pm Fri.-Sat., noon-5pm Sun.). Ten-inch handcrafted pizzas ($12) are made not only with Seal Cove's fresh goat and mixed-milk cheeses, but also with seasonal, farm-fresh produce. For dessert, don't miss the goat gelato. There's a small picnic pavilion. Human kids will get a kick out of watching the goat kids romping in the pasture or visiting them in the barn.

ACCOMMODATIONS

Most of the motels and cabin complexes along the Trenton stretch are small, family-owned operations—not fancy, but their rates are usually far lower than what you'll find on Mount Desert Island, and many are on the Island Explorer, so you can ditch the car. Those in Trenton are on Route 3, so expect traffic noise; the B&B in Lamoine is off the beaten path.

The **Isleview Motel & Cottages** (1169 Bar Harbor Rd./Rte. 3, Trenton, 207/667-5661 or 866/475-3843, www.isleviewmotel.com, from $79) comprises a motel, one- and two-bedroom cottages, and a few "sleep-and-go" rooms above the office, all decorated in country style. At these prices and with this location—eight miles from the park entrance, on the Island Explorer shuttle route, across from a lobster restaurant, and just 0.5 mile from the Thompson Island Picnic Area—don't go looking for fancy, but wallet-conscious travelers will be tickled with it. Although small, most guest rooms are equipped with a mini-refrigerator and a microwave. Cottages are pet friendly ($25/stay). Outside are picnic tables, grills, and a fire pit.

Perks at the pet-friendly **Acadia Sunrise Motel** (952 Bar Harbor Rd./Rte. 3, Trenton, 207/667-8452, www.acadiasunrisemotel.com, $90-125) include an outdoor heated pool, fire pit, patio, pirate-ship playground, and a guest laundry. Some rooms have kitchenettes. Ask for a room at the back, away from the street noise and overlooking the airport with the ocean and Acadia's mountains in the distance. Dogs are $15-25 per dog per night.

The family-owned **Open Hearth Inn** (Bar Harbor Rd./Rte. 3, Trenton, 207/667-2930 or

1: Scenic Biplane and Glider Rides **2:** Lobster trap tree at Trenton Bridge Lobster Pound **3:** Isleview Motel & Cottages **4:** goats at Seal Cove Farm

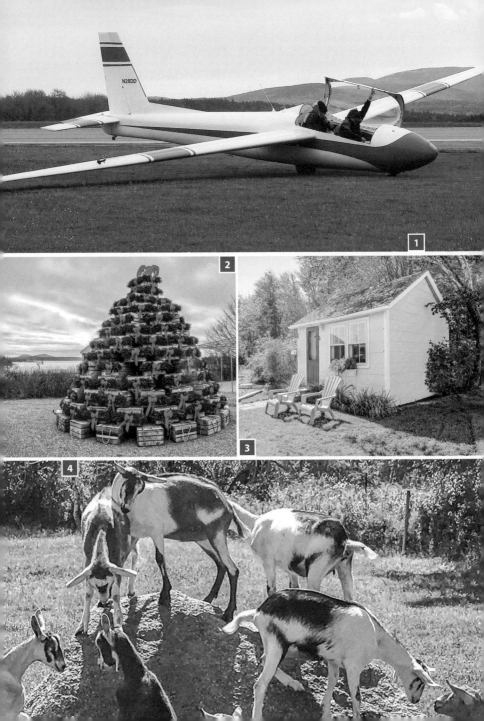

800/655-0234, www.openhearthinn.com, $95-165) is clean, convenient, and replete with retro charm. Choose an inn room, a 1950s tourist court-style cottage, a motel room, or an apartment. Free pickup at Bar Harbor Airport is offered during business hours. On most mornings, homemade muffins are available in the office, along with tea and coffee. It's less than 0.25 mile from the bridge connecting Trenton to Mount Desert Island and within walking distance of four lobster restaurants.

Chocoholics, take note: The **Chocolate Chip Bed & Breakfast** (720 Lamoine Beach Rd., Lamoine, 207/610-1691, www.chocolatechipbb.com, $135-160) treats guests to all kinds of chocolate treats, from muffins in the morning to cookies at night. Eric and Sue Hahn's lovingly rebuilt, early-19th-century, pond-side farmhouse has four comfy guest rooms decorated in country style, all with hardwood floors and beds topped with handmade quilts.

Camping

Equally convenient to the Schoodic region and Mount Desert Island is the 55-acre, oceanfront ★ **Lamoine State Park** (23 State Park Rd./Rte. 184, Lamoine, 207/667-4778, www.parksandlands.com, mid-May-mid-Oct., $20-30, reservations $5/night). Facilities include a picnic area with a spectacular view, a boat launch, a children's play area, a tree house, and a dump station. Camping is available at 62 mostly wooded sites; several are oceanfront. No hookups are available (except for one accessible site). The campground has a modern bathhouse with free hot showers. Reserve online with a credit card, or call 207/624-9950 or 800/332-1501

on weekdays. Leashed pets are allowed; cleanup is required.

INFORMATION AND SERVICES

The **Thompson Island Information Center** (Rte. 3, Thompson Island, 207/288-3411, 8am-6pm daily mid-May-mid-Oct.) represents the Mount Desert Island Regional Chambers of Commerce, which includes the Trenton Chamber of Commerce. Note: When the new Gateway Center with tourism information opens (planned for 2023) on Re. 3 in Trenton, this center will close.

The **Ellsworth Area Chamber of Commerce** (207/667-5584, www.ellsworthchamber.org) also covers Trenton.

GETTING THERE AND AROUND

Trenton is about 8 miles via Route 3 from Ellsworth. It's about 12 miles or 15-20 minutes, depending on traffic, to Bar Harbor.

Route 1 of the free **Island Explorer** (www.exploreacadia.com) bus system connects the Hancock County/Bar Harbor Airport in Trenton with downtown Bar Harbor. The Island Explorer runs late June-mid-October.

Before or after visiting Mount Desert Island, if you're headed farther Down East—to Lamoine, the eastern side of Hancock County, and beyond—there's a good shortcut from Trenton. About five miles south of Ellsworth on Route 3, just north of the Kisma Preserve, turn east onto Route 204, bear left at the T intersection, and then take your first right, following Route 204/Pinkhams Flats Road. Turn left onto Mud Creek Road, which wiggles through a salt marsh and eventually spits out on Route 1 just west of Franklin.

Background

The Landscape

IN THE BEGINNING

Maine is an outdoor classroom for Geology 101, a living lesson in what the glaciers did and how they did it. I tell anyone who will listen that I plan to be a geologist in my next life—and the best place for the first course is Acadia National Park.

Geologically, Maine is something of a youngster; the oldest rocks, found in the Chain of Ponds area in the western part of the state, are only 1.6 billion years old—more than two billion years younger than the world's oldest rocks.

But most significant is the great ice sheet that began to spread over Maine about 25,000 years ago, during the late Wisconsin Ice Age. As it moved south from Canada, this continental glacier scraped, gouged, pulverized, and depressed the bedrock in its path. On it continued, charging up the north faces of mountains, clipping off their tops, and moving south, leaving behind jagged cliffs on the mountains' southern faces and odd deposits of stone and clay. By about 21,000 years ago, glacial ice extended well over the Gulf of Maine, perhaps as far as the Georges Bank fishing grounds.

But all that began to change with melting, beginning about 18,000 years ago. As the glacier melted and receded, ocean water moved in, covering much of the coastal plain and working its way inland up the rivers. By 11,000 years ago, glaciers had pulled back from all but a few minor corners at the top of Maine, revealing the south coast's beaches and the intriguing geologic traits—eskers and erratics, kettle holes and moraines, even a fjord—that make Mount Desert Island and the rest of the state such a fascinating natural laboratory.

Mount Desert's Somes Sound (named after pioneer settler Abraham Somes)—a rare fjord—is just one distinctive feature on an island loaded with geologic wonders. There are pocket beaches, pink granite ledges, sea caves, pancake rocks, wild headlands, volcanic dikes, and a handful of pristine ponds and lakes. And once you've glimpsed the Bubbles—two curvaceous, oversize mounds on the edge of Jordan Pond—you'll know exactly how they earned their name.

CLIMATE

Acadia National Park fits into the National Weather Service's **coastal** category, a 20-mile-wide swath that stretches from Kittery on the New Hampshire border to Eastport on the Canadian border. In the park and its surrounding communities, the proximity of the Gulf of Maine moderates the climate, making coastal winters generally warmer and summers usually cooler than elsewhere in the state.

Average June temperatures in **Bar Harbor,** adjoining the park, range 53-76°F; July-August temperatures range 60-82°F. By December, the average range is 20-32°F.

The Seasons

Maine has four distinct seasons: summer, fall, winter, and mud. Lovers of spring weather need to look elsewhere in March, the lowest month on the popularity scale, with its mud-caked vehicles, soggy everything, irritable temperaments, tank-trap roads, and occasionally the worst snowstorm of the year.

Summer can be idyllic—with moderate temperatures, clear air, and wispy breezes—but it can also close in with fog, rain, and chills. Prevailing winds are from the southwest. Officially, summer runs June 21-September 23, but consider summer to be June, July, and August. The typical growing season is 148 days long.

A poll of Mainers might well show autumn as the favorite season—days are still warmish, nights are cool, winds are optimal for sailors, and the foliage is brilliant—particularly throughout Acadia. Fall colors usually reach their peak in the park in early-to-mid-October. Early autumn, however, is also the height of hurricane season, the only potential flaw with this time of year, although direct hits are rare.

Winter, officially December 21-March 20, means an unpredictable potpourri of weather along the park's coastline. But when the cold and snow hit this region, it's time for cross-country skiing, snowshoeing, and ice-skating. The park receives an average of 61 inches of snow over the season.

Spring, officially March 20-June 21, is the frequent butt of jokes. It's an ill-defined season that arrives much too late and departs all

Previous: Acadia's distinctive glacier-rounded peaks.

too quickly. Spring planting can't occur until well into May; lilacs explode in late May and disappear by mid-June. And just when you finally can enjoy being outside, blackflies stretch their wings and satisfy their hunger pangs. Along the shore, fortunately, steady breezes often keep the pesky creatures to a minimum.

Northeasters and Hurricanes

A northeaster is a counterclockwise-swirling storm that brings wild winds out of—you guessed it—the northeast. These storms can occur at any time of year, whenever the conditions brew them up. Depending on the season, the winds are accompanied by rain, sleet, snow, or all of them together.

Hurricane season officially runs June-November, but hurricanes are most active in late August-September. Some years, Maine remains out of harm's way; other years, head-on hurricanes and even glancing blows have eroded beaches, flooded roads, splintered boats, downed trees, knocked out power, and inflicted major residential and commercial damage. Winds—the greatest culprit—average 74-90 mph. A hurricane watch is announced on radio and TV about 36 hours before the hurricane hits, followed by a hurricane warning indicating that the storm is imminent. Find shelter away from plate-glass windows, and wait it out. If especially high winds are predicted, make every effort to secure yourself, your vehicle, and your possessions. Resist the urge to head for the shore to watch the show; rogue waves combined with

ultrahigh tides have been known to sweep away unwary onlookers. Schoodic Point, the mainland section of Acadia, is a particularly perilous location in such conditions.

Sea Smoke and Fog

Sea smoke and fog, two atmospheric phenomena resulting from opposing conditions, are only distantly related. But both can radically affect visibility and therefore be hazardous. In winter, when the ocean is at least 40°F warmer than the air, billowy sea smoke rises from the water, creating great photo ops for camera buffs but seriously dangerous conditions for mariners.

In any season, when the ocean (or lake or land) is colder than the air, fog sets in, creating nasty conditions for drivers, mariners, and pilots. Romantics, however, see it otherwise, reveling in the womb-like ambience and the muffled moans of foghorns.

Storm Warnings

The National Weather Service's official daytime signal system for wind velocity consists of a series of flags representing specific wind speeds and sea conditions. Beachgoers and anyone planning to venture out in a kayak, canoe, sailboat, or powerboat should heed these signals. The signal flags are posted on all public beaches, and warnings are announced on TV and radio weather broadcasts, as well as on cable TV's Weather Channel and the National Oceanic and Atmospheric Administration (NOAA) broadcast network.

Plants and Animals

In the course of a single day at Acadia National Park—where more than two dozen mountains meet the sea—the casual visitor can pass through a landscape that lends itself to a surprising diversity of animal and plant life. On one outing, you can explore the shoreline—barnacles encrust the rocks, and black crowberry, an arctic shrub that finds Maine's coastal climate agreeable, grows close to the ground alongside trails. On the same outing, you can wander beneath the boughs of the leafy hardwood forest that favors more southern climes, as well as the spruce-fir forest of the north. A little farther up the trail are subalpine plants more typically associated with mountain environments and neotropical songbirds providing background music.

Acadia's creatures and plants will endlessly intrigue any nature lover; the following are but a sampling of what you might encounter during a visit.

OFFSHORE

Acadia National Park is surrounded by the sea—from the rockbound Schoodic Peninsula jutting from the mainland Down East to the offshore island in Penobscot Bay that Samuel de Champlain named Isle au Haut. While the park's boundaries do not extend out to sea, the life that can be found there draws travelers and scientists alike.

The Maine coastline falls within the Gulf of Maine, a "sea within a sea" that extends from Nova Scotia to Cape Cod and out to the fishing grounds of Brown and Georges Banks. It is one of the most biologically rich environments in the world. Surface water, driven by currents off Nova Scotia, swirls in counter-clockwise circles, delivering nutrients and food to the plants and animals that live there. Floating microplants, tiny shrimplike creatures, and jellyfish benefit from those nutrients and once supported huge populations of groundfish, now depleted by overfishing.

These highly productive waters lure not only fishing vessels but also sea mammals. **Whales** may rarely swim into the inshore bays and inlets bounded by Acadia, but whale-watching cruises based on Mount Desert Island ferry passengers miles offshore to the locales where whales gather. Whales fall into two groups: toothed and baleen. Toothed whales hunt individual prey, such as squid, fish, and the occasional seabird; they include porpoises and dolphins, killer whales, sperm whales, and pilot whales. Baleen whales have no teeth, so they must sift food through horny plates called baleen; they include finback whales, minke whales, humpback whales, and right whales. Any of these species may be observed in the Gulf of Maine.

Harbor porpoises, which grow to a length of six feet, can be spotted from a boat in the inshore waters around Mount Desert Island, traveling in pods as they hunt schools of herring and mackerel. The most you'll usually see of them are their gray backs and triangular dorsal fins as they perform their graceful ballet through the waves.

Of great delight to wildlife watchers is catching glimpses of **harbor seals.** While the shores of Mount Desert Island are too busy with human activity for seals to linger, they are usually spotted during nature cruises that head out to the well-known "seal ledges." Check the tide chart and book an excursion for low tide. Seals haul themselves out of the ocean at low tide to rest on the rocks and sunbathe. Naps are a necessity for harbor seals, which have less blubber and fur to insulate them from the frigid waters of the Gulf of Maine than other seal species. Hauling out preserves energy otherwise spent heating the body, and it replenishes their blood with oxygen.

At high tide, you might see individual "puppy dog" faces bobbing among the waves as the seals forage for food. Harbor seals, sometimes called "sea dogs," almost disappeared along the coast of Maine in the early 20th century. It was believed they competed with fishermen for the much-prized lobster and other valuable catches, and they were hunted nearly into oblivion. When it became obvious that the absence of seals did not improve fish stocks, the bounty placed on them was lifted. The Marine Mammal Protection Act of 1972 made it illegal to hunt or harm any marine mammal, except by permit—happily, populations of harbor seals now have rebounded all along the coast.

Every now and then, park rangers receive reports of "abandoned" seal pups along Acadia's shore. Usually it's not a stranded youngster, but rather a pup left to rest while its mother hunts for food. If you discover a seal pup on the shore, leave it undisturbed and report the sighting to rangers.

ALONG THE SHORE

Whether walking the shore or cruising on a boat, there is no symbol so closely associated with the coast as the ubiquitous **gull.** Several species of gulls frequent Acadia's skies, but none is more common than the herring gull. Easily dismissed as brassy sandwich thieves (which, of course, they are), herring gulls almost vanished in the 20th century as a result of hunting and egg collecting. Indeed, many seabird populations declined in the early 1900s due to the demand for feathers to adorn ladies' hats. Conservation measures have helped some of these bird species recover, including the large, gray-backed herring gull, an elegant flyer that often lobs sea urchins onto the rocky shore from aloft to crack them open for the morsels within.

Common **eider duck** females, a mottled brown, and the black-and-white males, nicknamed "floating skunks," congregate in large "rafts" on the icy ocean during the winter to mate. When spring arrives, males and females separate. While the males provide no help in raising the young, the females cooperate with one another, often gathering ducklings together to protect them from predators. Adult eiders may live and breed for 20 years or more, though the mortality rate is high among the young. Present along Acadia's shore all year long, they feed on mussels, clams, and dog whelks, their powerful gizzards grinding down shells and all.

A smaller seabird regularly espied around Acadia is the **black guillemot,** also known as the "sea pigeon" and "underwater flyer" because it seems to fly through the water. Guillemots learn to swim before they learn to fly. Black-and-white with bright red feet, guillemots are cousins to puffins. They nest on rock ledges along the shore, laying pear-shaped eggs that won't roll over the edge and into the waves below.

Bald eagles and **ospreys** (also known as fish hawks) take advantage of the fishing available in Acadia's waters. Both of these majestic raptors suffered from the effects of the pesticide DDT, which washed down through waterways and into the ocean, becoming concentrated in the fish the raptors consumed. As a result, they laid thin-shelled eggs that broke easily, preventing the development of young. The banning of DDT in the United States has resulted in a strong comeback for both species and the removal of the bald eagle from the federal endangered species list. Along the coast of Maine, however, the bald eagle's return has been less triumphant than in other parts of the country. Biologists continue to seek explanations for the lag, and the bald eagle remains on state and federal lists as a threatened species.

Boat cruises, some with park rangers aboard, depart from several Mount Desert Island harbors and offer good chances for sightings. They allow passengers to approach (but not too closely) nesting islands of eagles and ospreys. Both species create large nests of sticks from which they can command a wide view of the surrounding area. Some osprey nests have been documented as being 100 years old, and researchers have found everything from fishing tackle to swim trunks entwined in the sticks of the nests.

Look also for eagles and ospreys flying

above inland areas of the park. Ospreys hunt over freshwater ponds and lakes, hovering until a fish is sighted, then plummeting from the sky into the water to grab the prey. For aerodynamic reasons, they carry the fish headfirst.

Acadia visitors often ask rangers if there are sea otters in the park. After all, there is an Otter Creek, which flows into Otter Cove, which is bounded by Otter Cliffs. At one time, Gorham Mountain was known as Peak of Otter! With all these place-names devoted to the otter, it would be logical to assume that Mount Desert Island teems with them. In fact, though, there are no sea otters along the entire Eastern Seaboard of the United States—perhaps the earliest European settlers mistook sea minks (now extinct) for sea otters. River otters do reside in the park, but they are reclusive and spend most of their time in freshwater environments. You might observe one during the winter frolicking on a frozen pond.

INTERTIDAL ZONE

Some of the most alien creatures on earth live where the ocean washes the rocky shoreline. The creatures of this intertidal zone are at once resilient and fragile, and always fascinating. Some of the creatures and plants live best in the upper reaches of the intertidal zone, which is doused only by the spray of waves and the occasional extra-high tide. Others, which would not survive the upper regions, thrive in the lower portion of the intertidal zone, which is almost always submerged. The rest live in rocky pockets of water in between, and all are influenced by the ebb and flow of the tide. Temperature, salinity, and the strength of crashing waves all determine where a creature will live in the intertidal zone.

As you approach the ocean's edge, the first creatures likely to come underfoot are **barnacles**—vast stretches of rock can be encrusted with them. Step gently, for walking on barnacles crushes them. Their tiny, white, volcano-shaped shells remain closed when exposed to the air, but they open to feed when submerged. Water movement encourages them to sweep the water with feathery "legs" to feed on microscopic plankton.

Despite the tough armor with which barnacles cover themselves, they are preyed on by **dog whelks** (snails), which drill through the barnacle shells with their tongues to feed on the creature within. A dog whelk can be distinguished from the common periwinkle by the elliptical opening of its shell. Periwinkles have teardrop-shaped openings.

Sea stars find blue mussels yummy. Blue mussels siphon plankton from the water and anchor themselves in place with byssus threads. Sea stars creep up on the mussels, wrap their legs around them, and pry open their shells just enough to insert their stomachs and consume the animal inside. Look for sea stars and mussels in the lower regions of tide pools.

Related to sea stars are **sea urchins**—spiky green balls most often seen as empty, spineless husks littered along the shoreline (they are frequently preyed on by gulls). If you come upon a live sea urchin, handle it with care. While their spikes are not poisonous, they are sharp. Gently roll a sea urchin over to see its mouth and the five white teeth with which it gnaws on seaweed and animal remains. (While the green sea urchins found in Acadia do not possess poisonous spines, some of their counterparts in other regions do.)

Limpets, with cone-shaped shells, are snails that rely on seaweed for food. They suction themselves to rocks, which prevents them from drying up when exposed at low tide. Do not tear limpets from rocks—doing so hurts the animal.

Many intertidal creatures depend on seaweed for protection and food. **Rockweeds** drape over rocks, floating with the waves, their long fronds buoyed by distinctive air bladders. **Dulse** (edible for people) is common along the shore, as is Irish moss, used as a thickener in ice cream, paint, and other products.

Puffins

The chickadee is the Maine state bird, and the bald eagle is our national emblem, but probably the best-loved bird along the Maine coast is the Atlantic puffin *(Fratercula arctica)*, a member of the auk (Alcidae) family. Photographs show an imposing-looking creature with a quizzical mien; amazingly, this larger-than-life seabird is only about 12 inches long. Black-backed and white-chested, the puffin has bright orange legs, "clown makeup" eyes, and a distinctive, rather outlandish red-and-yellow beak. Its diet is fish and shellfish.

Almost nonexistent in this part of the world as recently as the 1970s, the puffin (or "sea parrot") has recovered dramatically thanks to the unstinting efforts of Cornell University ornithologist Stephen Kress and his Project Puffin. Starting with an orphan colony of two on remote Matinicus Rock, Kress painstakingly transferred nearly 1,000 puffin chicks (also known fondly as "pufflings") from Newfoundland and used artificial nests and decoys to entice the birds to adapt to and reproduce on Eastern Egg Rock in Muscongus Bay.

In 1981, thanks to the assistance and persistence of hundreds of interns and volunteers, and despite predation by great black-backed gulls, puffins finally were fledged on Eastern Egg. Within 20 years, more than three dozen puffin pairs were nesting on Eastern Egg Rock, and still more had established nests on other islands in the area. Kress's methods have received international attention, and his proven techniques have been used to reintroduce bird populations in remote parts of the globe. In 2001, *Down East* magazine singled out Kress to receive its prestigious annual Environmental Award.

PUFFIN CRUISES

Puffin-watching, like whale-watching, involves heading offshore (although you might get lucky and spot them at the tip of the Petit Manan Point Division of the Maine Coastal Islands National Wildlife Refuge), so be prepared with warm clothing, rubber-soled shoes, a hat, sunscreen, binoculars, and if you're motion-sensitive, appropriate medication.

Petit Manan Island

Three tour operators in the Acadia region cruise to Petit Manan Island; some also visit EggRock. On all, you observe the birds from the boat. Most are about three hours, and cost around $60-75.

Bar Harbor Whale Watch (207/288-2386 or 800/942-5374, www.barharborwhales.com) cruises from Bar Harbor.

Acadia Puffin Cruise (207/598-7900, https://acadiapuffincruise.com) departs from Winter Harbor, on the Schoodic Peninsula.

Robertson Sea Tours and Adventures (207/546-3883, cell 207/461-7439, www.robertsonseatours.com, May 15-Oct. 1) heads out from Milbridge.

Machias Seal Island

If you want to visit the state's largest colony on Machias Seal island, you'll have to make reservations months in advance for Cutler-based Bold Coast Charters (207/259-4484, www.boldcoast.com), the only U.S. boat licensed to disembark passengers on the island. The five-hour cruise costs about $165. The *Barbara Frost* cruises to the island late May-mid-August, departing at about 7am from way down east Cutler, approximately 90 miles or two hours by car from Bar Harbor. Weather permitting, you'll be allowed to disembark on the 20-acre island and spy on the roughly 3,000 puffins who call it their summer home.

ADOPT-A-PUFFIN PROGRAM

Stephen Kress's Project Puffin has devised a clever way to enlist supporters via the Adopt-a-Puffin program. For a $100 annual donation, you'll receive a certificate of adoption and a biography about your adoptee. How's that for a special gift for the bird lover in your life? For information, visit www.projectpuffin.org.

Tides

Nowhere is the adage "Time and tide wait for no one" truer than along the Maine coastline. The nation's most extreme tidal ranges occur in Maine, and they become even more dramatic as you head "Down East," toward the Canadian Maritime provinces. Every six hours or so, the tide begins either ebbing or flowing, so you'll have countless opportunities for observing tidal phenomena.

Tides govern coastal life, and everyone is a slave to the tide calendar or chart, which coastal-community newspapers diligently publish in every issue. Each issue of the free *Acadia Weekly*, available widely on the island, also contains tide info (as well as times of sunrise and sunset), as does the *Park Ranger Program* issued by the park. In tidal regions, boats tie up with extra-long lines, clammers and worm-diggers schedule their days by the tides, hikers have to plan ahead for shoreline exploring, and kayakers need to plan their routes to avoid getting stuck in the muck.

Average tidal ranges (between low tide and high tide) in the area around Acadia National Park are 10-11 feet, and extremes are 12-13 feet.

Tides, as we all learned in elementary school, are lunar phenomena, created by the gravitational pull of the moon; the tidal range depends on the lunar phase. Tides are most extreme at new and full moons—when the sun, moon, and earth are all aligned. These are **spring tides,** supposedly because the water springs upward (the term has nothing to do with the season). And tides are smallest during the moon's first and third quarters—when the sun, earth, and moon have a right-angle configuration. These are **neap tides** (*neap* comes from an Old English word meaning "scanty"). Other lunar and solar phenomena, such as the equinoxes and solstices, can also affect tidal ranges.

The best time for shoreline exploration is on a new-moon or full-moon day, when low tide exposes mussels, sea urchins, sea cucumbers, sea stars, periwinkles, hermit crabs, rockweed, and assorted nonbiodegradable trash. Rubber boots or waterproof treaded shoes are essential on the wet, slippery terrain.

Caution is also essential in tidal areas. Unless you've carefully plotted tide times and heights, don't park a car, bike, or boat trailer on a beach; make sure your sea kayak is lashed securely to a tree or bollard; don't take a long nap on shoreline granite; and don't cross a low-tide land spit without an eye on your watch.

A perhaps apocryphal but almost believable story goes that one flatlander stormed up to a ranger at a Maine state park one bright summer morning and demanded indignantly to know why they had had the nerve to drain the water from her shorefront campsite during the night. When it comes to tides, you just have to go with the flow.

Tide Pool Tips

The best way to learn about the fascinating world that exists between the tides is to look for creatures in their own habitats, with a good field guide as a reference.

- Go at low tide—there are two low tides daily, 12 hours apart.

- Tread carefully. Shoreline rocks are slippery.

- Do not remove creatures from their habitats; doing so could harm them.

- Be aware of the ocean at all times. Sudden waves can wash the shore and sweep you to your death.

- Join a ranger-guided shoreline walk to learn more about this unique environment. Check the *Beaver Log*, Acadia's official park newspaper, for the schedule and details.

FRESHWATER LAKES AND PONDS

Known best for its rocky shoreline and mountains, Acadia National Park cradles numerous glistening lakes and ponds in its glacially carved valleys. Several lakes serve as public water supplies for surrounding communities, and swimming is prohibited in most. Echo Lake and the north end of Long Pond are excellent designated swimming areas. Freshwater fishing requires a state license for adults. Obey the posted regulations.

The voice of the northern wilderness belongs to the **common loon,** whose roots are so ancient it is the oldest bird species found in North America. During the summer months, loons are garbed in striking white-and-black plumage, which fades to gray during the winter when they migrate to the ocean's open waters. Graceful swimmers, loons are clumsy on land. Their webbed feet are set to the rear of their bodies, making them front-heavy. Land travel is a struggle. Consequently, they nest very close to the water's edge, which makes them vulnerable to such human hazards as the wakes of motorized watercraft.

The loon's mysterious ululating call can be heard echoing across lakes on most any summer evening, an eerie sound not quickly forgotten.

Evening is actually an excellent time to observe wildlife. Creatures that seem shy and reclusive by day tend to be most active at dawn and dusk (crepuscular) or at night (nocturnal). Carriage roads along Eagle Lake, Bubble Pond, and Witch Hole Pond make nighttime walking easy. (Hint: Go at dusk so your eyes adjust with the darkening sky, and keep in mind that abrupt flashlight use ruins night vision.)

Frog choruses form the backdrop to the cries of loons. In Acadia, there are eight **frog and toad** species, which tend to be most vocal during the spring mating season. Close your eyes and listen to see if you can distinguish individual species, such as the "banjo-twanging" croak of the green frog and the "snore" of the leopard frog.

The onset of moonlight may reveal small winged creatures swooping, darting, and careening over lakes and ponds. Acadia is home to several species of **bats,** including the common little brown bat. Don't scream! Bats have no desire to get entangled in your hair. Their echolocation (radar) is so fine-tuned that it can detect a single strand of human hair. Bats are far more interested in the mosquitoes attracted to your body heat. True insect-munching machines, a single pinky-size little

brown bat can eat hundreds, if not thousands, of insects in one evening.

Bandit-faced **raccoons** are also creatures of the night, and they sometimes can be found scampering along the shore. They are omnivorous, dining on anything from grubs, frogs, and small mammals to fish, berries, and garbage. Rabies is present in Maine, and raccoons are common carriers of the disease. Do not approach sick-acting animals (seeing them during the daytime may indicate illness), and report any strange behavior to a park ranger. When camping or picnicking, stow food items in your vehicle and dispose of scraps properly. Raccoons are opportunistic thieves that have been known to claw their way into tents to find food.

And where are the moose? The question is asked often at Acadia's visitors center, and wildlife-watchers are disappointed to learn that moose, the largest members of the deer family, are rarely sighted in the park. Moose are more frequently observed in western and northern Maine, in the Moosehead Lake and Baxter State Park regions. However, individuals are spotted from time to time on Mount Desert Island, and there may even be a small family group residing on the west side. Moose like to dine on aquatic vegetation, such as the tubers of cattails and lily pads, and they frequent marshes and lakes to escape biting flies. Bass Harbor Marsh is an inviting habitat for moose, but good luck spotting one.

A prehistoric-looking creature sometimes encountered on carriage roads near ponds is the **snapping turtle.** An average adult may weigh 30 pounds or more. Keep well clear of the snapper's powerful beak, which is lightning-quick when grabbing prey; it can do real damage, such as biting off fingers. Adult snappers have no predators (except people), and they will dine on other turtles, frogs, ducklings, wading birds, and beaver kits.

By midsummer, many of Acadia's ponds are beautifully adorned with yellow water lilies and white pond lilies. Lily pads are a favorite food of **beavers,** which emerge from their lodges—large piles of sticks and mud—at dusk and dawn to feed and make necessary repairs to their dams. Beavers create their own habitat by transforming streams into ponds. They move awkwardly on land, so they adjust the water level close to their source of building materials and other favored foods: aspen and birch trees. Doing so limits their exposure to dry land and predators.

Beavers are large rodents that were trapped excessively for centuries for the fur trade. They have since made a strong comeback in Acadia—to the point that their ponds now threaten roads, trails, and other park structures. Resource managers try to keep ahead of the beavers by inserting "beaver foolers" (PVC pipes) through dams that block road culverts. This moderates pond levels and prevents damage to roads by allowing water to drain through the culvert. Sometimes the beavers, however, get ahead of the resource managers. They have been known to plug the beaver foolers with sticks and mud, or to chew through them with their strong teeth.

Amazingly adapted for life in the water, beavers are fascinating to watch. A very accessible location along the Park Loop Road, just past Bear Brook Picnic Area, is Beaver Dam Pond, featuring a few lodges, a dam, and an active beaver population. The best viewing times are dawn and dusk. In the fall the beavers are busiest, preparing food stores for the winter to come. The park often presents a beaver-watch program at that time of year, which is a great way to learn more about the habits and adaptations of the beaver.

Beavers act as a catalyst for increasing natural diversity in an area. Their ponds attract ospreys, herons, and owls; salamanders, frogs, and turtles; insects and aquatic plants; foxes, deer, muskrats, and river otters. Their ponds help maintain the water table, enrich soils, and prevent flooding.

While beavers may bring diversity to a wetland, an invader has been endangering Acadia's ponds and lakes. Purple loosestrife, a showy stalked purple flower not native to North America, was introduced into gardens as an ornamental. Highly reproductive and adaptive and with no natural predators, purple loosestrife escaped the confines of gardens and has literally choked the life out of some wetlands by crowding out native plants on which many creatures depend, thus creating a monoculture. Few native species find purple loosestrife useful.

Purple loosestrife has been contained at Acadia, but it's an ongoing process. Uprooting it seems to encourage more to grow, and jostling stalks at certain times of the year disperses vast numbers of seeds, so resource managers have resorted to treating individual plants with an approved herbicide in a way that does not harm the surrounding environment.

WOODLANDS

A dark, statuesque spruce-fir forest dominates much of Acadia's woodlands and does well in the cooler, moist environs of Maine's coast. Red spruce trees are tall and pole-like and often cohabit with fragrant balsam fir. The spruce grows needles only at the canopy, sparing little energy for growing needles where the sun cannot reach. Because the sun barely touches the forest floor, little undergrowth emerges from the bump and swale of acidic, rust-colored needles that carpet the ground, except for more tiny, shade-loving spruce, waiting for their chance to grow tall.

The spruce-fir forest can be uncannily quiet, especially in the middle of the day. The density of the woods and the springy, needle-laden floor seem to buffer noise from without. Listen closely, however, and you may hear the cackle of ravens, the squabble of a territorial red squirrel, or the rat-a-tat of a woodpecker.

Red squirrels are energetic denizens of the spruce-fir forest, scolding innocent passersby or sitting on tree stumps scaling spruce cones and stuffing their cheeks full of seeds. Observant wildlife watchers will find their middens (heaps of cone scales) about the forest. Squirrels are especially industrious (even comical) in autumn as they frantically prepare for the winter by stocking up on food, tearing about from branch to branch with spruce cones poking out of their mouths like big cigars.

Woodpeckers favor dead, still-standing trees, shredding the bark to get at the insects infesting the trunk. The pileated woodpecker—a large black-and-white bird with a red cap—is relatively shy, so you are more likely to encounter evidence of its passage (rectangular and oval holes in trees) than the bird itself. Other common species you might observe are the hairy and the downy woodpecker.

The face of Acadia's woodlands changed dramatically in 1947. That fall, during a period of extremely dry conditions, a fire began west of the park's present-day visitors center in Hulls Cove. Feeding on tinder-dry woods and grasses, and whipped into an inferno by gale-force winds, the fire roared across the eastern half of Mount Desert Island, miraculously skirting downtown Bar Harbor but destroying numerous year-round and seasonal homes. In all, 17,000 acres burned, 10,000 of them in the park.

Researchers have studied 6,000 years of the park's fire history by pulling core samples from ponds to analyze the layers of pollen and charcoal that have settled in their bottoms over time. The charcoal indicates periods of fire, and the most significant layer of charcoal appeared in the period around 1947, indicating the intensity of the great fire.

The aftermath of the fire—the scorched mountainsides and skeletal, blackened remains of trees—must have been a devastating sight. Loggers salvaged usable timber and removed unsafe snags. Seed was ordered so replanting could begin in earnest. Soils needed to be stabilized and the landscape restored.

Then a curious thing happened the following spring: As the snow melted, green shoots began to poke up out of the soil among the sooty remains. "Pioneer plants," such as lowbush blueberry and Indian paintbrush, took over the job of stabilizing the soil. By the time the ordered seeds arrived two years later (demand had been overwhelming, for much of Maine had burned in 1947), nature was already mending the landscape without human intervention. What had been blackened showed promise and renewal in green growing things.

Over the decades since then, a mixed deciduous forest has grown up from the ashes of the fire, supplanting the dominance of the spruce-fir forest on Mount Desert Island's east side. **Birch, aspen, maple, oak,** and **beech** have embraced wide-open sunny places where shady spruce once thrived. The new growth not only added colorful splendor to the autumn landscape but also diversified the wildlife.

Populations of **white-tailed deer** benefited from all the new browse (and a lack of major predators), and by the 1960s, the island's deer herd had soared in numbers. Recent studies have shown the population to be healthy and stable—perhaps due to car-deer collisions and predation from the recently arrived eastern coyote.

Coyotes crossed the Trenton Bridge and wandered onto Mount Desert Island in the 1980s. They had been expanding their territory throughout the northeast, handily picking up the slack in the food chain caused when other large predators, such as the northern gray wolf and the lynx, were hunted and trapped out of the state. While coyote sightings do occur, you are more likely to be serenaded by yipping and howling in the night. Their vocalizations warn off other coyotes, or let them keep in touch with the members of their packs.

The **snowshoe hare,** or varying hare, is a main prey species of the coyote. The large hind feet of these mammals allow them to stay aloft in the snow and speed away from predators. Camouflage also aids these fleet-footed hares—their fur turns white during the winter and brown during the summer, hence the name varying hare. Not all hares escape their predators. It is not uncommon to encounter coyote scat full of hare fur along a carriage road or trail.

Also along a carriage road or trail, you might encounter a **snake** sunning itself on a rock. Five species of snakes—including the garter snake, milk snake, and green snake—inhabit Acadia. None of these snakes are poisonous, but they will bite if provoked.

While autumn may cloak Acadia's mountainsides in bright beauty, spring and summer

Peregrine Falcons

One of Acadia's great success stories is that of a seasonal mountain dweller, the peregrine falcon. DDT and other pollutants caused a decline in the number of falcons until the last breeding pair in Acadia was observed in 1956. Even before DDT, trappers, hunters, and nest robbers depleted peregrines. The peregrine was listed as a federal endangered species in the early 1970s and was removed from that list in 1999; it remains an endangered species in Maine.

In 1984, biologists reintroduced the falcons to Acadia, and in 1991, a breeding pair settled on the east-facing cliffs of Champlain Mountain and produced young. By 2014, more than 120 chicks had fledged from Acadia, including nesting sites on Jordan Cliffs, Valley Cove cliffs on Somes Sound, the Beech Cliffs above Echo Lake, and on privately owned Ironbound Island, where the park has a conservation easement.

Peregrines nest between late March and early August. Their nests, or scrapes, are shallow ledges on cliff sides, which provide them with an unimpeded view of potential prey (other birds) below. Their high-speed pursuits of prey—they can reach speeds of more than 200 mph—thrill those who are lucky enough to witness them.

Park staff usually is stationed at the **Precipice Trail Parking Area** (9am-noon Mon.-Thurs. spring-summer, weather permitting) with spotting scopes to help anyone who stops by view the peregrines and their scrapes and to provide information about their habits. Check the park's event schedule for the latest information.

During breeding and fledging season (Apr.-mid-Aug.), the trailhead for the Precipice Trail is gated, with an informational sign explaining the history and status of peregrines in the park. Other trails may be closed for the same reason; check at the Hulls Cove Visitors Center.

bring relief to Mainers weary of ice storms, shoveling, freezing temperatures, and short, dark days. Spring arrives with snowy clusters of star flowers along roadsides, and white mats of **bunchberry** flowers (dwarf members of the dogwood family) on the forest floor. Birdsong provides a musical backdrop. Twenty-one species of wood warblers migrate to Acadia from South America to nest—among them are the **American redstart, ovenbird, yellow warbler,** and **Blackburnian warbler.** At the visitors center, request a bird checklist, which names 273 species of birds that have been identified on Mount Desert Island and adjacent areas. Then join a ranger for an early-morning bird walk. Check the *Beaver Log* for details.

The fire of 1947 may have transformed a portion of Acadia's woodlands, but change is always part of a natural system. While the broad-leafed trees that grew up in the wake of the fire continue to grow and shed leaves as the cycle of nature demands, young spruce trees poke up through duff and leaf litter,

waiting in the shade for their chance to dominate the landscape once again.

MOUNTAINS

A hike up one of Acadia's granite-domed mountains will allow you to gaze down at the world with a new perspective. Left behind is the confining forest—the woods, in fact, seem to shrink as you climb. On the south-facing slopes of some mountains, you'll encounter squat and gnarled pitch pines. The fire of 1947 not only was beneficial to the growth of deciduous vegetation, but it also aided in the regeneration of **pitch pines,** which rely on heat, such as that generated by an intense fire, to open their cones and disperse seeds.

Wreathing rocky outcrops and the sides of trails are such shrubs as **low-bush blueberry, sheep laurel (lambkill),** and **bayberry.** In the fall, their leaves turn blood-red. In the spring, **shadbush** softens granite mountainsides with white blossoms.

Green and gray lichens plaster exposed rocks in patterns like targets. Composed of algae and fungi, lichens were probably among the first organisms to grow in Acadia as the vast ice sheets retreated 10,000-20,000 years ago. Sensitive to air pollution and acid rain, lichens have become barometers of air quality all over the world.

On mountain summits, the trees are stunted. These are not necessarily young trees—some may be nearly 100 years old. The tough, cold, windy climate and exposed conditions of summits force plantlife to adapt to survive. Growing close to the ground to avoid fierce winds is one way in which trees have adapted to life at the summit.

Other plants huddle in the shallow, gravelly soil behind solitary rocks, such as **three-toothed cinquefoil,** a member of the rose family that produces a tiny white flower in June-July, and **mountain sandwort,** which blooms in clusters June-September.

While adapted to surviving the extreme conditions of mountain summits, plants can be irreparably damaged by feet trampling off-trail or by removal of rocks to add to cairns (trail markers) or stone "art." One has only to look at the summit area of Cadillac Mountain to see the damage wrought by millions of roving feet: the missing vegetation and the eroded soils. It may take 50-100 years for some plantlife, if protected, to recover. Some endangered plant species that grow only at summits may have already disappeared from Cadillac due to trampling.

To protect mountain summits and to preserve the natural scene, follow Leave No Trace principles of staying on the trail and on durable surfaces, such as solid granite. Do not add to cairns or build rock art, a form of graffiti that not only damages plants and soils but also blemishes the scenery for other visitors.

Autumn provides a terrific opportunity to observe **raptors** of all kinds. In the fall, during their south migration, raptors take advantage of northwest winds flowing over Acadia's mountains. Eagles, red-tailed hawks, sharp-shinned hawks, goshawks, American kestrels, peregrine falcons, and others can be spotted. The peregrine, a seasonal mountain dweller, has been reintroduced to Acadia after a long absence. Late August-mid-October, join park staff for the annual hawk watch atop Cadillac Mountain (weather permitting) to view and identify raptors. In a typical year, hawk-watchers count an average of 2,500 raptors from 10 species. The most prevalent species are American kestrels and sharp-shinned hawks.

WILDLIFE-WATCHING TIPS

- Seek out wildlife at **dusk** and **dawn** when it is more active. Bring binoculars and a field guide.

- Leave Rover at home—**pets** are intruders into the natural world, and they will scare off wildlife. If leaving your dog behind is not an option, remember that in the park, pets must be restrained on a leash no longer than six feet. This is for the safety of both the pet and wildlife, and it is courteous to other visitors.

- **Never approach wildlife,** which could become aggressive if sick or feeling threatened. Enjoy wildlife at a distance.

- **Do not feed wildlife,** not even gulls. Feeding turns wild animals into aggressive beggars that lose the ability to forage for themselves, and it often ends in their demise.

- Join walks, talks, hikes, cruises, and evening **programs** presented by park rangers to learn more about the national park and its flora and fauna. Programs are listed in the *Beaver Log,* readily available at the Hulls Cove Visitors Center, the Acadia Nature Center, and park campgrounds, as well as online (www.nps.gov/acad).

- Visit the **nature center at Sieur de Monts Spring,** where exhibits show the diversity of flora and fauna in the park and the challenges that resource managers face in protecting it.

(The Plants and Animals *section of this chapter was written by Kristen Britain, former writer and editor for Acadia National Park.)*

Environmental Issues

You've already read about some of Acadia's major environmental issues, but still others exist. Tops among these are air pollution and overcrowding. Of utmost importance is the matter of "zero impact," addressed by the Leave No Trace philosophy actively practiced at Acadia.

AIR QUALITY

In 2002, a study by the private National Parks Conservation Association revealed that Acadia National Park had the fifth-worst air quality of all the national parks; Acadia allegedly has twice as much haze as the Grand Canyon. Most scientists and environmentalists attribute the problem primarily to smoke and haze from power plants in the Midwest and the South. New England is the end of the line, so to speak, for airborne pollutants, and it's estimated that 80 percent of Maine's pollution arrives from other regions. Maine has the highest asthma rate in the nation, rivers and lakes have high concentrations of mercury, and rainfall at Acadia is notably acidic. Maine's four federal legislators and others in the region have been especially active in their efforts to strengthen the Clean Air Act and improve conditions at Acadia and in the rest of New England.

To heighten public awareness of pollution problems, CAMNET, a public-private joint program, provides real-time pollution and visibility monitoring. Acadia is one of the nine New England sites with cameras updating images every 15 minutes. Log on to www. hazecam.net for data on current temperature and humidity, wind speed and direction, precipitation totals, visual range, and the air-pollution level (low, medium, or high). The site also includes a selection of photos showing the variations that have occurred in the past at Acadia. In the "clear day" photo, visibility was pegged at 199 miles! Ozone alerts, according to Environmental Protection Agency standards, usually occur at Acadia a couple of times each summer. When they do, rangers put out signs to caution visitors—particularly hikers and bikers—to restrict strenuous activity.

While pollution is an Acadia issue—affecting the park, its vegetation and wildlife, and its visitors—the solution must be a national one. Stay tuned.

PARK CAPACITY

With more than four million visitors in 2019, Acadia and National Park Service officials are wrestling with a question: How many people are too many people? Other national parks have initiated visitor limitations, and Acadia began rolling out its new transportation plan in 2020. It includes vehicle reservations for the Sand Beach Entrance station of the Park Loop Road and the Acadia Summit Road and parking reservations for the Jordan Pond North lot.

The establishment of the propane-powered Island Explorer bus service has greatly alleviated traffic (and thus also auto, SUV, and RV emissions) during the months it operates (late June-early October), but its popularity is growing more quickly than its capacity. Although efforts to identify peak routes and times and add extra service are being made, there's still a chance you may have to wait a bit.

Cruise-vessel visits in Bar Harbor have multiplied exponentially in recent years. Most passengers spend at least some time in the park, but it's a minimal amount of time—often just a carriage ride or a visit to Jordan Pond House or the Cadillac summit. (Bar Harbor merchants, of course, welcome the influx.)

The heaviest use of the park occurs in July-August, with marginally less use in September and early October, yet there are still quiet corners of the park; it's a matter of

Leave the Rocks for the Next Glacier

Acadia's relatively small size among national parks and high volume of visitors have necessitated a very active campaign to heighten sensitivity to the park's ecosystem. While you're in Acadia, do your part to "Keep Acadia Beautiful" by adhering to guidelines developed by the national organization Leave No Trace (LNT, www.lnt.org), based in Boulder, Colorado:

- Plan ahead and prepare.

- Travel and camp on durable surfaces.

- Dispose of waste properly.

- Leave what you find.

- Minimize campfire impacts.

- Respect wildlife.

- Be considerate of other visitors.

While all seven of these are important, two are especially critical for Acadia:

- Travel and camp on durable surfaces. Since there is no backcountry camping in Acadia, and park rangers do their best to monitor the park's three "front-country" campgrounds (two on Mount Desert, one on Isle au Haut), the focus is on hiking and use of the trails. Stay on existing trails—paying attention to signposts, blazes, and cairns—and don't be seduced by false trails where hikers have begun to stray. Walk single file down the center of a trail to avoid trampling the sensitive vegetation alongside; slow-growing lichens are particularly fragile. Remember, plants grow by the inch and die by the foot. Every footstep can make a difference. If you must step off the trail, step onto a durable surface. Acadia's most fragile sites are the summits and ridges. Especially vulnerable is the summit of Cadillac Mountain—it's a matter of sheer numbers. Yes, walk the summit loop for its great views, but above all, stick to the trail, or at least step on solid rock.

- Leave what you find. That means *take no souvenirs*. Save the wildflowers for the next visitors to enjoy, and leave the tide pool creatures where you find them. Above all, don't mess with cairns, the carefully constructed stone trail markers. Resist the urge to build or unbuild or rebuild cairns along the way—in some instances, removal or addition of a single stone can threaten a cairn's stability. It's a safety issue too—a collapsed cairn becomes a missing link in the trail-marking system. Follow cairns, don't build them. As the slogan has it, "leave the rocks for the next glacier." Imagine if every one of the park's two million visitors each year removed one cobble or rock. Unfortunately, enough already have. Bar Harbor Airport screeners, under heightened security regulations, have been seeing visitors departing with beach rocks. But what to do with them? Who can say exactly where they came from? If you're planning to camp at one of the park campgrounds, purchase firewood—you'll see dozens of Firewood for Sale signs along the roads leading to the park. Stop and buy a bundle; it'll set you back just a few dollars.

Also essential—anywhere, not just in Acadia—is the carry-in, carry-out message. If you're planning a picnic, enjoy it (on a durable surface—there's plenty of granite in Acadia), then remove all evidence of it. Carry trash bags and use them.

To keep wildlife wild, *do not feed* any of the park's wildlife—a problem of increasing concern at Acadia. Animals become dependent on humans and risk being hit by cars or otherwise meeting their end.

We all love the park, but we can't love it to death.

finding them: Head over to the Quiet Side, get out to the islands, hike less utilized trails or explore more remote carriage roads. The best advice, if possible, is to visit in shoulder seasons—May-June and mid- to late October.

You take your chances then with weather and temperatures, and some sights and businesses might not be open, but if you're flexible and adaptable, it could be the best vacation you've ever had.

History

INDIGENOUS PEOPLE

As the great continental glacier receded out of Maine to the northwest about 11,000 years ago, some prehistoric grapevine must have alerted small bands of hunter-gatherers—fur-clad Paleo-Indians—to the scrub sprouting in the tundra, burgeoning mammal populations, and the ocean's bountiful food supply. They came to the shore in droves—at first seasonally, then year-round. Anyone who thinks tourism is a recent phenomenon in this part of Maine need only explore the shoreline of Mount Desert Island, where cast-off oyster shells and clamshells document the migration of early Native Americans from woodlands to waterfront. "The shore" has been a summertime magnet for millennia.

Archaeological evidence from the Archaic period in Maine—roughly 8000-1000 BC—is fairly scant, but paleontologists have unearthed stone tools and weapons and small campsites attesting to a nomadic lifestyle supported by fishing and hunting, with fishing becoming more extensive as time went on. Toward the end of the tradition, during the late Archaic period, there emerged a rather anomalous Indian culture known officially as the Moorehead phase but informally called the Red Paint People; the name comes from their curious trait of using a distinctive red ocher (pulverized hematite) in burials. Dark red puddles and stone artifacts have led excavators to burial pits in Ellsworth and Hancock. Just as mysteriously as they had arrived, the Red Paint People disappeared abruptly and inexplicably around 1800 BC.

Following them almost immediately—and almost as suddenly—hunter-gatherers of the

Susquehanna Tradition arrived from well to the south, moved across Maine's interior as far as the St. John River, and remained until about 1600 BC, when they too enigmatically vanished. Excavations have turned up relatively sophisticated stone tools and evidence that they cremated their dead. It was nearly 1,000 years before a major new cultural phase appeared.

The next great leap forward was marked by the advent of pottery making, introduced about 700 BC. The Ceramic period stretched to the 16th century, and cone-shaped pots (initially stamped, later incised with coiled-rope motifs) survived until the introduction of metals from Europe. During this time, at Pemetic (their name for Mount Desert Island) and on some of the offshore islands, Native American fisherfolk and their families built houses of sorts—seasonal, wigwam-style birchbark dwellings—and spent the summers fishing, clamming, trapping, and making baskets and functional birchbark objects.

THE EUROPEANS ARRIVE

The identity of the first Europeans to set foot in Maine is a matter of debate. Historians dispute the romantically popular notion that Norse explorers checked out this part of the New World as early as AD 1000. Even an 11th-century Norse coin found in 1961 in Brooklin, near Blue Hill, west of Mount Desert Island, was probably carried there from farther northeast.

Not until the late 15th century, the onset of the great Age of Discovery, did credible reports of the New World, including what is now Maine, filter back to Europe's courts and universities. Thanks to innovations in naval architecture, shipbuilding, and navigation, astonishingly courageous fellows crossed the Atlantic in search of rumored treasure and new routes for reaching it.

John Cabot, sailing from England aboard the ship *Mathew,* may have been the first European to reach Maine, in 1498, but historians have never confirmed a landing site. There is no question, however, about the account of Giovanni da Verrazzano, a Florentine explorer commanding *La Dauphine* under the French flag, who reached the Maine coast in 1524. Encountering less-than-friendly Native Americans, Verrazzano did a minimum of business and sailed onward toward Nova Scotia. Four years later, he died in the West Indies. His brother's map of their landing site (probably on the Phippsburg Peninsula, near Bath) labels it "The Land of Bad People." Esteban Gómez, a Portuguese explorer sailing under the Spanish flag, followed in Verrazzano's wake in 1525, but the only outcome of his exploits was an uncounted number of captives whom he sold into slavery in Spain. A map created several years later from Gómez's descriptions seems to indicate he had at least glimpsed Mount Desert Island.

More than half a century passed before the Maine coast turned up again on European explorers' itineraries. This time, interest was fueled by reports of a Brigadoon-like area called Norumbega (or Oranbega, as one map had it), a myth that arose, gathered steam, and took on a life of its own in the decades following Verrazzano's voyage.

By the 17th century, when Europeans began arriving in more than twos and threes and getting serious about colonization, Native American agriculture was already under way, the cod fishery was thriving on offshore islands, Native Americans far to the north were hot to trade furs for European goodies, and the birchbark canoe was the transport of choice when the Penobscots headed down Maine's rivers toward their summer sojourns on the coast.

MOUNT DESERT ISLAND "DISCOVERED"

In the early 17th century, English dominance of exploration west of the Penobscot River (roughly from present-day Bucksport down to the New Hampshire border and beyond) coincided roughly with increasing French activity east of the river—including Mount Desert Island and the nearby mainland.

In 1604, French nobleman Pierre du Gua, Sieur de Monts, bearing a vast land grant for "La Cadie" (Acadia) from King Henry IV, set out with cartographer Samuel de Champlain to map the coastline. They first reached Nova Scotia's Bay of Fundy and then sailed up the St. Croix River. Mid-river, just west of present-day Calais, a crew planted gardens and erected buildings on today's St. Croix Island while du Gua and Champlain went off exploring. The two men and their crew sailed up the Penobscot River to present-day Bangor, searching fruitlessly for Norumbega, and next "discovered" the imposing island Champlain named l'Île des Monts Déserts because of its treeless summits. Here they entered Frenchman Bay, landed at today's Otter Creek in early September, and explored inlets and bays in the vicinity before returning to St. Croix Island to face the elements with their ill-fated compatriots. Scurvy, lack of fuel and water, and a ferocious winter wiped out nearly half of the 79 men in the St. Croix settlement. In spring 1605, du Gua, Champlain, and other survivors headed southwest again, exploring the coastline all the way to Cape Cod before returning northeast and settling permanently at Nova Scotia's Port Royal (now Annapolis Royal).

Eight years later, French Jesuit missionaries en route to the Kennebec River (or, as some allege, seeking Norumbega) ended up on Mount Desert Island. With a band of about three dozen French laymen, they set about establishing the St. Sauveur mission settlement at present-day Fernald Point. Despite the welcoming presence of amiable Native Americans (led by Asticou, an eminent Penobscot sagamore), leadership squabbles led to building delays, and English marauder Samuel Argall—assigned to reclaim this territory for England—arrived in his warship *Treasurer* to find them easy prey. The colony was leveled, the settlers were set adrift in small boats, the priests were carted off to the Jamestown colony in Virginia, and Argall moved on to destroy Port Royal.

Even though England yearned to control the entire Maine coastline, her turf, realistically, remained south and west of the Penobscot River. During the 17th century, the French had expanded from their Canadian colony of Acadia. Unlike the absentee bosses who controlled the English territory, French merchants actually showed up, forming good relationships with the Native Americans and cornering the market in fishing, lumbering, and fur trading. And French Jesuit priests converted many Native Americans to Catholicism. Intermittently, overlapping Anglo-French land claims sparked messy local conflicts.

In the mid-17th century, the strategic heart of French administration and activity in Maine was Fort Pentagoet, a sturdy stone outpost built in 1635 in what is now Castine, on the peninsula west of Mount Desert Island. From Pentagoet, the French controlled coastal trade between the St. George River and Mount Desert Island and well up the Penobscot River. In 1654, England captured and occupied Pentagoet and much of French Acadia, but thanks to the 1667 Treaty of Breda, title returned to the French in 1670, and Pentagoet briefly became Acadia's capital.

A short but nasty Dutch foray against Acadia in 1674 resulted in Pentagoet's destruction ("levell'd with ye ground," by one account) and the raising of yet a third national flag over Castine.

THE REVOLUTION AND STATEHOOD

From the late 17th to the late 18th centuries, half a dozen skirmishes along the coast—often sparked by conflicts in Europe—preoccupied the Wabanaki (Native American groups), the French, and the English. In 1759, roughly midway through the Seven Years' War, the British came out on top in Quebec, allowing Massachusetts governor John Bernard to divvy up the acreage on Mount Desert Island. Two brave pioneers—James Richardson and Abraham Somes—arrived with their families in 1760, and today's village of Somesville marks their settlement. Even as the American Revolution consumed the colonies, Mount Desert Island maintained a relatively low profile, politically speaking, into the early 19th century. A steady stream of homesteaders, drawn by the appeal of free land, sustained their families by fishing, farming, lumbering, and shipbuilding. On March 15, 1820, the District of Maine, which included Mount Desert Island, broke from Massachusetts to become the 23rd state in the Union, with its capital in Portland (the capital moved to Augusta in 1832).

ARRIVAL OF THE "RUSTICATORS"

Around the middle of the 19th century, explorers of a different sort arrived on Mount Desert Island. Seeking dramatic landscapes rather than fertile land, painters of the acclaimed Hudson River School found more than enough inspiration for their canvases. Thomas Cole (1801-1848), founder of the group, visited Mount Desert only once, in 1844, but his onetime student Frederic Edwin Church (1826-1900) vacationed here in 1850 and became a summer resident two decades later. Once dubbed "the Michelangelo of landscape art," Church traveled widely in search of exotic settings for his grand landscapes. After his summers on Mount Desert, he spent his final days at Olana, a Persian-inspired mansion overlooking the Hudson River.

It's no coincidence that artists formed a large part of the 19th-century vanguard here: The dramatic landscape, with both bare and wooded mountains descending to the sea, still inspires those who see it. Those pioneering artists brilliantly portrayed this area, adding a few romantic touches to landscapes that really need no enhancement. Known collectively as "rusticators," the artists and their coterie seemed content to "live like the locals" and rented basic rooms from island fisherfolk and boatbuilders. But once the word got out and painterly images began confirming the reports, the surge of visitors began—particularly after the Civil War, which had so totally preoccupied the nation. Tourist boardinghouses appeared first, followed by sprawling hotels—by the late 1880s, there were nearly 40 hotels on the island, luring vacationers for summerlong stays.

At about the same time, the East Coast's corporate tycoons zeroed in on Mount Desert, arriving by luxurious steam yachts and building over-the-top grand estates (quaintly called "summer cottages") along the shore north of Bar Harbor. Before long, demand exceeded acreage, and mansions also began appearing in Northeast and Southwest Harbors. Their seasonal social circuit was a catalog of rich and famous families—Rockefeller, Astor, Vanderbilt, Ford, Whitney, Schieffelin, Morgan, and Carnegie, just for a start. Also part of the elegant mix were noted academics, doctors, lawyers, and even international diplomats. The "Gay Nineties" earned their name on Mount Desert Island.

BIRTH OF A NATIONAL PARK

Fortunately for Mount Desert—and, let's face it, for all of us—many of the rusticators maintained a strong sense of noblesse oblige, engaging regularly in philanthropic activity. Notable among them was George Bucknam Dorr (1853-1944), who spent more than 40 years fighting to preserve land on Mount Desert Island and ultimately earned the title "Father of Acadia."

As Dorr related in his memoir, the saga began with the establishment of the Hancock County Trustees of Public Reservations, a nonprofit corporation modeled on the Trustees of Public Reservations in Massachusetts and chartered in early 1903 "to acquire, by devise, gift or purchase, and to own, arrange, hold, maintain or improve for public use lands in Hancock County, Maine (encompassing Mount Desert Island as well as Schoodic Point), which by reason of scenic beauty, historical interest, sanitary advantage or other like reasons may become available for such purpose." President of the new corporation was Charles W. Eliot, president emeritus of Harvard. Dorr became the vice president and "executive officer," and he dedicated the rest of his life to the cause.

Dorr wrote letters, cajoled, spoke at meetings, arrived on potential donors' doorsteps, and even resorted to polite ruses as he pursued his mission. He also delved into his own pockets to subsidize land purchases. Dorr was a fund-raiser par excellence, a master of networking decades before the days of instant communications. Gradually he accumulated parcels—ponds, woodlands, summits, trails—and gradually his enthusiasm caught on. But easy it wasn't. He faced down longtime local residents, potential developers, and other challengers, and he politely but doggedly visited grand salons, corporate offices, and the halls of Congress in his quest.

In 1913, Bar Harbor taxpayers—irked by the increasing acreage being taken off the tax rolls—prevailed on their state legislator to introduce a bill to annul the corporation's charter. Dorr's effective lobbying doomed the bill, but the corporation saw trouble ahead and devised a plan on a grander scale. Again thanks to Dorr's political and social connections and intense lobbying in Washington DC, President Woodrow Wilson created the Sieur de Monts National Monument on July 8, 1916, from 5,000 acres given to the government by the Hancock County Trustees of Public Reservations. Dorr acquired the new title of Custodian of the Monument.

After the establishment of the National Park Service in August 1916, and after Sieur de Monts had received its first congressional appropriation ($10,000), Dorr forged ahead to try to convince the government to convert "his" national monument into a national park. "No" meant nothing to him. Not only

Acadia's Human Contributions

Acadia reels in visitors with its heady scenery, but this spectacular chunk of Maine real estate is as much a monument to human ingenuity as to nature's grandeur. More than any other national park, Acadia is distinguished by human imprint. Unlike other parks, Acadia was created from donations of private rather than public or corporate lands. Because much of Acadia was carved out of backyards and woodlots, its borders are woven into the surrounding communities. "There is no other park I'm aware of that was assembled piece by piece from property owned by people of modest means," said the late Aimee Beal-Church, former communications and outreach coordinator for Friends of Acadia.

CREATING ACADIA

The region's human story reaches back millennia. Archeological digs document a Wabanaki presence dating back roughly 5,000 years. French navigator Samuel de Champlain mapped the island in 1604, naming it l'Isle des Monts-deserts. English settlement began in 1760, and by the mid-19th century, farmers, lumbermen, shipbuilders, and fishermen were well established. That's when Frederick Church, Thomas Cole, and Fitz Henry Lane arrived. Their plein air paintings wooed wealthy Northeasterners, who designed trails that took advantage of the landscape and the views. These summer rusticators needed lodging, giving rise to grand hotels, grander cottages, and a summer colony that rivaled Newport, Rhode Island, in social prominence. By the late 19th century, substantial portions of shoreline property had passed from local ownership to people from away, and these lands were privatized and taken out of the public domain.

Enter summer resident George B. Dorr. In 1901, concerned about the threats to Acadia's environment from development and the invention of the portable sawmill, Dorr established the Hancock County Trustees of Public Reservation and began soliciting donations of land and money. Fellow summer resident Eliza Homans made the first significant land donation, the Beehive and the Bowl, which got the momentum rolling. "So many people go up and down the Beehive and don't realize the historical moment it represents," Beal-Church noted. The Homans Trail honors Eliza's legacy.

MAN-MADE WONDERS

In addition to being a natural beauty, Acadia also offers incredible man-made wonders that are some of the park's most treasured assets.

- Sieur de Monts Springs is home to an ornamental house over the spring Dorr dubbed the "Sweet Waters of Acadia," a garden filled with native flora, and the trailside Abbe Museum, established in the 1920s by summer resident and amateur archeologist Dr. Robert Abbe to showcase his growing collection of Native American artifacts.

- Summer rusticator John D. Rockefeller Jr. earns kudos for the Park Loop Road and the carriage roads. The philanthropic-minded heir to the Standard Oil fortune sought advice from Frederick Law Olmsted Jr. when designing the 27-mile loop road. Rockefeller engaged renowned landscape architect Beatrix Farrand, when creating the carriage road network comprising broken-stone roads accented with 17 rough-stone bridges, and he hired New York architect Grosvenor Atterbury to design the two French Romanesque gatehouses. Atterbury also designed Rockefeller Hall in the Schoodic section in the same style.

- During the Depression, more than 3,000 young men spent six months in Acadia as part of the New Deal's Civilian Conservation Corps. They constructed fire roads, planted trees, built trails, and constructed the granite steps that ease the hike up many of Acadia's peaks. The Perpendicular Trail is best example of their craftsmanship, according to Jack Russell, Friends of Acadia board member. "It's the most constructed trail in Acadia. It was built by poor boys of 18, 19, and 20, many from Aroostook County, most of whom had never cut stone in their lives." They constructed steps spiraling up Mansell Mountain, lined the trail with granite coping stones, and added culverts, iron rungs, and a ladder.

did he schmooze with members of Congress, cabinet members, helpful secretaries, and even former president Theodore Roosevelt, he also provided the pen (filled with ink) and waited in the president's outer office to be sure Wilson signed the bill. On February 26, 1919, Lafayette National Park became the first national park east of the Mississippi River; George Bucknam Dorr became its first superintendent. Ten years later, the name was changed to Acadia National Park.

THE GREAT FIRE OF 1947

Wildfires are no surprise in Maine, where woodlands often stretch to the horizon, but 1947 was unique in the history of the state and of Acadia. A rainy spring led into a dry, hot summer with almost no precipitation and then an autumn with still no rain. Wells went dry, vegetation drooped, and the inevitable occurred—a record-breaking inferno. Starting on October 17 as a small, smoldering fire at the northern end of the island, it galloped south and east, abetted by winds, and moved toward Bar Harbor and Frenchman Bay before coming under control on October 27. More than 17,000 acres burned, including more than 10,000 in Acadia National Park.

Sixty-seven magnificent "cottages" were incinerated on "Millionaires' Row," along the shore north of Bar Harbor, with property damage of more than $20 million. Some of the mansions, incredibly, escaped the flames, but most of the estates were never rebuilt. Miraculously, only one person died in the fire. A few other deaths occurred from heart attacks and traffic accidents as hundreds of residents scrambled frantically to escape the island. Even the fisherfolk of nearby Lamoine and Winter Harbor pitched in, staging their own mini Dunkirk to evacuate more than 400 residents by boat.

THE PARK TODAY

If only George Dorr could see today's Acadia, covering more than 49,000 acres on Mount Desert Island, the Schoodic Peninsula mainland, and parts of Isle au Haut, Baker Island, and Little Cranberry Island. The fire changed Mount Desert's woodland profile—from the dark greens of spruce and fir to a mix of evergreen and deciduous trees, making the fall foliage even more dramatic than in Dorr's day. If ever proof were needed that one person (enlisting the help of many others) can indeed make a difference, Acadia National Park provides it.

People and Culture

Maine's population didn't top the one million mark until 1970. Forty years later, according to the 2010 census, the state had 1.3 million residents.

Despite the long-standing presence of several substantial ethnic groups, plus four Native American groups that account for about 1 percent of the population, diversity is a relatively recent phenomenon in Maine, and the population is about 95 percent Caucasian. A steady influx of refugees, beginning after the Vietnam War, forced the state to address diversity issues, and it continues to do so today. While Portland is the state's most

diverse city, tiny Milbridge has a surprisingly diverse population thanks to immigrants who arrive to pick blueberries and sometimes settle there.

POPULATION GROUPS
Natives and "People from Away"

People who weren't born in Maine aren't natives. Even people who were born here may experience close scrutiny of their credentials. In Maine, there are natives and there are *natives*. Every day the obituary pages describe Mainers who have barely left the houses in which they were born—even in which their grandparents were born. We're talking roots.

Along with this kind of heritage comes a whole vocabulary all its own—lingo distinctive to Maine or at least to New England. Part of the "native" picture is the matter of native produce. Hand-lettered signs sprout everywhere during the summer advertising native corn, native peas, even—believe it or not—native ice. In Maine, homegrown is well grown.

"People from away," on the other hand, are those whose families haven't lived here year-round for at least a generation. But people from away (also called "flatlanders") exist all over Maine, and they have come to stay, putting down roots of their own and altering the way the state is run, looks, and will look. You'll find flatlanders as teachers, corporate executives, artists, retirees, writers, town selectmen, and even lobstermen.

In the 19th century, arriving flatlanders were mostly "rusticators" or "summer complaints"—summer residents who lived well, often in enclaves, and never set foot in the state off-season. They did, however, pay property taxes, contribute to causes, and provide employment for local residents. Another 19th-century wave of people from away came from the bottom of the economic ladder: Irish escaping the potato famine and French Canadians fleeing poverty in Quebec. Both groups experienced subtle and overt anti-Catholicism but rather quickly assimilated into the mainstream, taking jobs in mills and factories and becoming staunch American patriots.

The late 1960s and early 1970s brought bunches of "back-to-the-landers," who scorned plumbing and electricity and adopted retro ways of life. Although a few pockets of diehards still exist, most have changed with the times and adopted contemporary mores (and conveniences).

Today, technocrats arrive from away with computers, smartphones, and other high-tech gear and "commute" via the Internet and modern electronics, although getting a cell phone signal is still a challenge in parts of the Acadia region.

Indigenous People

In Maine, the *real* natives are the Wabanaki (People of the Dawn)—the Micmac, Maliseet, Penobscot, and Passamaquoddy of the eastern woodlands. Many live in or near three reservations, near the headquarters for their governors. The Passamaquoddies are at Pleasant Point in Perry, near Eastport, and at Indian Township in Princeton, near Calais. The Penobscots are based on Indian Island in Old Town, near Bangor. Other Indigenous people population clusters—known as "off-reservation Indians"—are the Aroostook Band of Micmacs, based in Presque Isle, and the Houlton Band of Maliseets in Littleton, near Houlton.

In 1965, Maine became the first state to establish a Department of Indian Affairs, but just five years later the Passamaquoddy and Penobscot people initiated a 10-year-long land-claims case involving 12.5 million Maine acres—about two-thirds of the state—weaseled from their ancestors by Massachusetts in 1794. In late 1980, a landmark agreement, signed by President Jimmy Carter, awarded the tribes $80.6 million in reparations. Despite this, Indigenous communities still struggle to provide jobs on the reservations and to increase their overall standard of living.

One of the true Native American success stories is the revival of traditional arts as businesses. The Maine Indian Basketmakers Alliance has an active apprenticeship program, and a few renowned basket makers have achieved National Heritage Fellowships. Several well-attended annual festivals—including two in Bar Harbor—highlight Indian traditions and heighten awareness of Native American culture. Basket making, canoe building, and traditional dancing are all parts of the scene. The splendid Abbe Museum in Bar Harbor features Indigenous artifacts, interactive displays, historic photographs, and special programs. Fine craft shops also sell Native American jewelry and baskets.

LOCAL CULTURE

Mainers are an independent lot, many exhibiting the classic Yankee characteristics of dry humor, thrift, and ingenuity. Those who can trace their roots back at least a generation or two in the state and have lived here through the duration can call themselves natives; everyone else, no matter how long they've lived here, is "from away."

Mainers react to outsiders depending on how those outsiders treat them. Treat a Mainer with a condescending attitude, and you'll receive a cold shoulder at best. Treat a Mainer with respect, and you'll be welcome, perhaps even invited in to share a mug of coffee. Mainers are wary of outsiders, and often with good reason. Some outsiders move to Maine because they fall in love with its independence and rural simplicity, and then they demand that the farmer stop spreading that stinky manure on his farmlands, or complain about the noise from lobster boats heading out to haul traps at 3:30am, or insist that the town initiate garbage pickup, or build a glass-and-timber McMansion in the middle of historic white-clapboard homes. Or, my favorite, make a formal complaint to the Coast Guard about a fog horn's cry, as Joseph Pulitzer did, with other residents, in 1904.

In most of Maine, money doesn't impress folks. The truth is, that lobsterman in the old truck and the well-worn work clothes might be sitting on a small fortune, or living on it. Perhaps nothing has caused more troubles between natives and newcomers than the rapidly increasing value of land and the taxes that go with that. For many visitors, Maine real estate is a bargain they can't resist.

If you want real insight into Maine character, listen to a CD or watch a video by one Maine master humorist, Tim Sample. As he often says, "Wait a minute; it'll sneak up on you."

THE ARTS

Fine Art

In 1850, in a watershed moment for Maine landscape painting, Hudson River School artist par excellence Frederic Edwin Church (1826-1900) vacationed on Mount Desert Island. Influenced by the luminist tradition of such contemporaries as Fitz Hugh Lane (1804-1865), who summered in nearby Castine, Church accurately but romantically depicted the dramatic tableaux of Maine's coast and woodlands that even today attracts slews of admirers.

Another notable is John Marin (1870-1953), a cubist who painted Down East subjects, mostly around Deer Isle and Addison (Cape Split).

Fine-art galleries are clustered in Blue Hill, Bar Harbor, and Northeast Harbor.

Crafts

Any survey of Maine art, however brief, must include the significant role of crafts in the state's artistic tradition. As with painters, sculptors, and writers, craftspeople have gravitated to Maine—most notably since the establishment in 1950 of the **Haystack Mountain School of Crafts.** Started in the Belfast area, the school put down roots on Deer Isle in 1960. Each summer, internationally famed artisans—sculptors, glassmakers, weavers, jewelers, potters, papermakers, and printmakers—become the faculty for the unique school, which has weekday classes and 24-hour studio access for adult students on its handsome 40-acre campus. Many Haystack students have chosen to settle in the region. Galleries and studios pepper the Blue Hill-Deer Isle peninsula. Another craft enclave is in the Schoodic region.

Down East Literature

Maine's first big-name writer was probably the early 17th-century French explorer Samuel de Champlain (1570-1635), who scouted the Maine coast, established a colony in 1604 near present-day Calais, and lived to describe in detail his experiences.

Artists and Artisans: A Studio Tour

Given the inspiring scenery, it's no surprise that the Acadia region is home to dozens of immensely talented artists and artisans. Visiting them in their studios allows you to view the region through their eyes. Galleries are abundant on the Blue Hill Peninsula and Deer Isle and in the Schoodic region, and more and more artists and artisans are calling Mount Desert Island home.

MOUNT DESERT ISLAND

- Must-See Contemporary Craft: **Island Artisans** (99 Main St., Bar Harbor, 207/288-4214, www.islandartisans.com) and **Shaw Contemporary Jewelry** (100 Main St., Northeast Harbor, 207/276-5000 or 877/276-5001, www.shawjewelry.com)

- Wild about Wildlife: **Christopher Smith Galleries** (125B Main St., Northeast Harbor, 207/276-3343, www.smithbronze.com)

- Don't-Miss Museum: **Wendell Gilley Museum** (Herrick Rd. and Rte. 102, Southwest Harbor, 207/244-7555, www.wendellgilleymuseum.org)

SCHOODIC REGION

- Take It for Granite: Obadiah Bourne Buell's **Stone Designs Studio and Granite Garden Gallery** (124 Whales Back Rd., 207/422-3111, www.stonedesignsmaine.com)

- Must-See Contemporary Art: **Spring Woods Gallery and Willow Brook Garden** (40A Willowbrook Ln., Sullivan, 207/422-3007, www.springwoodsgallery.com or www.willowbrookgarden.com)

- Folk Art Favorite: **Arthur Smith** (Rogers Point Rd., Steuben, 207/546-3462)

- Best Sculpture and Sculptor: **Ray Carbone** (460 Pigeon Hill Rd., Steuben, 207/546-2170, www.raycarbonesculptor.com)

BLUE HILL PENINSULA

- Must-See Contemporary Art: **Cynthia Winings Gallery** (24 Parker Point Rd., Blue Hill, 917/204-4001, www.cynthiawiningsgallery.com)

- Best Sculpture and Sculptor: **Jud Hartmann** (79 Main St. at Rte. 15, Blue Hill, 207/374-9917, www.judhartmanngallery.com)

- Smithsonian-Worthy Pottery: **Mark Bell Pottery** (289 Rte. 15, Blue Hill, 207/374-5881)

DEER ISLE

- Just Plain Fun: **Nervous Nellie's** (600 Sunshine Rd., Deer Isle, 800/777-6845, www.nervousnellies.com)

- Most Dynamic Duo: **Greene-Ziner Gallery** (73 Reach Rd., Deer Isle, 207/348-2601, www.melissagreene.com)

- Must-See Contemporary Art: **The Turtle Gallery** (61 N. Deer Isle Rd./Rte. 15, Deer Isle, 207/348-9977, www.turtlegallery.com)

- Furnish Your Future: **Geoffrey Warner Studio** (431 N. Main St., Stonington, 207/367-6555, www.geoffreywarnerstudio.com)

Today, Maine's best-known author lives not on the coast but just inland in Bangor— Stephen King (born 1947), wizard of the weird. Many of his dozens of horror novels and stories are set in Maine, and several have been filmed here for the big screen. King and his wife, Tabitha, also an author, are avid fans of both education and team sports and have generously distributed their largesse among schools and teams in their hometown as well as other parts of the state.

CLASSIC WRITINGS ON THE REGION

Louise Dickinson Rich (1903-1972) entertainingly described her coastal experiences in Corea in *The Peninsula,* after first having chronicled her rugged wilderness existence in *We Took to the Woods.*

Ruth Moore (1903-1989), born on Gott's Island, near Acadia National Park, published her first book at the age of 40. Her tales, recently brought back into print, have earned her a whole new appreciative audience.

Mary Ellen Chase was a Maine native, born in Blue Hill in 1887. She became an English professor at Smith College in 1926 and wrote about 30 books, including some about the Bible as literature. She died in 1973.

A WORLD OF HER OWN

For Marguerite Yourcenar (1903-1987), Maine provided solitude and inspiration for subjects ranging far beyond the state's borders. Yourcenar was a longtime Northeast Harbor resident and the first woman elected to the prestigious Académie Française. Her house, now a shrine to her work, is open to the public by appointment in summer.

ESSAYISTS AND CRITICS, NATIVE AND TRANSPLANTED

Maine's best-known essayist was and is E. B. White (1899-1985), who bought a farm in tiny Brooklin in 1933 and continued writing for *The New Yorker. One Man's Meat,* published in 1944, is one of the best collections of his wry, perceptive writings. His legions of admirers also include two generations raised on his classic children's stories *Stuart Little, Charlotte's Web,* and *The Trumpet of the Swan.*

Writer and critic Doris Grumbach (born 1918), who settled in Sargentville, not far from Brooklin, but far from her New York ties, wrote two particularly wise works from the perspective of a Maine transplant: *Fifty Days of Solitude* and *Coming Into the End Zone.*

MAINE LIT FOR LITTLE ONES

Besides E. B. White's children's classics, *Stuart Little, Charlotte's Web,* and *The Trumpet of the Swan,* American kids were also weaned on books written and illustrated by Maine island summer resident Robert McCloskey (1914-2003), notably *Time of Wonder, One Morning in Maine,* and *Blueberries for Sal.*

Essentials

Getting There

ORIENTATION

Acadia National Park lies about three-fifths of the way up the Maine coast. The primary section, on Mount Desert Island, is located about 46 miles south of Bangor and 160 miles northeast of Portland. Here is where you'll find the park's visitors center. Although it's an island, Mount Desert is connected to the mainland by bridges and causeways, so you can arrive by car or by bus. Not so with Isle au Haut, the most remote section of the park. Isle au Haut is located off the tip of the Blue Hill-Deer Isle peninsula, southwest of Bangor, and can only

be reached by boat. Access is limited, unless you have your own boat, and facilities are few. The Schoodic section of the park tips a mainland peninsula east of Bar Harbor and is easily reachable by vehicle or via passenger ferry from Bar Harbor.

There are no direct commercial flights from overseas to any of Maine's airports, although one airline provides direct service to Halifax, Nova Scotia. The closest **international airport** is Boston's Logan Airport (BOS). **Bus service** to Portland, Bangor, and in season, Bar Harbor, is available from Logan; **train service** is available from Boston's North Station terminal to Portland and Brunswick, and both stations also are served by bus. Rental cars are available at all airports.

DRIVING ROUTES

The major highway access to Maine from the south is **I-95,** which roughly parallels the coast until Bangor. Other busy access points are **U.S. (Route) 1,** entering the state at the Kittery border with New Hampshire and exiting at the Canadian border in Fort Kent; **U.S. 302,** from North Conway, New Hampshire, entering Maine at Fryeburg; **U.S. 2,** from Gorham, New Hampshire, to Bethel; **U.S. 201,** entering Maine at the Jackman border with Quebec; and a couple of crossing points from New Brunswick into Washington County in northeastern Maine.

The maximum speed on I-95 and the Maine Turnpike is 70 mph, on some stretches 55 mph. In snow, sleet, or dense fog, the limit drops to 45 mph; only rarely does the highway close. On other highways, the speed limit is usually 55 mph in rural areas and posted in built-up areas. Published distances can be deceptive; you'll never average even 55 mph on the two-lane roads.

The Maine Department of Transportation (800/877-9171, www.state.me.us/mdot) has general road information on its website and also operates the Explore Maine site (www.exploremaine.org), which has information on all forms of transportation in Maine. For real-time information on road conditions, weather, construction, and major delays, dial 511 in Maine, 866/282-7578 from out of state, or visit www.511maine.gov. Information is available in both English and French.

If you're arriving by car, the **Maine Tourism Association** operates state visitors information centers in Calais, Fryeburg (May-Oct.), Hampden, Houlton, Kittery, and Yarmouth. These are excellent places to visit to stock up on brochures, pick up a map, ask advice, and use the restrooms.

The Interstate and the Maine Turnpike

The interstate can be a bit confusing to motorists; it's important to consult a map and pay close attention to the green directional signs to avoid heading off in the wrong direction. Between York and Augusta, I-95 is the same as the Maine Turnpike, a toll highway regulated by the Maine Turnpike Authority (877/682-9433, travel conditions 800/675-7453, www.maineturnpike.com). All exit numbers along I-95 reflect the distance in miles from the New Hampshire border. I-295 splits from I-95 in Portland and follows the coast to Brunswick before veering inland and rejoining I-95 in Gardiner. Exits on I-295 reflect the distance from where it splits from I-95 just south of Portland at exit 44.

Two exits off I-95 provide access to the Acadia region: From exit 113 in Augusta, take Route 3 east to Belfast, which joins Route 1 north (allow 1.5-2 hours without traffic). From Bangor, take exit 182A, merging onto I-395 east to Route 1A north, which joins Routes 1 and 3 in Ellsworth (allow 45-75 minutes, without traffic). Be sure to follow signs for Ellsworth and Bar Harbor; avoid Route 1A south to Hampden and Stockton Springs.

The Maine Turnpike becomes extremely

Previous: Passenger ferries carry visitors to the Cranberry Isles.

congested on summer weekends, especially summer holiday weekends. The worst times on the turnpike are 4pm-8pm Friday (northbound), 11am-2pm Saturday (southbound; most weekly cottage rentals run noon Saturday-noon Saturday), and 3pm-7pm Sunday (southbound). On three-day holiday weekends, avoid heading southbound 3pm-7pm Monday.

U.S. 1

Two lanes wide from Kittery in the south to Fort Kent at the top, U.S. (Route) 1 is the state's most congested road, particularly July-August. Mileage distances can be extremely deceptive, since it will take you much longer than anticipated to get from point A to point B. If you ask anyone about distances, chances are good that you'll receive an answer in hours rather than miles. Plan accordingly. If you're trying to make time, it's best to take I-95; if you want to see Maine, take Route 1 and lots of little offshoots. If you drive Route 1 without stops and without encountering slow-moving traffic, it's about a four- to five-hour trip from Kittery.

TRAVEL HUB: BANGOR
Airport

Bangor International Airport (BGR, 207/947-0384, www.flybangor.com) is northern and eastern coastal Maine's hub for flights arriving from Boston and points beyond. Bangor is the closest large airport to Bar Harbor, Acadia National Park on Mount Desert Island, and the park's other outposts. About 500,000 passengers move through Bangor International annually, a user-friendly facility on the outskirts of the city. Although flights tend to be pricier to Bangor than to Portland or especially Boston, there's a big convenience factor to flying in here.

Despite the "international" in the airport's name, passenger service from international destinations to Bangor tends to be limited to charter airlines, which sometimes arrive here to clear customs, refuel, and then continue on to points south and west; military flights; and

alerts, in which badly behaving passengers are removed from international flights. More typically, international visitors arrive in Bangor via New York or Boston gateways. Bad weather in Portland or Boston can also create unexpected domestic and international arrivals at Bangor's less-foggy airfield.

The airport's lower level has an interactive information kiosk, where you can contact local hotels and motels for rooms and airport shuttle service.

Suggested Driving Routes

Bangor is slightly fewer than 50 miles from Bar Harbor, but you'll be traveling almost entirely on two-lane roads; in summer, figure on 1.5 hours. Drive Route 1A to Ellsworth and then Route 3 to Bar Harbor. Do not take Route 1A to Hampden, or you'll end up on the wrong side of the Penobscot River. For the Schoodic section of the park, when Route 1 and Route 3 split in Ellsworth, take Route 1 north to Gouldsboro, then head south on Route 186. For the Blue Hill Peninsula, Deer Isle, and Isle au Haut, from Ellsworth take Route 1 south to Route 172, then in Blue Hill, Route 15 south to reach Stonington and the boat to Isle au Haut.

Car Rentals

Car rentals at the airport include **Alamo** (207/947-0158 or 800/462-5266, www.alamo.com), **Avis** (207/947-8383 or 800/831-2847, www.avis.com), **Budget** (207/945-9429 or 800/527-0700, www.drivebudget.com), **Hertz** (207/942-5519 or 800/654-3131, www.hertz.com), and **National** (207/947-0158 or 800/227-7368, www.nationalcar.com).

Bus and Taxi Services

Concord Coach Lines (1039 Union St./Rte. 222, Bangor, 207/945-4000 or 800/639-3317, www.concordcoachlines.com) provides daily bus service year-round from Logan Airport in Boston to the Bangor Transportation Center via Portland; $81 round trip. **Greyhound** (430 Coldbrook Rd., Hermon, 207/945-3000 or 800/231-2222, www.greyhound.com) offers less frequent service between Boston's South

Station and Dysart's Truck Stop in Hermon, a less convenient spot just west of Bangor; from $100 round trip. Neither bus line services Bar Harbor, but both offer connections to the Bar Harbor-Bangor Shuttle.

While there are ways to connect various points in the Acadia region via regional bus services (see www.exploremaine.org), most operate only one or two buses per day and often only on a few days each week. The most convenient and reasonably priced transportation between Bangor and Bar Harbor is provided by **Bar Harbor-Bangor Shuttle** (207/479-5911, www.barharborbangor-shuttle.com). Shuttle stops include Bangor Airport, Bangor Transportation Center, the Greyhound station, and most hotels in Bangor; Mike's Groceries in Ellsworth; the Hancock County-Bar Harbor Airport; and numerous lodging properties in Bar Harbor; from $50 one way.

Round-the-clock **taxi service** is available; check the Bangor Airport website for current options. Bar Harbor-based Bar Harbor Coastal Cab (207/288-1222, www.barharborcoastalcab.com) provides both local and long-distance service and accepts credit cards. Fare is approximately $100 from the airport to Bar Harbor.

Accommodations

Bangor International Airport is approximately 45 miles from Bar Harbor. Depending on when your flight arrives, you may wish to spend the night here and begin your journey refreshed. Most of the mid-rate chains have properties here. Your choice of a hotel or motel near the Bangor Mall or the Bangor Airport may depend on your frequent-flyer memberships or where you get the best auto club deal. There are lots of options, and most offer free shuttle service to and from the airport.

Many properties book far in advance for the fourth weekend in August, when the American Folk Festival is in town and traffic can be a bear.

For early-morning flights, you can't beat the convenience of the **Four Points**

Sheraton Hotel (307 Godfrey Blvd., Bangor, 207/947-6721 or 800/228-4609, www.fourpointsbangorairport.com, from $115), which is linked to the terminal by a skyway. It has a restaurant and an indoor pool. Pets are permitted for $20 per stay.

Next to the Bangor Mall, with restaurants and a food court, is the 96-room **Country Inn at the Mall** (936 Stillwater Ave., Bangor, 207/941-0200 or 800/244-3961, www.country-innatthemall.net, from $135), which includes a continental breakfast and offers free lodging for kids rooming with parents.

Hollywood Casino Hotel & Raceway (500 Main St., Bangor, 877/779-7771, www.hollywoodcasinobangor.com, from $129) is the best downtown hotel, but it is a casino and you have to deal with the hoopla that goes with it. Facilities include two restaurants. The location puts all of downtown within footsteps. Airport shuttles are available.

Camping

On Bangor's western perimeter are two clean, well-managed campgrounds convenient to I-95 and Bangor. The emphasis is on RVs, but tent sites are available. Closest to the city is the 52-site **Paul Bunyan Campground** (1862 Union St./Rte. 222, Bangor, 207/941-1177, www.paulbunyancampground.com, mid-Apr.-Oct., from $24), about three miles northwest of I-95 on Route 222 west.

About two miles farther out on Route 222, **Pleasant Hill Campground** (45 Mansell Rd., at Rte. 222, Hermon, 207/848-5127, www.pleasanthillcampground.com, from $24), also a Good Sam Park, has 105 sites on 60 acres.

Food

You'll find lots of fast food and family-friendly chains between the airport and the mall. Just south on I-95 at exit 180 is **Dysart's** (Coldbrook Rd., Hermon, 207/942-4878, www.dysarts.com, $5-16), a 24-hour trucker's destination resort with good grub. For a nicer meal, head downtown to **Fiddlehead** (84 Hammond St., Bangor, 207/942-3336, www.thefiddleheadrestaurant.com, 5pm-9pm

Tues.-Sun., $19-33) or **Mason's Brewing** (15 Hardy St., Brewer, 207/989-6300, http://masonsbrewingcompany.com, 11am-9pm daily, $14-18), a contemporary brewpub with riverside seating and a menu that includes burgers, sandwiches, salads, and pizzas.

TRAVEL HUB: PORTLAND

For anyone planning to go *just* to Acadia National Park, the primary gateway typically is Bangor. But if you're visiting Acadia as part of a Maine vacation, you might well choose Portland—160-180 miles south of Bar Harbor, depending on the route—as a springboard for getting to Acadia. Another consideration: Because the airport is served by JetBlue and Southwest, prices tend to be lower.

Airport

Although it keeps expanding, **Portland International Jetport** (PWM, 207/874-8877 or 207/774-7301 automated info, www.portlandjetport.org) remains an easily navigable airport, where all flights leave from and arrive at the same building. Don't be fooled by the "international" in the airport's name: there's only one airline serving Halifax, Canada. Note that, being on the coast, the Portland airport is more subject to fog shutdowns than is Bangor.

Trains

Amtrak's Downeaster (800/872-7245, www.thedowneaster.com) makes daily round-trip runs between Boston's North Station and Brunswick, with stops in Wells, Saco, Old Orchard Beach (May 1-Oct. 31), Portland, and Freeport; from $24 one way.

Amtrak trains from Washington via New York arrive in Boston at South Station, not North Station, and there's no direct link between the two. While you can connect via the T (Boston's subway), it's a real hassle with baggage. Instead, splurge on a taxi or take the bus north from South Station.

There are no train connections to the Acadia region.

Suggested Driving Routes

There are several routes for driving from Portland to Mount Desert Island. Route A follows the four-lane interstate for most of the way, and then finishes up on two-lane roads. Route B is half interstate, half two-lane roads. Route C is almost all on two-lane roads—it's also the most scenic and the slowest route. As with most other Maine auto explorations, it's particularly helpful to use the DeLorme *Maine Atlas and Gazetteer* (www.delorme. com, $20).

For **Route A,** depart Portland north on I-295 and continue to just south of Augusta, where it merges with I-95. Continue on I-95 to Bangor and take exit 182A, merging onto I-395 east toward Holden and Ellsworth (and Acadia). At the end of I-395, you're also at the end of four-lane highways; it's two lanes the rest of the way. Continue on Route 1A to Ellsworth, then Route 3 through Trenton to Mount Desert Island. Allow at least three hours.

For Blue Hill, Deer Isle, and Isle au Haut, from Ellsworth head south on Route 1 (Main St.) through town, then take Route 172 south to Blue Hill, and then Route 15 south to reach Stonington and the boat to Isle au Haut.

For the Schoodic Peninsula, in Ellsworth take Route 1 north to Gouldsboro, and then take Route 186 south to the park.

For **Route B,** start out the same way from Portland, on I-295 to I-95, then just north of Augusta, take exit 113 for Route 3 east. You'll be on two-lane roads the rest of the way. Route 1 doubles as Route 3 from Belfast to the southern end of Ellsworth. Allow at least 3.5 hours.

For the Blue Hill Peninsula, Deer Isle, and Isle au Haut, take Route 15 south from Orland. If your destination is Castine, take Route 175 south from Bucksport.

For the Schoodic Peninsula, stay on Route 1 to Gouldsboro, and then take Route 186.

Route C is the coastal route, where you'll be winding through and skirting small communities the whole way. This route lends itself to (no, requires!) stops—for photos, for exploring, for shopping, for overnights.

Stopping only for lunch and restrooms, you'll still need to allow 4.5-6 hours from Portland to Bar Harbor. And all bets are off on Friday afternoons in summer, when towns such as Wiscasset and Camden can be major bottlenecks. They're lovely towns, though—definitely worth a stop.

To take Route C from Portland, you can start off on two-lane Route 1, or you can go north on four-lane I-295 and I-95 to Brunswick, then cut over when you see the Coastal U.S. 1 sign. Follow Route 1 the rest of the way—through Bath, Wiscasset, Newcastle, Waldoboro, Thomaston, Rockland, Rockport, Camden, Belfast, Searsport, Bucksport, Orland, and the turnoffs for the Blue Hill Peninsula, and on to Ellsworth, where you'll split off onto Route 3 and head for Mount Desert Island, or stay on Route 1 to Gouldsboro and the Schoodic Peninsula.

Between Brunswick and Rockland, down each of the "fingers" east of Route 1, are even more towns and villages—Harpswell, Phippsburg, Georgetown, Boothbay Harbor, Damariscotta, Friendship, and Cushing.

Which brings us to the bottom line: You could spend *weeks* visiting Portland and making your way from there to Acadia.

Car Rentals

Car rentals at the airport include Alamo (207/775-0855 or 877/222-9075, www.alamo. com), Avis (207/874-7501 or 800/230-4898, www.avis.com), Budget (207/874-7501 or 800/527-0700, www.drivebudget.com), Enterprise (207/615-0030, www.enterprise. com), Hertz (207/774-4544 or 800/654-3131, www.hertz.com), and National (207/773-0036 or 877/222-9058, www.nationalcar.com).

Bus Services

Concord Coach Lines (800/639-3317, www. concordcoachlines.com) departs downtown Boston's South Station Transportation Center and Logan Airport for Portland almost hourly from the wee hours of the morning until late at night, making pickups at all Logan airline terminals (on the lower level); $50 round trip.

Most of the buses continue directly to Bangor; a few daily non-express buses continue along the coast to Searsport before turning inland to Bangor. The Portland bus terminal is the Portland Transportation Center, on Thompson Point Road just west of I-295.

Also serving Maine but with far less frequent service is Greyhound (800/231-2222, www.greyhound.com); from $23 one way.

Local Transportation

Portland airport's small size and practically downtown location are big pluses for many travelers. It's simple to get on I-95 headed north if you're heading right out. If you're planning on spending the night, you can be in downtown Portland within 10-15 minutes via taxi.

Accommodations

You'll find most of the major chain hotels in the Greater Portland area. Also here are some lovely B&Bs and excellent independent hotels and inns; see www.visitportland.com. Some offer airport and transportation center shuttle service. Rates vary wildly at the intown Portland hotels below, depending upon the date and demand: A room may be $99 or $399.

Right at the airport, with free shuttles, are Embassy Suites Hotel (1050 Westbrook St., 207/774-2200, www.embassysuites.com), with an indoor heated pool, a restaurant, free full breakfast and afternoon reception, and coin laundry, and the Hilton Garden Inn (145 Jetport Blvd., 207/828-1117, www.hiltongardeninn.com), with an indoor heated pool and coin laundry.

Railroad tycoon John Deering built The Inn at St. John (939 Congress St., 207/773-6481 or 800/636-9127, www.innatstjohn.com) in 1897. The comfortable (if tired), moderately priced 39-room hostelry is a good choice for value-savvy travelers who aren't fussy. The inn welcomes children and dogs ($10). Reimbursement for taxi from the airport or transportation center is available at a fixed price. Most guest rooms have private baths (some are detached). The downside is the lackluster neighborhood—in the evening you'll want to drive or take a taxi when going out.

The **Portland Harbor Hotel** (468 Fore St., 207/775-9090 or 888/798-9090, www.portlandharborhotel.com) is an upscale boutique hotel with restaurant built around a garden courtyard in the desirable Old Port neighborhood. The hotel has a cozy lounge, the restaurant has 24-hour room service, and a free local car service is available.

About 20 minutes north of Portland, the family-run **Casco Bay Inn** (107 U.S. 1, 207/865-4925 or 800/570-4970, www.cascobayinn.com, $150-170) is a budget-friendly motel with spacious guest rooms and a continental breakfast.

Food

Downtown Portland alone has more than 100 restaurants. The city's proximity to fresh foods from both farms and the sea makes it popular with chefs, and its growing immigrant population mean a good variety of international dining too. Do make reservations, whenever possible, and as far in advance as you can, especially for July-August. If you're especially into the food scene, check www.portlandfoodmap.com for a breakdown by cuisine of Portland restaurants, with links to recent reviews. Here are a few favorites.

Ask around and everyone will tell you the best seafood in town is at **Street and Company** (33 Wharf St., Old Port, 207/775-0887, www.streetandcompany.net, 5pm-9:30pm Sun.-Thurs., 5pm-10pm Fri.-Sat., entrées from $18). Fresh, beautifully prepared fish is what you get, often with a Mediterranean flair.

For lobster in the rough, head to **Portland Lobster Company** (180 Commercial St., 207/775-2112, www.portlandlobstercompany.com, 11am-10pm daily). There's a small inside seating area, but it's much more pleasant to sit out on the wharf and watch the excursion boats come and go. Expect to pay in the low $20 range for a one-pound lobster with fries and slaw. Other choices ($8-23) and a kids' menu are available.

Vegan and vegetarian cuisine comes with an Asian accent at **Green Elephant** (608 Congress St., 207/347-3111, www.greenelephantmaine.com, 11:30am-2:30pm Tues.-Sat. and from 5pm daily, $9-14). There's not one shred of meat on the creative menu, but you won't miss it.

Plan well in advance to land a reservation at the city's nationally lauded tables: **Fore Street** (288 Fore St., Old Port, 207/775-2717, www.forestreet.biz, from 5:30pm daily, entrées from $20); **Hugo's** (88 Middle St., at Franklin St., 207/774-8538, www.hugos.net, from 5:30pm Mon.-Sat., entrées from $20); **Five Fifty-Five** (555 Congress St., 207/761-0555, www.fivefifty-five.com, from 5pm daily, entrées from $22); and **Eventide Oyster Co.** (86 Middle St., 207/774-8538, www.eventideoysterco.com, 11am-midnight daily, entrées from $25).

TRAVEL HUB: BOSTON

Boston's Logan Airport is the region's closest international airport, and due to its larger size, it often has fares that are lower than those serving Maine's airports.

Airport

General Edward Lawrence Logan International Jetport (BOS, 800/234-6426 automated info, www.massport.com) has four terminals (A, B, C, E) grouped in a horseshoe pattern. Terminal E handles most, but not all, international flights. Blue-and-white Massport On-Airport Shuttle buses connect the terminals with the Rental Car Center and the MBTA's Airport Station for the subway's Blue Line: During peak midday hours: Bus 22 serves Terminals A and B; Bus 33 serves Terminals C and E. During late morning and late evening off-peak hours, Bus 55 serves all terminals. Shuttle Bus 66 serves all terminals, the subway station, and the Water Transportation Dock; Bus 11 circulates between all terminals, but doesn't go to the subway; Bus 88 serves all terminals and the parking garage. Buses usually run every 5-6 minutes. In addition, the MBTA's Silver

Line SL1 bus provides transportation between all terminals and South Station, with stops en route (free inbound); a free connection is offered to the Red Line (which connects to North Station).

Car Rentals

Car rentals at Logan's Rental Car Center include **Advantage** (617/567-4140, www.advantage.com), **Alamo** (888/826-6893, www.alamo.com), **Avis** (617/568-6600, www.avis.com), **Budget** (617/497-3733, www.drivebudget.com), **Dollar** (866/434-2226, www.dollar.com), **Enterprise** (617/561-4488, www.enterprise.com), **Hertz** (617/568-5200, www.hertz.com), **National** (888/826-6890, www.nationalcar.com), and **Zipcar** (866/494-7227, www.zipcar.com)

Bus

Concord Coach Lines (800/639-3317, www.concordcoachlines.com) departs downtown Boston's South Station Transportation Center and Logan Airport for Portland almost hourly from the wee hours of the morning until late at night, making pickups at all Logan airline terminals (on the lower level). Most of the buses continue directly to Bangor; a few daily non-express buses continue along the coast to Searsport before turning inland to Bangor. Roundtrip fares to Bangor are around $81.

Trains

Amtrak's Downeaster (800/872-7245, www.thedowneaster.com) makes daily round-trip runs between Boston's North Station and Brunswick, with stops in Wells, Saco, Old Orchard Beach (May 1-Oct. 31), Portland, and Freeport. Fares to Portland from $24 one way. From the Portland station, Portland's Metro municipal bus service will take you gratis to downtown Portland; just show your Amtrak ticket stub. Amtrak trains from Washington via New York arrive in Boston at South Station, not North Station, and there's no direct link between the two. While you can connect via the T (Boston's subway), it's a real hassle with baggage.

Instead, splurge on a taxi or take the bus north from South Station.

There are no train connections to the Acadia region.

Suggested Driving Routes

It would be interesting to know the statistics on how many people drive directly from Boston to Acadia National Park without stopping en route. I'd guess not many; perhaps mostly those who have summer homes on Mount Desert Island or nearby. The trip is around 270 miles (about six hours), and not all of the trek is on multilane highway. You can't count on averaging 60 mph when you hit the two-lane roads, especially in midsummer. Even on the 4-6-lane I-95, traffic can choke up at tollbooths. Also, you'll need bathroom breaks, snack breaks, maybe a gas fill-up—and all of Maine south of Acadia has its own attractions to lure you into detours (L.L.Bean and the Freeport outlet shops are major magnets).

But if you're determined to drive from Boston, the best route is I-95, through 18 miles of New Hampshire into Maine and directly toward Bangor (the Maine Turnpike and I-95 are the same road for some stretches). Take exit 182A for U.S. 395 and watch for signs for Route 1A to Ellsworth and then Route 3 to Bar Harbor. Do not take Route 1A to Hampden, or you'll end up on the wrong side of the Penobscot River. For the Schoodic section of the park, when Route 1 and Route 3 split in Ellsworth, take Route 1 north to Gouldsboro, then head south on Route 186. For the Blue Hill Peninsula, Deer Isle, and Isle au Haut, from Ellsworth take Route 1 south to Route 172, then in Blue Hill, Route 15 south to reach Stonington and the boat to Isle au Haut.

BAR HARBOR AIRPORT

The most convenient air access to Acadia is **Hancock County-Bar Harbor Airport** (BHB, 207/667-7329, www.bhbairport.com). It's located 12 miles from downtown Bar Harbor, and despite its name, the airport is located in Trenton, just north of Mount Desert Island. This isn't a big-jet airport, in case you're squeamish about small planes. United Airlines partner Silver Airways (801/401-9100, www.silverairways.com) and Jet Blue partner Cape Air (866/227-3247, www.capeair.com) provide summer service to Bar Harbor from Boston. Flight time from Boston to Trenton is about 80 minutes.

Suggested Driving Routes

This one's quick and easy. Take Route 3 west for Mount Desert Island and Bar Harbor (just take a left when exiting the airport). It's about 1.5 miles or fewer than 5 minutes to the Thompson Island Information Center, 10 miles or 15 minutes to the Hulls Cove Visitor Center, or 12.5 miles or 20 minutes to Bar Harbor.

For the Schoodic section of the park, head east on Route 3 to the junction with Route 1 in Ellsworth, then north on Route 1 to Gouldsboro, then south on Route 186.

It's about 30 miles or 45 minutes to Winter Harbor and the Schoodic section of Acadia.

For the Blue Hill Peninsula, Deer Isle, and Isle au Haut, take Route 3 east through Ellsworth to Route 172, then in Blue Hill, Route 15 south to reach Stonington and the boat to Isle au Haut. It's about 47 miles or 70 minutes to Stonington.

Car Rentals

Hertz (207/667-5017 or 800/654-3131, www.hertz.com) provides on-site rental cars year-round. Enterprise (207/664-2662 or 800/325-8007) operates May 1-October 31. In summer, be sure to reserve a car well in advance.

Bus

The free Island Explorer (207/667-5796, www.exploreacadia.com) stops at the airport late June-early October. Connections serve most of Mount Desert Island, including Bar Harbor, Southwest Harbor, and Acadia National Park.

Getting Around

How will you get around once you get here? Europeans are always shocked at Maine's minimal public transport. Among less-populated areas, Mount Desert Island stands out, thanks to its fare-free, propane-fueled Island Explorer bus system, subsidized by your park fees, Friends of Acadia, L.L.Bean, and local businesses. It serves most of the island as well as Bar Harbor Airport in Trenton. The good news is that it's a very efficient network; the bad news is that it runs only late June-mid-October. Try to come during the Explorer's season, when you can rubberneck all you want from the comfort of a bus seat. No missed turns, no near misses; less pollution, less frazzle. If you've arrived by car, leave it at your lodging and hop on the bus.

The Island Explorer also circulates around the southern end of the Schoodic Peninsula, from Winter Harbor to Prospect Harbor, with a loop through the park. It meets the passenger ferry that connects Bar Harbor to Winter Harbor, so you can visit the Schoodic section of the park from Mount Desert Island without needing a car.

The outer islands are also accessible from Mount Desert Island. Most islands can be explored on foot or bicycle (rentals are available in Bar Harbor, Northeast Harbor, and Southwest Harbor). Passenger ferries from Southwest Harbor and Northeast Harbor cruise to the Cranberry Isles. A state car ferry serves Swans Island and Frenchboro. From Stonington, a passenger ferry connects Deer Isle to Isle au Haut.

You'll need a car to explore the other regions covered in this book: Blue Hill

Peninsula, Deer Isle, the Schoodic region beyond the Island Explorer's reaches, and Ellsworth, although there are some regional bus services with limited schedules.

DRIVING

Almost all gas stations in Maine are self-serve. Pumps are marked "Self"; at those marked "Full," you'll pay more to have an attendant pump the gas for you. Most now allow you to pay at the pump with a credit card. Many also have ATMs, but you'll usually have to pay a bank surcharge.

Important Driving Regulations

Seat belts are mandatory in Maine. Unless posted otherwise, Maine allows right turns at red lights, after you stop and check for oncoming traffic. *Never* pass a stopped school bus in either direction. Maine law also requires drivers to turn on their car's headlights any time the windshield wipers are operating and to keep three feet away from bicyclists. Cell phones must be hands-free.

Roadside Assistance and Road Conditions

Since Maine is enslaved to the automobile, it's not a bad idea for vacationers to carry membership in AAA in case of breakdowns, flat tires, and other car crises. Contact your nearest AAA office or **AAA Northern New England** (425 Marginal Way, Portland, 207/780-6800 or 800/482-7497, www.aaanne. com). The emergency road service number is 800/222-4357.

For real-time information on road conditions, weather, construction, and major delays, dial 511 in Maine or 866/282-7578 from out of state, or visit http://newengland511.org.

Maps

Request a free state map through the **Maine Office of Tourism** (888/624-6345, www.visitmaine.com). Acadia National Park maps are available at the visitors centers. Most local chambers of commerce have free local maps.

The Maine Atlas and Gazetteer

Peek in any Mainer's car and you're likely to see a copy of *The Maine Atlas and Gazetteer*, often referred to as Delorme, its former publisher. Despite an oversize format inconvenient for hiking and kayaking, this 96-page paperbound book just about guarantees that you won't get lost (and if you're good at map reading, it can get you out of a lot of traffic jams). Scaled at one-half inch to the mile, it's revised annually and details back roads and dirt roads and shows elevations, boat ramps, public lands, campgrounds, picnic areas, and trailheads. It's widely available in Maine, but you can also order direct (800/452-5931, https://buy.garmin.com/en-US/US/p/575993/pn/AA-000014-000#). The atlas is $19.95.

BUS SERVICES

Hancock County, including the Blue Hill Peninsula and Deer Isle, Ellsworth and Trenton, Mount Desert Island, and east to Gouldsboro, is served by a patchwork of local transportation systems designed for commuters, seniors, and residents without access to a vehicle. Providing an umbrella for it all is **Downeast Transportation** (207/667-5796, www.downeasttrans.org), with maps and schedules online. You can piece the region together, but each entity acts independently. Check online for fare details, as bus drivers require exact change.

Travel Tips

FOREIGN TRAVELERS

Since 9/11, security has been excruciatingly tight for foreign visitors, with immigration and customs procedures in flux. For current rules, visit https://www.usa.gov/travel-and-immigration. It's wise to make two sets of copies of all paperwork: one to carry separately on your trip and another left with a trusted friend or relative at home.

For information on what can be brought into the United States, check the website of the Customs and Border Protection division of the Department of Homeland Security (www.cbp.gov).

Money and Currency Exchange

Since Maine's Down East (geographically, northeast) coast borders Canada, don't be surprised to see a few Canadian coins mixed in with American ones when you receive change from a purchase. In such cases, Canadian and U.S. quarters are equivalent, although the exchange rate may be different. Most services (including banks) will accept a handful of Canadian coins at par, but you'll occasionally spot No Canadian Currency signs.

Other foreign currencies are not easily convertible (without losing in the exchange) at the small local banks on Mount Desert Island. Acadia National Park has no ATMs within its boundaries, but there are ATMs in Bar Harbor and other communities on Mount Desert Island.

For the most current exchange rate info, visit www.xe.com.

ACCOMMODATIONS

For all accommodations listings, rates are quoted for peak season, which is usually July-August but may extend through foliage season in mid-October. Rates drop, often dramatically, in the shoulder seasons and off-season at many accommodations that remain open.

Especially during peak season, many accommodations require a 2-3-night minimum.

For the best rates, be sure to check Internet specials and ask about packages. Many accommodations also provide discounts for members of travel clubs such as AAA and to seniors, members of the military, and other such groups.

Unless otherwise noted, accommodations listed have private baths.

A note about B&Bs: If you've never stayed at a B&B, begin by putting aside any ideas you may have about them. No two are alike, but all are built on the premise that your experiences will be richer if it's easy to meet other travelers. That said, many provide private tables for breakfast—ask before booking—if you're just not up to being sociable first thing in the morning. The shared breakfast table does provide an opportunity to trade experiences with other guests. Some also provide afternoon refreshments, another opportunity to chat. Many B&Bs are quite exquisite and decorated with antiques and fine art, which means they're often inappropriate for young children. Others are equipped with all the latest techy conveniences. A number of Mount Desert Island B&Bs are in grand historic cottages that survived the fire, providing a taste of that lifestyle and a peek into those rambling homes. Most B&Bs are operated by folks who live here year-round, so they are able to provide recommendations based on their in-depth knowledge. B&Bs, especially, reflect their owners, so expect any of them to be different than described if ownership has changed.

FOOD

Days and hours of operation listed for places serving food are for peak season. These do change often, sometimes even within a season, and it's not uncommon for a restaurant to close early on a quiet night. To avoid

Everyone knows Maine is *the* place for lobster, but there are quite a few other foods that you should sample before you leave.

- **Fiddleheads**: The still-furled tops of the ostrich fern *(Matteuccia struthiopteris)*, sprout along Maine woodland streams in spring. Tasting vaguely like asparagus, fiddleheads appear on many menus, usually as specials, in May and early June. Chefs prepare them in creative ways, from pizza toppings to quiches.

- **Whoopie Pies**: The official Maine snack food comprises two cake-like rounds sandwiching a cream filling. Look for the traditional chocolate rounds at convenience and grocery stores, but you'll find creative flavors at bakeries such as the Mount Desert Bakery and the Pink Pastry Shop, both in Bar Harbor.

- **Maine Wild Blueberries**: Try Maine wild blueberry pancakes topped with wild blueberry syrup at Jordan's Restaurant, Bar Harbor; enjoy a slice of blueberry pie at the Quietside Café or buy a whole pie at Island Bound Treats, both in Southwest Harbor; quench your thirst with Atlantic Brewing Company's Blueberry Ale.

Be sure to try a Maine wild blueberry pie!

- **Maine-made Ice Cream or Gelato: Look for traditional, crazy, seasonal, and must-be-Maine flavors. Get the scoop at** Morton's Moo, Ellsworth (nana's ginger); Pugnuts, Surry (lavender-honey, pumpkin-spice); and MDI Ice Cream (maple walnut, bay of figs), Jordan Pond Ice Cream (blueberry, needham), and Ben & Bill's (lobster, KGB), Bar Harbor.

- **Farmers' Markets**: Find breakfast, lunch, or snacks at a farmers' market—almost every town in the Acadia region has one. In addition to fruits, vegies, and meats, look for maple syrup, smoked salmon, baked goods, cheeses, ethnic specialties, herb vinegars, exotic condiments, honey, jams, and prepared foods.

---

disappointment, call before making a special trip. No matter what the season, reservations are always wise.

ALCOHOL

As in the rest of the country, Maine's minimum drinking age is 21—and bar owners, bartenders, and serving staff can be held legally accountable for serving underage imbibers. If your blood alcohol level is 0.08 percent or higher, you are legally considered to be operating under the influence.

SMOKING

Maine laws ban smoking in restaurants, bars, and lounges as well as enclosed areas of public places, such as shopping malls. Only a handful of bed-and-breakfasts and country inns permit smoking, and increasingly motels, hotels, and resorts are limiting the number of rooms where smoking is permitted. Some accommodations ban smoking anywhere on the property, and most have instituted high fines for smoking in a nonsmoking room. If you're a smoker, motels with direct outdoor access make it easiest to satisfy a craving.

TIME ZONE

All of Maine is in the eastern time zone—the same as New York, Washington DC, Philadelphia, and Orlando. Eastern standard time (EST) runs from the first Sunday in November to the second Sunday in March; eastern daylight time (EDT), one hour later, prevails otherwise. Surprising to many first-time visitors, especially when visiting coastal areas, is how early the sun rises in the morning and how early it sets at night.

If your itinerary also includes Canada, remember that the provinces of New Brunswick and Nova Scotia are on Atlantic time—one hour later than eastern time—so if it's noon in Maine, it's 1pm in these provinces.

TRAVELING BY RV

Bringing a recreational vehicle (RV) to Mount Desert Island and Acadia National Park creates something of a conundrum. No question, the vehicles are convenient for carting kids and gear, but they're a major source of traffic problems on the island, and especially within the park. All of the island's roads are two lanes, and even though the island offers more designated bike lanes than almost anywhere else in Maine, bikes and RVs often have to share the road. RV parking is very limited, and even banned in some locales (such as downtown Bar Harbor). Ideally, you should consider bringing an RV to Acadia only between late June and Columbus Day—when you can park the vehicle in one of the island's dozen commercial campgrounds and travel around the island via the Island Explorer shuttle service.

Incidentally, be aware that the maximum trailer (or RV) length in the national park's two campgrounds is 35 feet, maximum width is 12 feet, and only one vehicle is allowed per site. Neither park campground has water or electrical hookups.

TRAVELING WITH CHILDREN

Acadia National Park isn't a turn-the-toddlers-loose kind of place—there are too many cliffs and other potential hazards—but for school-age youngsters and cooperative teenagers, it's a fabulous family vacation destination. Enroll kids in the Junior Ranger program and participate in the Acadia Quest

scavenger hunt. There are family-oriented kayak tours, park ranger tours, whale-watching trips, hiking and biking trails, carriage rides, and boat excursions. There's saltwater swimming (literally breathtaking for adults, but not for kids) at Sand Beach and freshwater swimming at several lakes and ponds. Incredibly, McDonald's and Burger King haven't invaded Mount Desert Island (although Subway has), but Bar Harbor and other towns have plenty of pizza and lobster joints, as well as two cinemas (one year-round, one seasonal) and several museums for rainy days.

Be forewarned that in-line skates and skateboards are not allowed anywhere within the park. The island communities surrounding the park are small and—especially at the height of summer—congested. In-line skates can come in handy, but use them sensibly; skateboards, on the other hand, are a major hazard in these villages (Bar Harbor does have a skateboard park). Bicycles are not allowed on any of the park's hiking trails, but the car-free carriage trail network is ideal for biking.

How about doing a family volunteer stint? Consider spending a morning on a trail-maintenance crew. You'll help cut back vegetation along trails and carriage roads, rebuild walls or drainages, clean up, and participate in other such activities. Bring water, insect repellent, and a bag lunch for a post-work picnic—the camaraderie is contagious. It's advisable to dress in layers, and do wear sturdy shoes. The nonprofit Friends of Acadia organization chalks up more than 8,000 volunteer hours every year. Check the website (www.friendsofacadia.org) before you come, or call 207/288-3934 when you get here for the recorded schedule of work projects. Volunteer crews meet at park headquarters (Rte. 233/Eagle Lake Rd.).

Earn a BA in Family Fun

Every summer, College of the Atlantic opens its doors to families, offering five sessions of its **Family Nature Camp** (800/597-9500, www.coa.edu/summer). This hands-on, participatory, naturalist-led program provides plenty of fodder for those "What I Did on My Summer Vacation" essays. The weeklong sessions are designed to cure nature-deficit disorder, and they include activities such as whale-watching, tide pool exploration, wildlife-viewing expeditions, and more. Minimum age is five; extended family is welcome. The fee is around $1,000 per person for age 16 and older, $500 per person ages 15 and younger. Camp runs Sunday afternoon through Saturday morning and includes campus lodging (bring your own sheets and towels), meals, and all scheduled field trips.

TRAVELING WITH PETS

In Acadia National Park, dogs are allowed only on leashes not exceeding six feet, and they are banned from several park locations: Sand and Echo Lake Beaches, Duck Harbor Campground on Isle au Haut, park buildings, and any of the "ladder" hiking trails, which have iron foot- and handholds. (When you see the ladder trails, you'll understand why pets are forbidden.) Don't take pets on the park ranger tours, and do not leave your dog unattended, especially in an RV at one of the campgrounds. Be considerate of your pet as well as of other visitors. Of course, service dogs are exempted from the pet rules.

To make the best of a visit to Acadia—so you can hike and bike and kayak without worrying about your pet—you might want to reserve kennel space for part of your stay. Mount Desert Island has the Acadia Woods Kennel (Crooked Rd., Bar Harbor, 207/288-9766, www.acadiawoodskennel.com), which offers both overnight and day boarding. In July-August, be sure to call well in advance for a reservation. If you'd prefer to have a dog-sitter come to your hotel or campground, contact Wendy Scott at Bark Harbor (150 Main St., Bar Harbor, 207/288-0404, www.barkharbor.com). She'll recommend someone who can help. If at all possible, make arrangements before you arrive, and when you get here, visit the store—a Toys R Us for pet owners. Bark Harbor maintains a list of pet-friendly restaurants and accommodations. Another resource is *Downeast Dog News* (www.downeastdognews.com), a free monthly tabloid available at pet-friendly locations and also online. It has a calendar of events.

SENIORS

Age does have its privileges. U.S. citizens and permanent residents age 62 or older can purchase a Senior Pass, valid for admission to more than 300 national parks (including Acadia), historic sites, and monuments for $80, a one-time fee. It also entitles you to half-price camping. Many lodgings and many attractions and sights offer discounts to seniors. It never hurts to ask. Age varies; some begin their discounts for those as young as 55 (egad!). In any case, you'll need proof of age, such as a driver's license or passport.

Age also often brings achy knees and hips or other such maladies. Many of the accommodations in this area are small inns and B&Bs. If you have mobility problems or difficulty carrying your luggage up a flight of stairs or two, you'll want to make sure that your lodging has either first-floor rooms or elevators.

ACCESSIBILITY

Acadia National Park has been conscientious about providing as much accessibility as possible to people with disabilities. For a start, the Hulls Cove Visitors Center (the park's spring, summer, and fall information center) has a special parking area for easy wheelchair access, bypassing the 52 steps from the main parking area. When you get into the center, request an Access Pass, which provides free lifetime entry to any national park and half-price camping at park sites for any citizen or permanent resident who is permanently disabled (if you've broken your leg or have another temporary disability, you're not eligible). The passport is also available at the park's two campgrounds, at park headquarters, and at the Sand Beach and Bar Harbor Village Green ticket booths.

Also at the Hulls Cove Visitors Center,

pick up a copy of the *Acadia National Park Accessibility Guide,* which provides detailed accessibility information—including parking, entry, restrooms, pay phones, and water fountains—for the park's visitors centers, the two campgrounds, picnic areas, beaches, and gift shops as well as carriage rides, some boat cruises, and nonpark museums on Mount Desert Island. A few of the park ranger programs are wheelchair-accessible, as are all of the evening programs at the park's two campgrounds. Access to the carriage road network depends on your ability (there are some steep grades); even the easiest trails may require some assistance. Each of the Island Explorer shuttle buses—operating late June-Columbus Day—has room for at least one wheelchair.

Parking lots at some of the park's most popular locales (such as Thunder Hole, the Cadillac Mountain summit, and Jordan Pond House) have designated accessible parking spaces.

To plan your Acadia trip in advance, order an Access Pass online, then download the accessibility information from the park's website (www.nps.gov/acad/accessibility.htm). If you're reserving a campsite at the Blackwoods Campground online (www.recreation.gov), you'll need the Access Pass beforehand.

For additional accessibility information, call 207/288-3338 (voice) or 207/288-8800 (TTY). For emergencies in the park or elsewhere on Mount Desert Island, dial 911.

While newer properties must meet the strict standards of the Americans with Disabilities Act, older and historic lodgings and restaurants often don't have accessible rooms or facilities. It's wise to ask detailed questions pertaining to your needs before booking a room or making a restaurant reservation.

Health and Safety

There's too much to do and see in Acadia National Park to spend even a few hours laid low by illness or mishap. Be sensible—get enough sleep, wear sunscreen and appropriate clothing, know your limits and don't take foolhardy risks, heed weather and warning signs, carry water and snacks while hiking, don't overindulge in food or alcohol, always tell someone where you're going, and watch your step. If you're traveling with children, quadruple your caution.

Even though Maine's public transportation network is woefully inadequate, and the crime rate is one of the lowest in the nation, it's still risky to hitchhike or pick up hitchhikers.

MEDICAL CARE
In the event of any emergency, dial 911.

Blue Hill and Deer Isle
Northern Light Blue Hill Memorial
Hospital (57 Water St., Blue Hill, 207/374-3400, emergency 207/374-2836).

Acadia
Northern Light Maine Coast Hospital (50 Union St., Ellsworth, 207/667-5311, emergency 207/664-5340); **Mount Desert Island Hospital** (10 Wayman Lane, Bar Harbor, 207/288-5081).

Alternative Health Care
Nontraditional health-care options are available on Mount Desert Island as well as on the Blue Hill Peninsula and Deer Isle. After some overambitious hiking or biking expeditions, a massage might be in order. Holistic practitioners as well as certified massage therapists and acupuncturists are listed in the yellow pages of local phone books, and most accommodations can make referrals. Also check the bulletin boards and talk to the managers at

local health-food stores. They always know where to find homeopathic doctors.

Pharmacies

The major pharmacy chain in and near Acadia is **Walgreen's**. Hannaford supermarkets also have pharmacy departments, and some towns have an independent drug store. All carry prescription and over-the-counter medications. There are no round-the-clock pharmacies. Some independent pharmacists post emergency numbers on their doors and will go out of their way to help, but your best bet for a middle-of-the-night medication crisis is the hospital emergency room.

If you take regular medications, be sure to pack an adequate supply as well as a new prescription in case you lose your medicine or unexpectedly need a refill. It's also wise to travel with a list of any prescriptions taken, in case of emergency.

AFFLICTIONS

Insect Bites and Tick-Borne Diseases

If you plan to spend any time outdoors in Maine April-November, take precautions, especially when hiking, to avoid annoying insect bites and especially the diseases carried by tiny deer ticks (not the larger dog ticks; they don't carry it): **Lyme disease, anaplasmosis,** and **babesiosis. Powassan,** carried by the woodchuck tick, is so far extremely rare. Mosquito-borne **eastern equine encephalitis** has been found in mosquitoes twice in Maine, once in 2014 and once in 2015. The type of mosquitoes carrying the Zika virus are not in Maine. After any hike or prolonged time outdoors in the woods, thick grass, overgrown bushes, or piles of brush or leaves, check for ticks—especially behind the knees and in the armpits, navel, and groin.

For more information, consult the Maine Medical Center's Vector-Borne Disease Laboratory's **Ticks in Maine: What Do I Need to Know** (www.ticksinmaine.com) or contact the **Maine Center for Disease Control** (800/821-5821, www.mainepublichealth.gov).

Rabies

If you're bitten by any animal, especially one acting suspiciously, head for the nearest hospital emergency room. For statewide information about rabies, contact the **Maine Center for Disease Control** (800/821-5821, www. mainepublichealth.gov).

Allergies

If your medical history includes extreme allergies to shellfish or beestings, you know the risks of eating a lobster or wandering around a wildflower meadow. However, if you come from a landlocked area and are new to crustaceans, you might not be aware of the potential hazard. Statistics indicate that less than 2 percent of adults have a severe shellfish allergy, but for those victims, the reaction can set in quickly. Immediate treatment is needed to keep the airways open. If you have a history of severe allergic reactions to *anything,* be prepared when you come to the Maine coast dreaming of lobster feasts. Ask your doctor for a prescription for EpiPen (epinephrine), a preloaded, single-use syringe containing 0.3 mg of the drug—enough to tide you over until you can get to a hospital.

Seasickness

If you're planning to do any boating in Maine—particularly sailing—you'll want to be prepared. (Being prepared may in fact keep you from succumbing, since fear of seasickness just about guarantees you'll get it.) Talk to a pharmacist or doctor about your options. Alternative precautions that may be effective include acupressure wrist bands and ginger.

Hypothermia and Frostbite

Wind and weather can shift dramatically in Maine, especially at higher elevations, creating prime conditions for contracting hypothermia and frostbite. At risk are hikers, swimmers, canoeists, kayakers, sailors, skiers, even cyclists.

To prevent hypothermia and frostbite, dress in layers and remove or add them as needed. Wool, waterproof fabrics (such as Gore-Tex), and synthetic fleece (such as Polartec) are the best fabrics for repelling dampness. Polyester fleece lining wicks excess moisture away from your body. Especially in winter, always cover your head, since body heat escapes quickly through the head; a ski mask will protect ears and nose. Wear wool- or fleece-lined gloves and wool socks.

Special Considerations During Hunting Season

During Maine's fall hunting season (Oct.-Thanksgiving)—and especially during the November deer season—walk or hike only in wooded areas marked No Hunting, No Trespassing, or Posted. And even if an area is closed to hunters, don't decide to explore the woods during deer or moose season without wearing a blaze-orange (eye-poppingly fluorescent) jacket or vest. If you take your dog along, be sure it wears an orange vest too. Hunting is illegal on Sunday.

During hunting season, moose and deer are on the move and are made understandably skittish by the hunters invading their turf. Moose are primarily found inland, but deer are everywhere, and even the occasional moose strays into coastal areas of Maine. At night, particularly in wooded areas, these huge creatures often end up alongside or on the roads, so ratchet up your defensive-driving skills. Reduce your normal speed, use high beams when there's no oncoming traffic, and remain extra alert. In a moose-versus-car encounter, no one wins, and human fatalities are common. An encounter between a deer and a car may be less dangerous to the humans (although the deer usually dies), but some damage to the vehicle is inevitable.

Sunstroke

Since Acadia National Park lies above the 44th parallel, sunstroke is not a major problem, but don't push your luck by spending an entire day frying on Sand Beach or the granite shoreline. Not only do you risk sunstroke and dehydration, but you're also asking for skin cancer down the road. Early in the season, slather yourself, and especially children, with plenty of PABA-free sunblock (PABA can cause skin rashes and eruptions, even on people not abnormally sensitive). If you're in the water a long time, slather on some more. When you're hiking, carry water.

Information and Services

MONEY

Typical banking hours are 9am-3pm Monday-Friday, occasionally with later hours on Friday. Drive-up windows at many banks tend to open as much as an hour earlier and stay open an hour or so after lobbies close. Some banks also maintain Saturday-morning hours. Automated teller machines (ATMs) are found throughout Maine.

Credit Cards and Travelers Checks

Bank credit cards have become so preferred and so prevalent that it's nearly impossible to rent a car or check into a hotel without one. MasterCard and Visa are the most widely accepted in Maine, and Discover and American Express are the next most popular; Carte Blanche, Diners Club, and EnRoute (Canadian) lag far behind. Be aware, however, that small restaurants (including lobster pounds), shops, and bed-and-breakfasts off the beaten track might not accept credit cards or nonlocal personal checks; you may need to settle your account with cash.

Taxes

Maine charges a 5.5 percent sales tax on general

Coronavirus in Acadia National Park

At the time of writing, Acadia National Park was significantly impacted by the effects of the coronavirus, but the situation was constantly evolving.

Now more than ever, Moon encourages its readers to be courteous and ethical in their travel. We ask travelers to be respectful to residents, and mindful of the evolving situation in their chosen destination when planning their trip.

BEFORE YOU GO

- For information on **Maine's requirements** for visitors, https://www.maine.gov/dhhs/mecdc/infectious-disease/epi/airborne/coronavirus/travel.shtml#quarantine.

- For answers to **frequently asked questions,** see https://www.maine.gov/dhhs/mecdc/infectious-disease/epi/airborne/documents/frequently-asked-questions.pdf.

- Visit the **National Park Service's website** for information about park closures and restrictions: https://www.nps.gov/planyourvisit/alerts.htm.

- If you plan to fly, **check with your airline** and the destination's health authority for updated travel requirements (the **Centers for Disease Control and Prevention** website, www.cdc.gov, is very useful).

- Check the website of any museums and other venues you wish to patronize to confirm that they're open, if their hours have been adjusted, and to learn about any specific visitation requirements, such as mandatory **reservations** or limited occupancy.

- Ask **accommodations** about any changes to housekeeping practices and meal service.

- Pack **hand sanitizer, a thermometer,** and plenty of **face masks.** Consider packing snacks, bottled water, or even a cooler to limit the number of stops as you explore the area.

- Assess the risk of entering **crowded spaces,** joining **tours,** and taking **public transit.**

- Expect **general disruptions.** Events may be postponed or cancelled, and some tours and venues may require reservations, enforce limits on the number of guests, be operating during different hours than the ones listed, or be closed entirely.

purchases and services; 8 percent on prepared foods, candy, and alcohol; 9 percent on lodging/camping; and 10 percent on auto rentals.

Tipping

Tip 15-20 percent of the pre-tax bill in restaurants. Note that the tip is often added to the bill for groups of six or more. Taxi drivers expect a 15 percent tip; airport porters expect at least $1 per bag, depending on the difficulty of the job. The usual tip for housekeeping services in accommodations is $2-5 per person, per night. Some accommodations add resort or service fees; ask before booking and scrutinize bills before adding a tip.

TOURISM INFORMATION

The **Maine Office of Tourism** (888/624-6345, www.visitmaine.com) has an excellent website with articles, photos, and links to tourism-related businesses. The state also operates **information centers** in Calais, Fryeburg, Hampden, Houlton, Kittery, and Yarmouth. These are excellent places to visit to stock up on brochures, pick up a map, ask for advice, and use restrooms and Wi-Fi.

The **Maine Tourism Association** (207/623-0363, www.mainetourism.com) also has information and publishes *Maine Invites You* and a free state map.

PHONE AND INTERNET

Maine still has only one telephone area code, 207. For directory assistance, dial 411.

Cell phone towers are now sprinkled pretty much throughout Maine; only a few pockets—mostly down peninsulas and in remote valleys and hollows—are out of cell-phone range. Of course, reception also varies by carrier, and getting it often requires doing the cell-phone hokey pokey—putting your left arm out, your right leg in, and so on to find the strongest signal.

Internet access is available widely.

Resources

Glossary

alewives: herring

ayuh: yes

barrens: as in "blueberry barrens," fields where wild blueberries grow

beamy: wide (as in a boat or a person)

beans: shorthand for the traditional Saturday-night meal, which always includes baked beans

blowdown: a forest area leveled by wind

blowing a gale: very windy

camp: a vacation house (small or large), usually on fresh water and/or in the woods

chance: serendipity or luck (as in "open by appointment or by chance")

chicken dressing: chicken manure

chowder: (pronounced "chowdah") soup made with lobster, clams, or fish, or a combination thereof; lobster version sometimes called "lobster stew"

chowderhead: mischief- or troublemakers, usually interchangeable with "idiot"

coneheads: tourists (because of their presumed penchant for ice cream)

cottage: a vacation house (anything from a bungalow to a mansion), usually on salt water

culch: (also *cultch*) stuff, the contents of attics, basements, and some flea markets

cull: a discount lobster, usually minus a claw

cunnin': cute (usually describing a baby or small child)

dinner: (pronounced "dinnah") the noon meal

dinner pail: lunchbox

dite: a very small amount

dooryard: the yard near a house's main entrance

downcellar: in the basement

Down East: with the prevailing wind; the old coastal sailing route from Boston to Nova Scotia

dry-ki: driftwood, usually remnants from the logging industry

ell: a residential structural section that links a house and a barn; formerly a popular location for the "summer kitchen," to spare the house from woodstove heat

exercised: upset; angry

fiddleheads: unopened ostrich fern fronds, a spring delicacy

finest kind: top quality; good news; an expression of general approval; also, a term of appreciation

flatlander: a person not from Maine, often someone from the Midwest

floatplane: a small plane equipped with pontoons for landing on water; the same aircraft often becomes a ski plane in winter.

flowage: a water body created by damming, usually beaver handiwork (also called "beaver flowage")

frappé: a thick drink containing milk, ice cream, and flavored syrup, as opposed to a milk shake, which does not include ice cream (but beware: a frappé offered in other parts of the United States is an ice cream sundae topped with whipped cream!)

from away: not native to Maine

galamander: a wheeled contraption formerly used to transport quarry granite to building sites or to boats for onward shipment

gore: a sliver of land left over from inaccurate boundary surveys. Maine has several gores; Hibberts Gore, for instance, has a population of one.

got done: quit a job; was let go

harbormaster: local official who monitors water traffic and assigns moorings; often a very political job

hardshell: lobster that hasn't molted yet (more scarce, thus more pricey in summer)

hod: wooden "basket" used for carrying clams

ice-out: the departure of winter ice from ponds, lakes, rivers, and streams; many communities have ice-out contests, awarding prizes for guessing the exact time of ice-out, in April or May.

Italian: long, soft bread roll sliced on top and filled with peppers, onions, tomatoes, sliced meat, and black olives and sprinkled with olive oil, salt, and pepper; veggie versions are available.

jimmies: chocolate sprinkles, like those on an ice cream cone

lobster car: a large floating crate for storing lobsters

Maine Guide: a member of the Maine Professional Guides Association, trained and tested for outdoor and survival skills; also called a Registered Maine Guide

market price: restaurant menu term for "the going rate," usually referring to the price of lobster or clams

molt: what a lobster does when it sheds its shell for a larger one; the act of molting is called "ecdysis" (as a stripper is an ecdysiast).

money tree: a collection device for a monetary gift

nasty neat: extremely meticulous

near: stingy

notional: stubborn, determined

off island: the mainland, to an islander

place: another word for a house (as in "Herb Pendleton's place")

pot: trap, as in "lobster pot"

public landing: see "town landing"

rake: hand tool for harvesting blueberries

rusticator: a summer visitor, particularly in bygone days

scooch: (or scootch) to squat; to move sideways

sea smoke: heavy mist rising off the water when the air temperature suddenly becomes much colder than the ocean temperature

select: a lobster with claws intact

selectmen: the elected men and women who handle local affairs in small communities; the First Selectman chairs meetings. In some towns, "people from away" have proposed substituting a gender-neutral term, but in most cases the effort has failed.

shedder: a lobster with a new (soft) shell; molting generally occurs in July-August, making shedders more common then, thus less expensive than hardshells.

shire town: county seat

shore dinner: the works: chowder, clams, lobster, and sometimes corn on the cob; usually the most expensive item on a menu

short: a small, illegal-size lobster

slumgullion: tasteless food; a mess

snapper: an undersize illegal lobster

soda: cola, root beer, etc., referred to as "pop" in other parts of the country

softshell: see *shedder*

some: very (as in "some hot")

spleeny: overly sensitive

steamers: clams (before or after they are steamed)

sternman: a lobsterman's helper

summer complaint: a tourist

supper: (pronounced "suppah") evening meal, eaten by Mainers around 5pm-6pm, as opposed to flatlanders and summer people, who eat dinner around 7pm-9pm

tad: slightly; a little bit

thick-o'-fog: zero-visibility fog

to home: at home

tomalley: a lobster's green insides; considered a delicacy by some

town landing: shore access; often a park or a parking lot, next to a wharf or boat-launch ramp

upattic: in the attic

whoopie pie: a high-fat cake-like snack that only kids and dentists could love

wicked cold!: frigid

wicked good!: excellent

williwaws: uncomfortable feeling

Suggested Reading

CARRIAGE ROADS

Abrell, D. *A Pocket Guide to the Carriage Roads of Acadia National Park.* 3rd ed. Camden, ME: Down East Books, 2011. A dozen excellent carriage-road loops ranging 1.2-11.1 miles for hiking, biking, or horseback riding—presented in a portable format.

Roberts, A. R. *Mr. Rockefeller's Roads.* 2nd ed. Camden, ME: Down East Books, 2012. The fascinating story behind Acadia's scenic carriage roads, written by the granddaughter of John D. Rockefeller Jr., the man who created them.

CHILDREN

Dohmen, E. L. *Rock Friends of Acadia: A Treasure Hunt for Children and Adults.* Bar Harbor, ME, 2015. An illustrated guide to finding rock formations throughout Acadia National Park.

Evans, Lisa Gollin. *An Outdoor Family Guide to Acadia National Park.* Seattle: Mountaineers books, 1997. An excellent resource for hiking, biking, and paddling with kids in Acadia.

Ogintz, Eileen. *The Kid's Guide to Acadia National Park.* Lanham, MD: Down East Books, 2019. A leading family travel expert shares kid-tested tips about exploring the park along with games and quizzes.

Robson, Gary D. *Who Pooped in the Park.* Helena, MT: Farcountry Press, 2006. A sweet story centered on a family exploring the park and learning about the animals through scat and tracks.

Rowan, Hope. *Ten Days in Acadia: A Kids' Hiking Guide to Mount Desert Island.* Yarmouth, ME: Islandport Press. 2017. This fabulous guide written for ages 8-12 doubles as a journal and includes trail maps, illustrated field notes, and what to look for along the way.

Scheid, M. *Discovering Acadia: A Guide for Young Naturalists.* Bar Harbor, ME: Acadia Publishing, 1987. A delightful book for children—as well as the adults who accompany them.

HISTORY

Collier, S. F. *Mount Desert Island and Acadia National Park: An Informal History.* Revised ed. Camden, ME: Down East Books, 1978. An oft-cited source for island and park history.

Dorr, G. *The Story of Acadia National Park.* 5th ed. Bar Harbor, ME: Acadia Publishing, 2012 (reprinted, combining 1942 and 1948 originals). How Acadia began, and the roller-coaster struggles involved, as related by George Dorr, "the Father of Acadia."

Epp, R. H. *Creating Acadia National Park: The Biography of George Bucknam Dorr.* Bar Harbor, ME: Friends of Acadia, 2016. A meticulously researched volume about the Father of Acadia.

Duncan, R. F., E. G. Barlow, K. Bray, and C. Hanks. *Coastal Maine: A Maritime History.* Woodstock, VT: Countryman Press, 2002. Updated version of the classic work.

Helfrich, G. W., and G. O'Neil. *Lost Bar Harbor.* Camden, ME: Down East Books, 2015 reissue. Fascinating collection of historic photographs of classic turn-of-the-20th-century "cottages," most obliterated by Bar Harbor's Great Fire of 1947.

Judd, R. W., E. A. Churchill, and J. W. Eastman, eds. *Maine: The Pine Tree State from Prehistory to the Present.* Orono: University of Maine Press, 1995. The best available Maine history, with excellent historical maps.

Morison, S. E. *The Story of Mount Desert Island.* Yarmouth, ME: Islandport Press, 2011 (reprint of 1960 book). A quirky, entertaining little history—from Native Americans to 20th-century Americans—by the late maritime historian, a longtime Mount Desert summer resident.

Schmidtt, C. *Historic Acadia National Park: The Stories Behind On of America's Great Treasures.* Lanham, MD: Lyons Press, 2016. Acadia's story told through its natural, social, and geological history.

Shettleworth, E. G., and L. Vandenberg. *Bar Harbor's Gilded Century: Opulence to Ashes.* Camden, ME: Down East Books, 2009. A pictorial history of Bar Harbor before the Great Fire; includes 250 photos, some not published previously.

Wilmerding, J. *The Artist's Mount Desert: American Painters on the Maine Coast.* Princeton, NJ: Princeton University Press, 1995. A respected art historian's perspective on Mount Desert's magnetic attraction to such American artists as Thomas Cole, Frederic Church, and Fitz Hugh Lane.

Workman, A. K. *Schoodic Point: History on the Edge of Acadia National Park.* Charleston, SC: History Press, 2014. Examines the history of Schoodic Point from settlement through the creation and evolution of the park.

NATURAL HISTORY AND NATURE GUIDES

Braun, Duane, and Ruth Braun, *Guide to the Geology of Mount Desert Island and Acadia National Park.* Berkeley, CA: North Atlantic Books, 2016. A richly illustrated guide to the region's geology, including explanations, history, and self-guided field trips.

Butcher, Russell D. *Field Guide to Acadia National Park, Maine.* Lanham, MD: Taylor Trade Publishing, 2005. Revised ed. A detailed, illustrated guide to Acadia's flora, fauna, and geology, including some trail descriptions with what to look for along the way.

Conkling, P. W. *Islands in Time: A Natural and Cultural History of the Islands of the Gulf of Maine.* 3rd ed. Rockland, ME: Island Institute, 2011. A thoughtful overview by the president of Maine's Island Institute.

Gilman, Richard A., C. A. Chapman, T. V. Lowell, and H. W. Burns. *The Geology of Mount Desert Island.* Maine Geological Society, 1988. An introduction to the "geological processes which formed the island's spectacular scenery."

Gregory, Linda L., Sally C. Rooney, Jill E. Weber, and Glen H. Mittelhauser. *The Plants of Acadia National Park.* Orono: University of Maine Press, 2010. A comprehensive guide to the plants found in and around Acadia National Park.

Grierson, R. G. *Acadia National Park: Wildlife Watcher's Guide.* Minocqua, WI: NorthWord Press, 1995. You're not likely to see any creature in the park that isn't mentioned in this handy guide.

Kavanaugh, J. *Acadia National Park Wildlife: A Folding Pocket Guide to Familiar Species.* Phoenix: Waterford Press, 2017. An easy-to-carry laminated guide.

Newlin, William V. P., K. S. Cline, R. Briggs, A. Addison Namnoum, and B. Ciccotelli. *The College of the Atlantic Guide to the Lakes & Ponds of Mt. Desert.* Bar Harbor, ME: College of the Atlantic Press, 2013. Tips for exploring Mount Desert Island's more than 25 lakes and 40 streams.

Perrin, S. *Acadia's Native Flowers, Fruits, and Wildlife*. Fort Washington, PA: Eastern National, 2001. This handy reference to the park's flora and fauna runs chronologically through three seasons (spring-fall). It's not a complete field guide but rather a selective collection of photos in a portable square format.

OFFSHORE ISLANDS
Cranberry Isles
Eliot, C. W. *John Gilley: One of the Forgotten Millions*. Bar Harbor, ME: Acadia Press, 1989 (reprint of 1904 book). Poignant story of 19th-century life in the Cranberries, as told by the Harvard president who was instrumental in the establishment of Acadia.

Frenchboro (Long Island)
Lunt, D. L. *Hauling by Hand: The Life and Times of a Maine Island*. Frenchboro, ME: Islandport Press, 1999. A sensitive history of Frenchboro (aka Long Island), eight miles offshore, written by an eighth-generation islander.

Isle au Haut
Greenlaw, L. *The Lobster Chronicles: Life on a Very Small Island*. New York: Hyperion, 2002. Essays on Isle au Haut life, warts and all, by the talented writer and lobsterwoman who first gained fame as a swordfishing skipper in *The Perfect Storm*.

Pratt, C. *Here on the Island*. New York: Harper & Row, 1974. An appealing, realistic portrait of life on Isle au Haut several decades ago.

RECREATION GUIDES
General
Monkman, J., and M. Monkman. *AMC's Outdoor Adventures Acadia National Park: Your Guide to the Best Hiking, Biking, and Paddling*. Boston: Appalachian Mountain Club

Books, 2017. Well-planned and well-written guide, in the Appalachian Mountain Club tradition, including a foldout map.

Biking
Minutolo, A. *Biking on Mount Desert Island*. 2nd ed. Camden, ME: Down East Books, 2012. A third-generation islander's expert advice; this book covers the whole island, not just the park.

Birding
Duchesne, B. *Maine Birding Trail: The Official Guide to More Than 260 Accessible Sites*. Camden, ME: Down East Books, 2009. Authorized guide to the Maine Birding Trail.

Lovitch, D., editor. *Birdwatching in Maine: A Site Guide*. Lebanon, NH: University Press of New England, 2017. Organized by county, this illustrated and comprehensive guide provides detailed info on sighting common as well as rare species.

Pierson, E. C., J. E. Pierson, and P. D. Vickery. *A Birder's Guide to Maine*. Camden, ME: Down East Books, 1996. An expanded version of *A Birder's Guide to the Coast of Maine*. A valuable resource for any ornithologist, novice or expert, for exploring Acadia and the rest of Maine.

Climbing
Simons, G. *Rock Climbs of Acadia*. Acadia Rock Press, 2015. The bible for climbers, with route descriptions for nearly 300 climbs. Available as a book or an app

Cruising Guides
Bilder, J. *A Visual Cruising Guide to the Maine Coast*. Camden, ME: Ragged Mountain Press, 2006. A spiral-bound guide, with 180 aerial photos providing visual guidance.

Taft, H., J. Taft, and C. Rindlaub. *A Cruising Guide to the Maine Coast.* 6th ed. Peaks Island, ME: Diamond Pass Publishing, 2017. Don't even consider cruising coastal Acadia without this thoroughly researched volume.

Hiking

Kish, C. *Maine Mountain Guide: AMC's Comprehensive Guide to Hiking Trails of Maine, Featuring Baxter State Park and Acadia National Park.* 11th ed. Boston: Appalachian Mountain Club Books, 2018. The definitive statewide resource for going vertical, in a handy format. Author lives on Mount Desert Island.

Kong, D., and D. Ring. *Hiking Acadia National Park.* 3rd ed. Guilford, CT: Falcon Guides, 2016. Excellent hiking guide, with useful, accurate descriptions of 94 trails on Mount Desert Island, Isle au Haut, and the Schoodic Peninsula. The authors include a list of their 25 favorites and advocate the Leave No Trace philosophy.

St. Germain Jr., T. A. *A Walk in the Park: Acadia's Hiking Guide.* 10th ed. Bar Harbor, ME: Parkman Publications, 2015. The book includes plenty of historical tidbits about the trails, the park, and the island. Part of the proceeds go to the Acadia Trails Forever campaign to maintain and rehabilitate the park's trails. The book is updated regularly; ask for the most recent edition.

Kayaking and Canoeing

Brechlin, E. D. *Paddling Acadia.* Camden, ME: Down East Books, 2013. Brechlin, a Registered Maine Guide and island resident, recommends 18 places to paddle your kayak or canoe—in salt water as well as freshwater ponds and lakes. This little handbook (72 pages) includes locations for parking and launching areas as well as route maps.

The Maine Island Trail Guidebook. Rockland, ME: Maine Island Trail Association, updated annually. Available only with MITA membership (www.mita.org, annual dues $45); details access to dozens of islands along the water trail, including many in the Acadia region between Schoodic Point and Deer Isle.

REFERENCE

The Maine Atlas and Gazetteer. Yarmouth, ME: Garmin, updated annually. You'll be hard put to get lost on the roads in this region or anywhere else in Maine if you're carrying this essential volume with full-page (oversize format) topographical maps with GPS grids.

Internet Resources

ACADIA NATIONAL PARK INFORMATION

Acadia National Park
www.nps.gov/acad
A comprehensive site with extensive, detailed information about Acadia. Download natural and cultural history articles, accessibility charts, ranger programs, select hiking trails, FAQs, park maps, and hints for avoiding crowds Also included is a link for online reservations at park campgrounds.

Friends of Acadia
www.friendsofacadia.org
A very active nonprofit organization that acts as a financial safety net for the park and also organizes frequent volunteer work parties for various maintenance projects in the park. Its newsletters are posted on the website, as is information about where and when you can volunteer.

Island Explorer Bus System
www.exploreacadia.com
Everything you need to know about using the propane-fueled, fare-free Island Explorer buses (late June-early Oct. on Mount Desert, late June-early Sept. on the Schoodic Peninsula). Included are suggestions for getting to Mount Desert without a car as well as for exploring the park with the bus.

Schoodic Institute
www.schoodicinstitute.org
An active nonprofit supporting science and research on Acadia National Park's Schoodic section. Sponsors lectures, ranger-led programs, and other activities.

GENERAL INFORMATION

State of Maine
www.maine.gov
Everything you wanted to know about Maine and then some, with links to all government departments and Maine-related sites. Buy a fishing license online, reserve a state park campsite, or check the fall foliage conditions via the site's Leaf Cam. (You can also access foliage info at www.mainefoliage.com, where you can sign up for weekly email foliage reports in Sept. and early Oct.) Also listed is information on accessible arts and recreation.

Maine Office of Tourism
www.visitmaine.com
The biggest and most useful of all Maine-related tourism sites, with sections for where to visit, where to stay, things to do, trip planning, packages, and search capabilities as well as lodging specials and a comprehensive calendar of events.

Maine Tourism Association
www.mainetourism.com
Find lodging, camping, restaurants, attractions, services, and more as well as links for weather, foliage, transportation planning, and chambers of commerce.

Maine Archives and Museums
www.mainemuseums.org
Information on and links to museums, archives, historical societies, and historic sites in Maine.

Maine Department of Agriculture
www.getrealmaine.com
Information on all things agricultural, including fairs, farmers markets, farm vacations, places to buy Maine foods, berry- and apple-picking sites, and more.

Maine Travel Maven
www.mainetravelmaven.com
Moon Acadia National Park author Hilary Nangle's site for keeping readers updated on what's happening throughout the state.

PARKS AND RECREATION

Bicycle Coalition of Maine
www.bikemaine.org
Tons of information for bicyclists, including routes, shops, events, organized rides, and much more.

Department of Conservation, Maine Bureau of Parks and Lands
www.parksandlands.com
Information on state parks, public reserved lands, and state historic sites as well as details on facilities such as campsites, picnic areas, and boat launches. Make state campground reservations online.

Island Institute
www.islandinstitute.org
The institute serves as a clearinghouse and advocate for Maine's islands; the website provides links to the major year-round islands.

Maine Audubon
www.maineaudubon.org
Information about Maine Audubon's environmental centers statewide. Activity and program schedules are included.

Maine Birding Trail
www.mainebirdingtrail.com
A must-visit site for anyone interested in learning more about birding in Maine; includes news, checklists, events, tours, and more.

Maine Campground Owners Association
www.campmaine.com
Find private campgrounds statewide.

Maine Department of Inland Fisheries and Wildlife
www.state.me.us/ifw
Info on wildlife, hunting, fishing, snowmobiling, and boating.

Maine Island Trail Association
www.mita.org
The mission and activities of MITA as well as information on becoming a member and receiving the annual guidebook to the island trail.

Maine Land Trust Network
www.mltn.org
Maine has dozens of land trusts statewide, managing lands that provide opportunities for hiking, walking, canoeing, kayaking, and other such activities.

Maine Professional Guides Association
www.maineguides.org
Find Registered Maine Guides for sporting adventures, including sea kayaking, hunting, fishing, and recreation (such as canoeing trips and wildlife safaris).

Maine Trail Finder
www.mainetrailfinder.com
Searchable database of trails statewide with interactive maps, descriptions, images, and trip reports.

The Nature Conservancy
www.nature.org/en-us/about-us/where-we-work/united-states/maine
Information about Maine preserves, field trips, and events.

TRANSPORTATION

Explore Maine
www.exploremaine.org
Explore Maine has information on and links to airports, rail service, bus service, automobile travel, and ferries as well as links to other key travel-planning sites.

511 New England
http://newengland511.org
Provides real-time information about major delays, accidents, road construction, and weather conditions.

Index

List of Maps

Photo Credits

All interior photos © Hilary Nangle except: page 12 © Joe Sohm | Dreamstime.com; page 14 © Earl Brechlin; page 20 © (bottom) Carey Kish; page 26 © (bottom) Cheri Alguire | Dreamstime.com; page 27 © Earl Brechlin; page 31 © Jim Ekstrand | Dreamstime.com; page 33 © Jerry Whaley | Dreamstime.com; page 34 © Zhukovsky | Dreamstime.com; page 37 © (top right) Tom Nangle; page 53 © (top) Tom Nangle; (bottom) Carey Kish; page 67 © (top left) Carey Kish; page 83 © courtesy Friends of Acadia; page 150 © (left middle) Tom Nangle; page 155 © (bottom) Carey Kish; page 177 © Tom Nangle; page 188 © (top left) Tom Nangle; (top right) Tom Nangle; page 191 © (bottom) Tom Nangle; page 239 © (top left) Tom Nangle

Acknowledgments

This book is dedicated to all the underappreciated tourism workers in Maine's Acadia region: the volunteers and lowly staffers, the waiters, waitresses, toll collectors, gatekeepers, park rangers, traffic cops, ferry attendants, housekeepers, hostesses and front desk workers, tour guides, the Friends of Acadia, and everyone else who has contact with visitors. You make the region sing. We do appreciate you. You're the real face of Acadia. Thank you.

I've lived on the Maine coast since childhood (yes, I will always be a "from away"), and have traveled extensively throughout the state for both work and pleasure, but every time I revisit a place, I find something new or changed, sometimes subtly, other times dramatically. Restaurants open and close. Outfitters change their offerings. Inns are sold. Motels open. New trails are cut. Museums expand. Hotels renovate. Pandemics happen: Researching this book during the Covid-19 pandemic truly tested my abilities. While I pray that every business in the region survives, the reality is that some, if not many, will close, unable to make enough during the too-short tourism season to keep afloat through the winter. Others will change formats, revise days and hours of operation, or do whatever possible to keep open. Please, be kind to them.

And on it goes. Which all goes to say, I couldn't have done this without the help of many people, who served as additional eyes and ears.

I'll start with the folks at Avalon Travel who shepherded me through the process: publisher Bill Newlin, vice president / acquisitions Grace Fujimoto, editorial director Kevin McLain, senior manager / contracts operations Meghan Tillett, acquisitions associate Kathryn Roque, associate marketing manager Crystal Tournau, publicity and marketing associate Erika Lara, and most especially to my team on this edition: editor Kimberly Ehart, production and graphics coordinators Suzanne Albertson and Rue Flaherty, and map editor Albert Angulo. Also thank you to all the behind-the-scenes worker bees at Avalon Travel Publishing.

More heartfelt thank-yous are due to those who sat down with me and shared insider info, sheltered me along the way, fed me, helped with arrangements, verified information, called me with updates, or simply encouraged me: Michelle and Eric Allvin, Christie Anastasia, Anne and Peter Beerits, Earl Brechlin, Gretchen Chauncey, Karen Curtis, Carla Tracy, Devin Finigan, Nick Fisichelli, Bill Haefele, Duncan Hamilton, Scott Hall and Nicole Neder, Alvion Kimball, Carey Kish, Kristin Levesque, Frank Leyman, Rosemary and Gary Levin, Sally Littlefield, Kristi and Matt Losquadro, Megan Moshier, Julie Van de Graaf, Kristina Zverjako.

I owe more thanks to friends who joined me on research trips: Leah Hobson, Nancy MacKinnon, and Shannon Hurst DalPozzal.

I save my biggest thanks for my husband, Tom, my frequent road-trip sidekick/driver, Martha Kalina (and her patient, left-at-home husband Rick Skoglund), and my always-up-for-an-adventure friend Leah Hobson. Between them, they drove me everywhere and didn't complain (too much) when I made them backtrack two or three times along the same stretch of road while seeking an elusive address; waited patiently while I visited practically every restaurant, inn, bed-and-breakfast, and attraction between Bucksport and Milbridge; let me order for them in restaurants, and supported me in every way possible throughout the entire process.

And you, dear reader, thank you for using this book to plan your visit to Maine's magical Acadia region. Please, do me a favor, will you? Provide feedback to help make the next edition even better. Visit www.MaineTravelMaven.com or my Maine Travel Maven page on Facebook to know what's new, changed, or happening in Maine, and please, drop a line through my website to share your thoughts and finds.

MOON
Hike the
APPALACHIAN
TRAIL

THE BEST TRAIL TOWNS, DAY HIKES,
AND ROAD TRIPS IN BETWEEN

TIMOTHY MALCOLM

MOON
BASEBALL
Road Trips
TIMOTHY MALCOLM

THE
COMPLETE GUIDE
TO ALL
THE BALLPARKS,
WITH BEER,
BITES,
AND SIGHTS
NEARBY

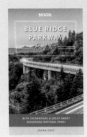

MOON
BLUE RIDGE
PARKWAY
Road Trip

WITH SHENANDOAH & GREAT SMOKY
MOUNTAINS NATIONAL PARKS

JASON FRYE

MOON
CALIFORNIA
Road Trip

SAN FRANCISCO, YOSEMITE, LAS VEGAS,
GRAND CANYON, LOS ANGELES
& THE PACIFIC COAST HIGHWAY

STUART THORNTON

MOON
NASHVILLE TO
NEW ORLEANS
Road Trip

NATCHEZ TRACE PARKWAY, MEMPHIS,
TUPELO, MISSISSIPPI BLUES TRAIL

MARGARET LITTMAN

MOON
NEW
ENGLAND
Road Trip

SEASIDE SPOTS, MAJESTIC MOUNTAINS &
FALL FOLIAGE, COZY GETAWAYS

MILES HOWARD

MOON
NORTHERN
CALIFORNIA
Road Trips

DRIVES ALONG THE COAST, REDWOODS, AND MOUNTAINS
WITH THE BEST STOPS ALONG THE WAY

STUART THORNTON & KAYLA ANDERSON

MOON
PACIFIC COAST
HIGHWAY
Road Trip

CALIFORNIA,
OREGON & WASHINGTON

IAN ANDERSON

MOON
Hike the
PACIFIC CREST
TRAIL

THE BEST TRAIL TOWNS, DAY HIKES,
AND ROAD FACTS IN BETWEEN

CAROLINE HINCHLIFF

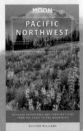

MOON
PACIFIC
NORTHWEST
Road Trip

OUTDOOR ADVENTURES AND CREATIVE CITIES
FROM THE COAST TO THE MOUNTAINS

ALLISON WILLIAMS

MOON
ROUTE 66
Road Trip

MOON
SOUTH FLORIDA
& THE KEYS
Road Trip

WITH MIAMI, WALT DISNEY WORLD, TAMPA &
THE EVERGLADES

JASON FERGUSON

MOON
SOUTHERN
CALIFORNIA
Road Trip

DRIVES ALONG THE BEST PCH, MOUNTAINS, AND DESERTS
WITH THE BEST STOPS ALONG THE WAY

IAN ANDERSON

MOON
SOUTHWEST
Road Trip

LAS VEGAS, ZION & BRYCE, MONUMENT VALLEY,
SANTA FE & TAOS, AND THE GRAND CANYON

TIM HULL

MOON
U.S. & CANADIAN
ROCKY MOUNTAINS
Road Trip

DRIVE THE CONTINENTAL DIVIDE AND
EXPLORE 8 NATIONAL PARKS

BECKY LOMAX

MOON
U.S.
CIVIL
RIGHTS
TRAIL

A TRAVELER'S GUIDE TO THE PEOPLE, PLACES,
AND EVENTS THAT MADE THE MOVEMENT

Deborah Douglas • With Foreword by Dion Fernandez-Bett

MOON
VANCOUVER &
CANADIAN ROCKIES
Road Trip

VICTORIA, BANFF, JASPER, CALGARY,
THE OKANAGAN, WHISTLER &
THE SEA TO SKY HIGHWAY

CAROLYN B. HELLER

MOON
YELLOWSTONE TO
GLACIER NATIONAL
PARK
Road Trip

JACKSON HOLE, CODY, THE GRAND TETONS
& THE ROCKY MOUNTAIN FRONT

CARTER G. WALKER

MOON
Road Trip
USA
25TH ANNIVERSARY EDITION
CROSS-COUNTRY ADVENTURES
AMERICA'S TWO-LANE HIGHWAY

MOON
the
OPEN
ROAD
50 BEST
ROAD TRIPS
in the
USA
From Weekend Getaways
to Cross-Country Adventures

JESSICA DUNHAM

Great Road Trips in the U.S. & Canada

MOON.COM | @MOONGUIDES

MOON

USA NATIONAL PARKS

THE COMPLETE GUIDE TO ALL 62 PARKS

BECKY LOMAX

Craft a personalized journey through the top National Parks in the U.S. and Canada with Moon!

MOON

ACADIA NATIONAL PARK

SEASIDE TOWNS · FALL FOLIAGE CYCLING & PADDLING

HILARY NANGLE

MOON

ARCHES & CANYONLANDS NATIONAL PARKS

HIKING · BIKING SCENIC DRIVES

JUDY JEWELL & W.C. McRAE

MOON

BANFF NATIONAL PARK

HIKE · CAMP SEE WILDLIFE

ANDREW HEMPSTEAD

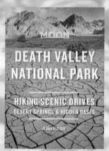

MOON

DEATH VALLEY NATIONAL PARK

HIKING SCENIC DRIVES DESERT SPRINGS & HIDDEN OASES

JENNA BLOUGH

MOON

GLACIER NATIONAL PARK

HIKING · CAMPING LAKES & PEAKS

BECKY LOMAX

MOON

GRAND CANYON

HIKE · CAMP RAFT THE COLORADO RIVER

TIM HULL

MOON

MOUNT RUSHMORE & THE BLACK HILLS

INCLUDING THE BADLANDS LAURAL A. BIDWELL

MOON

ROCKY MOUNTAIN NATIONAL PARK

HIKE · CAMP SEE WILDLIFE

ERIN ENGLISH

MOON

SEQUOIA & KINGS CANYON

HIKING · CAMPING WATERFALLS & BIG TREES

LEIGH BERNACCHI

In these books:

Coverage of gateway cities and towns

Suggested itineraries from one day to multiple weeks

Advice on where to stay (or camp) in and around the parks

MOON

GREAT SMOKY MOUNTAINS NATIONAL PARK

— HIKING · CAMPING SCENIC DRIVES —

JASON FRYE

MOON

JOSHUA TREE & PALM SPRINGS

MOON

YELLOWSTONE & GRAND TETON

— HIKE, CAMP, SEE WILDLIFE —

BECKY LOMAX

MOON

YOSEMITE SEQUOIA & KINGS CANYON

— HIKING · CAMPING REDWOODS & WATERFALLS —

MOON

ZION & BRYCE

WITH ARCHES, CANYONLANDS, CAPITOL REEF, GRAND STAIRCASE-ESCALANTE & MOAB

— HIKING · BIKING SCENIC DRIVES —

JUDY JEWELL & W. C. McRAE

Get inspired for your next adventure

Follow **@moonguides** on Instagram or subscribe to our newsletter at **moon.com**

#TravelWithMoon

MAP SYMBOLS

▰▰▰	Expressway	○	City/Town	✈	Airport	⚓	Golf Course
▰▰▰	Primary Road	◉	State Capital	✗	Airfield	🅿	Parking Area
▰▰▰	Secondary Road	⊛	National Capital	▲	Mountain	▱	Archaeological Site
- - -	Unpaved Road	✪	Highlight	✦	Unique Natural Feature	⛨	Church
······	Trail	★	Point of Interest			⛽	Gas Station
···········	Ferry	•	Accommodation	🏳	Waterfall	〰	Glacier
✕✕✕	Railroad	▾	Restaurant/Bar	⛰	Park	🔲	Mangrove
▰▰▰	Pedestrian Walkway	▪	Other Location	⛏	Trailhead	〜	Reef
▥▥▥	Stairs	Λ	Campground	⛷	Skiing Area	▱	Swamp

CONVERSION TABLES

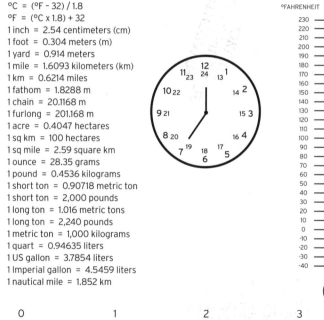

°C = (°F − 32) / 1.8
°F = (°C x 1.8) + 32
1 inch = 2.54 centimeters (cm)
1 foot = 0.304 meters (m)
1 yard = 0.914 meters
1 mile = 1.6093 kilometers (km)
1 km = 0.6214 miles
1 fathom = 1.8288 m
1 chain = 20.1168 m
1 furlong = 201.168 m
1 acre = 0.4047 hectares
1 sq km = 100 hectares
1 sq mile = 2.59 square km
1 ounce = 28.35 grams
1 pound = 0.4536 kilograms
1 short ton = 0.90718 metric ton
1 short ton = 2,000 pounds
1 long ton = 1.016 metric tons
1 long ton = 2,240 pounds
1 metric ton = 1,000 kilograms
1 quart = 0.94635 liters
1 US gallon = 3.7854 liters
1 Imperial gallon = 4.5459 liters
1 nautical mile = 1.852 km

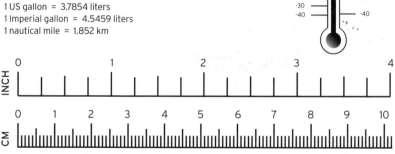

MOON ACADIA NATIONAL PARK

Avalon Travel
Hachette Book Group
1700 Fourth Street
Berkeley, CA 94710, USA
www.moon.com

Editor: Kimberly Ehart
Acquiring Editor: Grace Fujimoto
Graphics and Production Coordinators: Suzanne Albertson, Rue Flaherty
Cover Design: Faceout Studios, Charles Brock
Moon Logo: Tim McGrath
Map Editor: Albert Angulo
Cartographers: Brian Shotwell, Karin Dahl
Indexer: Greg Jewett

ISBN-13: 978-1-64049-479-4

Printing History
1st Edition — 2004
7th Edition — September 2021
5 4 3 2 1

Text © 2021 by Hilary Nangle.
Maps © 2021 by Avalon Travel.
Some photos and illustrations are used by permission and are the property of the original copyright owners.

Hachette Book Group supports the right to free expression and the value of copyright. The purpose of copyright is to encourage writers and artists to produce the creative works that enrich our culture. The scanning, uploading, and distribution of this book without permission is a theft of the author's intellectual property. If you would like permission to use material from the book (other than for review purposes), please contact permissions@hbgusa.com. Thank you for your support of the author's rights.

Front cover photo: sunrise from Boulder Beach at Otter Cliffs in Acadia National Park © Robert Garrigus / Alamy Stock Photo

Back cover photo: fall colors in Acadia National Park © F11photo | Dreamstime.com

Printed in Malaysia for Imago

Avalon Travel is a division of Hachette Book Group, Inc. Moon and the Moon logo are trademarks of Hachette Book Group, Inc. All other marks and logos depicted are the property of the original owners.

All recommendations, including those for sights, activities, hotels, restaurants, and shops, are based on each author's individual judgment. We do not accept payment for inclusion in our travel guides, and our authors don't accept free goods or services in exchange for positive coverage.

Although every effort was made to ensure that the information was correct at the time of going to press, the author and publisher do not assume and hereby disclaim any liability to any party for any loss or damage caused by errors, omissions, or any potential travel disruption due to labor or financial difficulty, whether such errors or omissions result from negligence, accident, or any other cause.

The publisher is not responsible for websites (or their content) that are not owned by the publisher.

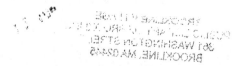